HESI A^2 Study Guide 2020

HESI A^2 Test Prep Guide & Practice Test Questions for the HESI A^2 Admission Assessment Exam Review

TABLE OF CONTENTS

Congratulations! You've decided to enter the world of nursing. You're in for a long journey ahead, but you've chosen an excellent profession. We wish you the best of luck in your new career.

The first order of business is to successfully pass the HESI. The HESI is an admissions exam used by many nursing schools to assess potential students and their likely future success. Nursing students who take the HESI must be prepared to complete reading, math, science and English language sections on the exam. The table below illustrates the question breakdown and time limits for the HESI test.

Section Questions
ENGLISH LANGUAGE
- Reading Comprehension 55 questions
- Vocabulary & General Knowledge 55 questions
- Grammar 55 questions

MATHEMATICS
- Basic Math Skills 55 questions

SCIENCE
- Biology 30 questions
- Chemistry 30 questions
- Anatomy & Physiology 30 questions

PERSONALITY PROFILE
- Personality Profile 15 questions
- Learning Style 14 questions
- Critical Thinking 25 questions

TOTAL 364 questions

Note: You are expected to complete the entire HESI A2 exam in 5.25 hours.

HESI English Language
The HESI English Language section consists of three subtests: reading comprehension, vocabulary & general knowledge and grammar.

HESI Mathematics
The HESI mathematics section contains only one subtest: basic math skills.

HESI Science
The HESI science section consists of three subtests: biology, chemistry and anatomy & physiology. This section is by far the most important and extensive section for the HESI exam...after all, you are working to become a nurse!

HESI Personality Profile
The HESI Personality Profile consists of three sections: personality profile, learning style and critical thinking. This section identifies several details about your personality and provides personalized suggestions to you based on your learning style.

Now that you know the overall structure of the HESI test, it's time to dig into the information.

Good luck, and let's get started!

READING

Finding the Main Idea

Many of the reading comprehension questions you will encounter on the exam are structured around finding the main idea of a paragraph. The last section on root words was all about finding the main idea of a word – notice a theme developing here?

In this section, you will need to find the main idea of a paragraph. Luckily, that's nice and simple once you know what to look for.

First of all, we're going to re-define a few terms you might think you already know, so don't rush through this part:

Paragraph

A paragraph is a tool for organizing information. It's simply a container for sentences in the same way that a sentence is a container for words. Okay, maybe you knew that already, but you'd be surprised how many professional writers get their minds blown when they realize that almost all books are structured in the same way:

Books are made of chapters, which are made of sections, which are made of paragraphs, which are made of sentences, which are made of words. It's a simple hierarchy, and smack in the center is the humble paragraph. For the purposes of the test, you need to be able to comb through given paragraphs to find two kinds of sentences: topic and detail.

Topic Sentence

A well-written paragraph, which is to say all of the paragraphs that you'll find on the test, contains just one topic. You'll find this in the topic sentence, which is the backbone of the paragraph. The topic sentence tells you what the paragraph is about. All of the other sentences exist solely to support this topic sentence which, more often than not, is the first or last sentence in the paragraph. However, that's not always the case, so use this foolproof method: Ask yourself, "Who or what is this paragraph about?" Then find the sentence that answers your question.

Detail Sentence

Detail sentences exist to support the topic sentence. They do so with all kinds of additional information, such as descriptions, arguments and nuances. An author includes detail sentences to explain why they're writing about the topic in the first place. That is, the detail sentences contain the author's point, which you'll need in order to find the main idea. To easily spot the author's point, just ask yourself, "Why is the author writing about this topic?" Then pay close attention to the detail sentences to pry out their motivations.

Got it? Good. Now, let's do some really easy math: The topic + the author's point = the main idea. Now, let's put that in English: What + Why = Main Idea.

In the Real World
All right, you've got the abstract concepts nailed down. Now, let's get concrete. Imagine a scenario where a friend is explaining the movie Toy Story to you. Also, imagine that she has already picked her jaw up off the floor, because seriously, how have you not seen Toy Story? You should fix that.

She tells you what the movie is about: There are these toys that get lost, and they have a bunch of adventures trying to get back to their owner. Then she tells you why you should see it: It's cute and funny, and it's a classic.

Two sentences: The topic (what the movie is about) and the author's point (why she's telling you about it.) And now you have the main idea: Your friend thinks you should see the movie Toy Story because it's a cute, funny classic about toys having adventures.

Illustrating the Main Idea
Here is a paragraph similar to one you might encounter on the test, followed by the types of questions that you will need to answer:

EXAMPLE 1 – from The Art of Conversation by Catherine Blyth:
"Silence is meaningful. You may imagine that silence says nothing. In fact, in any spoken communication, it plays a repertoire of roles. Just as, mathematically speaking, Earth should be called Sea, since most of the planet is covered in it, so conversation might be renamed silence, as it comprises 40 to 50 percent of an average utterance, excluding pauses for others to talk and the enveloping silence of those paying attention (or not, as the case may be.)"

This one is relatively easy, but let's break it down:

- Who/What is the paragraph about? Silence.
- Why is the author writing about this topic? It is often overlooked, but it's an important part of conversation.
- What is the main idea? Silence is an important part of conversation. Or, put it another way: "Silence is meaningful" - it's the first sentence!

Okay, you've seen the technique in action, so now it's your turn. Read the following paragraphs and determine the topic sentence, the author's main point, and the main idea.

To find the main idea of any piece of writing, remember: The topic + the author's point = the main idea or What + Why = Main Idea

Practice Time!
Let's see what you have learned about finding the main idea and focal points of a passage. Read the following passages below. Search for topic and main idea, and try to determine the focus of each one. Then answer the questions presented after each passage.

Good Luck!

Passage 1

Regardless of your reasons and motivations, if you choose to homeschool your child, there are many factors that must be considered. One of the most hotly debated is that of providing a means of socialization for students. The fear some people have is that students taught at home rather than a traditional school setting do not get the social interaction with peers that regular students do. There are many ways children can socialize and interact with others their age:

Group field trips- there are groups and certain organizations that help host group fields trips. Homeschooled students can also get together with other homeschool students or their friends and peers who are in public or private schools and attend field trips together. These trips also can serve as credit for the homeschooled student's class work- historical monuments can count as history credit and a report written about what was seen can count as an English assignment; they also get the benefit of having time with their friends and peers.

Community service- there is always an opportunity to get involved in the community and these are perfect opportunities to interact with others. Students can get together to work on a project or can work on their own and work alongside others who are volunteering at the same location. It helps get your child interacting with others and can also help to instill valuable life lessons at the same time.

Scouts, clubs, and programs- there are many organizations that offer the opportunity for students to work, learn, and grow alongside each other. Boy Scouts and Girl Scouts offer a chance for students to interact with their peers while developing their own life skills. The 4-H Program also offers a unique opportunity for homeschooled students to get life experiences and interaction; some 4-H clubs are set up especially for homeschooled students.

Co-op Groups- these exist to help families organize group events with fellow homeschool students. Group projects and study sessions are just some of the options that are available. Group study sessions can also be prepared to practice for things such as SAT testing, Finally, homeschooled families can take advantage of co-op groups to help set up study sessions and events for students. These are just a handful of simple ways home school families can answer society's question about how students can be socially active and interact with students their own age. Following the simple tips and taking a stab at any others that may be out there is a great way to meet your child's socialization needs while providing them with peace and protection and the education you want them to receive.

1. Which sentence best states the main idea of this passage?
A)   Homeschool children lack any good socialization and peer interaction.
B)   There are many ways children can socialize and interact with others their age.
C)   Children who are homeschooled lack major social skills.
D)   None of the above.

Answer: B. Throughout the piece, the author talks about how homeschooled children can still find ways to socialize and interact with their peers.

2. Which of the following is not a way homeschooled students can interact with their peers that was discussed in this passage?
    A) Join a club or social group
    B) Volunteer in the local community
    C) Go on field trips
    D) They all are ways homeschooled students can meet peers

Answer: D. All three of those methods of socialization were talked about in detail within the passage. Every one of them had several examples and explanations given as to why they were effective means of getting homeschooled students around their peer group.

Passage 2

The world around us is filled with the weird and usual. When we think of freaks of nature we usually bring to mind images of massive rabbits, six legged cows, and two headed dogs.
However, the usual species and 'freaks of nature' also spill over into the plant world. Usual plants offer a unique look at plant biology gone haywire. From excessive size to usual smell, these freaky plants are real and can be found today -if you know where to look.

Although more than 90% of plant types have leaves, used for photosynthesis, there are some scenes and varieties of plants that do not. The most common of these are members of the mushroom family that are parasitic in nature. They feed off the decaying material of plants or suck nutrients from healthy living plants. One such parasitic plant truly earns the title of usual. It is the Rafflesia arnoldii. This plant bears a bloom that can grow more than three feet in diameter. The flower smells like rotting flesh and has a hole in the center big and deep enough to hold up to six quarts of water. To top off the list of usual traits, this plant has no stems, roots, or leaves, a true freak of nature.

Flowers can range in size from a fraction of the size of the plant, to more than 80% of the plant itself. Flowers serve as the reproductive part of the plant and is responsible for producing seeds to further the next batch of plants to be grown according to that plant's individual biology. One of the plants that show this wide range in plant size is the group of plants known as Amorphophallus. Closely related to the peace lily, these plants have a similar flower. Found in the subtropics, more than 200 different species and varieties have been identified. One of these species, Amorphophallus titanum, has a bloom that is several times larger than the plant itself; the blooms can get so large on some plants that they can exceed the height and width of a grown adult. Truly amazing what plant biology is capable of.
Many species of trees and flowering plants are quite old. The methuselah trees of the desert and the great redwood giants of the forests are just two well-known examples of ancient species still living. But perhaps the most ancient of all is a plant that was believed to have been long extinct. Until 1944, the plant known as Wollemia nobilis was known only by the fossil remains. Then living plants of this

type were discovered in remote tropical areas. The bark is unique as it is a deep chocolate color and looks like it is comprised of many tiny bubbles. This is not tiny plant either as some specimens have been records at heights of over 120 feet. It is believed that there are maybe only 100 of these plants left in the wild.

Plant biology is an interesting branch of science. A great deal can be learned about nature and the world around us by studying plants. This field of study gets even more interesting when the unusual plant species that populate the world are taken into consideration. Every corner of the world hold surprises. Who knows, there may still be colossal giants hidden away in remote rainforests and miniscule plants hiding in the crevasse of a mountain side just waiting to be discovered.

1. Which point do the details in this passage support?
    A) Plants have many different features
    B) All plants are basically the same in their biologic makeup
    C) Plants must share similar characteristics in order to be plants
    D) None of the above

Answer: A. All the details in this passage talk about how plants are different from each other yet still are considered to be plants- some have leaves whole others do not and some are big while others are little. Plants can look vastly different from each other and still belong to the plant family.

2. What did the author want the reader to get out of reading this passage?
    A) That plants are amazing and very diverse in the way they look
    B) Not all plants look like the flowers and trees we are familiar with
    C) Some plants are very old and some are still waiting to be discovered
    D) All of the above

Answer: D. All of these points are correct because they are all mentioned within the passage and discussed and described in detail.

How did you do? If you still need some help figuring out the main idea and topics of passages like these, keep practicing!

Detail Questions

Reading passages and identifying important details is an important part of the critical reading process. Detail questions ask the reader to recall specific information about the main idea. These details are often found in the examples given in the passage and can contain anecdotes, data or descriptions, among other details.

For example, if you are reading a passage about certain types of dogs, you may be asked to remember details about breeds, sizes and coat color and patterns. As you read through the following passages, make sure you take note of numbers, figures and the details given about the topic. Chances are you will need to remember some of these.

There is a wealth of information, facts, pieces of data and several details that can be presented within any passage you read. The key to uncovering the main idea and understanding the details presented is to take your time and read through everything contained in the passage. Consider each example and figure presented. Think about how they relate to the main idea, how they support the focus, and how those details add to the information and value of the passage.

Read the following news article and answer the following questions.

Passage 1

Police of Chicago are searching for two men who under investigation for charges of impersonating cops. The men stopped a person on the city's Northwest Side. In a bit of an ironic twist, the two fake cops ended up pulling over an actual Chicago cop.

Officials say the officer who is in his 40's was finishing his shift and on his way home when he was pulled over. It was in Chicago's Avondale neighborhood just after midnight when the officer had a white SUV pull up behind him and flash its lights. The officer saw the signaling, said the SUV looked like a police issued undercover vehicle, and pulled over. According to reports, one of the two men exited of the unmarked car, wearing normal civilian clothes. The man approached the cop, who was still wearing his bullet proof vest, and said he was with the Chicago police.
The officer said that the civilian clothes and lack of standard police issued items alerted him that something was wrong and he challenged them on that statement. The two men ran back to the unmarked car and sped off and disappeared into the dark streets. The Chicago police describe the suspects as two Hispanic men in their early to mid 20s who are both around 6 feet tall and around 150 pounds. Anyone with tips should call the Chicago Police Department.

Questions:
1. What is the passage above mostly about?
A) Problems with the Chicago Police Department
B) A news report about people pretending to be police officers
C) Chicago Police are cracking down on crime
D) None of the above

Answer: B There is a sentence that specifically states that the report is about two men who were pretending to be Chicago Police officers.

2. According to the passage, what details were given about the incident?
A) Civilian clothes and lack of standard police issued items made the cop suspicious
B) The event occurred in Chicago's Avondale neighborhood just after midnight
C) The two men who posed as Chicago Police officers were of Hispanic decent
D) The police officer was in his 40's and the two fake cops were in their 20's
E) All of the above

Answer: E All of these details were mentioned throughout the news report.

3. All of the following are things we know about the real officer in this story except:
A) His Age
B) His duty status at the time
C) How long he's been with the Chicago Police
D) We know all these things

Answer: C Nowhere in the article is it mentioned how long the real officer has been serving with the Chicago Police Department.

Remember:
There is a wealth of information, many facts, countless pieces of data, and a lot of details that can be presented within any passage that you read. The key to uncovering the main idea and understanding all the details that are presented is to take your time and read through everything contained in the passage. Read everything and take the time to consider every example and every figure presented and see how it relates to the main idea and how to supports the focus and how those details add to the information and value of the passage you are reading.

Reading passages and picking out these important details is a big part of being an effective reader. Practice makes perfect and the more you read the more you analyze and the more you work on it the better you will get and the more you will be able to pull from any article, blog, story, or report you read!

Understanding Question Stems

In addition to careful reading of the passages (including marking up the text for topic and concluding sentences, transitional words and key terms), you must also be able to identify what is being asked of you in each of the questions. Recognition of the task in each question can be easily accomplished if you are familiar with the question stems, or the most commonly phrased wording that will be associated with each type of question on the test. Keep reading for an explanation of each question type, along with sample stems, and suggested approaches for tackling them.

Main Idea

Questions asking you to identify the main idea expect that you will be able to determine the overall point of the passage (often called the thesis), NOT secondary details or supporting points. Attempting to put the main idea into your own words after reading WITHOUT looking at the text again is a very helpful strategy in answering this type of question. If you can sum up the author's main point in your own words, then you will find it very easy to find the right "match" amongst the answers provided for you. Alternately, the main idea may often be found in the opening or concluding paragraphs, two common places where an author may introduce a topic and his perspective about said topic, or he summarize the main points.

Here are some common ways this type of question is asked:
- The main idea for this paragraph...
- The central point of the passage...
- A possible title for the passage...
- The author's primary point...

Supporting Details

Supporting details are those that back up the main ideas presented in the passage. These can include examples, clarifying explanations, or elaborations of basic ideas presented earlier in the reading. Supporting details are directly stated in the passage, so you must rely on your careful reading to guide you to the correct answer. Answers may not be stated in the original language of the passage, but the basic ideas will be the same.
Here are some common ways this type of question is asked:
- The passage states...
- The author says...
- According to what you read...

Inference

Inferences are those ideas which can be gleaned from the suggestions that may be implied in other statements made by the author. They are never explicitly stated, but we understand that they are true from "reading between the lines". The answers to inferences questions, therefore, are assumptions, and cannot be found from direct statements in the text. You will have to rely on your ability to logically deduce conclusions from your careful reading. More than one answer may sound correct, but only one is. Make sure that, whichever answer you choose, you can find statements in the text support that idea. If you cannot do that, then that choice is likely not the right answer.
Here are some common ways this type of question is asked:
- The passage implies...
- The author suggests...

- The reader could logically conclude that...
- The reader would be correct in assuming that...

Tone/Attitude

Some questions will ask you about the author's tone or attitude. A good place to start with this type of question is to consider whether the passage is positive, negative or neutral. Does the author seem angry? Maybe sad? Or torn between two points of view? The language that an author uses can be very telling about his tone and attitude. Is the author critical? Praiseworthy? Disappointed? Even if you find some finer details of passage difficult to understand, the tone and attitude are often fairly easy to identify. Look for adjectives and statements that reveal the author's opinion, rather than facts, and this will help you know his tone or attitude.

Here are some common ways this type of question is asked:

- The tone of the passage is...
- The attitude of the author is...
- The writer's overall feeling...

Style

Style refers to a writer's "way with words". Most seasoned writers have a well-developed and easily recognizable style. but often the topic of a written work can dictate style. If the topic is serious the language will likely be more formal. Works for academic settings may be heavy with the jargon of that discipline. Personal reflections can be rife with imagery, while instructional manuals will use simple and straightforward language. Identifying style is not difficult; simply pay attention to the words used (simple or fancy?), the sentence structure (simple or compound-complex?), as well as the overall structure of the piece (stream of consciousness or 5-paragraph essay?). You must answer these questions in order to determine the style of the passage.

Here are some common ways this type of question is asked:

- The overall writing style used in the passage...
- The author's style is...
- The organizational style of the passage is...

Pattern of Organization

Pattern of organization questions want you to consider how the writing of a piece was developed. What features did the writer utilize to make his point? Did he include personal anecdotes? Data or statistics? Quotes from authorities on the topic? These are all modes of organizing a passage that help the writer support his claims and provide a logical focus for the work.

Here are some common ways this type of question is asked:

- The author proves a point through...
- In the passage, the author uses...
- Throughout the passage, the author seems to rely on...

Purpose and Attitude

Questions asking about purpose and attitude require you to consider why the author took the time to write. The authors motivations are directly behind the purpose of the piece. What question did he wish to answer? What cause did he want to show support for? What action did he wish to persuade you to take? Identifying these reasons for writing will reveal the purpose and attitude of the passage.

Here are some common ways this type of question is asked:
- The purpose of the passage is...
- The author's intent for writing the passage is...
- The attitude the author displays is...

Fact/Opinion

There will be some questions on the test that will ask you whether a statement is a fact or an opinion. Without being able to fact-check, how will you do this? A rule of thumb would be that opinions reflect only the thoughts, feelings or ideas of the writer, whereas facts are verifiable as true or false, regardless of one's feelings. if a writer cites a statistic about the environmental effects of oil drilling on migratory mammals in the Pacific Northwest, then that is verifiable and can be considered factual. If, however, the writer claims that oil drilling in the Pacific Northwest United States is bad and should be stopped, then that is his opinion. He may at some point provide examples of why this is so, but that viewpoint is based on his thoughts and feelings about oil drilling, and can only be considered opinion.

Here are some common ways this type of question is asked:
- Which statement is a fact rather than an opinion?
- This statement is meant to be...
- An example of fact is when the author says...
- An example of opinion is when the author states that...

Eliminating Wrong Answers

An author often writes with an intended purpose in mind, and they will support their main idea with examples, facts, data and stories that help the overall meaning of their written text to be clear. You may be asked a question regarding one of these details or examples or about the overall theme or main idea of the passage. These types of questions require you to read the passage carefully for meaning and to look at all the supporting details used. However, it's also important to learn how to identify incorrect answer choices and eliminate them right away. This will help you narrow down the answer choices that are likely to be correct. Here's how you do it:

Strategies for Answering Specific Detail Questions:
• Identify the key words in the question that help you find details and examples that will help answer the question.

• Make mental notes as you read the passage about how words are used and the phrases that are repeated. Also look for the overall meaning of each paragraph and passage.

• Some questions will pull words or phrases from the passage and use them in the question. In this case, look through the passage and find those words or phrases and make sure they are being used the same way in both the passage and the question. Many questions will change the meaning of these to make the question wrong or confuse the reader.

• Some questions will ask you to determine if a particular statement about the passage or topic of the passage is true. In this case, look over the paragraphs and find the overall theme or idea of the passage. Compare your theme or idea to the statement in the question.

Now it is your turn to try it out and see how you do. Read the following passages and answer the questions, making sure you eliminate the wrong answers as you look for the right one. There will be three passages for you to read and several questions about each one- there will be one right answer and at least three wrong answers you will need to eliminate as you read. Good luck!

Passage 1
Online game play has become standard for many video games. While it allows your kids the opportunity to play with other fans of their favorite games, it also brings with it new risks and dangers. By being proactive and staying active with their children, parents can ensure video games remain safe and fun for their kids.

Parents need to stay current on several things- video game ratings, content clues, and their kid's use and involvement. The ratings on video games can help parents know what is and is not acceptable content for their kids.

Parents also need to keep an eye on the content of the games once the game play starts- peek in now and then to make sure there is nothing surprising lurking in a game you thought was fine. Also, parents need to monitor how often their kids are playing the games, the time spent playing, and how much time is spent thinking about the game. Balance is critical to make sure video game use remains fun and safe.

Make sure you keep communication lines open with your kids. They need to know that they can come to you with questions, concerns, or problems. They need to feel safe talking to you and not be fearful that you will be made or angry with them. When your child comes to you with a problem do not brush it off- be sure to give it the attention it deserves and make sure they know you are glad they are coming to you.

Questions:
1. Parents can ensure video games remain safe and fun for their kids by doing what?
A) Be proactive with your decisions
B) Be active and involved with your kids
C) Be willing to let your kids do what they want
D) A and B
E) B and C

Answer: D. Both A and B are correct since they were mentioned in one of the first sentences in the opening paragraph of the passage

2. What do parents need to do to keep their kids safe while playing video games?
A) Stay current on trends and news
B) Monitor kid's game activities
C) Communicate with kids often
D) All of the above
E) None of the above

Answer: D. All of these are things mentioned in the passage when it talks about the things people can do to keep their kids safe while playing games and playing online.

Remember reading all the paragraphs is a great way to get the overall idea of the passage. Also every paragraph of a passage should be discussing a different example or point that ties back to the main idea of the passage and helps further demonstrate the main idea.

Passage 2
Kids of all ages have long loved drawing and many kids will draw on anything and everything they can get their hands on. Thy will draw on paper, the floor, their clothes, themselves, and of course the walls! Many parents turn to the tried and true chalkboards for their kids' play room, or play area.

However, chalk can be messy, is harder to clean up, and some kids just don't like the light powdery look of their chalk artwork. If this is the situation you are in, you will want to consider dry-erase paint as the most practical solution to your dilemma. Years ago when dry erase was something you saw only in school or in office buildings, it was hard to come by if you wanted that option at home.

Dry erase easels and boards were cumbersome, bulky, heavy, and expensive. However, now you can actually get specially formulated dry erase paint that you can use on your walls to turn them into massive dry erase boards! Dry-erase has low odor, low-chemical content, and is suitable for a range of surfaces such as wood, brick, concrete, and many others.

Why stifle their creativity when you can unleash it and let them create, design, and explore the wonders of their own imagination? Many companies carry dry erase paint so you can transform your child's bedroom or play room into the best place in the world. Whether you want to give them a section of the wall, one entire wall, or all the wall space they can reach, this one little addition can help make it easy for you to give them ample room to be creative.

Image the smile on your child's face to see a daily message written to them on the wall when they wake up or when they come home from school. Send gentle reminders about chores and homework or use the dry erase space for a fun approach to the nightly homework sessions. Be creative and you will never run out of uses for the Create Pain dry erase paint.

Questions:

1. What are some reasons mentioned in the passage for why dry erase walls are a good choice for a kid's room?
   A) Easy to clean and helps kids be creative
   B) Safe and less chemicals
   C) Are able to be used for every day needs
   D) All of the above

   Answer: D All of the answers are correct and are mentioned in the passage- they are not all mentioned in one paragraph but they are mentioned throughout the passage and all tie back to the idea of dry erase being a good option for your kid's room.

2. Only a few companies carry dry erase paint to be used on walls, which makes it hard to find and use for kid's room designs. Is this statement *True* or *False*?

   Answer: False. In the passage it does mention getting dry erase paint from companies but says that many companies carry it. So this means it is fairly easy to find and use and is a good choice for kid's rooms.

Passage 3

We hear a lot of talk about recycling nowadays. We recycle glass, plastic, newspaper, and there are countless ways to reuse everyday items to keep them out of the landfill for a little longer. An equally important, but not as discussed method of recycling is scrap metal recycling. You may be wondering why it is such a big deal and what good metal recycling can make- well, let's take a look.

One of the biggest impacts this form of recycling has is it conserves raw resources and eliminated the carbon footprint for many metal production facilities. The Institute of Scrap Recycling Industries (ISRI) states that in 2010, more than $64billion was added to the United States economy; all of it came from the recycling, reuse, and production of new products from recycled metals. All of this metal scrap would otherwise end up in the landfills or in the environment and that much more raw material would have to be mined and refined and produced from scratch to make new tools, machines, and products. Scrap metal recycling is a very important aspect of conservation and pollution reduction.

In addition to the economic impact from profits of reusing scrap metal, the act of metal recycling also generates jobs. The ISRI estimated that in 2008, over 85,000 jobs were supported and made possible in some way thanks to scrap metal recycling. It also helps in trade sand exports, as it was estimated that over $28 billion and roughly 44 million metric tons of metal was shipped and sold overseas.

Scrap metal recycling comes in many forms. Sometimes it is a junk yard or scrap yard that buys scrap metal and then sells it to manufacturers who can melt it down, refine it, and use it to make new

products and materials. Or it could be the neighborhood scrap collector who visits yard sales and stops by your trash pile to pick up that old dishwasher or microwave you threw out.
There are also community sponsored recycling programs where cans are collected and turned in for cash, or programs such as the electronics recycling and business incentives for recycling scrap metal left over from production or building projects.

It is easy to see the benefits and importance of scrap metal recycling. Whether it is some materials left over after a home renovation project, tin cans your kids have collected, or the last remaining pieces to that old junk car you scraped, recycling the scrap metal can do a world of good and have a lasting impact on the environment, economy, and your local community. So do your part and be on the lookout for scrap metal to add to your recycling piles.

Questions:

1. The ISRI is a company that oversees scrap metal and recycling practices. True or False?

   True- the ISRI is the Institute of Scrap Recycling Industries and in the passage we see that they offer reports about money earned from scrap metal recycling and also talks about the job market associated with scrap metal recycling.

2. Recycling scrap metal helps the environment by keeping that junk out of landfills. True or False?

   True- the passage talks about recycling and how it is a very important aspect of conservation and pollution reduction.

   Good job- remember to read every passage you are given carefully and don't be afraid to go back and read something again or scan the passage for key words and phrases that show up in the questions.

Inferences and How to Make Them and Use Them
Inference is a mental process by which you reach a conclusion based on specific evidence. Inferences are the stock and trade of detectives examining clues, of doctors diagnosing diseases, and of car mechanics repairing engines. We infer motives, purpose and intentions.

You use inference every day. You interpret actions to be examples of behavioral characteristics, intents or expressions of particular feelings. You infer it is raining when you see someone with an open umbrella. You infer that people are thirsty if they ask for a glass of water. You infer that evidence in a text is authoritative when it is attributed to a scholar in that particular field.

You want to find significance. You listen to remarks and want to make sense of them. What might the speaker mean? Why is he or she saying that? You must go beyond specific remarks to determine underlying significance or broader meaning. When you read that someone cheated on his or her income taxes, you might take that as an example of financial ingenuity, daring or stupidity. You seek purposes and reasons.

Inferences are not random. While they may come about mysteriously with sudden recognition, you usually make inferences very orderly. Inferences may be guesses, but they are educated guesses based on supporting evidence. The evidence requires that you reach a specific conclusion.

Inferences are not achieved with mathematical rigor, and they do not have the certainty obtained with deductive reasoning. Inferences tend to reflect prior knowledge and experience as well as personal beliefs and assumptions. Thus, inferences tend to reflect your stake in a situation or your interests in the outcome. People may reason differently or bring different assumptions or premises to bear. This is why bias is addressed so carefully in our criminal justice system, so defendants are given a fair trial.

Given evidence that polychlorinated biphenyls (PCB) cause cancer in people and that PCB's are in a particular water system, all reasonable people would reach the conclusion that the water system is dangerous to people. But, given evidence that there is an increase in skin cancer among people who sun bathe, not all people would conclude that sunbathing causes skin cancer. Sun bathing, they might argue, may be coincidental with exposure to other cancer-causing factors.

*Daniel J. Kurland (www.criticalreading.com/inference_process.htm)

Inference Questions
Inference questions ask about ideas that are not directly stated, but rather are implied by the passage. They ask you to draw conclusions based on the information in the passage. Inference questions usually include words like "imply," "infer" or "conclude," or they may ask you what the author "would probably" think or do in a given situation based on what was stated in the passage.

With inference questions, it is important not to go too far beyond the scope of the passage. You are not expected to make any guesses. There is a single correct answer that is a logical, next-step conclusion from what is presented in the passage.
Let's take a look at some sample inference questions. Read through the following passages and use your inference skills to answer the questions. Remember that the inferences you make are not always obvious or directly stated in the passage.

Passage 1
Despite the fact that the practice is illegal in many states, some people set off their own fireworks at home each summer, especially on Independence Day. Most cities have public fireworks displays run by experienced professionals in a controlled environment, but many people still enjoy the thrill of setting off their own fireworks. However, this practice can be dangerous, and many people are injured each year from fireworks-related accidents. Having Independence Day fireworks in your own backyard is not worth the safety risk, especially when public fireworks display are available in most areas.

Questions:

1. The author of this passage would most likely support:
A. The complete legalization of fireworks nationwide
B. The reduction of public fireworks displays
C. More rigorous enforcement of restrictions on home fireworks
D. Promoting home fireworks use

Answer: C.

In the passage, the author takes a negative tone toward home fireworks use, citing the fact that the practice is dangerous, illegal in some areas and unnecessary since many areas have safe public fireworks displays on holidays. Someone who is critical of home fireworks use would support strong enforcement of restrictions on their use.

Passage 2

A man took his car to the mechanic because the engine was overheating. The mechanic opened the hood to inspect the situation. He removed the radiator cap and could see that there was a sufficient amount of coolant in the radiator. He took the car for a drive and also noticed that the engine would overheat at a stoplight, but not on the highway.

Questions:

1. According to the passage, what can you infer about the engine?
A. The engine needs to be replaced
B. The radiator is leaking
C. The engine is operating normally
D. The radiator fan is broken

Answer: D.

Although an overheating engine does indicate an abnormal condition, it does not necessarily indicate a catastrophic failure. Thus, the engine can be repaired instead of replaced. The radiator was full of coolant, so that eliminates the possibility of a leak. When a vehicle is moving, the airflow across the radiator cools the coolant. However, when a vehicle is stationary, the fan is responsible for cooling the coolant. If the fan is not working correctly, this would explain the overheating at a stoplight, but not on the highway.

Passage 3

One man in St. Paul Minnesota is making a difference for people in the community, and his impact was felt stronger than ever this Thanksgiving Holiday. Jeff Ansorge once was in charge of almost 20 staff members and earned $80,000 a year as the head executive chef at a classy downtown Minneapolis restaurant. Only for the very well-off, the restaurant featured items such as a 24-ounce dry aged Porterhouse steak that went for almost $50. However, Jeff gave it all up to and has taken on the job of head cook of a Salvation Army soup kitchen. Where meals would cost $40-$60, now his meals are free.

As head cook he is making salmon, ribs, and stews for those who come to The Salvation Army Eastside Corps Community Center in St. Paul. For the Thanksgiving meal that's Jeff had the traditional meal of turkey with stuffing, along with mashed potatoes and gravy, and even the extras like cranberry sauce and rolls. Even the ambiance was completed with dinner being served on tables covered with white tablecloths and simple decorations. Jeff Ansorge, who is 40, says that it was a spiritual awakening that prompted him make the move to the soup kitchen in October 2012, where he is now making just one-third of his previous salary.

Not only did Jeff bring his culinary skills but his eye for bargain shopping and his ability to make food stretch has allowed the Salvation Army to serve great food and actually save some money in the process. The Salvation Army works along with Second Harvest Heartland food bank and with Jeff's help, they can now get 40-pound cases of mixed poultry for as little as five bucks. Jeff Ansorge also does his best to bring nutritional value to every meal that he serves. He knows that for many who come to the soup kitchen, it may be the only meal they get for the day. He's eliminated desserts and is also working to cut back on the fat and sugars in meals, giving more room for fresh fruits and vegetables and healthy meats.

Questions:

1. Jeff is a caring and compassionate individual who has a deep sense of right and wrong and is likely governed by deeply held beliefs and ideas of mortality and civil duty. True or False?

   Answer: True. Several things mentioned in this passage can lead you to infer this about Jeff- he was raised in the Catholic faith, he works in a soup kitchen, volunteers, gave up a good job to help others, and genuinely seems to care about those who are less fortunate than himself.

2. All people who are well off and making good money dislike people like Jeff who make them look bad. True or False?

   Answer: False. Nowhere in the passage is this hinted to or implied at all.

<u>Remember inferences can be tricky things to master. Practice makes perfect so keep at it!</u>

MATHEMATICS

M1.1 Numbers and Algebra

- Convert among non-negative fractions, decimals and percentages
- Divide the numerator by the denominator
- Moving decimal points to make percentages
- Decimals into fractions by simplifying ratios

Essential to an understanding of fractions, is the concept of division. Whole numbers divided by whole numbers will always result in decimal answers. Continuing that division until a zero remainder will provide the complete decimal representation of the original fraction. A decimal answer less than one is the result for a proper fraction division. The answer greater than one is the result of an improper fraction division, when the numerator is greater than the denominator. This process of division will always allow conversion of fractions into decimals.

Every fraction represents a division problem. The decimal value of any fraction is represented by the numerator, (top value), divided by the denominator (bottom value). Certain combinations, such as $^1/_3$, will result in repeating decimals that will always require rounding in a testing situation.

The fraction $^1/_2$ has a decimal value of 0.5, which is the value of 1 divided by 2. The values of improper fractions such as $^3/_2$, $^5/_2$, or $^7/_2$ (larger numerator than denominator) are determined by dividing as previously stated or more easily by multiplying the numerator by 0.5. So the improper fraction of $^7/_2$ is 7 x 0.5 or 3.5. Often the determination of the unit fraction (1 divided by the denominator) followed by the decimal multiplication is simpler in a testing situation.

The fraction $^3/_5$ has a decimal value of 0.6, which is the value of 3 divided by 5. Alternately, the value of the unit fraction of $^1/_5$ is 0.2 and that unit fraction multiplied by 3 is 0.6. If you know the unit fractions for common fraction values, the test answer selection may be simplified.

When a fraction such as $^5/_7$ is evaluated the quotient of 5 divided by 7 results in a lengthy decimal value of 0.71428…. That extended value will never appear as a multiple-choice test answer selection. Typically, that value will be rounded to either 0.71 or 0.714. Remember that testing instructions say to choose the **best answer**. Your best choice may be a rounded number.

If we look at the fraction $^3/_4$, the division of numerator divided by denominator is 3 divided by 4. Since 4 cannot be divided into 3 evenly, the first division becomes 3.0 divided by 4 which is 0.7 with a remainder of 0.2. When we complete the next step of division, .20 divided by 4 has an answer of 0.05 with a remainder of zero. When the remainder is zero, the division is complete. The completed division answer is 0.75, the correct decimal representation of $^3/_4$.

The next step in the conversion process is the comparatively simple step of converting a decimal to a percentage. The term, "percent", means "per one hundred", which is simply a fraction with 100 in the denominator. Therefore, a decimal can simply be converted to a percentage by moving the decimal point in the correct direction. In the previous example where the answer was 0.75, that ratio is 75/100. Since percentage means "per one hundred", our percentage is 75%.

The remaining part of this process is the conversion of a decimal to a fraction, which completes the cycle and implies that we have a complete repertoire of skills to deal with fractions. The basic way to convert back to a fraction from a decimal is to write the decimal in fraction form. In our previous example, our answer was 75/100. This is the decimal representation of the percentage, and it is a fraction but not in simplest form. To simplify any fraction, we look for common factors in both the numerator and the denominator. If we choose 5 as a common factor 75/100 becomes (15*5)/(20*5). The common factors can be eliminated in both the numerator and denominator, so the fraction becomes 15/20. While this is a fraction, it is not yet in simplest form, since there are other common factors. The fraction becomes (3*5) / (4*5) which is ¾, the simplified form.

As you read this description, you may have thought that there was a simpler method. In fact, there was a common factor of 25 in both the numerator and denominator at the beginning. This process could have been executed in one step if you saw that 25 was the common factor. If you did not see that, please understand that this process of simplification can be accomplished in several steps if necessary. Whether it is completed in one step or more, as long as the final ratio has no common factors in the numerator and denominator, the simplification process is complete and successful. Most important is that you have completed the process of converting a decimal or percentage into a fraction. Your fraction skill set is on the way to completion. In the next section, the we will continue by adding, subtracting, multiplying and dividing fractions.

M.1.2. Perform arithmetic operations with rational numbers

- Add & subtract
- Like denominators
- Finding common denominators
- Multiply & divide
- Numerators times numerators etc.
- Invert the divisor before multiplying for division
- PEMDAS

Recall that rational numbers or fractions are made up of numerator and a denominator. The top number of the fraction, called the numerator, tells how many of the fractional parts are being represented. The bottom number, called the denominator, tells how many equal parts the whole is divided into. For this reason, fractions with different denominators cannot be added together because different denominators are as different as "apples and oranges". Therefore, when adding (or subtracting) fractions with different denominators, a "common" denominator must be found. In a later section (7. Multiples) there is a review of multiples, but the common denominator is an application of that principle that we will apply here first. In this case, simple geometric models will be used to explain the common denominator principle. Usually this principle is illustrated with circles divide into "pie slices". A simpler and more complete example involves the use of squares or rectangles divided into fractional parts.

Representing fraction parts $1/3$ and ¼ will be demonstrated with the following square diagrams. In this case a whole square is the number "1" and the fractional parts will be the slices of the square as follows:

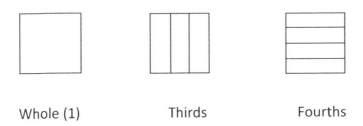

Whole (1)   Thirds   Fourths

If we superimpose the four horizontal slices over the three vertical slices, there are twelve separate parts of the whole as follows:

In the last diagram, any column that represents a third, has four of the twelve small rectangles from the diagram or $4/12$ as the equivalent fraction.

Similarly, any row of the last diagram that represents a fourth, has three of the twelve small rectangles from the diagram or $3/12$ as the equivalent fraction. With this modification of the two fractions, both have been modified in the form of a common denominator and the addition of the two fractions can be completed:

$$1/3 + 1/4 = 3/12 + 4/12 = 7/12$$

Notice that this result is directly analogous to the geometric diagram above. Common denominator fractions need not be simplified with a diagram, but it is a valuable example to explain the principle. The common denominator is required whenever fraction addition or subtraction is required but the denominators different. If the denominators are the same, then the addition or subtraction of numerators is all that is required. If more assistance is needed on how to find common denominators, start by finding the least common multiple which provides the required lowest common denominator for addition. The example below shows the multiples of 3 and 4

Multiples of 3:   3   6   9   <u>12</u>   15   18   21   <u>24</u>   27...

Multiples of 4:   4   8   <u>12</u>   16   20   <u>24</u>   28   32   36 ...

Notice that there are many common multiples of 3 and 4. We could have used 24 for example. But the **least** common multiple will provide the lowest common denominator that is easiest to use when adding and subtracting fractions. Using any other multiple usually means that there will be more simplification after you have performed the addition or subtraction.

Remember that the individual fractions will retain the same value only if the numerator and denominator are multiplied by the same value.

Multiplication of two fractions is a simpler operation because fractions multiply as follows:

$$7/8 \times 3/4 = {(7 \times 3)}/{(8 \times 4)} = 21/32$$

The fractional answer is in simplest form because there are no common factors. If common factors exist in the numerator and denominator of a fraction, then that fraction must be simplified.

Finally, division of fractions should never be attempted in the form of a ratio. The method is confusing and elaborate and unreliable in a testing situation. Instead, every fraction division can be a simple operation because the division operation can be rewritten as a multiplication as follows:

As noted previously, dividend / divisor = quotient.

This can be rewritten as:

$$\text{dividend} \times (1/\text{divisor}) = \text{quotient}$$

which is the same outcome as division. The quantity $(1/\text{divisor})$ is called a reciprocal and for a fraction it is as simple as flipping the fraction upside down.

Therefore:

$$(^5/_8) \div (^1/_4) \; = {^5/_8} \times {^4/_1} = {^{20}/_8} = 2\,{^4/_8} \text{ or } 2\,{^1/_2} \text{ (in simplified form)}$$

When a series of arithmetic operations are listed one after another, there is an method used to standardize results. The abbreviation **PEMDAS** stands for:

Parentheses, Exponents, Multiplication, Division, Addition and Subtractions

Which is a list of arithmetic operations in order of priority. Clearly operations inside of parentheses are performed first, followed by exponents since they occur second on the list.

Multiplication and Division are performed with equal priority but in left to right order as they are read. Addition and Subtraction are also performed with equal priority but in left to right order as they are read in the same manner.

Hints:
- Look for parentheses and exponents first.
- Execute those items in the correct order.
- Rewrite expression with remaining multiplication, division, addition and subtractions.
- Execute the multiplication and division in left to right order.
- Rewrite expression with remaining addition and subtractions.
- Execute the addition and subtractions in left to right order.

If you have executed this series of instructions in PEMDAS order, you will have the correct answer. One excellent way to check is that **EVERY** PEMDAS problem, if executed correctly, always ends in a series of additions and subtractions. Assuming you rewrote the expression as recommended, you will be able to go back and check your work to reassure yourself and build your confidence.

M.1.3. Compare and order rational numbers

- Decimals and comparison, place value and significance
- Comparison with like denominators
- Comparison with unlike denominators

Comparing and ordering rational numbers is about the determination of the inequality of two ratios, or which is the greater or lesser of two ratios. There are multiple ways to determine the comparison between two ratios.

In section M.1.1, we discussed the process of converting ratios into decimals. If the ratios can be converted into decimal form, then the comparison is a simple. If you choose this process, the comparison is a simple matter of evaluating two decimals. It is important to relate the matter of significance when considering this method. The decimal 0.751 is greater than 0.75. This may seem obvious but the evaluation is only complete when noting that 0.75 is equal to 0.750 and 750 is less than 751. The comparison is evaluated by looking at the third decimal place behind the decimal point (thousandths place). That value of zero in that third decimal place does not exist in the original form of the decimal. But the zero is implied because of the blank in that decimal place. The additional zero is allowed when comparing decimal numbers.

If the rational numbers are left in ratio form, there are two distinct possible outcomes. First, if the ratios have the same denominator, then the comparison is simply a matter of comparing the numerators. The larger numerator is the larger ratio. Obviously, one – fourth is less than three - fourths. One – fourth is also less than two - fourths which is another name for one – half. In the case of differing denominators, if a common denominator can be readily determined, this form of comparison can still be used.

Finally, if there are two ratios that can't obviously be converted to a common denominator, there is another simple but effective measure to allow comparison. If the two ratios are $^a/_b$ and $^c/_d$, the simple process of cross multiplication will allow a comparison. If the product bd is used as the common denominator, then the first fraction becomes $^{ad}/_{bd}$ while the second fraction becomes $^{bc}/_{bd}$. The comparison then becomes whether product "ad" is greater than or less than the product "bc". These two products are achieved simply by cross multiplying the numerators and denominators and maintaining the order of the two products. The final comparison is based upon the common denominator idea, but the algorithm is a simple matter of executing the products and comparing the results. It is not a trick but a simple mathematical process.

M.1.4. Solve equations with one variable

- Variable on one side and numbers on the other side
- Same operations on both sides of the equal sign
- Algebraic equation
- Combine like terms
- Constant
- Inverse Arithmetic Operation
- Reciprocal
- Variable
- Variable Terms

Solving equations is a basic foundation of Algebra skills. The term "equation" means that in between two algebraic expressions there is an equal sign. Section M.1.10 contains a table of what expressions can be. Simply, on either side of the equal sign there will be combinations of numbers and variables in various forms. The equation is solved when a single variable is on one side of the equal sign and a numerical value is on the other side. The steps involve combining like terms and applying inverse arithmetic operations. When we say "combine like terms" we mean that numbers will be manipulated to be one side of the equal sign (by convention, usually the right side), while the variable remains on the other (usually left) side. This may seem like a very general requirement, but the overriding issue is to make sure that all manipulation is completed while the equality is maintained between the left and right side of the equation. The guideline is that equality will **always** be preserved as long as the same operation is performed on each side of the equal sign. The question of which operations must be performed is determined by the expressions that are present in the equation. Specifically, the inverse operations are chosen to provide the results which we have specified in this paragraph. A few simple examples will illustrate the necessary steps.

Example 1: In the equation

$$X + 9 = 64$$

…there is a variable expression on the left side and a constant on the right side. Our goal is to end with the variable alone on the left and a constant on the right. That means we need to eliminate the number nine that is added to the variable on the left side. Elimination of the number nine is achieved by using the inverse operation of the addition. Equality is preserved by subtracting the same number on both sides of the equal sign. Specifically:

$X + 9 - 9 = 64 - 9$

The result is that x = 55. Using that value in the original equation is a correct solution. Because the original equation had an addition, the solution required a subtraction.

Example 2: A slightly more complex equation involves multiple operations in the solution:

$$9a - 14 = 67$$

$$9a - 14 + 14 = 67 + 14$$

$$9a = 81$$

$$9a/9 = 81/9$$

The result is that a = 9. Using that value in the original equation is a correct solution. Because the original equation has a subtraction and a multiplication, the solution required addition and division to solve. Notice that the addition is performed first. The process can be solved in either order but doing the addition and subtraction first means that addition and subtraction of fractions will not be required later in the solution. Until now the examples had only one variable expression. You will see that more complex equations will be solved with the same methods.

Example 3: A slightly more complex equation involves variable expressions on both sides of the equation:

$$17t + 52 = 9t + 68$$

$$17t + 52 - 52 = 9t + 68 - 52$$

$$17t = 9t + 16$$

$$17t - 9t = 9t - 9t + 16$$

$$8t = 16$$

$$8t/8 = 16/8$$

$$t = 2$$

The result is that t = 2. Using that value in the original equation is a correct solution. Subtraction was used twice, once with the variable terms and once with the constant terms until a single variable expression was equal to a single constant. Only then was the division process used to find a single variable equal to a constant with the inverse operation to find the value of t.

Could this solution have been achieved if the division was performed first? Of course it could, but it would mean that the solution would involve fraction addition and subtraction for both the constant terms and the variable terms. The best guideline to help you remember the correct order is that addition and subtraction are performed until the constant term is on one side of the equal sign and the variable term is on the other side. Once they are on opposite sides, division by the coefficient in the variable term will determine the value of one variable.

M.1.5. Solve real world one or multiple step word problems with rational numbers

- Interpreting verbal descriptions
- Formulating relations (equations)
- Checking and solving

Ratios and fractions are synonymous when discussing numerical values. The ratios or fractions always imply division of the numerator by the denominator as stated previously. The numerical values of ratios routinely occur in the testing situation. In previous section M.1.1, the conversion between fractions and decimals and back to fractions was discussed. In this section, the discussion is directed towards how words appear in ratio problems and how those words should be interpreted.

A commonly used ratio, defined by specific words, is contained in the term "miles per hour", usually abbreviated by mph. When the term "miles per hour" is interpreted numerically it is the ratio of the total number of miles traveled divided by the number of hours traveled. More details of this ratio will be discussed when converting units. The key word in this commonly used term is "per". It literally means for each hour of travel a specific number of miles will be traveled. It has the same implication when the term is "gallons per hour" (how fast the tub is filled or the lawn is watered) or "tons per year" (how much ore is mined in one year).

Another way that ratios can appear is when a phrase defines a ratio of one value to another. A common comparison is usually the ratio of "men to women" or vice versa. Test problems will often use the ratio "boys to girls" or "girls to boys". When this terminology is used, the first term is in the numerator and the second term is in the denominator by convention.

There is an inherent problem when this terminology is used as illustrated by the example below:

In a classroom setting, the ratio of girls to boys is 3 to 4 (or 3:4 in strictly mathematical terms). How many boys are there in the classroom if the total number of students is 28?

There are two ways that this word problem may be easily solved. If the ratio of $girls/boys$ is ¾, the actual numbers may be ¾ or $^6/_8$ or $^9/_{12}$ or $^{12}/_{16}$ and so forth. These fractions are all equivalent fractions since they all simplify to the value of ¾. The equivalent fractions are easily determined as the ratios of multiples of the numerator and denominator of the original fraction. There is only one fraction where the numerator and denominator add to a total of 28 and that is the ratio $^{12}/_{16}$. Therefore, the solution is the classroom has 16 boys and 12 girls.

Notice that the words specify which group, boys or girls, is which specific number in the original problem and in the solution. When choosing multiple-choice answers, make sure that the correct number is chosen based upon the original definition in the problem. Most often both numerical values are in the answer choices and only one selection is correct.

- Percentages are special rational numbers
- Percentages are most easily used with decimal equivalents
- Percent Increase
- Percent decrease

Solving word problems with percentages begins with the concept that percentages are ratios. In section M.1.5 we solved problems with rational numbers so in this section the specifics of percentage problems will be addressed. Percentages are ratios with 100 in the denominator; the "per cent" or per 100. A group of 14 students in a grade level with 140 students is a ratio of 14/140 or 10%. In section M.1.1 we looked at formulating percentages from ratios and ratios from percentages. In this section we will apply percentages to solving real world problems where they are commonly used.

The most common percentage problems involve finding what percentage a number represents. In this section, reading precisely what is given and what is requested will be of extreme importance. For example, we may be asked to find the percentage of boys in a classroom if there are 18 boys and 22 girls. The key to formulating the correct ratio first is that the numerator is the total number of boys and the denominator is **the total number of students in the classroom!** Students are often misled to the formulation of a ratio using just the two numbers given. But the words of the question specify that the number of boys (18) be compared to the total number in the class. So the ratio becomes 18/40. That percentage is determined by performing the division and the result is a decimal value of 0.45 which is represented as 45%.

Now, what would it look like if the problem was presented in the opposite order. If it were given that there were 18 boys in the class and they represented 60 % of the class, how would that solution be formulated? The solution is simply a one-step solution like we have already solved. The constant part of the equation is the 18, while the variable part is 60% of the classroom size which we will call the variable "x". The solution becomes:

$$.60 \ x = 18$$

$$.60 \ x/.60 = 18/.60$$

$$x = 30$$

If that question was reformulated with a slightly different wording, the mathematics would appear totally different. If instead you were given that only 20 students were in a class and you were asked to find the 60% of the class that were musicians the equations would appear as follows:

$$.60 * 20 = m$$

The solution is a simple multiplication with m = 12. But, you may not know that the simple solution works unless you formulate the equation guided by your understanding of the words that are in the problem. We have already seen how important the words are in ratio problems. Make sure that you read carefully and formulate an equation that is representative.

Another type of percentage question involves percent increase or decrease. You will see that this sort of problem involves quantifying a change relative to a given amount. Quite often this sort of problem involves money, so it's obvious that these problems will prove to be quite valuable.

For example, if the problem asks you to find your percent increase for your new raise that increases your pay from $10.00 to $13.50 per hour? In this case the unknown is the percent "p". The percent is defined as the ratio of the "increase"/ the original amount. Here again, there is a need to read carefully so that the comparison is understood completely. The equation looks like this:

$$P = (13.5\text{-}10) / 10$$

$$P = 3.5/10$$

$$P = 35\%$$

Did you remember to move the decimal point to make the decimal the percent? Notice that the subtraction was necessary to provide the "amount of change". Dividing that amount by the original pay rate provides the percent change.

We have addressed the "percent increase" question and the remaining question is about the opposite type of problem where we are asked to quantify the "percent decrease". As you might have guessed, the numerator will be another subtraction so we can calculate the decreased amount. As before, we are using the original amount as the denominator but in this case, it is the larger of the two values. So finding the percent decrease problems are solved as follows:

If your savings has has balance of $275 some of that total is deducted to pay bank service fees. If the new account balance is $263, what was the percent decrease in the account? The equation becomes:

$$P = (275\text{-}263)/275$$

$$P = 12/275$$

$$P = 4.4\% \text{ approximately}$$

Notice the beginning amount is in the denominator and the changed amount is in the numerator. Reading carefully is important once again to ensure that our ratio contains the correct amounts for the percentage calculation

M.1.7. Apply estimation strategies and rounding rules to real-world problems

- Rounding and significance
- Estimation and precision
- Primarily Metric system
- Distance
- Mass
- Temperature

In the world of quantifying numerical values, it is very common for us to estimate and round numbers for everyday use. If we are asked our age, we typically would not respond with the number of years, months, weeks and days. Of course we normally express our age in whole number of years. But also in that process we may round our age to the nearest year and that leads to the first topic in this section. When we are rounding a numerical value, we would normally want to understand the precision that is required. An example of the rounding process follows:

Example 1: Our calculated value when we solve a problem comes out to 256.739.

If we are asked to round to the nearest whole number, the 7 in the tenths place tells us that the whole number would be expressed as 257. A number in the tenths place equal to 5 or greater means that the ones place would be rounded to the next higher value. If it had been 4 or or less in the tenths place it would have remained at 256.

If our value is significantly more precise than needed, we may be asked to round to the nearest hundred. In that case, the 5 in the tens place means that the rounded value would be 300. Again the rounding rule is the same as the previous example except that it is applied to the number in the tens place.

In the world of scientific measurement, the precision is typically determined by the device used for the measurement. A metric balance scale would be more precise than required to weigh the amount of meat for a burger. Conversely, using a bathroom scale to measure a medical dose would never be considered precise enough. Having an introduction to precision helps us to estimate quantities. The difficult part is that for most of the scientific world, those estimations need to be within the metric system. We will use some examples to provide a means for you to compare your estimations. We will organize this discussion around the metric system units that you may be expected to use.

The largest unit of measure that you may be asked to use, is the kilometer. It is about 5/8ths of a mile so if you are asked to estimate your bus ride to school, you could take the number of miles and multiply by 8 and divide by 5. The decimal conversion is that a kilometer is about .625 miles or a mile is about 1.6 kilometers. A way to remember the conversion is that 55 miles per hour is approximately 88 kilometers per hour.
Shorter distances may be easier to convert and estimate. A meter is close to 39 inches or about 10% more than a yard. A football field then is about 110 meters.

The centimeter is one of the most useful units of metric measure. A way to compare is that 10 centimeters is close to 4 inches. 1 centimeter is very close to 3/8ths of an inch. An inch is about 25.4 millimeters. Since inches are usually broken down into sixteenths and thirty- seconds, a millimeter is easy to picture as a length between those small units that we often find on a tape measure or a ruler.

This discussion has provided some images that should help you in your effort to become fluent in using the metric system of length measurement. Unlike the standard system of measurement that is used in the U.S., there is a logical progression with powers of ten describing the relationship between these metric units we have discussed. Even better, the units of mass have a similar and logical relationship. Larger masses would typically be weighed in kilograms and small quantities would be weighed in grams. From your prior knowledge, you may remember that the relationship between a kilometer and a meter is 1000 m/km. In mass measurement the relationship is similar, 1000g/kg is the conversion. Relative to each other, we can compare and relate but the connections to real world objects may not be so obvious. However, it is actually simpler in the metric system than the standard system.

When the metric system was formulated, the unit of the gram was defined as the mass of one cubic centimeter of water. A cubic centimeter is about a teaspoon of water, so a gram is a very small unit of mass. A medical dose in a pill may be less than, but comparable to, a gram. But it provides a relative size to help you estimate. A letter in the mail may weigh a few grams. A milk carton is about a couple of kilograms. A soda bottle is just under a liter or 1000 cubic centimeters, so it weighs about 800 grams. Remember, your estimation may not be exactly the same as someone else's. But the comparisons from your knowledge base will increase the quality of your estimation.

Converting temperatures between Fahrenheit and Celsius scales can be accomplished using formulas that would be cumbersome for estimation purposes. They are however, linear scales that have a few points that will allow you to estimate temperatures that are close to the given values. Look at the following table for comparison:

F°	C°	
32	0	Freezing water
68	20	Cool Room
86	30	Warm day
212	100	Boiling water

Remember, you are estimating temperatures. Do you have an estimate for 50° C (halfway between 32 and 212)? Would you be comfortable at a temperature of 10° C? (halfway between 32 and 68)? To find the number halfway between add the two numbers and divide by two. 50° C is about 122° F and 10° C is about 50° F. Estimating is a challenge for everyone but practice makes everyone better and we all develop confidence when we practice.

M.1.8. Solve real world Problems involving proportions

- Proportion and ratios
- Constant of Proportionality

In previous sections, the topic of ratios has been addressed in various ways. In this section, real world examples will help you apply this to your problem solving. There are two features of all proportionality problems that you will use. First, proportionality means that two quantities will always compare in a constant ratio. This ratio is called the constant of proportionality (k) and it is often depicted as follows:

$$Y = K*X$$

And therefore:

$$K = Y/X$$

This may seem to be just a simple observation but in fact it results in a powerful problem solving tool. The following examples will illustrate how the proportionality is used.

A common example is the pay that is received for the hours that are worked. That ratio of dollars per hour is what we normally consider our rate of pay. If your rate is $17.50 per hour, then the following rates will apply:

$35/2 ($35 for 2 hours worked)
$87.50/5 ($87.50 for 5 hours worked)
$437.50/25 ($437.50 for 25 hours worked

How much money would you be paid for a 40-hour work week? The ratios that could be used are almost unlimited in number, but **one** solution would be as follows:

$$\$17.50/1 = X / 40$$

$$40 * \$17.50 = \$700.00$$

Of course this is a simple problem, but to illustrate how ratios are used, the problem could be solved with any of the other of the ratios:

$$\$437.50/25 = X / 40$$

$$25 X = \$437.50 * 40 \qquad \text{(cross multiplying)}$$

$$X = \$437.50 * 40/25$$

$$X = \$700$$

This is a simple example, but it illustrates an extremely valuable property of proportionality in problem solving. Once the proportionality constant is established, the rest of the problem solving is cross multiplying and dividing. The same answer resulted from using different numbers but they originated with the same proportionality constant.

Another example is to use proportionality to determine the completion of a work scope. If your workforce is able to generate 550 widgets (a common but fictional product) in a single 8-hour work day, how many hours are required to complete an order of 1750 widgets for your best customer?

The ratios are as follows:

$$550 / 8 = 1750 / X$$

$$550 * X = 1750 * 8 \quad \text{(cross multiplying)}$$

$$X = 1750 * 8 / 550$$

$$X = 25.45 \text{ hours}$$

This number tells you the how many hours are required to complete the order. There may be other questions to consider. The distribution of approximately 25-1/2 hours (rounded because we would never worry about .05 hours) is another question. The basic proportionality problem provides the information needed for the other real world questions of overtime or extra workers to be addressed separately.

- Rate
- Rate of change
- Ratio
- Unit Rate

Ratios have appeared in previous sections and we know that fractions, ratios and even rational numbers are all linked by the concept of a number divided by another number. We have used these ratios in mathematical problem solving examples. In this section our ratios will serve another purpose. Understanding the concept of rate give us another powerful problem solving tool. Understanding the terminology associated with rates and ratios is the first step in problem applications.

The term "rate", is defined as the ratio of two quantities with different units of measure. We used a pay rate in section M.1.8 because it is familiar to everyone. It represents "R" the number of dollars per hour that are earned for working. We also know if that we work "X" number hours we will earn R*X dollars for our efforts. If we double the number of hours, we earn double the amount of money. In terms of the rate "R", for each hour that is worked the rate of change in dollars earned is "R" the number of dollars per hour. Since "R" is the amount of money "per hour", it represents something called a "Unit Rate". As we shall see, this term is commonly applied even when we do not use the term.

Another widely used rate system is the one associated with driving a car. If we are driving and the speedometer reads 65, it means that we are moving at a rate of 65 miles per hour (mph). In terms of "rate" terminology, the rate of change in the position of our car, is 65 mph. In one hour our car will be 65 miles from the current location. Notice that 65 mph is a unit rate because the motion is 65 miles **per single hour.** Finally, for every hour that we apply the 65 mph rate, the car will be 65 miles further down the road. Simple examples will demonstrate the problem solving methods.

For example, at the 65mph rate, how much time (T) is required to travel 250 miles one way? The equation is modeled after "distance equals rate multiplied by time". The solution becomes:

$$250 = 65 * T$$

$$250/65 = T * 65/65$$

$$T = 3.85 \text{ hours (rounded)}$$

Note that this is not 3 hours and 85 minutes. Since 60 minutes are in one hour, .85 * 60 = 51 minutes (approximately). Our trip will take 3 hours and 51 minutes.

A similar example is how fast must we drive if we need to travel the 250 miles in 2 hours and 45 minutes? The equation becomes:

$$250 = R * 2.75 \text{ (45 minutes is ¾ or .75 hours)}$$

$$250 / 2.75 = R * 2.75 / 2.75$$

$$250 = R * 2.75$$

$$R = 91 \text{ mph} \qquad \text{(90.9 rounded to mph)}$$

If that sounds fast, it's a great lesson. Even though the correct ratios can be formulated, it doesn't mean that the ratio will be "reasonable". We can achieve 91 mph but traveling at that speed is not a reasonable outcome normally.

The rate problem leads to another example that is asked in a workplace situation. If you are in charge of workers, you may be asked to use this type of calculation to determine how to get the required productivity. The problem is to determine the rate of completion of a given task. Workers may have different rates of productivity in the workplace. We may be asked to combine the efforts of workers to finish in a shorter time.

In this example, worker A can complete a task working alone in 8 hours and worker B can complete the same task in 5 hours. How long will it take for them to complete the task if they work together? The individual rate for worker A is 1 task per 8 hours or 1/8 task/hour. Worker B completes 1 task per 5 hours or 1/5 task/hour. Their combined rate is 1/5 + 1/8 or 13/40 task /hour (remember the section where we found common denominators?) The final solution in the form of rate * time is as follows:

$$1 \text{ completed task} = 13/40 \text{ task/hour} *T \text{ (the task completion time)}$$

$$T = 40 / 13 \text{ (3.077 rounded)}$$

This solution says that the combined effort will require about 3 hours and 6 minutes (rounding to the nearest tenth of an hour). This may not seem to be intuitive or "reasonable". However, it's simply the outcome when the workers have two different work rates. Using two workers with the same rate would mean that the required time would be half the completion time for one worker. That makes sense intuitively but the mathematics allows you to evaluate the more complex problems.

- Equation (means a single answer)
- Expression
- Inequality (means ranges of answers that satisfy the condition "greater than or less than")
- Simplify

Algebra uses variables, numbers and operations as the basic parts. Variables are typically represented by letters and may have any number of values in a problem. Usually the variable is the unknown quantity in a problem. All letters can and often are used, but x, y, and z are letters that appear most often in algebra textbooks. In a testing situation, letters other than x, y, and z are often used to mislead test takers.

Algebraic expressions are variables and numbers with operations such as addition, subtraction, multiplication and division. The following are all examples of algebraic expressions:

x	y	a	(letters)
$7u$	$\frac{1}{2}q$	$3.9\,p$	(product of a variable and number)
$s + 5$	$u+v$	$2.3+r$	(sum of a variable and number)
$z - 3.5$	$k-n$	$t - 1.3$	(difference of a variable and number)
$m/6$	$z/2$	$3.9\,/p$	(quotient of a variable and number)
c^2	$b^{0.5}$	$\sqrt{3}$	(variable or number w/ an exponent)

Notably, the sum, difference, product or quotient of these items are also expressions.

Equations are defined as algebraic expressions that are set equal to a number, variable or another expression. The simplest identifier of an equation is the equal sign (=). When an equation is written to express a condition or represent a situation for problem solving, the solution is normally completed by manipulating the equation correctly so that a variable or unknown quantity is on one side of the equal sign and the numerical answer (s) are on the other side of the equal sign.

An example of an expression is "X − 35". An equation results if that expression is set equal to a number or another expression. For example, a simple equation results if "X − 35" is set equal to the number 78. To solve that equation, we use the steps from M.1.5. Our answer becomes X = 113. That value establishes the value of X that makes the left side equal to the right side. The reason that this terminology is important is that we need to determine what happens when we establish an Inequality.

If the equation was changed to an inequality, the result would be either the expression "greater than" or "less than" the numerical value on the other side of the sign. In the case of the inequality, there are signs which we use for "less than" or "greater than" as follows:

"<" means the left side is less than the right side
">"   means the left side is greater than the right side

These signs are normally read left to right. It can be confusing but, there is a definitive way to make sure that the signs are interpreted correctly. Simply, the signs when viewed as arrowheads, always point toward the smaller side. Evaluating these "inequalities" is simply a matter of solving the equality and checking to see if the result is consistent with the original inequality. In the example of

$$X - 35 > 95$$

$$X - 35 + 35 > 95 + 35$$

$$X > 130$$

This solution means that any value greater than 130 means that the original inequality is true. Solving other inequalities is similar. If it is necessary to multiply both sides of and equation by a negative number to solve, then the direction of the inequality sign is reversed. If you check your result for reasonableness, the correct value will provide the correct result.

Expressions may require simplification. In this section we look at the methods of simplification that may be useful as steps to problem solution.

In the expression:

$$8X + 18$$

there are common factors that allow the expression to be simplified. Since 8 and 18 are both even numbers they have a common factor of 2. Therefore, the expression is simplified by writing it as follows:

$$2(4x+9)$$

The common factor appears outside the parentheses and the 4 and the 9 are left inside since they have no common factors.

If that expression was:

$$8X + 16$$

the common factor could be 2 ,or 4, or 8. Choosing the largest common factor provides the best choice for simplification.

Another simplification example is a rational expression with common factors in the numerator and denominator. The rational expression:

$$X^7 / X^3$$

can be simplified into just: X^4

To illustrate how this simplification occurs, we can rewrite the original expression in expanded form:

$$X^7 / X^3 = X^4 * X/X*X/X*X/X$$

In the expanded form, there are seven "X" factors in the numerator and three "X" factors in the denominator. Clearly the three factors of X/X can be cancelled since they always equal one. The remaining factor is the simplified form of the expression.

After looking at the simplification of expressions, a few examples will be used to illustrate problem-solving methods.

If the simple equation is written in word form, the first step must be to write the equation that represents that written question. The simple problem of ages of individuals is a common example:

Example 1: Jane is 8 years older than Nancy. In 5 years she will be 27 years old. What is Jane's age now?

The variable J will represent Jane's age and the expression J+5 will represent Jane's age in 5 years. In this example we read that this expression is equal to a number, in this case 27. Our equation becomes:

$$J+5 = 27$$

In the words of the problem, we have the correct expression set equal to a number. Our basic principle is to perform algebraic operations until the "J" is alone on one side of the equation and the numerical answer is on the other side. This type of solution involves the opposite of the addition (+5) so 5 is subtracted from both sides.

$$
\begin{array}{r}
J+5 = 27 \\
\underline{-5 \quad -5} \\
J+0 = 22
\end{array}
$$

Therefore, the answer says that Jane's age is now 22 years of age. What happened to Nancy's age? Often, extraneous information is left in the problem as a distractor from the problem at hand. In Example 2, the more complex version of this problem will be addressed.

If the simple equation involved a multiplication the steps would involve an opposite operation which in this case would be division such as:

$$
\begin{array}{c}
7J = 84 \\
7J / 7 = 84/7 \\
J = 12
\end{array}
$$

These examples are typical of "one step solutions" since a single operation is involved to solve the problem.

Of course, there are multiple step solutions in more involved problems. But the rules are still the same, i.e.

- Opposite (or inverse) operations are performed to solve
- The same operations must be performed on both sides of the equation.
- The solution is complete when a variable is on one side and the numbers are on the other side

<u>Example 2:</u> Jane is 8 years older than Nancy. In 5 years she will be twice as old as Nancy. What is Jane's age now?

The first step to solving this type of problem is to identify the variable. In this solution we will select the variable "J" to represent Jane's age and "N" to represent Nancy's age.

The two equations from the word description, become:
$$J - 8 = N$$
and
$$J + 5 = 2(N+5)$$

Dividing both sides of the second equation by 2 means that it becomes:
$$(J+5)/2 = N+5$$
Adding 5 to the original equation we have:
$$J - 8 + 5 = N + 5$$

In this method, there are two expressions which contain "J" and they are both equal to "N + 5". Mathematically, they must be equal to each other. The completed equality becomes:
$$J - 3 = (J + 5)/2$$

To solve, multiply both sides by 2 (same operation on both sides) and the equation is:
$$2J - 6 = J + 5$$

Subtract J and add 6 to both sides and the answer becomes:

$$
\begin{array}{rcl}
2J - 6 & = & J + 5 \\
-J + 6 & & -J + 6 \\
\hline
J & = & 11
\end{array}
$$

With this solution, the problem is completed and the following statements are clarified:
- Now Jane is 11 years old and Nancy is 3 years old.
- In 5 years Jane will be 16 years old and Nancy will be 8 years old.

We are able to answer the question, "What is Jane's age now?" and all the other ages in the question because of an algebra principle that requires two equations for two unknowns. In the problem, there are two variables (J and N) and two relationships between them (now and 5 years from now). If we are able to formulate two equations with the two unknowns, then algebra principles will allow for the solution of a complex problem.

M.2.1. MEASUREMENT AND DATA

Interpret relevant information from tables, charts, and graphs:

- Axis
- Bivariate
- Cartesian Coordinate
- Chart
- Graph
- Legend
- Scale
- Table

In this section, the important systems for presenting data in graphic ways will be discussed. The purpose of the tables, charts or graphs is to formulate a representation of specific data in a system that is informative and meaningful to an audience or in the workplace to coworkers who may not have had direct contact with the presented data. An often overlooked benefit of presenting data in these forms is to allow trending, interpolation and extrapolation based upon the existing data. If these terms are not familiar to you now, they will be discussed after some basic concepts are presented.

Graphic data is normally presented on an x-y coordinate system. The x values are normally scaled on the horizontal number line called the "x axis". The vertical axis is the "y axis". The scale of the two axes does not necessarily need to be exactly the same. Plotting real data often means that the axes will be different because the x and y data will use numerically different data. If there are differing he scales of the axes, this information would normally be included in the label for the individual axis. The labels may include the units (cm for example), a scale factor (100's of mm), and the type of data represented. The data presented is termed "bivariate" because there are two variables that are paired together in the presentation of the data. Before the data is plotted on this two axis system, it is normally represented in "x-y pairs" which are written as ordered pairs inside of parentheses (x, y). Often, students are confused on the formulation of the ordered pairs. The guidelines will be discussed for you to apply when your data is ready to plot.

The ordered pairs are usually gathered in (x, y) form, where the x value is first and the y value is second inside the parentheses. The horizontal axis is always first and the vertical axis is always second. If there is some confusion, the "x, y" pair is always in alphabetical order, x first, y second. These two values are normally referred to as Cartesian coordinates and the graphing system is called the Cartesian plane. The horizontal axis is normally used to plot the "independent" data, and the vertical axis is use to plot the "dependent" data. A medical example is an excellent way to illustrate how data is categorized as dependent or independent.

A critical patient may have his vital signs taken several times a day. When plotted, the data would be presented with the time of day on the x axis and the blood pressure, for example, on the vertical axis. For clarity, the horizontal axis would be labeled, "time", along with the AM / PM format (24-hour time formats are standard in the military). The vertical axis would be labeled "blood pressure" and probably include both systolic and diastolic values as two different points for single timed entry.

If this is not enough to clarify the choice for "x data" and "y data", then it may be worthwhile to use this questioning method to help you decide. In the case of the vital signs, do the vital signs depend on the time of day or does the time of day depend on the vital signs? The second part of this question is silly, so the vital signs are dependent and are graphed on the y axis. The time is graphed on the x axis. If there is any question on the formulation of the graph, a legend is normally used so the viewer has a clear picture of the intent and content of the graph. In the example of the critical care patient, it would possibly be labeled "Blood Pressure Data for Marcus Jones, May 19 – 21, 2016". The patient's name means that the graph is dedicated to his folder and the dates allow the graph to be viewed relative to previous and subsequent blood pressure data. More specific information will be discussed in the section below discussing evaluation of data.

If the plotted data is depicted in the form of a connected line between data points, it would normally be called a line graph or just a graph. There are two other forms of data representation. They can be shown on a coordinate axis such as the original data graph. If the data is demonstrated in the form of solid vertical bars the data is in chart form for a display called a histogram. If multiple data items are depicted with adjacent vertical bars, the display form is called a bar chart. Both of these displays are typically done on graph paper but instead of the line, the representation is simplified in the form of vertical bars. A significant benefit in this data form is the possible use of color the further enhance the significance of your data display.

Another type of chart is valuable for multiple data items that can be viewed as "parts of a whole". If we are depicting budgetary items, for example, a pie chart is often used for viewing the items that make up the total budget. The term "piece of the pie", refers to the concept of parts of the whole in the shape of pie slices. Again, a legend is used to clarify the percentages of the "pie slices" and the description of the budgetary items represented. In the makeup of the pie chart the central angle of each item is directly proportional to the percentage represented. A 35% item in a budget would have a central angle determined by 35% of the $360°$ in the full circle. In this case the central angle would be $.35*360°$ or $126°$. The complete pie represents 100% of the budget and the sum of all the budgetary items.

A final representation can be very useful in the form of a table. The following example will be analyzed to show how useful a table can be:

X	Y
5	7
11	19
14	25
23	43

Of course, this table could be used as the basis for a graph on a Cartesian coordinate system. In the following sections, examples such as this will be used to demonstrate how valuable trending data can be determined by direct analysis of the table itself.

- Measures of central tendency
- Outlier
- Range
- Shape
- Spread
- Data Trend
- Expected value (Interpolate and Extrapolate)
- Point on a graph

In a set of numerical data, the concept of central tendency is an important quality with several different ways that it may be characterized. Mean, median, mode and range are commonly used terms of central tendency that are defined and demonstrated in this section.

To determine the Mean, the elements of the data set are simply added together and that sum is divided by the total number of items in the set. You may have used the word "average" to describe this same quality and the two are the same calculation. It is possibly the most known quantity and has simple yet powerful applications.

In the first example, the number set will be defined as follows:

6, 5, 8, 11, 23, 14, 7, 9

In this calculation, the order of the sample need not be considered. The next step is to find the sum of the sample:

Sum of the sample = 83

83/ 8 = 10.375 (rounded to 10.4)

Dividing by 8, the sample mean is 10.4. It is important to note from this example that the mean is not necessarily an element of the original set. We can use the calculated mean value to compare with the other central tendencies to be determined.

To determine the median, the numbers of the set must first be assembled in order. The given set, in order, appears as follows;

5, 6, 7, 8, 9, 11, 14, 23

Once the set is ordered, the median is the number that appears exactly in the middle of the set with equal numbers of the set to the left and the right of median. Note that the given set in this problem has an even number of elements. In this case the median is determined to be the average of the two center elements. In this sample the two center elements are 8 and 9 so the average of the two and therefore the median is 8.5.
The mode of a set is the number that appears most often in the set. Specifically, the mode must appear at least twice and in this set the mode is undefined.

The range of the set is sometimes considered as measure of central tendency. It is defined as the largest element of set minus the smallest element. In our example above, the range is defined as:

$$23 - 5 = 18$$

The range in this example is once again not an element of the set. Further in most cases it is the least likely to represent the original set of data. If the data is represented on a number line or as a bar graph of data, the range is a measure of the spread from the greatest to the least of the data elements.

In this section the data sets have been limited in number, depicting only eight elements in the sample. For samples that are larger in number, there are qualities of the set that can be viewed as shapes of the data distribution. The normal distribution is a large set of numbers with as single peak in the distribution and symmetrical values mirroring the data on the opposite side of the peak. Sometimes called the "bell curve", the ideal distribution has the mean, median and mode centered at the central value of the distribution. With a table of the "Standard Normal Distribution" models of the "bell curve" type of distribution can be quantified numerically. For the purposes of this discussion the shape of the curve will be adequate to describe the distribution. If there are two peaks in this distribution, it is called "bi-modal". In the previous discussion of the mode, the values were the ones that appeared most often. The mode is the value that has the highest peak of the distribution and if there are two or more peaks, the data is said to be "bimodal" (or multi-modal for more peaks).

In the analysis of the shape of the data sets, there may be an asymmetry to the shape which is a quality called skewness. If there is an excess of data to the left of the distribution (with data tailing to the left of the main peak of the distribution) it is said to be "skewed left". The opposite condition is called "skewed right". Skewness is a common feature of a data distribution in the real world. If the skewed data can be characterized as a single data point, (an extreme case) that data point is called an outlier. Once a data point is labeled as an outlier, it is not unusual that the qualities of the data distribution would be quantified without using the single outlier data point.

There are two other types of data sets to be considered when discussing the shape. If the data has no clear peaks and no identifiable trends it is termed a "uniform" distribution. Throughout the range of the data, there is a uniform number of data points at each value. The data is said to be "without trend" or "correlation".

If the data has a randomness but has a tendency to decrease to the right, the trend is said to be negative (as in the slope of the graph) or a negative correlation. If there is a tendency for the data to increase to the right, the trend is positive or increasing with a positive correlation. This level of evaluation is extremely valuable for characterizing experimental data that is expected to be "linear" in nature.

Further, a single straight line drawn along and following the trend of the random data is called a "line of bet fit". This is a graphic method for the purposes of this instruction, but advanced mathematical analysis or calculators can perform this estimation precisely for a limited data set. This technique is a valuable tool, since the line of best fit will allow the user to predict a y value for any value on the x axis. A point on the line of best fit allows for interpolation, the determination of a point between two actual data points. By extending the line of best fit past the range of the original date set, a point on the line can be used to extrapolate or predict values beyond the range of the original data.

The specifics of this simplified method of characterizing experimental data, is often the basis for analyzing simple high school level physics problems. The effectiveness of this method makes it valuable in the analysis of real world data.

A data table may not seem to be a representation useful for data analysis. The previous example will be used to demonstrate how a table can be used to illustrate linear data qualities.

This table was used earlier in this section:

X	Y
5	7
11	19
14	25
23	43

Of course, this table could be used as the basis for a graph on a Cartesian coordinate system but to find rate of change we can look at how variables change with the following work on the table:

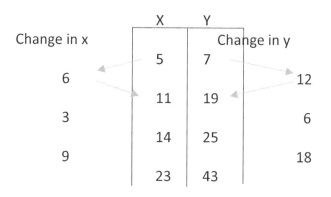

The rate of change in the table is defined as Change in y/ Change in x. On a graph this quantity is called the slope and provides a measure of how fast the data is rising or falling (if negative). The entries in the "Change in x" (and Change in y) columns are just the difference between the two adjacent x or y entries in the table. Any table that you encounter can be analyzed in this manner. The linearity is not obvious in the original table but the simple analysis in this example shows that the data is linear in nature, with a slope of positive 2 and a positive correlation.

In earlier examples we discussed interpolation and extrapolation in the data and the example can be used to demonstrate these qualities for a data table.

	X	Y	
Change in x	5	7	Change in y
	11	19	
	14	25	
	23	43	

Knowing that the slope is 2 allows you to determine a y value for x = 17. For x = 17 the change in x is 3 (measured from 14). Knowing that the Change in y/ Change in x is 2 means that the change in y must be 6 (measured from 25).   Therefore, the value for x = 17 would be y = 31 simply using the numerical values from the table. Since x=17 is inside the range of the data, this is interpolation.

Extrapolation, finding data points that are outside the range of the table, is also possible with this method. Can you see that x = 37 and y = 71 is an extension of the linear table that we began with in this section?

M.2.3. Explain the relationship between two variables.

- Covariance (positive and negative)
- Dependent variable
- Independent variable

The nature of the dependent and independent variable was discussed in section M.2.1. The topic of covariance will be explained with selected example to illustrate the concepts associated with covariance.

Covariance is defined as the property of how two variables change relative to each other. Since we have stated that y values are dependent and x values are independent, this becomes more of a description of how y changes with x.

Covariance of a data set that has a tendency to decrease to the right, is said to have a negative trend (as in the slope of the graph) or a negative covariance. If there is a tendency for the data to increase to the right, the trend is positive and increasing with a positive covariance. This level of evaluation is extremely valuable for characterizing experimental data that is expected to be "linear" in nature. The concept of covariance and correlation for the purposes of this text are the same. Only with more advanced data analysis would these two concepts differ. For this reason, most secondary education focuses on correlation rather than covariance.

- Linear Units
- Length
- Arc
- Subtend
- Circumference
- Perimeter
- Area
- Irregular Shape
- Square Units
- Sum
- Surface Area

In this section on geometric qualities, the general focus will be on one-dimensional and two-dimensional geometry. The specific focus will be on length and area. Under the heading of length and area, we can formulate a substantial knowledge base to problem solve real world geometric questions. This study will not address three dimensional objects and their volume or surface area.

Section M.1.7. contained the information on length units of measure in both the standard and metric systems. The length units of measurement are an important beginning of the geometry discussion because the two geometry topics apply the linear units of measure directly. Perimeter is defined as the distance around the outside of a two dimensional figure. A two dimensional figure is one that can be completely contained in a single plane. For this reason, they are sometime called planar figures

For example, the perimeter of a square is the sum of the four sides. Since the sides are equal in length, the perimeter of the square is the length of one side multiplied by four. In general, the perimeter is the sum of the length of all sides of the planar figure. This assumes that the sides are all line segments.

To determine the distance around the outside of a circle requires a quantity known as π (the Greek letter pi). The quantity π is defined as the ratio of the circumference / diameter for every circle. Therefore, the circumference which is the length of the outside curve of a circle is found by multiplying π times the diameter. The diameter is simply the straight line distance from one side to the other side of a circle, measured through the center. The curved segment which is part of a circumference is known as an arc. The arc length is a fraction of the circumference. That length is calculated with the following formula:

$$\text{Arc length} = \pi * \text{diameter} * \text{central angle} / 360°$$

The central angle is the angle with the center at the vertex. The central angle rays cut (or subtend) that part of the circumference that is in the interior of the angle. The ratio of that central angle / 360 is the fraction of the circumference. Can you see that the arc length of a semi-circle (1/2 of the circle) is π * diameter/2 or just π * radius? This π ratios is usually approximated as 3.14 although it is actually an irrational number with an unlimited number of decimal places. In this case it is precisely known as a ratio but never precisely known as a single number. In the following discussion of area, the ratio π appears in the formula for the area of a circle.

The concept of surface area begins with the length unit of the side of the figure. The shape that is considered the basis of area calculation is the square that measures one unit in length for each side. That unit may be metric or standard, but the square unit is defined as the measure of space inside that unit square. As we measure larger and more complex shapes, including circles, the areas will all be expressed in terms of square units.

The following table is a summary of the formulas for the area calculations associated with the triangular and quadrilateral shapes:

Shape	Formula	Description
Square	$A = L * L = L^2$	L is the length of the side
Rectangle	$A = L * w$	L and w are the different side lengths
Isosceles Triangle	$A = \frac{1}{2} b * h$	b is the base length, h is the Perpendicular distance to the opposite Vertex.
Parallelogram	$A = b * h$	b is the base length, h is the Perpendicular distance to the opposite Side
Trapezoid	$A = \frac{1}{2} (b_1 + b_2) * h$	b_1 and b_2 are the two base length, h is the Perpendicular distance between the bases
Rhombus	$A = \frac{1}{2} (d_1 + d_2)$	d_1 and d_2 are the lengths of the diagonals

To determine the area inside of a circle again requires the quantity π. Instead of the diameter, the area calculation for a circle uses the radius which one half the diameter. It is defined as the distance from the center of the circle to the circumference. The area is calculated with the formula of π times the radius squared or $\pi * r^2$. The units are the square unit of the radius, either standard or metric.

The shapes that have been discussed in this section may be used to add and subtract from each other to calculate the area of complex shapes. The following examples will illustrate these methods.

Example 1: Find the area inside a rectangle but outside the circle in the diagram (not to scale):

The rectangle has length of 6cm and width of 5cm

The circle has radius of 2cm

Area of the rectangle is 5*6 = 30 cm^2

Area of the circle is π * 2*2 = 4 π cm^2

The required area is 30 - 4 π cm^2

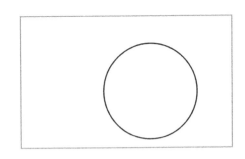

If you expected a single number, the value of 3.14 can be used for π and the decimal value becomes:

$$30 - 12.56 = 17.44 \text{ cm}^2$$

Remember that the decimal number is not a precise answer. The answer that has the "pi" in the answer is a precise answer.

Example 2: Find the area inside the circle but outside the square in the diagram (not to scale):

The radius of the circle is 3"

The length of the side is 3"

Area of the square is 3*3 = 9 sq. inches

Area of the circle is π * 3*3= 9 π sq. inches

The required area is 9 π − 9 sq. inches

Again If you expected a single number, the value of 3.14 can be used for π and the decimal value becomes:

$$28.26 − 9 = 19.26 \text{ cm}^2$$

The combinations of all figures is impossible to duplicate in a limited text, but the concept of adding and subtracting areas and perimeters is a simple matter of identifying the specific parts that need to be added or subtracted. As you can see simple creativity is needed!

- Conversion
- Conversion factors within the standard or metric system.
- Conversion factors between standard and metric systems.
- Unit Conversion

Converting the units of measured or calculated quantities is simply a multiplication process that allows data to be presented in the preferred units of measure. The multiplication is simple if the conversion factor is known. A simple example of this process using familiar, well known units of measure will be helpful.

A football field is 100 yards from goal line to goal line. If we are asked to convert this measurement to feet, we know that there are 3 feet in every yard. The mathematical conversion factor is 3 $^{feet}/_{yard}$. The method to convert looks like this:

$$100\ ^{yards}/_{field} * 3\ ^{feet}/_{yard} = 300\ ^{yards}/_{yard} *^{feet}/_{field} = 300\ ^{feet}/_{field}$$

In the conversion, the "yards" units cancel each other since one is in the numerator and one is in the denominator. The final units are left in the form that is required to answer the question in feet. This cancellation process not only tells us how to calculate but it also helps us to decide whether to multiply or divide. Writing the conversion factor with the units in the form of a ratio will help us decide on the process to use. Since 3 $^{feet}/_{yard}$ has feet in the numerator, it also shows us that the yards will cancel and the conversion process will provide the information that we require.

Can you see that this football field is also 3600 inches long?

To illustrate the other way that conversion factors may be used, we need to solve the problem of expressing this same football field in terms of miles. The readily known conversion factor is 5280 $^{feet}/_{mile}$. Since we need "miles" to be in the numerator, the conversion factor tells us that we must divide by 5280 $^{feet}/_{mile}$. The method to convert looks like this:

$$300\ ^{feet}/_{field} * 1/5280\ ^{mile}/_{feet} = 300/5280\ ^{miles}/_{field} = 0.062\ miles\ (rounded)$$

That's not even a tenth of a mile!

Within the standard system of measurement, most of the conversion factors are quantities that we know. Feet, inches, yards and miles are well known by most people that need to measure or calculate data. The other type of conversion involves the metric system and converting standard units to metric. The main unit of conversion is 2.54 $^{centimeters}/_{inch}$. The football field that is 3600 inches long can be converted to centimeters as follows:

$$3600\ ^{inches}/_{field} * 2.54\ ^{centimeters}/_{inch} = 9144\ centimeters$$

The conversion to other units within the metric system is simplified by the fact that the units contain the information that helps choose the conversion factor. For example, the centimeter units that we used contain the metric prefix "centi" which means one hundredth. Therefore, the 9144 centimeters in the football field is converted as follows:

9144 centimeters *1/100 ^{meter}/$_{centimeters}$ = 91.44 meters

That also tells you that a meter is about 91 % of a yard.

If we need to look at the field in terms of a kilometer, the prefix "kilo" means one thousand so, the 91.44 meters in the football field is converted as follows:

91.44 meters *1/1000 ^{meter}/$_{centimeters}$ = 0.09144 kilometers

Meters, kilometers, centimeters are commonly used metric units. The other commonly used unit is the millimeter. Since the Prefix "milli" means "one thousandth", we are readily able to convert using powers of ten.

Can you see that there are ten millimeters in one centimeter? Can you also see that there are 1000 times 1000 millimeters in one kilometer? That means that a millimeter (close to one thirty second of an inch) is about one millionth of a kilometer.

SCIENCE

Science Section 1

The questions contained in the science sections of the ATI-TEAS are designed to evaluate one's level of knowledge of the chemical basis of life, cellular biology, human anatomy and human physiology. This includes virtually the entire range of content of a full year of introductory high school level biology and general chemistry. Additionally, the ATI-TEAS will likely include questions that test for knowledge of topics that are often not well covered by the introductory high school level courses in biology and general chemistry. In particular, these question topics may include material that is usually addressed in higher level courses such as organic chemistry biochemistry, cell physiology, human physiology, human anatomy, human embryology and human genetics.

It is obviously not practical to provide a complete science review within a single manual that includes the entire range of material that is covered in multiple years of science coursework at a high school and/or college level. No study manual can claim that is covers everything in the TEAS. The information provided in this manual is - in our opinion - likely to be high-yield. In other words, it is material that is very likely to be encountered as topics of actual HESI science questions. We also present the material as a logical progression of topics - as a storyline that makes sense and is (we hope) reasonably interesting. It is also our judgement that by far most of lower yield science information that is actually encountered on HESI science questions is likely within this section of the manual.

We also - when necessary - may introduce concepts that are unlikely to be directly tested for on the TEAS, but which greatly clarify and simplify the explanation of high-yield information. This material will allow one to avoid the need to use rote memorization of a large amount of high yield facts as preparation for the TEAS. It will also provide a deeper level of understanding of a large amount of otherwise confusing information and allow us to introduce much of the more advanced science topics in an efficient and more easily grasped manner. Although we cannot guarantee that this manual will prepare you for every possible HESI science question we are confident it will prepare you to succeed at the highest levels of the HESI Science section.

Life and Physical Sciences
A discussion of the physical and life sciences is virtually impossible without providing the basics of physics. Although there are few if any purely physics type questions on the TEAS, one is at a huge disadvantage without an understanding of several basic topics in physics. This understanding begins with the fact that the physical universe consists of essentially four things, space, time, matter and energy. These four things have various measurable properties. The properties are measured in standardized units called metric or **SI units**

Space
There are three spatial dimensions on our universe and one may define these as length, width and height. The SI unit of measurement for space is the **meter**. The abbreviation for a meter is "m". If we define two points in space, we can measure the **linear distance** between the two points. The magnitude of this distance can vary greatly, from the incredibly small to the unimaginably large. At a human level the meter (m) is often used since many of the things we encounter as humans are in the meter scale. The height of an average adult male in the U.S is about 1.7 meters. For larger scales we often use 1000 meter units called **kilometers** (km). The circumference of the earth is about 40,000 km. For very large distances we use scientific notation in meters or kilometers. The distance from the earth to the sun is about 1.5×10^8 km. For the largest

distance scale, we use the distance that a beam of light would travel (in a vacuum) in one year - a light year. One light year is equal to 9.46×10^{12} km. For small human-scale distance we use **centimeters** (cm) which are 1/100th of a meter and **millimeters** - which are 1/1000th of a meter. At the microscopic scale we use **micrometers** (μm) which are one millionth of a meter or 1×10^{-6} m. For the atomic scale we often use **nanometers** (nm) which are 1×10^{-9} m.

Area

A 2-dimensional region in space can be defined as an area or a surface. The simplest of these is a is a flat or planar rectangular surface with a length "L" and a width "W" The resulting area is equal to the product of the length and the width. For instance, a flat rectangular surface with a length of 4 m and a width of 5 m has an area (A) of

$$A = (4 \text{ m})(5 \text{ m}) = 20 \text{ m}^2$$

Notice that the units "m" or meters are multiplied in the equation to give a new metric - meters-squared (m^2) or "**square meters**". Meters-squared" is a distance squared and areas in general have units of distances squared.

In the life sciences, square meters is usually too inconveniently large a scale. More often surface areas are defined as square centimeters. One centimeter is equal to 100 centimeters but 1 square meter is not equal to 100 square centimeters. A square with sides of 1 meter has an area of 1 m^2. This means it has sides that are 100 cm in length, so the area of the square in square centimeters is (100 cm)(100 cm) = 10,000 cm. While 1 meter is equal to 100 centimeters, one square meter is equal to 10,000 square centimeters

Volume

A 3-dimensional region in space can be defined as a volume. The simplest of these volumes is a rectangular volume with a length "L", a width "W" and a height "H". The resulting volume is equal to the product of the length, width and height. For instance a rectangular volume (V) with a length of 4 m, a width of 5 m and a height of 6 m has an volume of

$$V = (4 \text{ m})(5 \text{ m})(6 \text{ m}) = 120 \text{ m}^3$$

the units "m" or meters are multiplied together three times in the equation to give a new metric - meters-cubed (m^3) or "**cubic meters**". Meters-cubed" is a distance cubed and volumes by definition have units of distances cubed. Notice that 1 cubic meter can be the volume of a cube with sides each equal to 1 meter in length, width and height. This means the cube can also be said to have sides equal to 100 centimeters in length, width and height. Therefore the volume of the 1 m^3 cube in centimeters is (100 cm)(100 cm)(100 cm) = 1,000,000 cm^3. A Volume of 1 m^3 is equivalent to a volume of one million or $1 \times 10^6 cm^3$.

 A common non-SI unit of volume particularly in the laboratory is the **liter** (L). The liter is defined as a volume of exactly 1,000 cubic centimeters (cm^3). One milliliter (mL) is 1/1000th of a liter or 1×10^{-3} L. The milliliter scale is also a very common volume scale for the life sciences.

Circular metrics

A linear distance in space often is a displacement distance. Displacement represents the shortest distance between a starting point and ending point location of an object when an moves from one location to another object. An object may travel any arbitrary distance in a circle and end up exactly where its motion began. The object will have no overall or net displacement but the object has traveled a distance. This distance - if it is a complete circle - is equal to the diameter of the circle "D) times a constant called pi (π). This is the circumference (C) of the circle.

$$C = \pi D$$

The value of pi is a transcendental number - a number that has no exact value but can be calculated to any arbitrary level of preciseness beyond the decimal point. For our purposes we will use the value of pi to two places to the right of the decimal point, this value is 3.14.

A **circular area** (A) is calculated by multiplying the square of the radius (r) of the circle by pi

$$A = \pi r^2$$

A **spherical volume** (v) is given by the formula

$$V = 4/3 \, \pi r^3$$

Frequently in the laboratory, volumes are measured in **cylinders**, the formula for the volume (V_c) of a cylinder is height (h) of the cylinder times the cross sectional area of the cylinder (r^2)

$$V_c = h(\pi r^2)$$

Mass

Nearly everything in the universe relevant to the HESI can be defined as matter or as energy. Matter is essentially everything that has mass. Nearly all matter on earth is composed of atoms, and atoms are composed of three basic subatomic particles, the proton, the neutron and the electron. All three of these subatomic particles have a fundamental physical property called mass. Any physical object on earth should be thought of as being composed entirely of atoms. All physical objects on earth therefore have mass. This mass is the sum of the mass of all of the atoms that comprise the object. The mass of the atoms of the object is the sum of the masses of all of the protons, neutrons and electrons that compose the atoms of the object.

For macroscopic objects such as a rock, a glass of water, or a balloon full of helium gas, The SI units of mass is the kilogram (kg). In the laboratory it is more common to work with smaller units of mass than kilograms. The most common of these mass units are grams and milligrams. Grams (g) are 1/1000th of a kilogram and milligrams (mg) are 1/1000 that of a gram. It is unusual that the kilogram is the standard SI unit for mass since a kilogram is by definition equal to 1000 grams.

At the atomic scale masses are incredibly small. The mass of a proton is 1.6726 x 10^{-27} kg, the mass of the neutron is slightly more than the mass of a proton but the mass of the electron is 1827 times lighter than the mass of the proton. For atomic scales, masses are given in atomic mass units (AMUs). The AMU unit is vastly smaller than a kilogram unit. The mass of a proton in AMUs is approximately 1.007 AMU. The mass of the electron is so small that it can be approximated as zero for most cases likely to be encountered in the TEAS

Density

In addition to mass, all matter also has a volume, For any given sample of matter, that volume is the volume of space that the sample occupies. The mass of a sample of matter divided by the volume of the sample of matter is the mass per unit volume of the sample (m/V). This property of matter is defined as the density of matter. The scientific symbol for density is the Greek letter rho (ρ). There are no commonly used specific SI units of density, density is by definition units of mass divided by units of volume. Density is usually given in units of grams per liter (g/L) or in SI units of kilograms per cubic meter (kg/m^3) or grams per cubic centimeter (g/cm^3). The density of liquid water at a temperature of 4°C is equal to 1 gram per cubic centimeter (1 g/cm^3)

Weight

As we proceed through our review of the science section of the TEAS, we will often introduce terms and concepts that we have not already carefully described. Most students should already have a least somewhat general understanding of these commonly referenced items. If you are uncertain about the meaning of these items, you should still be able to follow the discussion and consider that we are previewing concepts that will be addressed in detail in other sections of the review. This section is an example where we address the topic of "weight" and explain the topic in terms of forces and accelerations. We are jumping ahead of ourselves in a sense - we are describing one concept using other concepts that have not yet been addressed. We do this because we are presenting this review in the format of a logical progression of ideas. The topic of weight is very closely related to mass, and this is also a logical stage to preview the concepts of forces and accelerations.

The physical quantities of weight and mass are often misunderstood. Mass is an intrinsic property of matter that is determined by the type and number of atoms that comprise a given sample of matter. Weight is a force that acts on matter in a gravitational field. On earth this force is equal to the mass of an object times the acceleration that the object experiences due to the strength of the Earth's gravitational field. This acceleration is 9.8 m/s^2. For instance the weight of a 20 kg object on the surface of the earth will be (20 kg)(9.8 m/s^2) = 196 kg-m/s^2.

The units "kg-m/s^2" are defined as the SI units of force - the "newton (N)". One newton equals 1kg-m/s^2, therefore the weight of a 20 kg mass on earth is 196 newtons (N). When samples of substances are weighed in the laboratory the "weight is usually given in units of mass. Since mass is directly proportional to weight this is an acceptable but technically inaccurate description of the sample weight. Almost always in experiments a sample weight is given in mass units, but in reality what is measured is the weight of the mass due to earth's gravity. And the correct units are not units of mass (i.e kilograms) but units of force (i.e. newtons). One way to keep this distinction in mind is to consider that in an environment where there is no significant force of gravity, one could not "weigh out" a sample of a substance on a scale. The sample mass would exert no force of the scale and would be literally weightless.

Atomic and Molecular Weights

The terms atomic and molecular weights are often used in science and should be considered to be equivalent to the terms atomic mass and molecular mass where the units of mass in grams is substituted for the number of AMU units. If , for example, an atom has an atomic mass of is 10 AMU then the corresponding atomic weight is 10 grams. This is actually equivalent to the number of atoms, that as a sample, would have a mass total mass of 10 grams. We have discussed that a single atom's atomic mass is approximately the sum of the masses of the protons and neutrons contained in the atom's nucleus. The unit of mass at the atomic level is the atomic mass unit (AMU). When the term atomic weight is used it is referring to the average mass of an atom of an element.

Elements

An element is the group of all atoms that have the same number of protons in their nucleus. For instance, the element carbon refers to all atoms that have exactly four protons in their atomic nuclei. Most carbon atoms also have four neutrons in their nuclei so most carbon atoms have an atomic mass of approximately 8 AMU (4 protons + 4 neutrons). Some carbon atoms have more than 4 neutrons in their nuclei so these carbon atoms have a mass larger than 8 AMU. On average the mass of a carbon atom is somewhat larger than 8 AMU due to the existence of the carbon atoms that have nuclei with more than 4 neutrons. The actual average value depends on the naturally occurring percentages of heavier carbon atoms. This average elemental atom mass is defined as the element's atomic mass - but also is frequently described as the element's atomic weight. In the laboratory the term atomic weight is considered to be the equivalent to the element's atomic mass in grams. This is a very important definition to understand because it is used as a scientific basis for designing almost all chemical experiments. The reason for this is because the atomic masses of all of the elements have been determined experimentally. The absolute values of these elemental masses are less important than the fact that we also know what the elemental masses are relative to the other elemental masses. For instance, the atomic mass (average mass) of a carbon atom is approximately 12 AMU (21.01) and the atomic mass of an oxygen atom is approximately 16 AMU.

Molar Mass

We cannot work with individual atoms in the laboratory but since we know what the relative values of the masses of carbon and oxygen atoms are (12-to-16 or 12:16), then we can weigh out 12 grams of carbon and 16 grams of oxygen and since this is the ratio of the masses of carbon and oxygen atoms we know that there are theoretically exactly the same number of carbon atoms in the 12-gram sample of carbon as there are oxygen atoms in the 16-gram sample of oxygen. This knowledge allows scientists to conduct experiments and make measurements that reveal import and detailed information about chemical reactions. This knowledge of the relative masses or mass ratios of elements is so useful that scientists have adopted a working version definition of an element's atomic mass as being the element's atomic weight in grams.

Molecular weights are defined in the same manner as atomic weights, for instance the mass of one molecule of water (H_2O) is the sum of the atomic masses of two hydrogen atoms and the atomic one oxygen atom. This is (2)(1)+16=18 AMU. The molecular weight of H_2O is the molecular mass of H_2O in grams, so the molecular weight of H_2O is 18 grams. This mass in grams of an atomic or molecular mass is also called the **molar mass** of the atom or molecule.

An example is a single molecule of oxygen which consists of two chemically bonded oxygen atoms. The atomic mass of oxygen is 16 AMU so the atomic weight of oxygen is 16 grams. The molar mass of oxygen atoms is also 16 grams. The oxygen molecule O_2 contains two oxygen atoms so it has a molecular mass of 32 AMU (16+16) and a molecular weight of 32 grams and a molar mass of 32 grams. This can also be stated as "the atomic weight of oxygen is 16 grams per mole (g/M)" or " the weight of one mole of oxygen atoms is 16 grams."

Avogadro's Number

For the molecule of O_2 one can say "the molecular weight of O_2 is 32 grams per mole (g/M)" or "the mass of one mole of O2 is 32 grams". The mole is actually a number without units. It is equivalent to the number 6.022×10^{23}. This number is also called Avogadro's number. This is the number (1 mole) of particles present in any sample of a pure molecular substance where the mass of the sample of the substance is equal to the molecular weight of the substance. It is an awkward concept to express in words but easier to show by example.

Scientific Methods and Reasoning

Suppose that a student is in chemistry lab and is asked to measure out 5 moles of liquid ammonia. First the student must determine what the molecular formula for ammonia is. It is NH_3 meaning that individual ammonia atoms consist of three hydrogen atoms and one nitrogen atom. Next the student must determine the molecular mass of an ammonia molecule. This can be determined by referring to the periodic table of the elements which generally will list the atomic mass of every element beneath the atomic symbol for the element. For nitrogen (N) this is 14 AMU and for hydrogen this is 1 AMU. The molecular mass of ammonia is therefore 14+ (3)(1)=17 AMU. The molecular weight or the molar mass of ammonia is therefore 17 grams.

The student can weigh out a sample of liquid ammonia on laboratory scales such as a triple beam balance scale or on an electronic scale. The scales will give values in grams. It is true that grams is a mass unit not a weight unit, but this is usually not relevant because metric or SI unit scales are calibrated so that the weight the scale indicates for the sample in grams is actually the true mass of the sample in grams. (The true weight of the sample would be $(17g)(9.8 \text{ m/s}^2) = 166.6$ newtons). This 17-gram sample of ammonia is equivalent to one mole of ammonia. The number of ammonia molecules in the sample is 6.022×10^{23} molecules.

Next the student is asked to obtain a 3 mole sample of carbon tetrachloride. The molecular formula for carbon tetrachloride is CCl_4 meaning one molecule of carbon tetrachloride contains one atom of carbon (C) and four atoms of chlorine (Cl). The atomic masses of a carbon atom and a chlorine atom according to the periodic table of the elements is 12 AMU for carbon and 36.45 AMU for chlorine. The molecular mass of CCl_4 is therefore 12+(4)(36.45)=157.8 AMU. This means 1 mole of carbon tetrachloride will "weigh"157.8 grams on a laboratory scale. The molar mass of CCl_4 is 157.8 grams/mole (g/M). Notice that this one molar mass is equal to the mass of 6.022×10^{23} molecules of CCl_4. Since not one, but three moles of CCL_4 are required, the student must weigh out (3 moles)(157.8 grams/mole) = 473.4 grams of CCl_4

The concept of the mole (M) and molar mass is encountered continually in the physical and life sciences. It is more common to think of a chemical reaction as representing the reaction of moles of molecules rather than individual molecules. For instance the chemical equation $2H_2 + O_2 \rightarrow 2H_2O$ can be interpreted as two molecules of hydrogen (each molecule consisting of two atoms of hydrogen) reacting with one molecule of oxygen (the "2" in O_2 indicating the molecule consists of two atoms of oxygen) to produce two molecules of H_2O (the molecular formula "H_2O" indicates that one molecule of H_2O consists of two atoms of hydrogen and one atom of oxygen).

It is often more useful, however, to think of this reaction as being one where two moles of molecular hydrogen (H_2) react with one mole of oxygen molecules (O_2) to produce two moles of H_2O molecules. Molar masses are often inconveniently large for research purposes and it is frequent that experimental procedures use millimolar (mM) units which are equal to 1/1000th of a mole.

Concentrations

Molar masses are almost always the units used to describe concentrations. Nearly all biochemical reaction occurs in liquids. The concentration of chemicals in a liquid is the number of molecules dissolve in the fluid per unit volume of the liquid. The dissolving liquid is called the "solvent" and the dissolved molecules are called the solute or solute particles. Together, the solvent and dissolved solutes are called a "solution". A one molar solution of a molecular substance contains one mole of the substance dissolved in one liter of solution (1Mol/L) The term "molarity" is closely related - it is the molar concentration of a solution phrased as "the molarity of the solution is". For example, a solution a given molecular substance with a concentration of 0.45 moles/liter (M/L) has a molarity of 0.45, or equivalently - a molar concentration of 0.45. Millimolar concentration units are also frequently used in the life sciences. A one millimolar solution of a chemical has 1/1000th of a mole of molecules dissolved in one liter of solution.

The Four Fundamental Forces

All matter interacts through space by one or more of the four fundamental forces. These forces are the strong force, the weak force, the electromagnetic force and the gravitational force.

The Strong Force

The strong force is the force that interacts between protons and neutrons in the nucleus of atoms to bind the individual protons and neutrons tightly together within the nucleus. The strong force is significant for the HESI because it is the force that is acting during the fusion of hydrogen nuclei into helium nuclei at the center of the sun. This fusion reaction produces unimaginable amounts of energy that reaches the earth in the form of photons. This energy is the energy that is used to power nearly every physical and chemical reaction That occurs on our planet. It is the energy that raises the temperature of the planet to a level that can support the chemical processes of life and it is the energy in the form of photons of visible light that is absorbed by plants to convert carbon dioxide and water into carbohydrates and oxygen. this process - called photosynthesis - is the reaction that allows plants to form the base of the food chain upon which nearly all other forms of life depend and it is the process that continually replenishes the atmospheric oxygen that is essential to all multicellular forms of life including humans.

The Weak Force

The weak force is the force within an atomic nucleus that can induce the radioactive decay (or breakdown) of an atomic nucleus. These radioactive decay products are of two types; alpha particles which are helium nuclei consisting of two protons and two neutrons, and beta particles (previously called beta rays) rays, which are very high energy electrons (or positrons). The weak force is significant for the HESI because it is process that generates many of the harmful types of radiation that humans encounter that can cause damage to human cells. The radiation hazard from radon gas is an example.

The Electromagnetic Force

The electromagnetic force is the force that interacts between charged particles. Charge is a fundamental property of subatomic particles. Electrons have an electric charge of -1, protons have an electric charge of +1 and neutrons have zero charge. Particles with opposite electric charges are attracted to one another by the electromagnetic force and particles with the same electric charge repel each other. It is the electromagnetic force that attracts electrons to an atom's positively charged nucleus.

When an atom contains the same number of electrons and protons, the positive charge due to the protons in the nucleus and the negative charge of the electrons surrounding the nucleus cancel out. As a result, the atom has a net electric charge of zero. When this is the case, the atom is called a neutral atom.

Ions

Atoms can have fewer or more electrons than protons. When the number of electrons exceeds the number of protons, the atom has a net negative charge. When the number of protons exceeds the number of electrons, the atom has a net positive charge. The net charge is equal to the sum of the positive charges due to protons and negative charges due to electrons. For instance, if an atom has eight electrons and six protons, then the net charge of the atom is (-8)+(6)= -2.

Atoms (and molecules) with net charges are called ions. Negative ions are called anions and positive ions are called cations. Larger particles such as molecules and even macroscopic objects can have a net charge, but this net charge always is due to an unbalanced number of electrons and protons within the particle or object

We will discuss the electromagnetic force at the atomic and molecular level in greater detail in the chemistry review section, but it is important to note that nearly all of the macroscopic mechanical forces such as mechanical friction, air resistance and the pressures exerted by fluids and gases are actually due to the repulsive electromagnetic force at the atomic level between the electrons of different atoms.

The Electromagnetic Force Equation

The mathematical formula that describes the electromagnetic force between charged objects is as follows:

$$F_e = k_e(q_1q_2)/r^2$$

Where F_e is the magnitude (amount) of the electrical force between two charged objects, q_1 and q_2 are the magnitude of the charge on the two objects and r is the distance between the two charged objects. Is the electric force constant that converts the right side of the equation into the SI units of force - the Newton (N).

The Gravitational Force

The gravitational force is a purely attractive force between objects separated in space. The gravitational force between objects depends on the mass of the objects and the distance between the centers of mass of each of the objects

$$F_g = G(m_1m_2)/r^2$$

Notice that the gravitational force equation is very similar to the electromagnetic force equation. F_g is the force of gravity (in Newtons) between two objects with masses m_1 and m_2 respectively,, r is the distance between the centers of mass of the two objects and G is the universal gravitational constant that converts the right side of the equation into Newtons (the SI unit of force).

General Features of Forces

We have defined the electromagnetic and gravitational forces but we still need to explain what these forces are and how they interact with matter. The nature of a force is best explained using **Newton's second law of motion**. This law describes what a force is in general, rather than describing a particular type of force, such as the electromagnetic force or the gravitational force. To understand this second law, we must describe three other physical concepts; the concepts of motion, velocity and of acceleration. This is because Newton's second law states that force (F) equals mass (m) times accelerations (a) or F=ma. It is unlikely that you will be asked questions that require calculations as given in the following discussion, but the concepts of a force, of velocity and acceleration are so fundamental it is very difficult to explain human physiology at the level of complexity expected by the HESI without this essential background information

Motion

Physical objects at any instant in time have a precise location in the three spatial dimensions. If an object's spatial location does not change over time, the object is said to be at rest or motionless. If an object continuously changes its spatial location over time it is said to be in motion.

When an object moves from one spatial location to another spatial location, this motion is called translational motion. The simplest type of translational motion is motion in a straight line. This is called linear motion.

Velocity

When an object is undergoing linear motion, the linear distance that the object travels during a given period of time is defined as the speed of the object. A car that travels 100 meters in 10 seconds has a speed of 100 meters/ 10 seconds or 10 meters per second (10 m/s).

The velocity of an object includes not only the speed of the object - which is the magnitude (size or amount) of the object's velocity - but also the direction in which the object is traveling. For instance, a car traveling 10 m/s due north has a different velocity than a car traveling 10 m/s due south. For the HESI one usually does not need to consider the direction of an object's motion. And therefore an object's speed may be considered to be the same as the object's velocity.

The exception to this may be when one is considering velocity in one direction vs. velocity in the opposite direction. For instance, an object that is traveling due north at 10 m/s can be assigned a positive velocity of 10 m/s. In this case, another object that is traveling due south (the opposite direction) at 10 m/s would be assigned a negative value velocity of -10 m/s.

The general equation to determine an object's linear velocity is

$$V = \Delta d / \Delta t$$

V is the object's velocity. The character "Δ" indicates "the change in". Δ d is the linear distance the object has traveled over a certain period of time and Δt is "that certain period of time". This is also called the change in position divided by the change in time.

Acceleration

Acceleration is the change in an object's velocity per unit time. If an object's linear velocity remains constant the object's acceleration is zero. If an object is increasing its velocity at a constant rate it is undergoing a constant acceleration. The general formula for the acceleration of an object is:
a= Δv/Δt

An example is a car that has an initial velocity of 10 m/s. Assume the car begins to accelerate at a constant rate. After 5 seconds the car's new velocity is 60 m/s. The change in the car's velocity, Δv, is (60 m/s) - (10 m/s) = 50m/s. The time span over which this change of velocity occurred - the change in time - or " Δt" - is 5 seconds (5 s). The car's acceleration is therefore:

a= (50 m/s)/ (5 s) = 10 m/s^2

This "second squared" or s^2 term is commonly called seconds per second - it means that, in the case above, the car is increasing its velocity by 10 m/s for every second that the car is traveling.

One aspect of acceleration to remember for the HESI is that acceleration can be negative. In the example above, if the car had an initial velocity of 60 m/s and slowed down at a constant rate resulting in a final velocity of 10 m/s after a time span of 5 seconds, the car would be accelerating in the opposite direction of its initial velocity. Under these circumstances, the car has a negative acceleration equal to -10 m/s^2.

Forces in Action

At the macroscopic (large scale) level the forces that act on an object resulting in changes in motion of the object are usually mechanical forces or the gravitational force. Mechanical forces at the microscopic level are the result of interactions of matter through the electromagnetic force. Mechanical forces at the macroscopic (large) scale can be generated, for example, by muscle contractions resulting in pushing and pulling mechanical forces that can be applied to an object. Another common means of applying a mechanical force is through chemical reactions such as the combustion of gasoline to exert a mechanical force on the pistons in an internal combustion engine.

Net Force

A force has a magnitude and a direction just as velocity and acceleration have magnitudes and directions. There are usually a number of different forces acting on an object, such as air resistance and surface frictional forces. Depending on their magnitude and direction, all of these forces added together can produce a net force; a single force of a specific magnitude that acts in a specific direction on the object. Often, all of the forces acting on an object cancel each other out and the net force acting on the object is zero.

If a net force is applied to an object, the object will begin to accelerate in the direction in which the force is applied. This is given by the general formula
$$F=ma$$

An example is an object with mass m =20 kg, that is experiencing an unknown net force. As this net force is exerted upon the object, it experiences an acceleration of 5 m/s^2. We can calculate the force acting on the object by substituting these values into the general force equation

$$F = (20 \text{ kg}) (5 \text{ m/s}^2); F = 100 \text{ kg} \cdot \text{m/s}^2$$

The unit kg·m/s^2 is the SI units for force. 1 kg·m/s^2 is equal to 1 Newton (N). Therefore, the object in the example above is experiencing a net force of 100 newtons (100 N)

We can rearrange the general force equation to determine an unknown mass or unknown acceleration of an object. For instance, if a 50 N force is applied to a 25 kg object, we can calculate the object's acceleration by rearranging the force equation to

$$a = F/m$$
$$a = 50 \text{ N}/25 \text{ kg}$$
$$a = 2 \text{m/s}^2$$

Notice that by definition, an object at rest has no net force acting upon it. Additionally, and often overlooked, is the fact that an object that has a constant velocity is also experiencing no net force. If a net force was acting on the object, as the equation F=ma shows, the object would be accelerating. An object with a constant velocity is not accelerating.

Pressure - Force per unit Area
Pressure is a physical quantity that is defined as the amount of force that is exerted by a substance per surface area (F/A). For example, gases that are confined in a sealed container will exert a pressure against the walls of the container. The individual gas molecules exert a force on the container walls when they collide with the interior surface of the container. The amount of force exerted per unit area by the gas on the container walls depends on how many gas molecules are inside of the container and how much force the average gas molecule exerts on the container wall when it strikes the container walls.

The SI unit of pressure is the pascal (Pa). One pascal is defined a 1 newton per square meter (1N/m or 1 kg-m/s^2). Atmospheric pressure is the pressure that the earth's atmosphere exerts on surfaces exposed to the atmosphere. At sea level this is defined as 1 atmosphere (atm) of pressure. One atmosphere of pressure is equal to approximately 1x10^5 pascals (the precise ratio is 1 atm = 101325 Pa). pressure is often measured in a barometer by the displacement height of mercury (Hg) within a U-shaped tube. The pressure unit as measured in this manner is the torr, 1 torr of pressure is equal to 1 mm displacement of mercury. One atmosphere will register in a barometer as a displacement height of 760 millimeters of mercury (760 mmHg), therefore 1 atm = 760 torr.

In human physiology, pressures effects are important factors in the respiratory system, the circulatory system, the renal or kidney excretory system. There are numerous others instances where pressure or pressure differences are a critical factor in a wide variety of physiological processes. In particular pressure effects are encountered in several physiological processes that involve diffusion of substances. Osmotic pressure is an important phenomenon that is produced when diffusion is occurring across semipermeable membranes within the body.

Energy
Energy is a fundamental quantity that - along with time and space - defines the physical universe. Energy and matter are intimately related. Matter is a form of condensed energy that has acquired the property of mass. Matter can be created from energy and matter can be converted to energy. This relationship is expressed mathematically by Einstein's famous equation E=mc^2, where E is a quantity of energy, m is a quantity of mass and "c" is the universal constant of the speed of light in a vacuum.

Still we are left with the question "what IS energy?" and that is a very difficult question at the fundamental level but it can be generally understood as a substance that can be absorbed by matter and emitted by matter and can be transferred between material objects. This interaction can change the properties of matter by increasing or decreasing the velocity of matter or by altering the interactions of matter in the form of chemical bonds between atoms and electromagnetic bonds between molecules and other larger particles of matter.

Electromagnetic Energy

Pure energy exists everywhere in the universe in the form of electromagnetic radiation. This energy consists of fundamental subatomic particles called photons. At the atomic level the notion of a particle as a solid object with a definite size and location is no longer valid. Photons can behave as if they are solid particles under certain conditions, but they more often behave as if they are waves of energy. The energy of a photon is related to its wave-like nature. Waves have a wavelength and a frequency. The energy of a photon can be almost zero or almost any higher value. The higher the energy of a photon the shorter the photon's wavelength and the higher the photons frequency. This range of energy wavelengths is referred to as the electromagnetic energy spectrum.

Electromagnetic waves are unique compared to other types of waves in that they do not require a medium within which to travel. Sound waves and all other waves must travel through matter in the form of a continuous gas, liquid or a solid medium. Electromagnetic waves can and do travel through the vacuum of empty space.

Beginning at the lowest energies and therefore the longest photon wavelengths (and lowest frequencies) of the electromagnetic spectrum are the radio waves followed with increasingly high energies by microwaves, infrared radiation, wavelengths of the visible light spectrum, ultraviolet wavelengths, x-rays and gamma rays. Infrared radiation is also referred to as thermal or heat radiation because it is emitted by all objects in proportion to the temperature of the objects and the absorption of infrared radiation generally results in an increase in the temperature of the substance that absorbs the infrared radiation. This type of transfer of energy in the form of heat is called radiation or radiative heat transfer (the other modes of heat transference are conduction and convection). Excessive heat transference to the body can of course cause thermal injury to cells ranging from mild 1st degree burns to 3rd or 4th degree burns resulting in permanent injury and frequently fatal injury.

The visible light spectrum is significant in that these are the photons that are detected by the human visual system. The light receptors of the eye - the rod and cone cells- actually absorb visible light and convert this energy to electrical signals that are relayed to the brain. Visible light photons are also absorbed by chlorophyll molecules in chloroplast in plant cells and are used as a source of energy for converting carbon dioxide and water into carbohydrates and oxygen.

The ultraviolet spectrum in significant in that photons at ultraviolet energies are emitted by the sun are able to damage DNA in the skin and are a primary cause of skin cancer including the extremely deadly form of skin cancer - malignant melanoma. Prolonged exposure of unprotected skin to sunlight dramatically increases the risk for the development of malignant melanoma. X-rays and gamma rays are even more damaging to DNA and even brief exposure can cause severe and widespread cell injury and - at high enough levels - rapid death from radiation poisoning.

In chemical reactions photons are absorbed and emitted by electrons as electrons rearrange themselves within and among the atoms that are participating in the chemical reactions. At the most fundamental level this is why chemical reactions occur. Electrons are always trying to achieve their lowest possible energy state and this requires that they find a means to release energy in the form of the emission of photons. Chemical reactions are one of the types of processes that allow this lowering of electron energy to occur through the emission of photons.

Heat

All forms of energy - kinetic energy and potential energy in particular - can be converted into work and that work can be converted back into any form of energy. Work and energy are therefore equivalent and the units of energy and work are the same. Heat ("H" or sometimes "Q")) is also equivalent to energy and to work and the units of heat are also given in joules. Heat can be converted to all forms of energy including kinetic and potential energy and all forms of energy including kinetic and potential energy can be converted to heat.

Temperature

In most cases heat - on the atomic and molecular scale - is energy that ultimately is converted to kinetic energy. Although an object that is motionless has no net kinetic energy, every object has a temperature. The temperature of an object is proportional to the average kinetic energy of the atoms that are contained in the object (to be precise the temperature of a substance is directly proportional to the square root of the statistical mean of the kinetic energy of the particles - atoms or molecules - that comprise the substance). This is true not only for substances in the solid state, but for substances in the liquid and gas states as well. The higher the temperature of a substance the greater the average kinetic energy of the individual particles contained in the substance. The addition of heat to a substance usually increases the temperature of the object.

The Temperature Scales - Celsius, Kelvin and Fahrenheit

The Fahrenheit (F) temperature scale defines the freezing point of water as 32 °F and the boiling point of water as 212 °F. The Celsius (C) temperature scale defines the freezing point of water as 0°C and the boiling point of water as 100°C

The Kelvin (K) temperature scale is equivalent to the Celsius scale with the exception that the Kelvin scale defines absolute zero as 0 °K, and the triple point of water as exactly 273.16 degrees (we will discuss what a triple point is in the "phases of matter" discussion). Absolute zero on the Celsius scale is -273.15 °C.

Absolute zero is the theoretically lowest possible temperature of matter. It corresponds to a state where the atoms of matter have no kinetic energy at all - in other words, they are completely motionless. The laws of quantum mechanics show that this temperature can never occur in nature - it is physically impossible to cool anything down to a temperature of absolute zero.

The conversion formula for Celsius to Fahrenheit is

$$T \ (°C) = (T \ (°F) - 32) \times 5/9$$

The Celsius to Kelvin conversion is

$$T \ (°C) = T \ (°K) - 273.15$$

Entropy

Chemical energy also can be acquired or released by changes in the entropy of the atoms and molecules that participate in a chemical reaction. Entropy (S) is related to the amount of order that exists in a system. There is a fundamental tendency for all systems to progress from a more highly ordered or arranged state to a more disorganized state. The amount of disorder of a system is called the entropy of the system. For instance, an ionic crystalline solid is very highly ordered - it has a very precise and tight arrangement of atomic ions. This crystalline solid has very low entropy. This low entropy state can be utilized as a source of potential chemical energy that can be liberated during chemical reactions. The precise amount of chemical energy associated with a given entropy level can be calculated. it is related to the minimum amount of energy that would be required to assemble a system of particles to the level of order of a given entropy state - the entropy of the ionic crystal for example - from a completely random arrangement of individual particles (the highest possible entropy state or the most disordered state. During chemical reactions where ionic crystals are dissolved the entropy of the system - in this case the chemicals participating in the reaction - increases by a large amount, since the highly ordered crystalline ions become very disordered and randomly distributed ions in a solution. In any chemical reaction the change in entropy (ΔS) of the reaction can be calculated. When the change in entropy for the reaction is positive the reaction is progressing from a more highly ordered state to a more disorganized state. The greater the positive change in entropy the greater the amount of chemical potential energy that is liberated by the reaction. This energy is equal to "$T\Delta S$" where T is the temperature at which the reaction occurs.

Acids, Bases and pH

An important category of chemical reactions for the HESI is acid-base reactions. Acids are - according to the Bronsted-Lowry definition proton donors or more specifically - substances or compounds that in a solvent (almost always water) dissociate, and one of the dissociation products is H^+ (the +1 hydrogen ion - which is actually a single naked proton). The general formula for the dissociation of an acid is

$$HA \rightleftharpoons H^+(aq) + A^-(aq)$$

Strong Acids

Strong acids will completely dissociate in water. The classic example of a strong acid is hydrochloric acid (HCl). To determine the pH of a strong acid, consider an aqueous solution of HCL that has a concentration of 1×10^{-2} Mol/L.

$$HCl \rightarrow H^+(aq) + Cl^-(aq)$$

Notice there is a single arrow in this equation, indicating the dissociation of HCL is complete. There is actually no concentration of HCL in solution. The HCl molecules have completely dissociated into $H^+(aq)$ and $Cl^-(aq)$ ions. Since one molecule of HCl dissociates into one $H^+(aq)$ ion (and one $Cl^-(aq)$ ion), 1×10^{-2} Mol/L of HCl will dissociate into 1×10^{-2} Mol/L of $H^+(aq)$ ion. The negative log of 1×10^{-2} is 2, therefore the pH of the HCl solution is 2.

Weak Acids

Weak acids do not dissociate completely in aqueous solutions. The pH of weak acid solutions depends on the equilibrium concentrations of the weak acid "HA" and its dissociation components "$H^+(aq)$" and "$A^-(aq)$". For weak acids, " $A^-(aq)$" is referred to as the conjugate base of the acid "HA".

$$HA \rightleftharpoons H^+(aq) + A^-(aq)$$

The equilibrium constant for acids is called the K_A and is given by the formula

$$K_A = [H^+(aq)] \; [A^-(aq)]/[HA]$$

In chemistry K_A values are converted to pK_A values. pK_A values are the negative log of the K_A value, just as pH and pOH values are the negative logs of the H^+ and OH^- concentration values of a solution.

The K_A equation can be rearrange to solve for the H^+ concentration as shown below (the "aq" notation has been eliminated to simplify the equation)

$$[H^+] = K_A \; [HA] / [A^-]$$

If we convert this equation to negative log values, the equation becomes the **Henderson-Hasselbalch equation**

$$pH = pK_A + \log([A^-]/[HA])$$

Scientific Methods and Reasoning

The primary importance of the Henderson-Hasselbalch equation is that it identifies the isoelectric point for a weak acid. This is the the pH level of the weak acid solution where $[A^-] = [HA]$. this means that $\log [A^-]/[HA] = 1$ and since the log (negative or positive) of 1 is equal to zero, $\log([A^-]/[HA]) = 0$. Therefore, at the isoelectric point, the weak acid solution pH is equal to the pK_A

$pH = pK_A$; the isoelectric point of a weak acid "HA" solution

This isoelectric pH value is important in chemistry because it is the optimum pH for a buffered solution - a solution that is resistant to changes in pH when additional acids or bases are added to the solution. In the human body the bicarbonate buffering system plays a crucial role in maintaining fluid pH values between a range 0f 7.35 and 7.45

A classic weak acid is acetic acid (the acid found in vinegar). The chemical formula for acetic acid is CH_3CO_2H. The partial dissociation of acetic acid in water is

$$CH_3CO_2H \rightleftharpoons H^+(aq) + CH_3CO_2^-(aq)$$

The pK_A of acetic acid is 4.76, and 1 molar aqueous solution (1 Mol/L) of acetic acid has a pH of 2.4, meaning the equilibrium $H^+(aq)$ ion concentration of the solution is between 1×10^{-2} Mol/L (a pH of 2) and 1×10^{-3} Mol/L (a pH of 3). We will not describe the mathematics required to determine the precise concentration of acetic acid in solution that would result in a solution pH that is equal to the pK_A of acetic acid, but this is a common calculation in chemistry used to prepare an optimally buffered solution with a pH of 4.76. The choice of which weak acid to use to prepare buffered solutions depends on the pH level that one wishes to maintain and then to select a weak acid with a pK_A that is as close to possible to the desired pH level

Bases

Bases are substances that according to the Bronsted-Lowry definition are proton acceptors or more specifically - substances or compounds that in a solvent (almost always water) dissociate, and one of the dissociation products is (usually) the OH^- ion. The general formula for the dissociation of a base is
$$BOH \rightleftharpoons B^+(aq) + OH^-(aq)$$

The concepts discussed for acids are nearly exactly analogous for bases. Strong bases completely dissociate in aqueous solutions and weak bases partially dissociate in aqueous solutions. There are K_b, pK_b and pOH values for base dissociations and. The B^+ in the above equation is called the conjugate acid of the base (analogous to the conjugate base, A^- of an acid dissociation reaction).

We will revisit acid-base reactions in greater detail in our later discussion of specific types of chemical reactions. The relationship of acid and base dissociations to equilibrium concentrations and associated equilibrium constants as we have discussed in this section are key concepts to an understanding of chemical equilibriums and future discussions of acid-base reactions.

In Section one we discussed many of the features of atoms, molecules and chemical reactions in general terms and with respect to underlying physical principles of chemical reactions. These topics are important to understand as a basis for the more in depth discussion of atoms, molecules and chemical reaction that are addressed in this section. Section 1 provides all of the information required to understand how chemical reactions behave without regard (for the most part) for what type of atom or unique types of molecules are participating in chemical reactions. In this section we address the concepts that determine what makes one type of atom or molecule unique and how these unique characteristics of particular atoms or molecules result in the huge variety of chemical interactions that make the processes of life possible.

There is material throughout this section that has been be introduced with varying levels of detail in section 1. We are restating some topical information already covered in section 1, but this is a useful method of active review and reinforcement of the previous material. Since many of these concepts are now somewhat familiar, they are more easily discussed in this section often in a different context and often in more detail. By reinforcing concepts in this manner, the relationships of topics become more clearly understood and more easily recalled. This also allows for a more efficient presentation of new material. Finally, this repetition of information allows the sections to stand on their own. An understanding of section 2 does not require a pre-reading of section 1. Taken together these two sections reinforce one another and provide a logical progression of scientific concepts

The Atom
The atom is the smallest unit of matter that can retain the physical and chemical properties of a specific substance. Atoms are composed of three subatomic particles; electrons - which are fundamental (not composed of smaller subatomic particles), and protons and neutrons which are each composed of quarks. Quarks are fundamental subatomic particles.

Atomic Radius
The electrons of an atom orbit the atom's nucleus. The outermost orbiting electrons define the surface boundary of the atom and define the size of the atom. Usually this size is given in terms of atomic radius or atomic diameter.

The Atomic Nucleus
The central region of an atom - the nucleus - is composed of protons and the neutrons. The only exception to this statement is that one isotope of the element hydrogen - hydrogen 1 - consists of atoms that have a nucleus that contains one single proton and no neutrons. Protons and neutrons are more generally classified as "nucleons". The nucleons of an atomic nucleus are held together by the strong nuclear force.

Atomic Mass
By definition, the mass of a proton is equal to exactly one atomic mass unit (1 AMU). The mass of a neutron is nearly equal to but slightly higher than that of the proton. For the HESI the mass of the neutron is also 1 AMU. The mass of an electron is several thousand times less than 1 AMU and for the HESI the mass of the electron is so small that it will irrelevant in comparison to proton and neutron masses. The mass of a single atom therefore is almost entirely due to the sum of the masses of the nucleons (protons and neutrons) in the

atom's nucleus. For example, an atom whose nucleus contains six protons and seven neutrons has an atomic mass of 6 AMU + 7 AMU = 13 AMU.

Nuclear Radius

The radius of an atom's nucleus is thousands of times smaller the atomic radius. Nearly all of the mass of an atom and almost none of the volume of an atom are contributed by the atomic nucleus. This means that the atom is almost entirely empty space and that the nucleus is incredibly dense.

Electrons and Atomic Charge

The nucleus is surrounded by electrons. Electrons have an electric charge of -1, protons have an electric charge of +1 and neutrons have zero charge. Particles with opposite electric charges are attracted to one another by the electromagnetic force (particles with the same electric charge repel each other). It is the electromagnetic force that attracts electrons to an atom's positively charged nucleus. When an atom contains the same number of electrons and protons, the positive charge due to the protons in the nucleus and the negative charge of the electrons surrounding the nucleus cancel out. As a result, the atom has a net electric charge of zero. When this is the case, the atom is called a neutral atom.

Ions

Atoms can have fewer or more electrons than protons. When the number of electrons exceeds the number of protons, the atom has a net negative charge. When the number of protons exceeds the number of electrons, the atom has a net positive charge. The net charge is equal to the sum of the positive charges due to protons and negative charges due to electrons. For instance, if an atom has eight electrons and six protons, then the net charge of the atom is (-8)+(6)= -2.

Atoms (and molecules) with net charges are called ions. Negative ions are called anions and positive ions are called cations.

The Elements

A specific element is defined as the group of all atoms that individually contain the same number of protons within their nuclei. Atoms with nuclei that contain different numbers of protons are different elements. The atoms of every individual element have a unique set of physical and chemical properties. Isotopes of an element have virtually identical chemical properties but can have different physical properties due to the difference in mass among the isotopes.

Isotopes

The simplest atom is the hydrogen atom. Any atom that has one and only one proton in its nucleus is an atom of the element hydrogen. Hydrogen atoms may also have one or two neutrons in their atomic nucleus. These three types of hydrogen nuclei - one with one proton only, one with one proton and one neutron and one with one proton and two neutrons - all have one proton in their nucleus, but the nuclei have different numbers of neutrons. Elemental atoms with different numbers of neutrons in their nucleus are designated as isotopes of the element. Therefore, there are three isotopes of the element hydrogen. The other elements have varying numbers of isotopes.

Atomic Weight

The atomic weight of an element is defined as the average atomic mass of atoms of an element. Since almost every element has at least two isotopes, the average mass of the elemental atoms depends on the masses of the isotopes and the fractional percentage (relative abundance) of the isotopes that occur in nature.

Hypothetically, imagine that hydrogen's three isotopes occur naturally in percentages of 50% H-1 (one proton or 1 AMU), 20% H-2 (1 proton and 1 neutron or 2 AMU) and 30% H-3 (one proton and 2 neutrons or 3AMU). The average atomic weight of hydrogen atoms in general would be
(0.5)(1 AMU) + (0.2)(2 AMU) +(0.3)(3 AMU) = 0.5 + 0.4 + 0.9 =1.8
If these were the actual percentages of hydrogen's three isotopes, the average mass of hydrogen atoms would be 1.8 AMU and the atomic mass of the element hydrogen would be 1.8. In reality, nearly all hydrogen (99.99%) is the isotope H-1, therefore the tiny fractions of heavier isotopes are too small to change the mass except at several digits to the right of the decimal point. Therefore, the atomic mass of the element hydrogen is very nearly equal to that of the hydrogen-1 isotope, which is 1.008.

For the lighter elements, usually the most common isotope by far is the isotope that has equal numbers of protons and neutrons, so most atomic weights are close to twice the element's atomic number (the number of protons in the elemental atom nucleus). This is not always true. For instance, the element chlorine has an atomic number of 17 and an atomic weight of 35.45. This indicates that the element chlorine contains a relatively large percentage of the heavier chlorine isotopes.

The Periodic Table
The periodic table arranges all of the elements in a modified grid-like chart. Each element occupies a unique position in the table. The position correlates with the element's atomic number (as we have mentioned, the atomic number of an element is equal to the number of protons contained in the nucleus of atoms of the element). The first element - hydrogen- occupies the upper left corner position in the table. Elements of sequentially increasing atomic number are added to the next available position in the same row of the chart immediately to the right until the row of the table is complete. The element with the next higher atomic number is assigned to the first position on the left of the row immediately below the completed upper-row of the table.

Groups and Periods
The rows of the periodic table are called periods; the columns of the table are called groups. The first two columns on the left side of the table, beginning with the first column on the left, are the group I elements and - for the adjacent column on the right - the group II elements. The last column on the right side of the table is designated as the group XIII elements. The columns that are located to the immediate left of the group VIII column, beginning with the adjacent column, are the group VII, VI, V, IV and III elements,

The first period (top row) of the table has only a group 1 position - hydrogen - and a group VIII position - helium. They are separated by a wide gap in the periodic row. The second period has eight positions that include all of the groups I-VIII. The group I and group II positions are separated by another large gap from the group III-VIII positions. The third period has eighteen positions. Between the group II and the group III positions are ten new positions. The elements corresponding to these ten new positions are designated as transition metal elements.

The gaps in the periods ultimately reflect differences and similarities in properties of the elements that emerge as electrons arrange themselves in various configurations. We will describe the manner in which electrons are arranged around an atomic nucleus shortly.

Atomic Energy States
All atoms strive to attain their lowest possible energy states. First this is favored by achieving charge neutrality for the atom. The nuclei of atoms have a positive charge equal to the number of protons in the atom's nucleus. All protons have a charge of +1. The most energetically favorable state for an atom in terms

of charge is the neutral state. An electron has charge of -1 the exact opposite charge of proton. When an atom contains equal numbers of protons and electrons the proton and electron charges cancel out and the atom's net charge is zero. By definition, neutral atoms have a net charge of zero. Neutral atoms however can lower their overall energy state even further if they can achieve a particular arrangement of electrons.

Electron Shells - the N levels

Electrons that are electromagnetically bound to an atom arrange themselves in concentric electron shells around the nucleus. In an atom, the innermost electron shell is the "n=1" electron shell. The "n=1" electron shell contains the lowest energy level positions available to electrons. For this reason, the n=1 shell is the first to be filled by electrons. The n level can be any positive integer n=1,2,3... the larger the integer value for n, the higher the energy of the n electron shell.

Electron Subshells (Orbitals)

The regions within a electron shell that electrons may occupy are called subshells or electron orbitals. The n=1 level shell has only one type of subshell/orbital. This is a spherical orbital called an "s" orbital. Since this s orbital is located at the n=1 shell, it is designated as the "1s" orbital. Individual subshell orbitals can accommodate no more than 2 electrons. There is only one s orbital at any n shell level. Therefor only two electrons can be accommodated at the n=1 level.

An atom achieves a significant lowering of its energy state when it fills its n=1 shell. Atoms of the element helium have two protons and therefore will achieve charge neutrality by acquiring 2 electrons. Additionally, these two electrons will fill the 1s orbital. This also simultaneously completes the n=1 electron shell. There is no additional electron configuration that will further lower the energy state of helium atoms. Helium is therefore chemically inert - it will almost never participate in any chemical reactions with other elements.

Period 2 Elements and p Orbitals

For elements with atomic numbers higher than 2 (by definition, atoms that have nuclei containing more than 2 protons), additional electrons must be acquired for the atoms to achieve charge neutrality. Beginning with helium, the n=1 electron shell is filled. For all elements with atomic numbers greater than 2, additional electrons must occupy higher energy positions within orbitals beginning at the n=2 electron shell.

At the n=2 level, there are two types of orbitals - the s orbital and a new type of orbital, the "p" orbital. At the n=2 shell level, and at all subsequently higher shell levels (n= 3, 4 ...) There are one "s" orbital and three "p" orbitals. Within any n level electron shell, this new type of orbital - the p orbital - is at a higher energy level in comparison to the s orbital.

Since the maximum electron capacity of any single orbital is always 2 electrons, the n=2 shell can accommodate a total of eight electrons; 2 in the single s orbital and 2 electrons in each of the three p orbitals. These orbitals at the n=2 level are designated as the 2s orbital and the $2p_x$, $2p_y$ and $2p_z$ orbitals.

Elements in the second period (row) of the periodic table have electrons that occupy positions within the orbitals of the n=2 electron shell. There are eight elements in the second period of the table, beginning with lithium on the left in the group I column directly beneath hydrogen. The elements to the right of lithium sequentially add one additional electron to the n=2 level orbitals. At the final position on the right (and the 8th position of the period) is the element neon (atomic number 10). Notice that neon has completed the n=2 electron shell and that neon is in the group VIII column directly below helium.

Electron Configuration Notation

The electron configuration (positions) of an atom can be specified by listing the electron shells and orbitals that contain electrons. The electron positions are specified beginning with the lowest energy orbital on the left and then to progressively higher energy orbitals. For hydrogen this would be indicated by the following notation: $1s^1$

For helium (atomic number 2) this would be: $1s^2$
For neon (atomic number 10) this would be: $1s^2\ 2s^2\ 2p^6$

Since at any given n electron shell level, the s orbitals are lower energy than the p orbitals, the s orbitals fill before electrons begin to occupy positions in p orbitals. For example, the electron configuration for boron (atomic number 5) is:

$$1s^2\ 2s^2\ 2p^1$$

NOT

$$1s^2\ 2s^1\ 2p^2$$

AND NOT

$$1s^2\ 2p3$$

NOTE: The electron energy level notation indicates the lowest possible electron energy state for an atom. This is called the **ground state** for electrons in an atom. Electrons can acquire energy by absorbing photons and consequently jump to higher energy level orbitals. This is termed an **excited energy state**. If an electron absorbs sufficient energy, it can escape from the parent atom entirely. The energy required for this is equal to the parent atom's elemental ionization energy.

Valence Electrons

At this point we can begin to explain and even predict the chemical properties of the elements as well as many physical properties of the elements. For the ten period 2 elements, the n=2 electron shell is the outermost electron shell. Recall that all ten of the period 2 elements have an innermost n=1 electron shell that is filled by 2 electrons. These electrons are very tightly bound to their atomic nuclei and under normal circumstances never participate in chemical reactions. It is the electrons in the outermost or highest energy shells of an atom that participate in chemical reactions. These outermost shell electrons are usually called valence electrons.

The Octet Rule

The energy of an atom is lowered by a large amount when the n=1 electron shell is completed by the acquisition of 2 electrons that occupy the 1s orbital. Beginning at the n=2 energy level, an additional large reduction of energy occurs when the 2s orbital and the three 2p orbitals of the shell are filled by electrons. This is an underlying explanation for the octet rule. The octet rule states that there is a fundamental reason that atoms engage in chemical reactions. The reason is atoms strongly desire to acquire exactly eight valence electrons in their valence s and p orbitals. The reason for this desire is that this eight-electron configuration in the valence s and p orbitals results in a large reduction in an atom's electron energy level. Atoms that do not have a filled valence octet can "fill" the octet by taking electrons from other atoms (and consequently becoming an anion). Alternatively, **atoms may achieve a valence octet by sharing additional electrons with other atoms through the formation of covalent chemical bonds with those other atoms.**

Lewis Dot Structures

The s orbital and three p orbital valence electron configuration of an atom can be represented by Lewis dot structures. The Lewis dot structures are useful because they provide additional information about the valence electron configurations of an atom. To illustrate this, consider **the Lewis dot structure for nitrogen** (atomic number 7)

Notice that there are four positions to place dots on the Lewis dot structure. These are the top, bottom and left and right sides of the atomic symbol (in this case N for nitrogen). These four locations represent the s and each of the three p valence shell orbitals of the atom. Nitrogen has 5 valence electrons; two in the 2s orbital and one each in each of the three 2p orbitals.

Electrons in an electron shell will not pair up in a p orbital until there is at least 1 electron in the other p orbitals. The two dots on the left side of the nitrogen symbol indicate there are 2 electrons in the 2s orbital of the nitrogen atom. This is an arbitrary position; the s orbital may be represented at any of the four positions surrounding the atomic symbol. The Lewis dot structure for nitrogen has single dots above, below and to the right of the nitrogen symbol. This indicates that there is one electron in each of nitrogen's three 2p orbitals.

The Trends in the Periodic Table - From Left to Right
Electronegativity

The ability of an elemental atom to draw electrons from other atoms to share in a covalent bond or, in extreme cases, to take an electron away from an atom is determined by the electronegativity of the atom. The electronegativity of elemental atoms is primarily determined by how near the atom is to completing a valence octet. The group VII element atoms (the halogens) are one electron short of completing their valence octets and are therefore the most electronegative of the group I through VII elemental atoms.

The group I elemental atoms (the alkali metals) are 7 electrons short of completing their valence octets. They are the farthest away from completing their valence octet and have little to gain by attempting to acquire additional electrons. The group I elemental atoms therefore have the lowest electronegativity of the groups I through VII elemental atoms.

The trend in the electronegativities of elements in the periodic table is that electronegativities increase from left to right across a period. This trend is broken at the last element on the right of a period. This is the group VIII element. The noble gases (group VIII) have no desire for additional electrons and therefore have almost zero electronegativity.

Ionization Energies

The ionization energy for an atom is the amount of energy required to overcome the electrons attraction to its nucleus. The extraction of the first electron from an atom requires the lowest amount of energy. This is called the first ionization energy. This process results in a +1 charged atomic ion. Extracting a second electron requires a larger amount of energy. This process results in a 2+ atomic ion. Each subsequent ionization requires progressively higher amounts of energy.

An elemental atom's ionization energies are usually correlated to the elemental atoms electronegativity. Elements with the lowest first ionization energies are the Group I elements and those with the highest first ionization energies are the group VIII elements. The exception to this correlation is the noble gases. The noble gases have the lowest electronegativities of the all of the periodic groups but have the highest ionization energies of all of the periodic groups.

The trend in the ionization energies of elements in the periodic table is that ionization energies increase from left to right across a period.

Atomic Radius

The trend from left to right in the periodic table for the atomic radii of the elemental atoms is that the atomic radius decreases from left to right. The reason for this is that in the periodic table the progression from left to right correlates with an increasing number of protons contained in the nucleus and therefore an increasing positive nuclear charge of the elemental atoms. This increasing positive nuclear charge exerts a stronger electromagnetic force on the electrons orbiting the nucleus. As a result, the electrons are physically drawn closer to the nucleus, including the electrons located in the outermost electron shell. Since the outermost electron shell determines to outer boundary surface of an atom, increasing nuclear charge will decrease the atom's atomic radius.

The Trends in the Periodic Table - from Top to Bottom

Electronegativities and ionization energies decrease from top to bottom in the periodic table and atomic radii increase from top to bottom in the periodic table. There is a common phenomenon that explains all three trends. This is the phenomenon of electron shell shielding of the atomic nucleus.

Electron Shell Shielding of Nuclear Charge

When an electron shell is filled, it partially shields higher energy shell electrons from the positive electric charge of the atomic nucleus. This reduces the electromagnetic force that the positive charge of the nucleus is able to exert on electrons that occupy positions outside of the lower filled electron shell or shells. As a result, the outer electrons move farther away from the nucleus. Of course they must be farther away simply because they must be located outside of the lower electron shells, but the shielding phenomenon results in a larger actual radius of the outer shell electrons than is required by the geometry of the concentric shell arrangement.

Since electronegativity and ionization energies are a result of the strength of the electromagnetic attraction of the positively charged nucleus for electrons, the reduction in the charge due to shielding reduces the energy required to ionize an atom (ionization energy) and also reduces the ability of the atom to attract additional electrons (electronegativity). Shielding does not occur among electrons in unfilled shells. Adding electrons in a given shell does not result in any shielding of other electrons in the shell.

Chemical Bonding

With the exception of the group VIII elements, all elemental atoms to varying degrees will engage in chemical reactions with other atoms. The groups I through VII elemental atoms attempt to satisfy the octet rule either by taking one or more electrons away from other atoms (ionization) or by sharing electrons with other atoms through the formation of interatomic bonds.

Ionic Bonds

When an atom succeeds in taking one or more electrons from another atom, the atom that takes the electrons becomes a negatively charged ion (an anion). The atom that loses the electron(s) becomes a positively charged atom (a cation). Usually the electron donor and the electron acceptor atoms become strongly bonded due to the electromagnetic force between the negative and positive charges of the two atoms. This type of interatomic or molecular bond is called an ionic bond.

Atoms with very high electronegativities are able to take electrons away from atoms with very low electronegativities. Ionic bonds therefore occur between atoms of very high electronegativity and those with very low electronegativity. The tendency to form ionic bonds is highest for elements located on the left and right of the periodic table -groups I and II as cations and groups VI and VII as anions - and progressively lower towards the middle of the table. The formation of the cation in an ionic bond requires less energy and is therefore more likely progressing from top to bottom, but the formation of an anion is less energetically favorable and therefore less likely progressing from top to bottom in the periodic table.

Ionic Solids

When two different types of atoms form ionic bonds the atoms arrange themselves in crystal - **a three dimensional lattice of alternating anions and cations**. There is no sharing of electrons in a pure ionic bond. The force that holds the ionized atoms in place is the attractive electromagnetic force between positively and negatively charged atomic ions. This is a very strong type of bonding and ionic crystalline solids have very high melting and boiling points since all of the ionic bonds in the solid and liquid phase must be weakened in the solid to liquid transition (melting) and completely broken in the liquid to gas transition (boiling).

An example of an ionic crystalline solid is common table salt, sodium chloride (NaCl). Solid sodium chloride consists of sodium cations (Na+) and chloride anions (Cl-) arranged in an alternating three-dimensional crystalline structure that is typical of ionic compounds.

An important characteristic of many ionic solids is that they are easily dissolved in polar liquids such as water. The partial positive and negative charges on polar molecules are able to weaken the ionic attractions between the ionic solid ions and stabilize them as individual atomic ions within the dissolving polar liquid.

Covalent Bonds

 In most cases, the difference in electronegativity between bonding atoms is insufficient for one atom to take an electron away from the other bonding atom. The two atoms instead share one electron each through a covalent bond. Atoms can share additional electrons through the formation of additional covalent bonds with other atoms or by forming additional covalent bonds with the same atom resulting in double or triple covalent bonds.

The number of covalent bonds that an atom forms depends on how many electrons the atom requires to complete its valence octet. For instance, oxygen, with 6 valence electrons, is 2 electrons short of completing its valence octet. Therefore, oxygen typically forms two covalent bonds with other atoms. This results in the sharing of two additional electrons by the oxygen atom through the two covalent bonds with other atoms. In this manner, the oxygen atom has completed its valence octet.

Polar Bonds

In covalent bonds, electrons are not equally shared when there is a significant difference in electronegativity between the bonding atoms. For example, in the molecule hydrogen fluoride (HF), fluorine is much more electronegative than hydrogen and the hydrogen fluoride molecule has a partially negative pole near to the fluorine atom and a partially positive pole near to the hydrogen atom. The covalent bond between hydrogen and fluorine is said to have a partial ionic character.

Ionic bonds also have some covalent character, more so as the difference in electronegativities between the bonding atoms decreases.

Some covalent bonds are pure covalent bonds; in particular, when the molecule consists of atoms of the same element such as O_2 or N_2. Importantly, the carbon-hydrogen bonds in hydrocarbon atoms have almost no ionic character and hydrocarbon molecules are nonpolar molecules. This is significant because nonpolar molecules will not dissolve in polar liquids such as water. Water molecules are very polar and liquid water is a powerful polar solvent. Hydrocarbons and molecules composed in large part of hydrocarbons (fats and other lipid molecules) or insoluble in water but will dissolve in nonpolar liquids such as benzene or other hydrocarbon liquids.

Chemical Reactions

Throughout or previous discussions we have described general features of chemical reactions and the fundamental physical processes that drive chemical reactions. We have addressed in considerable detail major features of several types of one major form of chemical reaction - the decomposition reaction. In particular, we described the concept of chemical equilibrium - where chemical reactions will proceed from initial conditions to reach an equilibrium state. This equilibrium state refers to the concentration of chemical participants that exist when a chemical reaction appears to have stopped - with no further changes in the concentrations of chemical participants occurring over time. This chemical equilibrium state can be defined by an equilibrium constant - Keq for chemical reactions in general; Ksp for one type of decomposition reaction the dissolving of solids or liquids in a liquid solvent to form solutions and, Ka and Kb in acid and base decompositions respectively in a solvent; and Kw for the decomposition of pure liquid water in hydrogen and hydroxide ions. In the following section we will review several of these basic principles of chemical reactions and discuss several types of reactions in greater detail.

General Form of a Chemical Reaction

The convention for writing chemical reactions is to place the reactants on the left followed by a rightward pointing arrow followed by the products of the reaction.

aA + bB $\rightarrow$ cC + dD

The small letters, a,b,c,d are the relative amounts in number of particles for each participant A,B,C,D in the reaction (These are called the stoichiometric coefficients of the reaction). Of course there may be more or less than two individual reactants and/or products of a specific chemical reaction.

The General Types of Chemical Reactions

Simple chemical reactions can be categorized as one of four types of reactions. These are the synthesis reaction, decomposition reaction, single-replacement reaction and double -replacement reaction. The General formula for each of these types of reactions are shown below

Synthesis
$A + B \rightarrow AB$

Decomposition
$AB \rightarrow + A + B$

Single Replacement
$AB + C \rightarrow + A + BC$

Double Replacement
$AB + CD \rightarrow + AD + BC$

The general formulas for these four types of reactions should be self-explanatory in terms of what occurs during the reactions. There are more complex reactions where combinations of these four basic reactions occur simultaneously. This categorization of reactions actually provides very little useful information, other classifications of reaction types are much more important to recognize, in particular whether the reaction is an acid-base reaction, a reduction- oxidation reaction a hydrolysis or dehydration reaction, a polymerization reaction or phosphorylation or dephosphorylation reaction.

Balancing Reactions

Balancing chemical reactions is a process that begins with the elements and elements of molecules that constitute the reactants and products of a chemical reaction but with no ratios of the elements that compose molecules nor stoichiometric ratios of elements and/or molecules that participate in the reaction. To balance a chemical reaction, the total numbers of each type of atom on the left must equal the total numbers of each type of atom on right. When the ratios of elements are unknown for the molecules that participate in chemical reactions, the information provided in the periodic table and in particular the octet or equivalent rule for individual elements can be used to predict what the ratios of elements should be. Once this information is known, the stoichiometric coefficients can be reasoned out using common sense or simple algebra, to illustrate this balancing process, several examples are provided below

Reaction 1: Synthesis of liquid water from molecular hydrogen gas and molecular oxygen gas

Perhaps the most basic chemical reaction is the reaction of hydrogen molecules (H_2) and oxygen molecules (O_2) to form a hydrogen-oxygen molecule

$H_2(g) + O_2(g) \rightarrow HO\ (l)$

The reaction shown above is an **unbalanced chemical reaction** where hydrogen and oxygen combine to form a molecule consisting of hydrogen and oxygen The (g) for H_2 and O_2 indicate that, in this reaction, both O_2 and H_2 react as gasses. The (l) for HO indicates the product "HO" is a liquid.

There are two atoms of hydrogen and two atoms of oxygen on the right and one atom each of hydrogen and oxygen contained on the molecule HO on the left. One could write a balanced reaction 1 as

$H_2(g) + O_2(g) \rightarrow 2HO\ (l)$

This is a balanced reaction - there are the same number of hydrogen and oxygen atoms on the left and right sides of the reaction, but it is incompatible with what we know atoms are attempting to do in chemical reactions - namely to satisfy the octet rule. Recall that oxygen requires two additional electrons to satisfy the octet rule. Hydrogen is unique in that it does not have an octet rule, but does have the equivalent.

When hydrogen has 2 electrons it achieves a substantial lowering of energy by filling the n=1 electron shell. Oxygen therefore wishes to share 2 electrons by creating two covalent bonds and hydrogen wishes to share one electron by creating one covalent bond. Therefore, we can predict that one oxygen atom will form 2 covalent bonds, one with each of 2 hydrogen atoms. The Lewis dot structure for this is as follows;

The two dots between the hydrogen and oxygen atoms represent covalent bonds between hydrogen and oxygen atoms. Each atom is sharing one of its valence electrons in each covalent bond.
This structure demonstrates that both hydrogen and the oxygen atoms have all attained a desired electron configuration; each hydrogen has 2 electrons that are shared in a covalent bond with oxygen and oxygen has eight octet valence electrons, an additional two which are acquired through sharing of electrons in single covalent bonds with the two hydrogen atoms. This indicates the correct chemical reaction for reaction 1 is

$2H_2(g) + O_2(g) \rightarrow 2H_2O\ (l)$

Chemical Reactions in Solutions - Review
Nearly all biological chemical reactions occur in solutions. In a solution, the liquid that dissolves particles is called the solvent. For the HESI the solvent in a solution will almost certainly be water. The dissolved particles within the solvent are called solutes. Solutions where water is the solvent are called aqueous (aq) solutions.

Molar Concentration of Solutions - Review
The concentration of substances in solutions is usually given in unit of moles per liter. A mole is a numerical amount. The amount is 6.022×10^{23} particles. That is a huge number but atoms and molecules are incredibly small so it works out that this is a convenient number of particles to use experimentally for chemical reactions. A substance that has a concentration of 1 mole of substance/per liter of solution is defined to be a 1 molar solution of the substance or a 1M concentration of the substance

Aqueous (water) Solutions - Review
Liquid water is the ideal medium for acid-base reactions. Although water by definition is neutral, water exists in an equilibrium with hydrogen and hydroxide ions. This is because water undergoes the following reaction

$H_2O\ (l) \rightleftarrows H+(aq) + OH-(aq)$

At equilibrium, pure liquid water contains concentrations of 1×10^{-7} M of H+ and 1×10^{-7} M OH- ions.

pH - Review
For solutions that contain hydrogen ions (H+), the negative log of the hydrogen ion concentration is defined as the pH of the solution. As we discussed, in pure liquid water, the hydrogen ion concentration is 1×10^{-7}. Therefore, the ph of pure liquid water is 7. This is by definition a neutral pH, Solutions with higher concentrations of H+ have pH values lower than 7. These solutions are defined as acidic solutions. Solutions with lower concentrations of H+ have pH values higher than 7. These solutions are defined as basic solutions. The pH of body fluids in humans is tightly regulated to an ideal pH of 7.4

Acids - Review

Acids are molecules that, in solution, partially or nearly completely dissociate into hydrogen ions and a conjugate base. One definition of an acid is that an acid is a proton (hydrogen ion) donor molecule.

A general formula an acid dissociation reaction is $HA(aq) \rightleftarrows H+(aq) + A- (aq)$

HA is the acid and A- is the acid's conjugate base

Strong Acids

The strongest acids, in aqueous solutions at 1 molar concentrations, will completely or nearly completely dissociate into hydrogen ions and the acid's conjugate base. For the TEAS, hydrochloric acid (HCl) is almost always the strong acid that is participating in chemical reactions. One should also know that sulfuric acid (H_2SO_4) is also a strong acid

For example, in an aqueous solution a 0.1 M solution of the strong acid HCL will completely dissociate as given by the following reaction

$HCL \rightarrow H+ + Cl-$
Since one molecule of HCL dissociates into one proton and one Cl- ion, the concentration of H+ in the solution will be 0.1 M or 1×10^{-1} moles/liter, Therefore the pH of the solution will be 1

Weak Acids

In aqueous solutions, weak acids only partially dissociate into a hydrogen ions and conjugate bases. As a general example consider a 1 molar aqueous solution of the weak acid HA with a measured pH of 5. The pH of the solution indicates that 1 mole of the weak acid HA partially dissociates into 1×10^{-4} moles of hydrogen ion and 1×10^{-5} moles of the conjugate base. This means only one acid molecule in 100,000 has dissociated into hydrogen ion and conjugate base. A 1M concentration of a strong acid such as HCL would nearly completely dissociate into 1 M of hydrogen ion and 1 M of conjugate base. This would result in a pH of 0 for the solution (since the H+ concentration written in exponential form is 1×10^{0} M). In this example, a 1M solution of HCl is 100,000 times stronger than the 1M solution of the weak acid HA.

Bases

Bases, by one definition, are molecules that accept hydrogen ions. Notice the general reaction for this definition of a base is the reverse of the general acid reaction

$A- + H+ \rightleftarrows HA$
This is why A- is referred to as the conjugate base of an acid.

In aqueous solutions the hydrogen ion acceptor is usually the hydroxide ion OH^-. When this is the case, another way to represent a general dissociation of a base is
$BOH \rightleftarrows B+ + OH-$

Strong bases will completely dissociate in 1 M solutions. For instance, a 1 molar solution of potassium hydroxide NaOH (a strong base) will completely dissociate as follows

$NaOH(aq) \rightarrow Na+(aq) + OH-(aq)$

For the HESI assume that strong bases have a 1 molar solution pH of 14. In contrast, weak bases do not completely dissociate and for the HESI assume that they have 1 molar solution pHs of greater than 7 and less than 14.
Acid-Base Reactions

The general formula for an acid (Ha) and base (BOH) reaction is shown below

HA + BOH ⇄ BA + H$_2$O

The compound "BA" is referred to as the "**salt**" of an acid -base reaction.
An example of an acid base reaction between a strong acid (HCl) and a strong base (NaOH) is shown below

HCl + NaOH → NaCl + H$_2$O

Notice that the salt produced by this reaction is an ionic compound; in this case the ionic compound NaCl. It is typical that salts formed by acid-base reactions are (in their solid form) ionic compounds. In water - which is a strong polar solvent - a substantial fraction of the salt that is produced by an acid -base reaction often is dissolved in the form of the ions that compose the crystal structure of the salt. In the case of the aqueous HCl/NaOH acid -base reaction, at equilibrium, there will be substantial amounts of Na+ and Cl- ions dissolved in the aqueous solution.

The actual amounts of dissolved ions in an aqueous solution for a given acid base reaction depend on the properties of the specific salt that is formed. Many salts are very insoluble in water and will precipitate out of the aqueous solution as solid salt crystals rather than remain dissolved as ions in the aqueous solution.

Enzymes
Enzymes are biological catalysts. They are not simple metallic surfaces but extremely complex three dimensional protein structures. They lower activation energies of biological reactions by attracting reactants to a specific site on the enzyme known as the active site. As reactants bind to the active site, the configuration of the site changes in a manner that orients the reactants in the optimum manner for the chemical reaction to occur. This process is called the "induced fit" mechanism for enzymatic activity. The activity of an enzyme is defined as the rate at which the reaction catalyzed by the enzyme occurs. The higher the enzyme activity, the greater the rate of enzyme catalyzed reaction

Enzyme Activity
The activity of an enzyme depends on the concentration of the reactants and products of the reaction and the temperature and pH under which the reactions occur. Enzymes will have an optimum temperature and pH range for maximal activity. In general, the reaction rate doubles for every increase of 10 degrees Celsius, but beyond an upper-temperature level the enzymes structure is thermally disrupted and the enzyme ceases to function. Similar structural disruptions occur at pH ranges outside of the enzymes activity range.

Enzyme Denaturation and Inhibition
The term for both the thermal and pH disruptions that deactivate enzymes is denaturalization. A denatured enzyme or other protein is usually permanently dysfunctional. The activity of enzymes can also be reduced by molecules that can interfere with the chemical reactions at the active site. This process is called enzymatic inhibition. Inhibitor molecules can reduce enzyme activity by various mechanisms, commonly by physically blocking the active site. This form of inhibition is called competitive inhibition. Other forms of inhibition are termed noncompetitive or uncompetitive inhibition. These other forms of inhibition are often utilized as a means for the body to regulate the activity of enzymes.

This concludes the discussion of the basic chemical level of organization that is found in living organisms. The following section addresses the next level of organization the specific biochemical and chemical and physical processes that occur in living organisms

Proteins and Biology

We have now discussed most of the basic chemical reactions and the basic molecules involved in the processes that generate energy in cells and that form the physical building blocks of cells and extracellular substrates. We have also discussed the fundamental physics that underlie nearly all of the chemical and physical processes that are essential to the functioning of living organisms. In the following Section we will continue with discussions of proteins and their role in living organisms. These discussions will also be used to begin to introduce many of the most important aspects of human cellular and general anatomy and physiology.

Structural Proteins

One of the primary functions of proteins in the human body is to provide a physical structure for elements within the body. These may be microscopic structures inside of cells and in the extracellular spaces between cells or they may be macroscopic structures that extend over body surfaces These structural proteins are designed to provide the mechanical properties that are required by the structural role that they provide. These properties also are designed to respond in particular ways to the forces that the proteins experience in their structural roles. Some roles require that the proteins have the ability to stretch or flex in one or more directions, but to resist forces in other directions. In general, structural proteins have an overall **fibrillar** (fiber-like) shape - as opposed to globular proteins, which typically have enzymatic or transport functions.

Collagen

 The most important extracellular structural protein is collagen. There are many different forms of collagen, each with its own unique mechanical properties. The collagen found in bone is rigid, in in tendons that connect muscles to bone, collagen is elastic and able to stretch and relax as muscles contract and relax. Collagen in cartilage has mechanical properties intermediate between rigidity and elasticity in its role of providing a protective layer over the ends of bones at movable joints and as structural elements in the nose, ears and within the skeletal system and elsewhere throughout the body. Collagen also is a major component of ligaments - which connect bones at joints - and in the integumentary system where it provides the ability of skin to stretch but to resist mechanical penetration by foreign objects and to contain the internal contents of the body.   Collagen is also a major structural element of blood vessels.

Overall collagen comprises approximately 30% of the total protein mass of the human body. Collagen is synthesized by many types of cells but the most important producer is the fibroblast cells. These cells are found throughout the body and are constantly producing collagen particularly in inflammation and tissue regeneration and repair processes.

Collagen is a three peptide-chain protein with a quaternary triple-helix structure composed of two alpha-1 single strand proteins and an alpha-2 strand protein. Therefore, two genes are required to produce collagen - an alpha-1 collagen gene and an alpha-2 collagen gene. As we mentioned helical molecular structures are often able to stretch and compress in response to mechanical forces but resist such forces in other directions. This is a primary structural property of collagen

After the collagen strands are constructed they undergo post-translational modification where some of the amino acids of the collagen strand are hydroxylated (a hydroxyl group is created on the amino acid). This type of modification of proteins is common in protein synthesis. In collagen this hydroxylation process allows covalent bonds to form cross-links between the three collagen strands as they form a triple helix. Vitamin C is required to this cross-linking process. Vitamin C deficiency results in a failure of the collagen fiber crosslinking which severely weakens the strength of collagen leading to structural failure of the cartilage in skin, tendons, ligaments and blood vessels. This is the disease process known as scurvy. Scurvy is fatal if not corrected by adequate vitamin C intake.

Keratin

Keratin is the other major extracellular structural protein in humans. It provides protective and mechanical support to the outer layers of skin and also is the primary component of hair and nails in humans. In other animals it also forms horns and claws. Keratin is composed of individual keratin filaments which are single polypeptide chains. These chain combine to form intermediate filaments which are multiple keratin filaments that are held together first by hydrogen bonds, then by disulfide bonds and finally by covalent fiber cross links similar to those found in collagen. The keratin intermediate filaments then form a three dimensional supercoiled helix that is extremely tough but has very high elasticity in the long axis of the supercoiled helix. This can be seen macroscopically by plucking a hair from one's head and pulling the strand from either end. In young healthy persons the hair strand when wet can be stretched to up to 50% of its original length.

Fibrillin and Elastin

Fibrillin is a protein and elastin is a glycoprotein that combine to form elastic fiber which is found throughout the extracellular regions of the body. Both fibrillin and elastin form fibers. In elastic fibers elastin fibers are randomly arranged and fibrillin fibers embedded linear arrangements. The result - elastic fibers are extremely resilient - they can flex, stretch and compress in all directions in response to external mechanical forces and then rapidly return to their original shape after the forces have dissipated. This ability allows elastic fiber to act as a "shock absorbers' in regions of the body subject to strong mechanical forces, such and the intervertebral discs of the spinal; column. Elastic fibers are found usually with collagen fibers in the skin and throughout the body. Elastic fiber is an important component of the extracellular matrix which forms internal frameworks for the cells that form tissues and organs and also form larger framework structures within the body. This structural matrix surrounds and supports internal organs and larger structures, allowing these structures to expand and contract, bend and shift positions within the body but to retain their overall relative positions within the body. Fibrillin also has many functions within cells as well.

Intracellular Structural Proteins

In humans, cells are not simple distensible balloon-like structures - they have an internal structure called the cytoskeleton. The cytoskeleton is a complex three dimensional framework the provides structural support to the cell and also is involved in intracellular transport and other cellular functions. The cytoskeleton is not a static construct, it is constantly undergoing disassembly and reassembly in response to the needs of the cell. The cytoskeleton is composed of a cytoskeletal matrix. The matrix is primarily composed of three types of protein filaments (thread-like structures) - microfilaments, microtubules and intermediate filaments.

Microtubules

Microtubules are the largest diameter of the three general types of cytoskeletal filaments. Microtubules are hollow cylinders that are composed of two types of protein monomers (single-unit building blocks) -alpha-tubulin and beta-tubulin. The tubulin proteins are spherical and form alpha-beta pairs called dimers. These dimers often self-assemble and disassemble rapidly in response to various conditions within the cell. The microtubules participate in many functions of the cytoskeleton including vesicle transport but their most notable role occurs during mitosis and meiosis phases of a cell cycle.

During these **cell division** phases, microtubule organizing structures called **centrosomes** coordinate the formation of **microtubule "spindles"** that are composed of microtubules attached to chromosomes and two one of two centrosomes located at opposite poles of the cell during mitosis and meiosis. When the microtubules begin to disassemble near the centrosome, the tubules shorten and chromosomes are pulled apart to opposite sides of the cell.

Microtubules are also major elements of the flagellum of sperm cells. They form the core of the flagellum and interact with a centrosome-like microtubule organizing center at the base of the flagellum that coordinates sliding motions between microtubules within the flagellum. These sliding motions are powered by protein complexes called dynein arms located along the length of the microtubules. The sliding motions cause the flagellum to bend laterally - alternately in one direction and then the opposite direction. This results in a rapid whip-like motion of the flagellum that propels sperm cells in their journey through the uterus in an attempt to fuse with a female ovum.

Intermediate Filaments

Intermediate filaments are the most stable elements of the cytoskeleton. These filaments organize to form a complex three dimensional framework throughout the cell that provides local support and spatial organization to all of the cell organelles - the nucleus, endoplasmic reticulum, golgi, mitochondria, cell vesicles and cell vacuoles. It also provides an underlying structural framework for the cell membrane which results in the specific three dimensional shape of the cell. Intermediate filaments are formed from keratin like protein fibers. In addition to their structural role, the intermediate fiber framework also serves as a convey belt system for the transport of vesicles and their contents from the golgi or other regions inside to cell to the cell membrane, where the vesicles merge with the cell membrane and release the vesicle contents to the extracellular environment. This process is a specific example of the general process of exocytosis.

Microfilaments

Microfilaments are the smallest diameter of the three intracellular structural filaments. They are composed primarily of subunits of actin. Actin is a protein that has ATPase activity - it can hydrolyse ATP and use the energy of ATP hydrolysis to interact with other proteins and when organized into microfilaments - actively move along the length of the other proteins. This ability allows microfilaments to engage in a wide variety of functions within cells. It can serve as the "vehicle" that transports vesicles along the cytoskeleton of cell and can organize at the interior of cell membranes to dynamically reshape membranes - resulting in the ability of cells to phagocytize external substances (including other cells) by extending local regions of cell membrane around external substances and enveloping the external substance.

Actin Microfilament Related Cellular Processes

Cytokinesis

Actin microfilaments are also responsible for the physical separation of a single cell into two cells in a process that occurs at the end of a mitotic or meiotic cell replication cycle. The microfilaments create a encircling belt at the cell membrane that is drawn progressively tighter and eventually pinches the original cell into two new separate cells.

Cell Contraction

Many cell types are capable of actively contracting or shortening. All types of muscle cells - skeletal, cardiac and smooth muscle cells - are designed to contract and relax in response to various types of stimuli. In all cases actin microfilaments play a central role in the contraction and relaxation process.

Thin and Thick Filaments in Muscle Cells

In skeletal and cardiac muscle cells, actin and tropomyosin protein filaments and attached troponin protein molecules form a composite filament called a thin filament. During cell contraction, thin filaments slide between myosin protein thick filaments. This shortens or contracts the cell. The process is powered by ATPase (ATP hydrolysis) sites located on the myosin molecule. The free end of the myosin thick fibers has "heads" which are specialized regions of the protein that can swing back and forth and can also form crosslink bonds with troponin molecules, Troponin molecules are evenly spaced a short distance apart along the entire length of the thin fibers located on the thin fibers that are attached to actin microfilaments.

Electrical signal from nerves or adjacent muscle cell membranes trigger the release of calcium ions (Ca++) from a vesicular intracellular structure in the muscle cells called the sarcoplasmic reticulum. The calcium ions diffuse to and bind with troponin proteins which then form crosslink bonds with adjacent myosin fiber heads. The Myosin heads pivots or shifts the crosslink bond site backwards and draws the thin filament further along myosin thick filament. The crosslink it subsequently broken during ATP hydrolysis occurring at myosin ATPase sites and the myosin head site swings forward and can then bind to another troponin molecule located further along the thin filament. In this manner actin fibers are grabbed like rungs of a ladder and pulled progressively further along the myosin fiber and the muscle cell progressively shortens.

Cell Motility

A wide variety of cell types in the human body are capable of independent locomotion. In particular, macrophages and other types of white blood cells, and fibroblasts are capable of actively traveling from virtually any region of the body to any other region of the body. This motion is accomplished by a coordinated extension and retraction of portions of the cell membrane. These local cellular extrusions are called pseudopods. Pseudopods are capable of attaching to various molecules in the extracellular matrix. This process is called cellular adhesion. Using pseudopod motions and cellular adhesion, motile cells are able to continuously creep along and squeeze through intercellular spaces. Pseudopod motion depends on a continuous reshaping of cell membranes that is produced by the activity of actin microfilaments.

Diapedesis

A closely related activity to pseudopod motion in motile cell is diapedesis. Motile cells generally begin their journeys to a particular target destination when they are circulating in blood vessels. When they detect signal molecules that have diffused from a target site that trigger the motile cells to leave the blood vessel and move into the intracellular space. This movement out of the blood vessel requires that the motile cell adheres to the interior wall of the vessel and then deform in a manner that allows it to ooze or squeeze in between adjacent cells that form the vessel wall. This process is called diapedesis and predictably it is also an active cell reshaping process that depends on the movements of actin fibers.

Chemotaxis

Chemotaxis is a process where motile cells are recruited to move to a region of the body where their particular functions are required. The process begins with the production of chemoattractant molecules at the target site that subsequently diffuse outward. This diffusion process creates a concentration gradient extending from the site where the chemoattractant was produced. When a motile cell detects chemoattractant molecules that it is designed to respond to, the cell begins to move in the direction of the molecules. The cell continues moving towards the target site by selecting a direction of motion that corresponds to progressively higher concentrations of the chemoattractant. In this fashion the cell follows the chemoattractant molecules concentration gradient back to its source.

Endocytosis

Phagocytosis is an extreme example of the general process of endocytosis. While most cell types in the human body are not capable of phagocytosis, many cell types are capable of ingesting small molecules from the cell membranes and internalizing them in small membrane bound vesicles. This general process of endocytosis occurs in the same fashion as described for phagocytosis.

Phagocytosis

Usually phagocytized substances are bacteria, injured or virally infected cells or remnants of cells and extracellular matrix substance fragments that require clearance during immune response and tissue repair and regeneration activities. Phagocytosis begins with the binding of a substance, virus or cell to the outer cell membrane, actin microfilaments and other proteins begin to envelop the target substance, the enveloping cell membrane segment invaginates (draws into the cell) and pinches off forming an intracellular membrane bound vesicle. These vesicles can be transported within the cell and other vesicles can be brought to the phagocytic vesicle and merged with the vesicle. Often this cellular vesicle is a lysosome or a proteasome - which contains powerful oxidizing chemicals or digestive enzymes. When the two vesicles merge the contents of the phagocytized vesicle are subjected to the effects of the lysosome or proteasome and the contents are chemically and enzymatically digested.

Exocytosis
The general process of transporting intracellular vesicles to a internal surface of a cell membrane and then fusing the vesicle membrane to the cell membrane so that the vesicle is turned inside out and empties its contents to the external environment is called exocytosis. Antigen presentation is a variation of exocytosis where the antigens within the vesicle remain bound to the vesicle membrane and thus become molecules attached to the external surface of the cell membrane. In all other cases the contents of intracellular vesicle are released into the extracellular environments. Nearly all of the products of cells are delivered to the rest of the body beginning with the process of exocytosis. The transport and vesicle-membrane fusion events of exocytosis are carried out by the movements of actin microfilaments.

Antigen Presentation
There are a wide variety of cell types in the human body that are capable of phagocytosis. The primary function of several of these cell types is phagocytosis The most notable type of these in the human body are macrophages. Macrophages play central roles in tissue repair and regeneration activities and are critical to many immune system responses. This role is complex but it often begins with the phagocytosis of a foreign biological product - a virus infected cell, an infectious foreign cell such as bacteria, or other foreign substances.

After these infectious elements are phagocytized and broken down into smaller digestive molecular remnants, actin filaments can transport these small molecular remnants to the cell membrane of the macrophage. These small molecular sub regions are classified as antigens. Antigens have unique molecular structures that can be recognized by other immune cells as foreign or non-self. The detection of foreign antigens by the immune system triggers the body's immune response. These antigens can be anchored to the external surface of the macrophage cell membrane. This process is call antigen presentation and cell that have the ability to phagocytize foreign substances and then present the antigens derived from the ingested foreign substance are called antigen presenting cells. We will discuss additional features of antigen presentation shortly.

General Biology
Primary Functions of Living Organisms
On a continuous basis, complex multicellular organisms must continuously adapt to external conditions in order to identify and acquire needed resources and to identify and avoid risks to survival that are present in the external environment. For animals this includes the abilities of the nervous system to sense the external environmental conditions and to adapt as needed to these conditions.

Adaptation and Voluntary Movements
An important method that animals use to adapt - as the nervous system deems necessary - to their environment is locomotion – are voluntary movements generated by the musculoskeletal system. Pursuit of prey, avoidance of predators and gathering all manner of physical resources requires locomotion. At a higher level, the propagation of a species requires that male and female members sexually reproduce and subsequently rear offspring. All of these activities require continuous adaptation and physical activities of the voluntary muscle to generate these long-term and complex behaviors.

General Body Functions

At a more fundamental level, the physical acts of ingesting water and nutrients and of obtaining oxygen and expelling carbon dioxide via breathing are also functions that require muscular motion. The absorption of water and processing of nutrients into a form that can be distributed throughout the body require digestion and the transport of oxygen, water, nutrients and waste products requires a circulatory system. The elimination of wastes requires an excretory system. Production of offspring requires sexual reproductive systems and the regulation of overall body functions requires both a nervous and an endocrine system.

The Cell

The cell is the smallest unit of life. There are other biological entities that show many characteristics of living organism. Most notable of these are viruses and infectious protein particles called prions. Viruses and prions are incapable of survival without parasitizing living cells.

Universal Features of Cells
Cell Membranes - Review

We have discussed the details of the structure of human cells membranes. In Summary: All cells have a number of universal features. First all cells have a cell membrane that separates the internal contents of the cell from the cell's external environment. This membrane is a bilayer of long, linear phospholipid molecules - hydrocarbon chains that are attached as chain pairs to a phosphate group at one end of the molecule. The phosphate "heads" of molecules face outward in the outer layer of the membrane bilayer and inward in the inner layer; thus forming the exterior and interior surfaces of the cell membrane. The hydrocarbon chains or "tails "of the molecule aligned and face inward toward the center of the bilayer.

Cytoplasm: All cells contain cytoplasm. Cytoplasm consists of the material enclosed within a cell membrane with the exception of the material enclosed within the membrane of the cell nucleus (the nuclear membrane). The contents of the nucleus are called the **nucleoplasm**. Cytoplasm includes all of the cell organelles and the **cytosol** which is the gel-like aqueous (watery) solution the fills the interior of the cell. The cytosol consists primarily of water but also contains countless other dissolved chemicals and proteins.

Nucleic Acids, Enzymes and other Proteins: All cells contain nucleic acids - DNA and RNA molecules These are the genetic information molecules of the cell. All cells have proteins that can replicate DNA within the cell. All cells have enzymes that can convert an energy source - sunlight or chemicals obtained from the outside environments - into high energy molecules that can drive other chemical reactions within a cell.

Ribosomes: All cells contain ribosomes. Ribosomes are small spherical complexes of proteins and RNA that can read messenger RNA transcripts and assemble the proteins coded for in the mRNA. The ribosomes assemble these proteins from individual amino acids that are dissolved in the cell cytosol. The ribosomes of bacterial cells are considerably different in structure compared to the ribosomes of human cells. For this reason, many antibacterial drugs are designed to attack the bacterial ribosome. The differences between the bacterial ribosome and human ribosomes are sufficient that the antibacterial drugs will not affect the human ribosomes

Cytoskeleton -Review: All human cells contain a cytoskeleton. We have discussed the elements of the cytoskeleton in detail, to summarize this structural system provides mechanical support and numerous other intracellular functions. The three primary components of the cytoskeleton are actin-protein microfilaments, intermediate filaments and microtubules.

Common Features of Cells
Cell Walls

Depending on the type of cell, there are common structures and organelles that cells often possess. Cell walls are physical barriers or envelopes that exist exterior to the cell membrane. They are constructed of various types of molecules and are several times thicker than a cell membrane. Bacterial cells have cell walls are composed of complex structural arrangements of several types of molecules. Plants have cell walls composed of cellulose - a relatively simple sugar polymer and fungal cells have cell walls composed of chitin - another relatively simple sugar polymer. Animal cells do not possess cell walls. Human cells do not possess cell walls

Bacterial cell walls are significant for medical science because they are not a feature shared with human cells and are therefore a prime target for antibiotics and other antibacterial treatments. A primary classification system for pathogenic (disease causing) bacteria is based on the Gram-stain. The Gram stain identifies two types of cell walls in bacteria - the gram-positive and the gram-negative bacteria have different molecular cell wall structures. This feature is very useful in the early stage of diagnosis and treatment of bacterial infections. In addition, a molecular component of gram-negative bacterial cell walls is lipopolysaccharide (LPS) is an extremely potent toxin that is a primary cause of gram-negative sepsis and toxic shock. Gram-negative sepsis a major cause of medical complications and death in hospitalized patients.

Flagella, Cilia and Pilli

Flagellum cilia and pilli are extensions of cell membranes or attachments of cell membranes. Flagella are long whip-like energetically driven structures that can generate locomotion of a cell. The structure varies greatly. The flagella of bacteria are completely different than the flagella of protist or animal cells. Cilia are found on many unicellular organisms and on many specialized cells of multicellular organisms. They often have powered independent movement ability. Pilli are tubular structures found in most bacterial cells that can transfer DNA from one bacterial cell to another.

Internal organelles
The Nucleus

The nucleus is a major intracellular organelle. Cells that contain a nucleus are defined as eukaryotic cells. Those without a nucleus are defined as prokaryotic cells. Nearly all human cells contain a nucleus (mature red blood cells are a notable exception). Bacterial cells do not have a nucleus and are therefore prokaryotic cells. All other cells - plant, animal, protist and fungal cells -contain a nucleus and are therefore eukaryotic cells.

The nucleus is a membrane-bound structure that contains the DNA of a cell and the nucleolus. The nucleolus is a structure where ribosomes are constructed. There are membrane pores in the nuclear membrane that allow various small molecules to enter - primarily building blocks of DNA and RNA molecules. Nuclear pores also allow messenger RNA (mRNA) molecules and ribosomes to exit from the nucleus into the cell cytoplasm.

A much simpler, non-membrane-bound structure called the nucleosome contains the majority of DNA in prokaryotic cells.

Mitochondria and Chloroplasts

Mitochondria and chloroplasts are complex organelles that possess with both an inner and outer encapsulating membrane. Mitochondria are found in most of the cells of every eukaryotic organism. Chloroplasts are found in cells of all plants and a few types of protist cells. Chloroplasts contain the enzymes that are involved in photosynthesis -the conversion of sunlight water and carbon dioxide into carbohydrates and oxygen.

Mitochondria are present in nearly all eukaryotic cells including most human cells (again - as is the case with the cell nucleus - mature red blood cells are a notable exception.) We have discussed in detail the metabolic pathways of aerobic cellular respiration that occur in mitochondria - the Krebs or citric acid cycle, the electron transport chain and oxidative phosphorylation in detail to review: Mitochondria contain enzymes that extract chemical energy from nutrients - usually glucose molecules - and convert the energy into potential energy stored in high energy molecules - usually ATP or NADH. These high energy molecules are coupled to chemical reactions that require energy to proceed. Without this coupling most of the synthesis of complex chemicals in the cell could not occur. Mitochondria and chloroplast are never found in prokaryotic cells.

Rough and Smooth Endoplasmic Reticulum (ER)

The endoplasmic reticulum (ER) is found in eukaryotic cells and is a convoluted network of membrane passageways that is connected to the cell nucleus and then continues extensively into the cell cytoplasm. Smooth ER is involved in synthesis of lipid compounds and the transport and packaging of various compounds produced by the cell. Smooth ER functions in close coordination with the Golgi apparatus. Rough ER (RER) is so called because ribosomes are distributed in the RER membranes, giving a granular or rough appearance to the RER membranes. Cells that produce large amounts of proteins for transport outside of the cell contain prominent amounts of RER.

The Golgi Apparatus (the Golgi)

 The Golgi apparatus is found in almost all eukaryotic cells and in a much simpler form in prokaryotic cells. The Golgi is a highly folded series of membrane compartments that resembles a stack of pancakes. The Golgi functions with the smooth ER to process, package and transport a wide variety of products synthesized with the cell. Most often these products are packaged into secretory vesicles that are subsequently carried to the cell membrane and then secreted out of the cell into the external environment. In some types of cells, these vesicles remain inside the cell and are involved in intracellular digestion of phagocytized substances.

Centrosomes

Centrosomes are structures in eukaryotic cells that assemble and organize microtubule structures. These are required for a wide variety of purposes within the cell. They are for example central elements in the construction of flagella in human sperm cells and in the construction of the spindle apparatus during mitosis and meiosis stages of cell division.

Cellular Functions

At the most basic levels all of these higher adaptive and general functions require cellular functions - growth (cell division) cellular differentiation (production of specific cell types) and cellular repair mechanisms. All of these cellular functions require cellular metabolism and the ability of cells to process the genetic instructions encoded on DNA into proteins and to replicate DNA.

Homeostasis

Homeostasis for living organisms is the maintenance of a stable and specific internal environment that is distinctly different from the external environment. All living organisms must achieve homeostasis as a necessary condition for continued life.

Homeostasis for all living organisms must be achieved first at the cellular level. For unicellular organisms - such as bacteria, this is sufficient. For multicellular organisms there are several additional levels of homeostasis that must be achieved. For humans these mechanisms for the maintenance of higher levels of homeostasis are described in the human physiology sections.

Cellular Homeostasis
Cell membranes

 For biological cells, homeostasis requires a physical barrier in the form of a cell membrane to separate the cell's internal environment from the surrounding external environment. The external cell membrane is a selective, semi-permeable membrane. The cell membrane is permeable to water, oxygen and carbon dioxide molecules. These molecules are free to cross the membrane but most other atomic ions and molecules are not.

Molecular Genetics and Protein Synthesis
Nucleic acids
We have already discussed several aspects of nucleic acids in the carbohydrate biology section of or review. Namely the role of the sugars ribose and deoxyribose in the sugar-phosphate backbones of DNA and RNA molecules and of the structural roles of theses sugars in nucleotides - the subunits of DNA and RNA molecules that a polymerized to form complete RNA and DNA molecules. The integrated roles of DNA and RNA in human biology are discussed below.

Nitrogenous Bases
All cells contain the nucleic acids DNA and RNA. The DNA molecules within a cell contain all the genetic information required to synthesize all of the proteins that the cell requires to carry out its metabolic, physiological and structural functions. This information is stored as a linear sequence of nitrogenous bases. The nitrogenous bases occur in two forms, purines and pyrimidines. Both forms are small nitrogen-containing molecules that have either one structural ring - the pyrimidines, or a double ring - the purines.

The nitrogenous bases in DNA are the purines adenine (A) and guanine (G) and the pyrimidines thymine (T) and cytosine (C). The nitrogenous bases found in RNA molecules are the same as those found in DNA molecules with the exception that in RNA, another pyrimidine, uracil, is substituted for thymine.

The DNA Double-Helix
The structure of a DNA molecule in a cell is usually the double-stranded form of DNA. This double-stranded structure is a spiraling (helical) ladder consisting of linear backbones of alternating deoxyribose sugars and phosphate groups. One deoxyribose phosphate polymer backbone forms the left side rail of the DNA ladder and another one forms the right side rail of the DNA ladder.

Complementary Base Pairing in Double -Stranded DNA
Each deoxyribose sugar is also bonded to a single nitrogenous base. Additionally, in double-stranded DNA, each of these bases is hydrogen bonded to its complementary base, which is similarly bonded to a deoxyribose sugar on the opposing sugar-phosphate backbone of the DNA molecule. These hydrogen bonded nitrogenous base pairs form the rungs of the double stranded DNA ladder.

The term "complementary" in complementary base pair bonding refers to the fact the each nitrogenous base will pair bond with one and only one specific complementary base, Adenine (A) will only pair bond with thymine (T) and guanine (G) will only pair bond with cytosine (C). There are two hydrogen bonds formed between base-pairing adenine and thymine and three hydrogen bonds formed between base-pairing guanine and cytosine in double stranded DNA.

Nucleotides - Review
 A "nucleotide" is the term for a nucleic acid molecular subunit consisting of either a ribose or a deoxyribose sugar bonded to a phosphate group and to a nitrogenous base is referred to as a nucleotide. Any DNA molecule can be assembled entirely from deoxyribose containing nucleotides. Any RNA molecule can be assembled entirely from ribose containing nucleotides.

Chromosomes
In eukaryotic cells, DNA is usually in an extended linear form that allows the cells to access the nitrogenous base sequences for DNA replication and for transcription of DNA base sequences into messenger RNA molecules. During cell division these DNA strands are highly condensed into structures called chromosomes. The formation of chromosomes during cell division cycle involve a series of coiling and supercoiling actions of

the DNA molecule This process involves the physical wrapping of the DNA molecule around specialized spherical proteins called histone proteins or "**histones**".

Chromatids
Each chromosome can exist in two forms. One is as a single condensed strand of DNA. The other form consists of two condensed identical strands of DNA. These two condensed DNA strands are called chromatids individually, and together they are called "sister chromatids". The sister chromatid form occurs only after replication of an entire DNA strand is completed.

Homologous Chromosomes
Human somatic cells have 46 chromosomes. These 46 chromosomes occur as 23 pairs of chromosomes - 22 pairs of autosomes and 1 pair of sex chromosomes. The pairs of chromosomes are called homologous chromosomes. The sex chromosome pair in males is not an actual pair - it consists of one "X" chromosome and one "Y" chromosome. In females, the sex chromosomes are a chromosome pair - consisting of two X chromosomes.

Alleles
Each single chromosome in an autosomal homologous chromosome pair contains the same genes - but the two chromosomes of a homologous chromosome pair are not necessarily exact copies of one another. There are often two or more variations of a gene. These gene variants are called alleles. Frequently the individual chromosomes of a homologous chromosome pair will contain different alleles of a given gene. At a molecular level alleles have variations in the base sequences that code for a particular single-chain protein that is designed to severe a specific function within an organism. Alleles of a particular gene will ultimately generate single chain proteins that have variations in their amino acid sequences. This will often result in an alteration in the protein's function. Often the variant proteins will not be optimally functional but sometimes they have enhanced functional abilities. This is how the succeeding generations of organisms are able to continuously evolve more effective biological adaptations to their environment.

Diploid and Haploid Cells
Cells that contain a full set of chromosome pairs are called diploid cells. All human somatic cells are diploid cells. Most organisms including humans can create haploid cells - cells that contain only single chromosomes rather than homologous chromosome pairs - These haploid cells have exactly half of the total number of chromosomes as a corresponding diploid cell.

Germ-Line Cells
In humans, haploid cells are produced by germ-line cells, the cells that undergo meiosis to produce gametes. Gametes are the sex cells of the male and female that can fuse to form a new hybrid diploid cell called a zygote. The zygote is capable of developing into a new individual organism. In humans the gametes are, in the male - sperm cells and in the female - ova or egg cells. These haploid cells contain 23 chromosomes; one of each of the 23 chromosome pairs of a human somatic cell. During successful fertilization, the human gametes fuse - one sperm and one ovum - to form a zygote with 23 pairs of chromosomes.

Notice this is now a new human diploid cell with a total 46 chromosomes in the form of 23 homologous pairs of chromosomes. Each homologous pair of chromosomes includes one chromosome from the male sex cell and one from the female sex cell

In Humans, when male and female gametes fuse during fertilization, the resulting cell - the zygote- contains a full complement of 46 chromosomes, 22 pairs of homologous autosomes and 1 pair of sex chromosomes. In Female zygotes exactly half of the DNA is contributed by the mother and half by the father (in male zygotes, slightly more DNA is contributed by the mother. Her X chromosome contains somewhat more DNA than the father's Y chromosome. Y chromosomes can only be contributed by the father. In male zygotes the X chromosome is always contributed by the mother. This method of generating offspring is called sexual reproduction. and

The purpose of sexual reproduction is to vastly increase the range of genetic variability among offspring. This allows a species to enhance the chances of continued survival through the process of natural selection. Increased genetic variability in a species increases the likelihood that some offspring will have an optimum set of genetic traits to more successfully adapt to the external environment and to outcompete other species for the limited essential resources available in the environment

During the replication of new complementary DNA strands or during the transcription of DNA gene sequences into mRNA molecules, the DNA is not organized into a chromosome since chromosome are a highly condensed configuration of the DNA molecule - one whose base sequences cannot be accessed by DNA or RNA polymerases.

Protein Synthesis
When a cell begins the process of constructing a protein, it first must expose the DNA base sequences of the gene that codes for the desired protein. During protein synthesis, the region of the DNA that contains the gene that will be transcribed is exposed by disrupting the hydrogen bonds between the nitrogenous base pairs. This separates the left and right halves of the DNA ladder as if it were being unzipped down the middle of the nitrogenous base pair rungs.

Transcription of DNA into mRNA - The 3' to 5' Direction
A protein complex called RNA polymerase then inserts itself into the cleft created by the disruption of the hydrogen bonds between complementary base pairs. The RNA polymerase then begins to assemble a single-strand RNA molecule that is complementary to the DNA strand that contains the base sequence code for the protein that will be constructed. The DNA strand that is transcribed is transcribed beginning at the 3' end of the DNA molecule and continues in the 5' direction.

The Sense and Antisense Strands of DNA
The DNA strand that is transcribed by RNA polymerase is called the "antisense strand" The other DNA strand - the complementary strand of the sense strand - is called the sense strand. Since the base sequence of the sense strand is the complementary sequence of the antisense strand, the sense strand does not code for functional proteins and it is not read by RNA polymerase. The mRNA base sequence is identical to the sense strand DNA sequence with the exception that the nitrogenous base uracil in the mRNA base sequence replaces the nitrogenous base thymine in the sense strand of the DNA molecule

Genes
The base sequence in the sense strand that codes for a single-chain protein is called a gene. One gene always codes for one and only one polypeptide chain - a polypeptide chain is a linear molecule composed of amino acids. All polypeptide chains are single-chain proteins. Some complex proteins are composed of more than one type of polypeptide chain.

Codons
The individual amino acids that will form the protein's chain are coded for by three-base sequences. These three-base sequences are called codons. Since there are four different bases that can occur at any point in the DNA base sequence, there are statistically 64 possible combinations of three-base sequences. Therefore, there are 64 possible codons. There are only 20 amino acids that are used to assemble proteins, so there may be more than one codon that specifies for a given amino acid. The reverse is NOT true - None of the individual codons ever codes for more than one specific amino acid.

Transcription of DNA

As RNA polymerase assembles an RNA molecule, a new nitrogenous base, uracil (U), is used in place of the base thymine, Uracil is the RNA base that is complementary to adenine. The process of constructing an RNA molecule that contains a complementary base sequence to a DNA gene sequence is defined as "transcription".

Anticodons and Ribosomes

Once a complete RNA transcript of a gene has been completed, the transcript, known as a messenger RNA (mRNA) molecule leaves the nucleus and enters the cell cytoplasm. Eventually the mRNA molecule encounters a ribosome that attaches to the mRNA transcript. The ribosome then reads the RNA as three-base compliments of the DNA codons. These three- base RNA sequences are called anticodons.

Translation of mRNA

When the ribosome reads an anticodon, it inserts the amino acid that corresponds to the anticodon onto a growing polypeptide chain. When the entire mRNA molecule has been processed by the ribosome the result is a newly synthesized single chain protein. This polypeptide chain is the protein coded for by the gene that was transcribed at the beginning of this process. The reading of mRNA by ribosomes and the construction of the corresponding protein is called "translation".

Transfer RNA

During the assembly of a protein chain at a ribosome, the individual amino acids are transported to the ribosome by transfer RNA (tRNA) molecules. These molecules are short segments of RNA that have a three-leaf-clover configuration. One end of the "stem" of the clover binds to a particular amino acid. There are 20 different types of tRNA molecules and each binds to one and only one type of amino acid. There is a complementary tRNA molecule type for each of the 20 amino acids.

DNA Replication

During DNA replication, the unzipping of double-stranded DNA is accompanied by the construction of a new complementary DNA for each of the original strand of the double stranded DNA. The synthesis of these two new complementary strands continues for the entire length of the DNA molecule. The result is that exact two copies of the original DNA molecule are created. Each of the new DNA molecules contains either the right or the left strand of the original DNA molecule and a complete newly synthesized complementary strand. This type of replication of DNA is called semi-conservative replication.

DNA polymerase

During the replication of DNA, DNA polymerases are the enzyme complexes that insert themselves into gaps created by disruption of complementary base pair hydrogen bonds. These DNA replication molecules synthesize complementary DNA strands to both the original DNA sense and antisense strands simultaneously.

Mutations of the Genetic Code

During the replication process, the polymerase molecules occasionally make errors. For example, as the polymerase molecule is synthesizing complementary DNA strands, it may erroneously emplace or mismatch a complementary base. For instance, an adenine on an original DNA strand may be mismatched on the complementary DNA strand. This mismatch would be a substitution of guanine or a cytosine in place of the correct complementary base -thymine.

This is a mutation at the genetic level. The mismatched base will probably (but not necessarily) code for a different amino acid in the gene of which it is a part. If the error is in the antisense strand, then upon the next round of DNA replication, the new sense strand will base pair correctly with the mutated base. This will likely result in an alteration in the amino acid that is coded for in the mRNA molecule.

Even more seriously, some codons are "stop" codons that signal that signal RNA polymerase to terminate the transcription of a gene sequence. This stop codon is placed at the end of a normal gene sequence. If the stop codon is created within the gene sequence by a mismatch or other type of mutation, RNA polymerase will terminate transcription of the gene at the moment that it reads this stop codon. This almost always results is a completely nonfunctional and possibly toxic gene fragment protein.

DNA Repair Mechanisms
Mismatch errors are substitution errors -one base (the correct base) is substituted for by another base (an incorrect base). DNA polymerases have a highly accurate method of repair for this type of mutation. Essentially the DNA polymerase double-checks the base pairing and nearly always detects this type of error before the replication process goes much further. The error is then corrected by DNA polymerase. This type of error correction is called "proofreading repair". When the proofreading repair mechanism for a substitution error fails, there is a second type of error correction that DNA polymerase also utilizes before completion of replication. This mechanism is called mismatch repair.

Somatic Cell Mutations
The overall substitution error rate in human DNA is very low due to proofreading and mismatch repair mechanisms. Some errors - mutations - are not corrected by proofreading or excision repair functions. These mutations can become permanent alterations in the genetic code of all subsequently replicated DNA. If this occurs in a somatic cell the mutation may be amplified over many mitotic cycles resulting in a clonal population of mutated cells. These may be dysfunctional cells or even cancerous cells.

Germ-line Cell Mutations
When mutations evade detection and correction by proofreading and excision repair in a germ-line cell, the mutation becomes a hereditary mutation that can be passed to future generations. These mutations will commonly be present in nearly every cell of organisms that developed from a mutated germ-line cell. While it is most likely these mutations will be harmful or at least harmless - some actually result in better versions of genes.

Mutagens and Carcinogens
After the replication of a DNA molecule is complete, there are numerous ways that the DNA can be damaged or altered. During mitosis or meiosis, sections of chromosomes can be lost or fail to separate resulting in chromosomal abnormalities. Radiation and chemicals can cause direct damage to DNA. Agents that have been shown capable of inducing mutations to DNA are called mutagens. Those that have been shown capable of inducing cancerous mutations are termed carcinogens.

Excision Repair of DNA
There are several types of DNA repair genes and DNA repair processes that can correct various types of post-replication damage to DNA. One of these is the excision repair mechanism. This mechanism can identify short segments of damaged DNA and can then snip the damaged DNA section out. The repair enzymes then use the complementary segment as a template to create a correct DNA base sequence replacement for the excised damaged DNA segment.

Genetic Adaptation and Natural Selection
These mutated versions of gene are alleles of genes found on chromosomes. This mutation process is how different alleles of a gene are first created. And the creation of new alleles is the means through which natural selection and evolution of species occurs. Therefore, some level of germ-line DNA mutation must occur so that the offspring of organisms may continue to successfully adapt to a changing environment and to survive the competitive challenges of other species that are themselves continuing to adapt through

genetic mutations. This is essentially the definition of the process of natural selection through genetic adaptation.

Cell Division
The Cell cycle
Cells that are capable of replication have a cell cycle that corresponds to specific activities related to cell replication. The cycle consists of interphase and mitosis/meiosis. The interphase phase of the cell cycle consists of two growth phases (G1 and G2) that are separated by an intervening synthesis (S) phase. The G1 and G2 phases correspond to the periods where there is active transcription of DNA into mRNA and the translation of mRNA into proteins. Replication of the entire cell genome occurs during the S phase. Mitosis (and meiosis 1) begins upon the completion of the G2 phase of the cell cycle.

Mitosis
Prophase
In prophase of mitosis, the nuclear membrane begins too disintegrates, and a centrosome - a microtubule assembly structure - forms and divides into two centrioles. The centrioles begin to move to opposite poles of the cell. Microtubule spindle fibers begin to form and DNA begins to condense into chromosomes.

Since the DNA of every chromosome has been replicated, the mitotic chromosomes at this stage have twice the amount of DNA that they possess during the interphase stage of the cell cycle. This is apparent in the structure of the chromosomes which consist of two sister chromatids connected at their central region. Each sister chromatid of a given chromosome has an identical sequence of base sequences (unless one or more mutations had occurred during the replication process).

Chromosomes with duplicated sister chromatids have an X shape (but they are not X chromosomes - the X chromosome is one of two forms of the sex chromosome. The other form is the Y chromosome)

Metaphase
During metaphase of mitosis, all 46 individual chromosomes form a single file line arrangement at the center of the metaphase plate. Centrioles- have settled at opposite poles of the cell to the left and right of the aligned chromosomes. Microtubule spindle fibers then begin to form between the centrioles and between the centrioles and the chromosomes. Spindle fibers to attach to the central connecting regions of the sister chromatids of every chromosome with a single spindle fiber attached to theses central regions from the right centriole and a single fiber from the left centriole.

Anaphase
In anaphase of mitosis, the left and right microtubule spindle fibers attached to each central region of every chromosome begins to shorten. This action pulls the sister chromatids of each chromosome apart. The left chromatids are pulled toward the left centriole and the right chromatids are pulled toward the right centriole. At this time the entire cell begins to divide into two separate daughter cells. This process is called cytokinesis,

Telophase
During telophase of mitosis, cytokinesis progresses to completion. The chromatids drawn to the left are separated into the left daughter cell and the chromatids drawn to the right are separated into the right daughter cell. Nuclear membranes then form to contain each daughter cell's compliment of 46 individual chromosomes. Once cytokinesis is complete, the original cell has now divided into two daughter cells that have a full set of chromosomes that are identical to the full set of chromosomes contained in the original cell. With subsequent generation of mitosis, a single progenitor cell can generate a huge number of identical daughter cells.

Meiosis

The cells that participate in meiosis are called germ-line cells. All other cells in the body are somatic cells. Meiosis consists of 2 separate stages, and two rounds of cell division. The first stage of meiosis, meiosis 1, occurs during the first round of cell division. Meiosis 2 occurs during the second round of cell division

In contrast to mitosis, meiosis does not produce identical daughter cells; rather it produces gametes, sex cells that have exactly one half of the number of individual chromosomes as the progenitor cell. rather than 23 pairs of chromosomes (homologous chromosome pairs), These cells, beginning with the first two daughter cells resulting from the first cell division of meiosis (meiosis I), contain only one of the two chromosomes from each of the 23 homologous chromosome pairs contained in the progenitor cell.

Meiosis 1

Meiosis I begins with a diploid, germ-line progenitor cell. The progenitor cell replicates its entire chromosomal DNA just as occurs in somatic cells prior to mitosis. During metaphase of meiosis 1, in contrast to mitosis, the chromosomes align at the metaphase plate not as a single file line of individual chromosome but instead as homologous chromosome pairs. The chromosome pairs then separate in the same fashion as occurs in mitosis, Notice this does not result in the separation of the sister chromatids of individual chromosome. Instead, one chromosome from each homologous chromosome pair, with each chromosome still consisting of both sister chromatids, is separated into separate daughter cells. These daughter cells now contain one chromosome from each of the 23 pairs of chromosomes contained in the progenitor cell.

Genetic Variability

Recall that homologous chromosome pairs do not in general have identical genes, but often have variants of each gene, different versions of a gene called alleles. Therefore the two daughter cells resulting from the first cell division of meiosis have one half of the total number of chromosome - 23 instead of 46 and these cellular sets of genes, but these are not identical sequences of DNA . The individual chromosomes from homologous chromosome pairs which are now in different cells, almost certainly have a wide variety of differing alleles for a wide variety of individual genes. Also, during the pair separation process in anaphase of meiosis 1, small segments from chromatids on different chromosomes of the homologous pairs can be exchanged. This creates hybrid chromatids. This process is called "crossing over" and it increases the genetic variability of the chromosomes.

Meiosis 2

The next round of cell division follows immediately without any replication of DNA. This is the Meiosis 2 phase of meiotic cell division. The events of Meiosis 2 cell division are identical to the events of mitosis cell division. In each of the two daughter cells created by the meiosis 1 cell division, the 23 individual chromosomes align at the metaphase plate of each daughter cell and individual sister chromatids of each chromosome are pulled apart and separated into the second generation of daughter cells.

This process - beginning with the original diploid progenitor cell - results in the production of four haploid cells. Each haploid cell contains one chromosome on the form of a sister chromatid, from each of the 23 pairs of chromosomes contained in the progenitor cell. In the human male, meiosis results in the production of sperm cells. In the human female, meiosis results in the production of ova.

Molecular Genetics

In individual members of a species, the total amount of genetic information contained in the genes of a diploid cell of the individual represents the individual's genome. The specific types of genes within the genome are the individual's genotype. The manner in which an individual's genotype is expressed in physical form is the individual's phenotype.

Calculating Gene Frequencies

For species where there are multiple alleles for a given gene, individual members of the species may have different combinations of these alleles in their individual genomes. When there are two alleles for a given gene - for instance if we indicate these to be the alleles "A" and "a" for a specific gene, individuals may possess one of have three possible combinations of the two alleles within their genotype. These are "AA", "aa" and "Aa". The combinations AA and aa are the two possible homozygous genotypes and the combination Aa is the heterozygous genotype. When a mating male and female pair of a species create a zygote, the probability or predicted frequencies of the alleles in the zygote can be calculated using a Punnett square.

	A	a
A	AA	Aa
a	Aa	aa

The Punnett square above shows the possible combinations of zygotes resulting from a mother and father where both are heterozygous for the gene with alleles A and a. Since each parent can contribute only one allele to any particular zygote, the alleles for one parent are separated into an "A" column and an "a" column. The other parent's alleles are represented by an "A" row and a little "a" row. The four squares show the combination of alleles that results from combining a parental row with a corresponding parental column.

Notice that for two heterozygous individuals there is one AA square, one aa square and two Aa squares. This indicates that there is a 1 in 4 probability (25% chance) that the parents with produce a zygote with AA alleles, a 1 in 4 probability (25% chance) that the parents with produce a zygote with aa alleles and a 2 in 4 probability (50% chance) that the parents with produce a zygote with Aa alleles. Since zygotes can develop into children, for humans these are the probabilities of heterozygous parents having children with the AA, Aa and aa genotypes.

The expected gene frequencies resulting from matings between parents with other genotypes can be calculated in the same fashion using the Punnett square technique.

Dominant and Recessive Alleles

Often the phenotypic appearance or the physical trait that results from a gene depends on whether the alleles for the gene are dominant or recessive. The classic example is eye color where the brown allele is "B" and blue allele is "b".

Brown (B) is the dominant allele and blue (b) is the recessive allele. Homozygous brown eyed individuals - those who are BB, and heterozygous individuals - who are Bb, always have brown eyes. Only homozygous blue (bb) individuals have blue eyes. Notice that the offspring of parents who are heterozygous for eye color (Bb), will have the same expected genotype frequencies as shown in the Punnett square example above; but the blue-eyed phenotype is only the bb genotype. Therefore, heterozygous brown-eyed parents will have a 1 in 4 or 25% chance of having a blue-eyed child.

Notice that two blue-eyed parents will never have brown-eyed children, since both parents possess only the blue eye color allele. Finally notice that in any couple where at least one parent is homozygous brown (BB), there is no possibility of offspring who will be homozygous blue (Bb) and therefore these parent have no chance of having a blue eyed child.

Cell Differentiation
Once a human sperm cell and a human ovum have fused to form a zygote, the process of the development of a new human being begins. During this process the zygote will undergo countless rounds of cell division. As the zygote proliferates into a large collection of cells, the process of cell differentiation begins. This process involves a vast, complex and still poorly understood interaction of cell markers, cell receptors, extracellular matrix molecules and cell signaling molecules That cause undifferentiated cells to begin to change into specific mature cell types and to begin to organize into tissues and organs. The first stage of this process is called embryogenesis

Embryogenesis
Almost immediately after a zygote is formed the first stage of embryogenesis - the development of an **embryo** begins. First, the single-cell zygote undergoes an initial mitotic cell division. The two daughter cells then undergo a second round of mitotic cell division. Each new generation of daughter cells continues this cycle of mitotic divisions. During these early rounds of cell division, the daughter cells undergo divide simultaneously. This results in a doubling of the number of cells derived from the original zygote with each round of cell division.

The Morula Stage
During these divisions there is little if any individual cell growth so the increasing mass of cells retains a total volume that is approximately equal to the original zygote. These types of divisions are called cleavages. After the first four rounds of cleavage the original zygote has become a solid spherical cell mass consisting of 16 cells. This cell mass is called a morula - The morula stage is the first stage of embryological development. These 16 (or so) cells are completely undifferentiated, each cell has the capacity to differentiate further into any mature cell type in the human body. Cells that have this capacity are called totipotent stem cells.

As subsequent rounds of cell division occur the progeny cells of the cells of the morula begin the process of cell differentiation. Through cell-cell interactions, these progeny cells begin to rearrange themselves into a more complex structure. As this structure develops the cells also begin to express new cell markers and cell membrane receptors. Further increasingly diverse cell-cell interactions and other intracellular processes lead to selective activation and deactivation of genes within individual cells. This allows cells to become further differentiated with subtypes of cells emerging that are capable of new functions. This increasingly diverse cell mass transforms from the morula stage to the next phase of embryogenesis - the blastula stage.

The Blastula Stage
At the beginning of the blastula stage of embryological development, the cells of the morula begin to increase in mass with subsequent cell divisions and the cell divisions are no longer simultaneous. Cells in differing local regions of cell mass begin dividing faster than others. Cells also begin to develop the ability to move or migrate from one location to another. This process leads to the formation of two separate cell layers - an inner cell layer and an outer cell layer. The outer layer is called the trophoblast and the inner layer is called the inner-cell mass. The two layers separate except at one specific site called the embryonic pole.

The Embryonic Disc
The cells of the trophoblast and most of the cells of the inner cell mas will proliferate and differentiate into extraembryonic structures - those that do not continue as part of the developing embryo. Instead these go no to form the yolk sac, amniotic sac and portions of the placenta and fetal umbilical cord. The cells that do proliferate and differentiate into the developing embryo are the cells of the inner cell mass located at the embryonic pole. The space created between the two cell layers begins to expand and fill with fluid. After the seventh round of cell division the resultant 128 cell mass has differentiated into a structure called the blastula. In humans the blastula consists of a spherical outer cell layer called the blastoderm and an inner fluid-filled cavity called the blastocoel. In humans a local region of the blastoderm begins to differentiate into

an inner-cell mass called the blastocyst. The blastocyst further proliferates and differentiates into a fluid-filled substructure that includes cells that will form the amniotic sac and a small region of cells the embryonic disc. The cells of the embryonic disc are the cells that will proliferated and differentiate into the human embryo. This differentiation process begins with the formation of the cells of the primary germ layers.

The Gastrula Stage and The Primary Germ Layers
The blastoderm cells of the embryonic disc continue to proliferate, differentiate and migrate to form three layers of cells. The upper layer of cells are ectoderm cells. Ectoderm is one of the three primary germ layers. The middle cell layer is composed of mesodermal cells. Mesoderm is the second of the three primary germ layers. The bottom layer of cells is composed of endodermal cells. Endoderm is the third of the three primary germ layers. All subsequent cells, tissues and organs of the human body are composed of cells derived from these three primary germ layers. This three-layer cell structure consisting of the three primary germ layers is called the gastrula.

Differentiation of the Primary Germ Layer Cells
With the creation of the three primary germ layers of the gastrula, the development of the human embryo proceeds with further cell proliferation and differentiation of the three primary germ layer cells. There are two methods to describe the differentiation process of the germ layer cells. One is to describe the germ cell derivation of the four primary tissues, The other is to describe germ cell derivation of the organs of the human body.

The Four Primary Tissue Types
Tissues are organized collections of one or a few types of cell that share the same functions and by many definitions have the same primary germ-cell origins. The four primary tissue types are epithelial, connective, muscle and nervous tissues. It is important to recognize that functional tissues are composed of a not only a particular type of cells but also of an extracellular component that includes structural matrices of proteins and other substances. Together these form an organized assembly of cells and extracellular material that are integrated to provide a common set of functions within the body. There are many subsets of the four basic tissue types and theses tissues can perform many different functions throughout the body. In many cases a particular tissue is composed primarily of extracellular materials with actual tissue cells only sparsely distributed throughout the tissue.

Epithelial Tissue
The definition that a tissue is - in part -comprised of cells that are derived from the same germ layer is somewhat confused since epithelial tissues by most definitions include epithelium derived from ectoderm - which forms the epidermis of the skin, subcutaneous glands, mammary glands; from endoderm - which forms the linings of the digestive tract. The respiratory tract, the urinary bladder and urethra; and from mesoderm - which forms endothelium, the cells that line the interior surfaces of blood vessels the chambers of the heart and lymphatic vessels and mesothelium, the cells that line the surfaces of internal body cavities such as the peritoneum, the pleura and the pericardium.

The alternative view is that epithelia tissue of mesodermal origin - endothelium and mesothelium - are not true epithelial tissue. Regardless of either definition there is agreement that true epithelial tissue includes types of epithelium derived from ectoderm and epithelia tissue derived from endoderm.

Structural and Functional Characteristics of Epithelial Tissue
Epithelial tissue is typically organized in one of two general structural forms; one is as sheets of tissue, Where the tissue may provide structural /protective functions, absorptive functions, filtering functions and secretory functions. the other form is as globular arrangements of epithelial tissue called glandular epithelium where the tissue functions as glandular tissue. The primary role of glandular epithelium is the secretion of

substances, such as sweat, sebaceous material, mucous, digestive fluids and enzymes, and hormone molecules.

Epithelial tissue cells are notable for their high regenerative capacity - they can and do frequently undergo mitosis to replace cells that have been damaged or lost due to mechanical or other types of injury. Another notable feature of epithelial cells is that they do not have a direct blood supply but they are innervated (have connections to the nervous system)

Characteristics of Epithelial Cells
A primary feature of all epithelial cells is the three dimensional shape of the cells; squamous epithelial cells are flattened and have an irregular polyhedral shape. Cuboidal epithelial cells are -as the name implies - shaped like a cube and columnar epithelial cells are elongated in the form of a rectangular solid - with the height of the sides of the cell being significantly greater than the length and width of the top or apical surface of the cell and of the length and width of the bottom or basilar surface of the cell.

Within a particular type of epithelial tissue, the sheet or membrane form of epithelial tissues can have one of several arrangements of the epithelial cells. Simple epithelial tissue consists of a single layer of cells. Simple epithelium is usually found in regions where the function of the epithelium is to absorb or to filter substances such as in the alveoli of the lungs, in the glomerulus of the renal tubules of the kidney in the digestive tract and in the capillaries of the circulatory system. Simple epithelium can have secretory functions particularly as the epithelial linings of the peritoneal cavity of the abdomen and the pleural cavity of the chest where they secrete pleural and peritoneal fluid which acts as a lubricant and shock absorbing substance. Stratified epithelium consists of two or more layers of epithelial cells. Stratified epithelium is typically located where the tissue serves a protective or structural role and therefore is subject to mechanical, chemical or environmental or other types of stress. Stratified cuboidal epithelium is located in the ducts of sweat glands and mammary glands and typically has two layers of cuboidal cells.

Together epithelial tissue can be described as a combination of these two features- These include simple squamous, cuboidal and columnar tissue and stratified squamous and stratified cuboidal. In some cases, the epithelial tissue is a stratified arrangement where the lowermost layer is columnar or cuboidal and progressively higher layers become more squamous shaped. This is most notably seen in the dermis and epidermis of the skin. Columnar epithelial cells are almost always arranged is a single layer as simple columnar tissue. In some cases, columnar tissue is irregularly shaped and arranged in a fashion that creates the appearance that there are two layers of cells. This arrangement is known as pseudostratified columnar tissue.

In addition to the shape of epithelial cells and to the number of layers of epithelial cells there are several other features of non-glandular epithelial tissue that most or all specific epithelial tissues have in common. A near universal feature of non-glandular epithelium is that the epithelium has a barrier function - this requires that the tissue prevent substances from crossing between epithelial cells and passing into underlying regions of the body.

Tight Junctions and Desmosomes
The bottom or basal layer of such epithelial tissue (and the only layer in the case of simple epithelium) are densely packed and connected to adjacent cells by specialized intercellular structures called tight junctions and desmosomes. Tight junctions are located at the upper or apical regions of the epithelia cells. Tight junctions form a leak proof seal between epithelial cells and also help to keep specialized elements of certain cells localized to the apical region of the cell. Desmosomes are "spot-welds between epithelial cells, were intermediate filaments inside adjacent cells are linked together by intercellular connections. Desmosomes

provide a remarkable degree of tensile strength to the epithelial tissue while allowing the tissue to remain flexible.

Basement Membranes
At the base of the epithelial cells the cells are attached to an extracellular membrane consisting primarily of collagen fibers. The basement membrane serves as an additional barrier to the leakage of substances past the epithelial cells and also provides additional structural support and mechanical resilience to the epithelial tissue. The basement membrane is semipermeable - this is important because epithelial cells do not have a blood supply Oxygen, nutrients and other essential molecule are able to diffuse through the basement membrane and then gain access to the epithelial cells. Similarly, substances that are absorbed by epithelial cells and waste products from epithelial cells are able to diffuse across the basement membrane into the interior of the body.

Polarity of Epithelia Cells
Another key feature of non-glandular epithelium is cell polarity. The apical surfaces of epithelial cells that facing outward toward the interior of lumen (passageways) of anatomical structures - such as the bronchial airways of the lungs and the lumen of the gastrointestinal tract - frequently have specialized structural and molecular features that enable the cells to perform absorptive or transport functions. Since these features are localized to the apical surface the cells are described as polar - one end of the cell is different than the other end of the cell. Polarity is most commonly seen in simple columnar and pseudostratified columnar epithelium.

Cilia and Microvilli
Two of the most common polar specializations of the apical end of endothelial cells are cilia and microvilli. Cilia are densely packet thread-like extensions of the apical membrane that are capable of active movement. As a group on a cell and as a continuous layer on epithelial tissue surfaces, cilia generate a coordinated wavelike motion that move across epithelial surfaces. This is particularly important in the airways of the lungs, where this cilia-generated motion moves substances within the airways progressively out of the lungs and into the trachea and then the oropharynx. This phenomenon is called the mucociliary conveyor belt. The ciliated epithelium in the bronchial airways are pseudostratified epithelium

MIcrovilli are the other common specialized feature of the apical region of epithelial cells. These are also densely packed tubular extrusions of the cell membrane. In the small intestine microvilli greatly increase the surface area of the epithelial cells increasing their ability to absorb water and nutrients. Microvilli form an outermost region of the epithelial tissue called a brush border. In addition to increasing the absorptive capacity of the epithelial cells, there are several types of digestive enzymes - called the brush border enzymes -that are attached to the microvilli of epithelial cells in the small intestine. The majority of these are disaccharidases - enzymes that break disaccharides down into simple sugars. The epithelium of the digestive tract are simple columnar epithelium.

Connective Tissue
Connective tissue is derived from mesoderm. The adjective "connective" if frequently misunderstood as a description of the functions of connective tissue. Some connective tissues - literally connect - in the mechanical sense - separate structures to one another within the body. This is a function of some types of connective tissues in some cases, for instance ligaments and tendons are composed of connective tissue and they do physically bind bones to bones and muscles to bones. Connective tissues have many other functions however. They can connect in a broader sense - by providing protective and structural support to organs and other body structures as well as providing an interactive biological ground substance that extends throughout the body - filling the spaces between body structures and providing the underlying framework the results in the shape of the body.

Connective tissues networks are the source of the many of the overall mechanical and physical properties of the body. The distribution of substances throughout the body and many of the functions of organs and organ systems depend on processes that occur within the this continuous and complex network of connective tissue.

Connective tissue is also an important component of organs and blood vessels lymph nodes where among other functions they provide a structural framework of **reticulin fibers** that organize the cells within organs, blood vessels and lymph nodes.

Ground Substance
a general features of most types of connective tissues is the ground substance of connective tissue. Ground substance is a extracellular often gel-like mixture of fluids and various embedded proteins such as elastic and collagen fibers as well as and other molecules and molecular complexes including proteoglycan and glycosaminoglycan molecules. Proteoglycans and glycosaminoglycans are macromolecules that serve as osmotic particles to retain water within the ground substance and also provide various structural and cell-signaling functions. The connective tissue cells are also embedded within this ground substance. There is a wide range of variation in the specific types of materials, concentration of materials, organization of structural components and types of connective tissue cells that comprise the ground substance of any particular type of connective tissue. The actual overall content of the ground substance depends on the structural and functional roles that the connective tissue is designed to provide at any given location within the body.

Dense Connective Tissue
Dense connective tissue has a high content of fibrous proteins within the connective tissue ground substance. These fibers are composed primarily of collagen and also of variable amounts of elastic fibers. Fibroblasts are distributed among the extracellular fibers. Dense connective tissue forms ligaments, tendons and cartilage and the lower structural layers of the dermis of the skin.

Loose Connective Tissue
The composition of loose connective tissue varies widely but in general loose connective tissue includes a high content of ground substance fluid, with lesser amounts of fibrous proteins, adipose cells, fibroblasts, monocytes, macrophages and neutrophils. Adipose tissue is connective tissue with a high content of adipose (fat) cells. Fibroblast synthesize and secret most of the proteins including collagen and elastin that is found in the ground substance of loose connective tissue. Macrophages, and neutrophils are white blood cell leukocytes that clear the connective tissue matrix of cellular debris through phagocytosis and also engage in immune system surveillance and response functions. Several other types of immune system cells are frequently distributed within loose connective tissue including mast cells, eosinophils and plasma cells.

Adipose Tissue
Adipose tissue is a specific type of loose connective tissue. Large collections of adipose tissue function as a fat storage depot for the body by more loosely arranged adipose tissue is distributed throughout the body where it provides cushioning, shock absorbing functions and a flexibility and freedom of movement to the organs and other body structures which the adipose tissue surrounds. Other types of connective tissue provide similar functions throughout the body.

Bone and Blood
Although bone can be considered to be a dense connective tissue and blood can be considered to be a loose connective tissue, this is not a very helpful definition for either. Bones have a high content of dense connective tissue but they also or composed of several other types of tissues and most authorities consider bones to be organs. Bones also play key roles in the immune system and in the endocrine system and in the

overall metabolic homeostasis mechanisms of the body. Blood has many of the characteristics of a loose connective tissue - where the fluid component of the blood - plasma - can be considered the ground substance and the circulating cells - red blood cells white blood cells and platelets are the cellular components. Blood is a dynamic substance and a key element of the circulatory system. The extracellular proteins and cells of the blood are critical participants in the immune system as well as nearly all of the organs and organ systems of the body. We will therefore discuss bones and blood in the context of their function within these systems.

Nervous Tissue

Nervous tissue is derived exclusively from ectoderm. Neural tissue of the primary tissue of the central nervous system - the brain and the spinal cord - and of the peripheral nervous system. Nervous tissue is almost entirely composed of nervous tissue cells - neurons and glial cells. We have described the anatomy and physiology of neurons in the context of the creation and transmission electrical impulses. Glial cells are nervous tissue cells that play critical roles in the development maintenance and repair of nervous and enhance the functional roles of neurons. The a several different types of glial cells. These are oligodendrocytes, astrocytes, ependymal cells and microglia, and in the peripheral nervous system cells. Schwann cells and satellite cells.

Microglia are not technically nervous tissue cell because they are derived from mesoderm. They are phagocytic cells that are mobile and constantly patrol nervous tissue for cellular debris and infectious agents and participate in immune and cell repair activities within the central nervous system. Astroglia (astrocytes) are notable for their shape which includes numerous branching arm-like structures. Astroglia or astrocytes are arranged around blood vessels within the CNS and form an important element of the blood-brain barrier; they also regulate the levels of electrolytes in the extracellular regions of the CNS. Schwann cells and oligodendroglia provide extensions of their cell membrane which ensheath the axons of neuron providing an insulating layer to the axons that is called myelin.

Muscle Tissue

Muscle tissue is exclusively derived from mesoderm. There are three distinct types of muscle tissue - skeletal/voluntary muscle, cardiac muscle and. Skeletal or voluntary muscle is a syncytium - individual cells have intercellular connections called gap junctions that allow the cytoplasm of cells to move freely among the other cells of the syncytium. Cardiac muscle is the muscle tissue that forms the heart. Cardiac muscle is also a syncytium. We have discussed the structural and biochemical process that occur during the contraction of skeletal and cardiac muscle. Smooth muscle is the muscle type that is located throughout the body particularly in the muscular layers of the respiratory airways, the walls of the digestive tract and in the walls of circulatory vessels. Cardiac and smooth muscle are not under voluntary control but are regulated by the autonomic nervous system.

General Human Anatomy

Anatomical positions

The anatomy of the human body and the discrete structures within the human body are described in part by their spatial orientations and relationships. The terms used to describe the relative positions of anatomical structures to one another are also used to describe specific regions of individual anatomical structures. There is some overlap in the definitions of these terms and occasionally they may be used interchangeably. Most of the terms are best understood as pairs of opposing directions or relative locations.

Dorsal vs. Ventral: Dorsal means towards the back of the body and ventral means towards the front of the body. At the outer body surface, the back of the head, neck, torso, upper and lower legs and arms, the back of the hands and the upper surface and the top (vs. the soles) of the feet are the dorsal exterior surfaces. The most significant dorsal region landmarks are the midline of the spine and the shoulder blades or left and right scapulae.

The exterior ventral surfaces are the front of the neck, chest, abdomen, pelvis, upper and lower arms and upper and lower legs and the soles of the feet. Prominent ventral surfaces landmarks include the trachea (or windpipe) in the midline ventral neck, the sternum (or breastbone), the clavicles (or collarbones), the breasts in the ventral thorax (chest), the umbilicus (belly button) in the midline of the ventral abdomen, and the external genitalia in the ventral pelvis. The ventral surfaces of the arms are the surfaces that face upward when the arms are extended straight out with palms facing upward.

Important dorsal/ventral regions are the dorsal and ventral regions of the spine and spinal cord, and the dorsum of the hands and feet (vs. the palms of the hands and the soles of the feet).

Anterior vs. Posterior These terms are to a large extent analogous to the terms dorsal and ventral, but they are usually the terms preferentially used to describe relative positions. It is common to describe one structure as being "anterior to" or "posterior to" another structure rather than to say "dorsal to" or "ventral to". For instance, the esophagus is correctly described as being located "dorsal to" the heart, but usually the esophagus is described as located "posterior to" the heart and conversely the heart is described as being located "anterior to" the esophagus.

Notable anatomical regions identified with these terms include the anterior and posterior pituitary (sub regions of the pituitary gland) and the coronary arteries (arteries that supply oxygenated blood to the muscle tissue of the heart), the left anterior descending coronary artery for example.

Lateral vs. Medial: Lateral means "to the side" or "the side(s) of". Medial means "toward the center" or "closer to the midline". Lateral and medial are often used in combination other positional terms to produce a more precisely defined location such as dorsolateral, ventromedial, anterolateral etc. The ventromedial hypothalamus is a notable region described in this manner.

It is common to say that one anatomical structure is located "lateral to" or "medial to" another anatomical structure. Externally, the major lateral regions are the lateral chest regions, the lateral abdominal regions and the lateral thigh and knee regions. The prominent medial regions of the external surfaces of the body are the medial thigh and medial knee regions.

Inferior vs. Superior: Superior means "above", "over" or "towards the top of the head". Inferior means "below", "underneath" or "towards the feet". These terms can be combined with other positional terms to identify more precise and discrete anatomical regions, such as the anterior-superior ischial spine region of the pelvis.

Rostral vs. Caudal: This pair of descriptive terms is somewhat analogous to the terms superior and inferior. Rostral means "towards the head or cranium" and caudal means "towards the pelvis or the base of the spine". These terms are comparatively rarely used. They are most often used in reference to the regions between the head and pelvis and are not used to describe the appendages (arms and legs).

Superficial vs. Deep: Superficial means "shallow" or "towards the surface of" or "closer to the skin". Deep means "closer to the center of" or "farther from the surface of". Superficial body structures include skin, hair, facial structures such as the eyes, nose and mouth; nipples of the breast, the umbilicus and external genitalia.

The deepest structures in the appendages of the body (arms and legs) include the medullary cavities of the long bones. The deepest regions of the skull are the ventricles at the center of the brain. The heart, the digestive organs, the kidneys, urinary bladder and female reproductive organs are deep structures with respect to the external body surfaces.

When describing relative positions of two or more anatomical structures or locations, the superficial structure or location is closer to the external surface of the body compared to the deep structure or location. The esophagus is posterior to the trachea, but it is equally correct to describe the esophagus as being deep to the trachea.

Proximal vs. Distal: Proximal means "close" or "nearer to" and distal means "distant", "further away from" or "towards the end of". The reference point that is used to define what is proximal or distal varies depending on what is being described. In the broadest sense, proximal is closer to the center of mass of the body within the deep chest or abdomen. Distal is nearer to the tips of the toes or fingers or the top of the head.

Usually the reference point is more specific; the main artery of the body, the aorta begins at the heart and passes from the chest into the abdomen with a first major branch at the femoral arteries. The reference point in this case is the heart; the abdominal aorta is proximal to the femoral arteries and distal to the thoracic aorta with respect to their proximity to the heart. In the kidneys, small filtering units have structures called renal tubules. The tubule is divided into proximal and distal renal tubule segments. In this case the reference point is Bowman's capsule, a central region of these filtering units of the kidney.

Prone vs. Supine: This term pair defines two general positions of the entire human body. The supine position is when one is lying flat on one's back, the arms and legs are extended (straight, not bent at a joint such as the knee or elbow) The palms of the hands are facing upward, and the heels of the feet are in contact with the ground.

The prone position is the reverse of the supine position, occurring when one is lying flat and face down, with the palms of the hands and the tops of the feet in contact with the ground. In the supine position all of the ventral anatomical surfaces of the body are facing upward. The reverse is true for the prone position where all of the dorsal surfaces of the body are facing upward (except for the upper arms, where the lateral surfaces face upward).

Cross Sections
 The anatomy of the body can be visually displayed as cross sections, either of the entire body or of body structures, (the heart or the brain for example). These sections are defined in relation to a human body that is in an upright standing position. There are three primary types of cross-sectional views; the transverse, the sagittal and the coronal cross-sectional views.

Transverse sections are the views represented as if the body has been sliced cleanly in two on the horizontal plane - a mid sagittal view will divide the upper body - head, arms, chest and upper abdomen and the lower body - lower abdomen, pelvis, and legs at about the waistline of a typical individual. Cross-sections of the body may occur at any higher or lower horizontal height either moving toward the top of the head or toward the soles of the feet.

Sagittal sections divide the body into a left and a right side. The mid-sagittal section will divide the body into equal right and left sides, as if a knife had cut cleanly through the body beginning at the top of the head and then proceeded downward through the midline axis of the body. The left section will include the left side of the face, neck, chest, abdomen, pelvis and the left leg. The reverse is true for the right section of the body.

Coronal sections are identical to sagittal sections except that the dissection plane is rotated by 90 degrees. This results in a transection of the body that results in a front, ventral or anterior section and a back, dorsal or posterior section. A mid-coronal section divides the body into front and back sections at the midline of the body.

 Any sagittal section of the body may be obtained by moving the dissection plane parallel and lateral to the midsagittal section. Any coronal section of the body may be obtained by moving the dissection plane parallel and lateral to the mid coronal section.

Direction of motions of the parts of the human body
Nearly all voluntary movements of the human body occur through muscle contractions that result in motions of bones at joints that are designed for body movement (notable exceptions are facial expression movements and the motion of the diaphragm during breathing).

Generally, these motions refer to movement of the arms and legs (the appendages), but considerable numbers and types of movements occur along the skull -spine and spine-pelvis axis. The appendages in particular are capable of quite complex motions, particularly at the shoulder, wrist and ankle regions.

For the HESI the primary types of motions one should know are abduction vs. adduction and flexion vs. extension

Flexion vs. Extension. At a joint, the adjacent ends of bones may be able to move such the joint angle between the bones increases (opens) or decreases (closes), in a simple hinge-like fashion, usually within a maximum range of 180 degrees. This simple, hinge-like joint motion notably occurs at the elbow and knee joints, but most joints can produce this motion.
Extension is the increase in the angle of the joint (opening or extending out). Flexion is the opposite or reverse of extension. Flexion at a joint causes the bones at the joint to move in a manner that causes the joint angle to decrease (close or bend inward).

Abduction vs. Adduction. This type of motion is almost always in reference to motion of the upper arms at the shoulder joints and the upper legs at the hip joints. Abduction results in movement of the arms or legs outward or away from the midlines of the body. Adduction is the reverse of the motion of abduction, the movement of arms or legs towards the midlines of the body.

The Axial Skeleton
The axial skeleton consists of the bones of the skull and the spinal column, the ribs and the sternum.
The Spine
The spine is in many respects the fundamental structural element of the human body. It consists of individual bones known as vertebrae arranged linearly to form a continuous, flexible, bony column.

There are 5 regional spinal segments, the cervical, thoracic and lumbar spinal segments, the sacrum and the coccyx. The cervical segment begins with the vertebra that articulates with the base of the skull (this vertebra has a specific name - the "atlas") There are seven cervical vertebrae. These are the vertebra found in the neck.

The thoracic spinal segment begins with the 8th vertebra. There are 12 thoracic vertebrae. They are notable in that they articulate laterally with the 12 pairs of ribs that are important structural components of the chest or thoracic walls. The lumbar vertebrae begin with the 19th vertebrae, there are 5 lumbar vertebrae.

The final lumbar vertebra connects to the sacrum (which is actually 5 or 6 fused vertebrae). The sacrum is fused medially to the other bones of the hip and together they form the bony pelvis. At the most distal end of the sacrum are four small partially fused vertebrae that together are referred to as the coccyx. In many other species the coccyx is the base of the tail. The terminal vertebra of the coccyx represents the caudal end of the spine.

The Vertebral Canal
The surfaces and underlying sub-regions of the spine and the individual vertebrae are identified as the dorsal, ventral, lateral and central regions. The central vertebral-spinal region is hollow and forms the vertebral canal. The vertebral canal contains the spinal cord of the central nervous system. The spinal cord begins as the distal extension of the brainstem and enters the vertebral canal through the foramen magnum - a large opening in the posterior base of the skull.

The spinal cord does not extend for the entire length of the vertebral canal. It terminates distally (or caudally) at the junction level of the 1st and 2nd lumbar vertebrae. The dorsal and ventral spinal nerve roots that combine to form the 31 sets of spinal nerves of the somatic or voluntary nervous system emerge from the spinal cord at the dorsolateral and ventrolateral intervertebral junctions in the cervical, thoracic and lumbar spinal regions.

The Skull
The skull consists of the tightly fused bones that form the cranial vault, which contains the brain and pituitary gland, and the facial bones; including the upper jaw bones - the maxillae and the lower jaw - the mandible. The mandible is the only moveable bone of the skull. The inner surfaces of the bones that form the cranial cavity (cranial vault) correspond to the adjacent underlying regions of the cerebral cortex of the brain. The frontal bone overlies the left and right frontal cortices. The midline parietal bones overlie the parietal cortices. The laterally positioned temporal bones overly the temporal cortices and the posteriorly positioned occipital bones form the back of the skull and overly the occipital cortices.

The cerebellum and brainstem of the brain also occupy the occipital region of the cranial cavity at the base of the brain. A small depression called the sella turcica is located in the medio anterior inner surface of the base of the skull. The pituitary gland is partially contained within the sella turcica. The 12 pairs of cranial nerves emerge from the brain through various openings in the skull. Together with the 31 pairs of spinal nerves, these form the peripheral portion of the somatic nervous system.

The Thoracic Skeleton
The thoracic (the chest and upper back) skeleton is comprised of the thoracic vertebrae, 12 sets of ribs, the sternum (breastbone) and the medial sections of the clavicles (collarbones). The ribs connect to the lateral surfaces of the thoracic vertebrae then extend laterally to form the dorsal thorax. Next, the ribs curve anteriorly to form the lateral walls of the thorax and then curve medially, continuing to their medial

articulations with the sternum. The sternum is located in the midline of the anterior (ventral) wall of the thorax. The medial ends of the clavicles articulate to the superolateral angles of the sternum.

The thoracic skeleton creates a cage-like structural framework. When the associated muscles and connective tissues are added to this framework, an interior thoracic cavity is created. This cavity will contain the heart, lungs and several other important anatomical structures. The floor of the thoracic cavity will be formed by a single dome-shaped sheet of muscle - the diaphragm.

The Appendicular Skeleton

The upper appendicular (attached) skeleton consists of the bones of the shoulder girdles, arms, wrists, hands and fingers. The shoulder girdles are formed by the clavicles and the scapulae. The medial ends of the clavicles articulate with the superolateral angles of the sternum. This is the only direct bony connection of the upper appendicular skeleton to the axial skeleton. The distal end of the scapula and a lateral extension of the clavicle - the acromion, articulate distally and, along with the proximal end of the humerus, together form the bony elements of the rotator cuff - the complex shoulder joint.

The distal end of the long bone of the upper arm - the humerus, forms the elbow joint with the proximal ends of the two lower arm bones - the radius and the ulna. The distal ends of the radius and the ulna articulate with several of the wrist bones -the carpals, to form the complex wrist joint. The carpals articulate with the metacarpal bones of the hand. The distal ends of the metacarpals articulate with the bones of the fingers - The phalanges.

The Lower appendicular skeleton consists of the bones of the pelvis (except for the sacrum -which is part of the axial skeleton), and the bones of the legs, ankles, feet and toes. The left and right portions of the bony pelvis are fused to the axial skeleton medially at the lateral edges of the sacrum. The proximal end or "head" of the femur fits into a semicircular depression of the inferolateral borders in the bones of the pelvis. Along with associated muscles and connective tissues these form the ball and socket joint of the hip. The distal end of the femur articulates with the proximal ends of the tibia and fibula at the knee joint. The distal ends of the tibia and fibula articulate with several tarsal bones to form the complex ankle joint. Tarsal bones in the ankle region articulate with proximal ends of metatarsal bones in the foot. Distal ends of metatarsal bones articulate with the bones of the toes, the phalanges.

Skeletal Muscles

Most of the skeletal structure of the body is covered by layers of muscles. The anterior surface of the tibiae or shins and the wrists, ankles, cranium and dorsal surface of the spine the ribs and the sternum and the clavicles have comparatively thin or extremely thin overlying layers of muscles. Major skeletal muscle groups include the upper arm muscles, the biceps and triceps; the deltoid muscles of the shoulders, the large muscles of the anterior chest - the pectoralis major muscles; the large lateral muscles of the back - the latissimus dorsi; the large muscles of the pelvis (hips) - the gluteal muscles; the anterior muscles of the upper leg - the quadriceps; The large muscles of the posterior upper leg - the hamstrings, and the largest muscle of the lower leg - the gastrocnemius (calf) muscles.

Body cavities

There are two major cavities of the human body - the dorsal and the ventral body cavities. These cavities are almost completely sealed off from the external environment by surrounding bone and or muscle and other connective tissue. The dorsal body cavity consists of the cranial cavity and the spinal canal. The dorsal cavity is enclosed by the inner surfaces of the bones of the cranium and the vertebra walls of the central vertebral canals. The dorsal cavity contains the brain and the spinal cord. The ventral cavity is enclosed by the inner walls of the thorax - thoracic muscles, ribs sternum and thoracic vertebrae - the inner surfaces of the ventral, lateral and dorsal abdominal wall muscles, and the inner surface bones and associated muscles of the pelvis.

The ventral cavity is divided into an upper cavity - the thoracic cavity - and a lower cavity - the abdominal/pelvic cavity - by a transverse dome-shaped muscle - the diaphragm. Major contents of the thoracic cavity are the heart and lungs. Major contents of the abdominal/pelvic cavity are the intestines, associated digestive organs - liver, gallbladder and pancreas - the urinary bladder and, in females, the uterus and ovaries.

The Integumentary System
The integumentary system of the human body - or simply "the integument" - is a multilayered sheath of tissues and associated cells and extracellular structural and functional components that completely encloses the interior of the body. The most superficial layer of the integumentary system is exposed to the external environment and forms the external surface of the body. Two of the most general primary functions of the integumentary system are to provide a physical containment of the internal body contents and to provide a physical and biochemical barrier to elements of the external environment. There are several secondary functions of the integumentary system as well. Most of these functions as a group can be categorized as homeostatic functions in the sense that they all provide mechanisms to maintain a controlled and stable yet adaptable internal environment that is distinctly separate from the external environment.

Defensive Barrier Functions
The external surface of the integumentary layer in humans is relatively impermeable to water and atmospheric gases. This feature prevents the loss of water (dehydration) and soluble substances from the body. The surface layer of the integument is resistant to radiation damage by ultraviolet wavelength light which is a component of sunlight. The surface layer of the integument is also resistant to penetration by potentially harmful toxic chemicals and infectious biological agents such as viruses, bacteria, fungi, and other eukaryotic unicellular and multi-cellular parasites. Therefore, the integument provides a critical role as the first line of defense in the body's immune system,

Thermoregulation
Another important homeostatic function of the integument is thermoregulation - which allows the body to maintain a constant optimum internal temperature range. The integument regulates internal body temperature by several mechanisms. The lowest layer of the integument - the hypodermis contains adipose tissue that has poor thermal conduction and therefore acts as an **insulator** to protect against excessive heat transfer between the internal regions of the body and the external environment.

Sweat and Evaporative Heat Loss
The insulation capacity of the integument is a passive form of thermoregulation but there are several active thermoregulatory mechanisms possessed by the integument. The integument possesses sweat glands which transport an aqueous solution (sweat) to the surface of the skin. The secretion of sweat can be regulated by neural and hormonal signals. The evaporation of sweat from the skin surface absorbs heat energy from the body as it undergoes a phase change from the liquid phase to the gas phase, thereby lowering the internal body temperature when it exceeds the optimum internal temperature range.

Vasoconstriction and Dilation
The integument is also highly vascularized and the dense capillaries near the skin surface can constrict or dilate in response to local conditions and also in response to neural and hormonal signals. When the internal body temperature is too high, superficial blood vessels dilate and blood flow increases near the surface of the skin. Heat energy can flow from the blood via conduction to the skin surface where it can radiate to the environment or be removed via sweat evaporation. Conversely when internal body temperature is too low, superficial blood vessels constrict and decrease the loss of heat from the body via the bloodstream.

Somatosensory Functions

The integument plays a major role in the sensory functions of the nervous system. The middle layers of the skin are richly innervated and contain several types of sensory cells that are distributed throughout the entire volume of these integumentary layers. The sensory receptors are designed to provide nearly all of the specific types of sensory information that comprise the **somatosensory sense** including sensations of pain, heat, cold, light touch, pressure and vibration. Specific examples of these integumentary sensory receptors include Meissner's corpuscles which detect changes in texture and slow vibrations, Pacinian corpuscles which detect deep pressure, fast vibrations, Merkel's discs which detect sustained touch and pressure and free nerve endings which are pain receptors

Excretory Functions

The integument does arguably play a minor role is as an excretory organ. Alcohol and several metabolic waste products including urea and several types of organic acids are excreted from the bloodstream onto skin surfaces and excess body water and electrolytes contained in sweat may be excreted in the form of sweat. It should be noted however that the primary method of clearing alcohol by the body is by metabolic functions provided by the liver and excretion of urea and organic acids is a primary function of the kidney which is completely capable of providing excretion of these substances without any contribution of excretion through the skin. The excretion of these substances through the skin is simply a result of the forces of diffusion. They are not regulated excretory process of the body.

The secretion of some types of organic acids are a design feature of the integument, but not as an excretory process but as an element of the innate immune system - where the organic acids generate a low surface skin pH level that is unfavorable to the growth of fungi and bacteria. The loss of water and electrolytes through sweat is more likely to result in excessive loss of water and electrolytes leading to dehydration and electrolyte abnormalities within the body which can be dangerous and even fatal. In this sense this form of excretion is undesirable and is disruptive to the maintenance of homeostasis of the body.

Non-Barrier Immune Functions

The extracellular matrix and highly keratinized cells of the outer surface of the integument provide physical barriers in the form of tight cytoskeleton-keratin protein and extracellular phospholipid interconnections. Hydrolytic enzymes, short polypeptide segments with antimicrobial activity and organic acids provide biochemical resistance to infectious organisms. Active immune functions of the integument are provided by other cells and molecular substances located within the integument including antigen presenting cells called dendritic cells, T-cells and other cells of the immune system.

Vitamin D Synthesis

The integument has metabolic functions, most notably in the synthesis of vitamin D where ultraviolet radiation travels into the skin where it participates in chemical reaction stage required for the conversion of vitamin D precursors - which are also located in the skin to -to vitamin D. The hypodermis of the integument stores energy in the form of fat contained in adipose cells.

Layers of the Integument

The integument consists of a dermal or cutaneous layer and a subcutaneous or hypodermal layer. The dermal layer consists of two sub layers- the dermis and the epidermis.

The Hypodermis (Subcutaneous Layer)

The lowermost or deepest layer of the integument the hypodermis or the subcutaneous layer of the integument consist primarily of loose adipose connective tissue, blood vessels, lymphatic vessels and nerves. The hypodermis provides a transitional connective zone between the overlying dermal layer and the adjacent underlying body contents, usually outer skeletal muscle layers, but in some areas bony structures - particularly over the knee and elbow joints and the anterior surfaces of the lower leg (the shins).

The adipocytes of the hypodermis are organized into small collections called lobules that are enmeshed in collagen fibers. Fibroblasts are sparsely distributed throughout the hypodermis. The hypodermis- dermis boundary is a continuous series of interdigitating invaginations of both layers into the other with direct structural connections provided by collagen and elastic fibers. One of the four major types of mechanoreceptors - Lamellar or Pacinian corpuscles, are located at the boundary region between the hypodermis and the dermis. These sensory receptor cells provide tactile information those results in the perception of pressure or vibration.

The Dermis
The dermis is the middle layer of the three major integument layers. It is composed of three primary cell types, fibroblasts, macrophages and adipocytes, but there are numerous other types of cells interspersed within the dermis, including chromophores or melanocytes and various cells associated with the immune system including dendritic cells and T-cells.

The extracellular matrix of the dermal layers contain collagen, elastin and reticulin fibers and several types of macromolecules that help to retain water within the matrix and also serve other functions. The most common types of these extracellular macromolecules are glycosaminoglycans, proteoglycans and glycoproteins.

The Dermal Reticular Layer
The dermis consists of two sub layers - the deep layer -adjacent to the hypodermis - is the reticular layer. The reticular layer is composed of dense connective tissue. This tissue contains dense amounts of collagen fibers and elastic fibers and reticular fibers. These fibers provide the mechanical properties of tensile strength and elasticity to the integument. The roots of hair follicles, sweat glands, sebaceous glands and sensory receptor cells are also implanted within the reticular layer of the dermis.

The Dermal Papillary Layer
The second sub layer of the dermis - the papillary layer - is immediately superficial to the reticular layer. The primary type of tissue contained in the papillary layer is areolar connective tissue. Areolar connective tissue is a very loose arrangement of adipocytes and collagen and elastin fiber with an abundance of gel-like extracellular matrix. These features of areolar connective tissue allow substances to readily diffuse through the tissue.

The Dermal-Epidermal Interface
At the interface between the papillary layer of the dermis and the overlying superficial layer of the integument - the epidermis - the papillary layer projects numerous knob like extension of tissue called papillae between interdigitating ridges of the epidermis -called rete ridges. The result is a tight enjoining of the two integumentary layers. The papillae of the papillary layer contain tufts of capillaries or Meissner's corpuscles. Meissner's corpuscles are sensory receptor cells that are adapted to provide information that is interpreted in the CNS as the sensation of light touch. Mid portions of hair follicles, sweat and sebaceous glands nerves and lymphatic vessels also travel through the papillary dermis toward the epidermis.

The Epidermis
The most superficial layer of the integument is the epidermis. The epidermis has no direct blood supply and depends on diffusion for the supplies of oxygen and nutrients and for transport of CO_2 and other waste products. The epidermis begins immediately adjacent at the superficial surface of the papillary layer of the dermis. The two layers are separated by a basement membrane. The basement membrane is a common feature of almost all epithelial tissues and serves as an attachment surface for the lowermost layers of epithelial cells and also creates anchoring connections with loose connective tissue located beneath the basement membrane. The basement membrane of the epidermis provides the biomolecular features that

allow the epidermis to adhere to the dermis. The basement membrane has several additional functions including immune system functions and cellular repair functions. The basement membrane has a complex structure consisting of multiple layers of fibrous proteins including anchoring collagen fibers, substrate adhesion molecules (SAMS) integrins and several other types of macromolecules. The basement membrane is also the last line of defense of the spread of cancerous cells that originate within the epithelium.

Regions of the Epidermis
The epidermis is composed of either four or five stratified regions depending on the local anatomical areas where the epidermis is located. Most areas consist of four regions - the stratum basale stratum spinosum, stratum granulare and the stratum corneum. The epidermis of the palms of the hands and the soles of the feet soles is known as "thick skin" because it has 5 epidermal regions and is referred to as thick skin. The additional region of thick skin is the stratum lucidum which is interposed between the stratum spinosum and the stratum granulare.

The Malpighian Layer
The deepest layer of the epidermis is the Malpighian layer which is subdivided into the stratum basale or inner basal layer and the overlying stratum spinosum layer.

The Basal Layer (Stratum Basale)
The basal layer is composed of columnar epithelial cells that are attached to the superficial surface of the underlying basement membrane by connective structures called hemidesmosomes. These cells are germinal epithelium that undergoes mitotic division to produce a continuous supply of cells which migrate toward the outer surface of the epithelium. As these cells migrate, they undergo progressive stages of differentiation with varying characteristics that define the overlying regions of the epidermis. Melanocytes, Merkel cells and associated cutaneous nerves and cells that participate if the inflammation reactions of the immune system are also present in the basal layer. Melanocytes connect to keratinocytes and provide the pigment melanin to keratinocytes. Melanin provides a barrier to ultraviolet radiation and is also the pigment that determines the degree of darkness of skin tone that is a component of human racial characterizations. Merkel's cells and associated cutaneous nerves provide sensory information associated with the perception of light-touch.

The Stratum Spinosum (Spinous or Prickle Cell Region)
The stratum spinosum is the second of the two sub layers of the Malpighian layer of the epidermis The stratum spinosum region is located directly superficial to the inner basal layer. This region consists of polyhedral-shaped cells that are daughter cells of the basal epithelial progenitor cells. The stratum spinosum cells also undergo mitotic division contributing to the approximately five layers of epidermal cells within the region. The cells have a spiny or prickly appearance due to microfilament shortening within desmosomes that interconnect among the cells. The stratum spinosum cells synthesize large amounts of fibrillar proteins called cytokeratin. Cytokeratin aggregates within the cells to form tonofilaments. Tonofilaments are assembled into desmosomes which form tight junctions between the epidermal cells as they continue to differentiate and migrate toward the epidermal surface.

As keratinocytes within the stratum spinosum continue to migrate upward and differentiate, the Golgi within the keratinocytes begin to produce lamellar bodies that contain a complex assortment of phospho and glycosphingolipids, free fatty acids and enzymes that have antibiotic activity. These products will eventually participate in the formation of the complex extracellular matrix of the outer epidermal layers.

The Stratum Granulosum
The region of the epidermis adjacent and superficial to the stratum spinosum is the stratum granulosum. The region is three to four cells in thickness. The cells of the granular region have a high content of keratin granules that produce a granular microscopic appearance - hence the name "granulosum" that is given to

this layer. The cells of the stratum granulosum are classified as keratinocytes. Keratinocytes do not divide - in contrast to the cells of the stratum basale and the stratum spinosum. As keratinocytes continue to be displaced toward the outer surface of the epidermis, they become progressively flatter and more tightly compacted. In the palms and soles of humans the stratum lucidum is a two-to-three cell-thickness region of the epidermis is adjacent and superficial to the stratum granulosum.

The Stratum Corneum
The most superficial region of the epidermis is the 10 to 30 cell-layer-thick stratum corneum. Keratinocytes proceed through the final stages of cell differentiation to become corneocytes as they moving from the stratum spinosum or stratum lucidum region to the stratum corneum. Corneocytes have ejected their cell nucleus (mature red blood cells also eject their cell nuclei) and are enveloped in a keratin protein matrix that in turn is surrounded by stacked layers of lipid molecules. The keratin proteins are connected to the cytoskeleton of corneocytes by structures called corneodesmosomes. This interconnection of corneocytes through keratin-corneodesmosomes-cytoskeleton networks provides the exceptional mechanical durability of the epidermis.

Extracellular Matrix of the Stratum Corneum
The contents of the lamellar bodies within corneocytes are transported out of the cells and serve as the raw materials for the construction of the extracellular matrix of the stratum corneum. The lipid molecules within this matrix are arranged parallel to the skin surface and form a barrier that is impermeable to water. Organic acids, hydrolytic enzymes and short chain peptides with antimicrobial activity are interspersed throughout the extracellular matrix and provide an environment that is hostile to disease causing organisms including bacteria and fungi.

The stratum corneum has very low water content and supports a community of non-harmful microorganisms that provide additional hostile conditions to potentially harmful microorganisms. Finally, the continuous shedding and replacement of superficial skin cells enhances the protective functions of the epidermis. The entire epidermal region above the basal layer is completely regenerated approximately every 48 days.

Glands of the Integument
The integument contains a variety of glands, most notably apocrine and eccrine sweat glands and sebaceous or oil glands. All of these glands are exocrine glands. Exocrine glands secrete substances through a glandular duct (tube) onto the surface of epithelial tissue, either on the surface of the skin on the luminal surface of an epithelial-lined hollow organ such as the small intestine. In contrast, endocrine glands secrete substances directly into the bloodstream or lymphatic system.

Holocrine, Apocrine and Merocrine Glands
Glands are also categorized based on the manner in which they secrete substances. There are three general types of secretory process, holocrine, merocrine and apocrine. Holocrine secretion occurs through the disintegration of the secretory cells - the disintegration of holocrine glandular cells releases the secretory substances present in the cytoplasm of the cells. Sebaceous glands of the integument are holocrine glands. The fragments of disintegrated glandular cells are also constituents of the secretions of holocrine glands.

Apocrine secretion occurs through a budding of cell membrane segment which form vesicles that contain the secretory substances of the gland. Apocrine sweat glands are one of the two types of sweat glands located in the integument. The cell membrane segments that bud off of apocrine glandular cells are constituents of apocrine secretions. Human mammary glands are also apocrine glands.

The cellular fragment components of both holocrine and apocrine glands can obstruct the ducts of the glands. Obstructed glandular ducts can result in the formation of abscesses of the gland. The contents of these abscesses may become infected by bacteria resulting in acne and other types of localized infections within the integument.

Merocrine glands utilize exocytosis to secrete their glandular products. No disintegration or budding of cell membranes occurs in the secretory cells of merocrine glands. The exocrine glands of the pancreas and virtually all endocrine glands are merocrine glands. The second type of sweat glands found in the integument - the eccrine sweat glands - are merocrine glands.

Sebaceous (Oil) glands
Sebaceous or oil glands are widely distributed within the integument with the exception of the soles of the feet and the palms of the hands. Sebaceous glands have ducts that most commonly communicate with the spaces adjacent to hair shafts within hair follicles but a small percentage open directly onto the external epidermal surface. The glandular cells are located in the dermis usually adjacent to a hair follicle. Sebaceous glands are holocrine glands that synthesize and secrete a substance called sebum. Sebum is an oily or waxy substance consisting of triglycerides, lipid esters and free fatty acids.

Sebum provides an oily medium that contributes to the composition of the sweat layer on the surface of the skin. The oily component of sweat extends the cooling effects of evaporative sweating and prevents dehydration by increasing the adherence of the sweat layer to the surface of the skin. The free fatty acids contained in sebum lower the pH of the skin surface to a range of 4.5 to 5.0 - a level that strongly inhibits the growth of potentially harmful microorganisms. In addition to the indirect antimicrobial effect provide by the lowering of skin pH, free fatty acids in sebum also provide strong, direct antimicrobial activity. The production of sebum can be influenced by various hormone levels, in particular, testosterone stimulates sebum production and estrogen inhibits sebum production.

Eccrine Sweat Glands
Eccrine glands are merocrine glands. They are by far the most numerous and widely distributed type of sweat glands. Eccrine sweat glands secrete a watery solution containing sodium and chloride ions. In addition, eccrine sweat contains bicarbonate ions, cytokines, immunoglobulins and short-sequence polypeptides that have antimicrobial activity. The secretory cells of the glands are coiled deep in the dermis. Myoepithelial cells surround the secretory cells and contraction of these cells propels sweat solution through the eccrine duct and onto the skin surface. Eccrine sweat glands are innervated by autonomic nerve fibers that modulate sweat secretion in response to core body temperature levels and to emotional stress such as excitement or fear.

Apocrine Sweat Glands
The secretory cells and surrounding myoepithelial cells of apocrine sweat glands are located in the dermis near the dermis-hypodermis interface. The duct of apocrine sweat glands - like those of most sebaceous glands- communicate with the spaces adjacent to hair shafts within hair follicles the distribution of apocrine sweat glands is limited to only a few regions of the surface of the body, primarily the axillae (armpits). The composition of apocrine sweat gland secretions differs significantly from eccrine sweat compositions. Apocrine secretions have a high protein and carbohydrate content. Apocrine sweat combines with sebaceous gland secretions in hair shafts located in the axillae resulting in a cloudy viscous solution that clings to axillary hair and supports colonization by bacteria. Colonizing bacteria break down components of axillary sweat and these breakdown products are responsible for the characteristic odor associated with the axillary regions.

Abnormalities of the Integument
Notable abnormalities (pathologies) of the integument include impetigo - a superficial staphylococcal bacterial infection and cellulitis a deep bacterial infection that extends into the hypodermis. Superficial viral infections typically are caused by papilloma virus (warts) but many generalized viral infections produce

surface viral-containing vesicles such as those associated with the herpes virus. Superficial tinea-species fungal infections cause the condition known as athlete's feet. Generalized viral and other infections often produce immune related skin rashes and many drug hypersensitivities also produce skin rashes and mild temporary blistering in the form of hives. In more serious cases deep blistering and skin loss can occur with poison ivy reactions and severe drug sensitivity, infectious and autoimmune reactions. Eczema is a common hereditary hypersensitivity reaction of the skin. Psoriasis is an often severe and debilitating condition resulting from excessive rates of cell division in the epidermis. Malignant melanoma is a particularly deadly and common cancer of melanocytes usually related to excessive sun exposure. The resistance of the integument to infection in generally is impaired by high levels of cortisol - often associated with prolonged periods of psychological stress.

Bone
While the discussion of bones may seem to be a comparatively simple task it is much more complex than a one might imagine. An efficient means to begin the discussion is with the process of bone development.

Bone tissue cells are derived from mesoderm. The cells that produce the extracellular matrix of bone tissue are chondrocytes, fibroblasts and osteoblasts. Osteoblasts, fibroblasts and chondrocytes are all capable of independent motion and can migrate to sites of bone formation throughout the body. Osteoblasts are derived from osteoprogenitor cells. Osteoblasts secrete substances that form the first stage in the production of the extracellular matrix of mature bone tissue.

Membranous Bone Formation
During embryological and fetal development, bone formation occurs through one of two processes, either intramembranous formation or endochondral formation. Intramembranous bone formation occurs by the conversion of a region of mesenchymal connective tissue membrane into a bone. Membranous bone formation generally results in the creation of flat bones, including most of the bones of the skull.

Endochondral Bone Formation
Endochondral bone formation results in the creation of most other skeletal bones. The first stage of endochondral bone formation begins with the production of a preliminary cartilaginous version of a particular bone. This cartilage model of the future mature bone is constructed from substances secreted from fibroblasts and chondrocytes. These initial versions of bones have the same shapes as the mature bones that they will be converted to. This conversion process is called ossification.

Ossification
Endochondral Ossification begins with various physiological processes that progressively break down and reabsorb the cartilage version bone while osteoblasts simultaneously invade the collagen matrix. Osteoblasts synthesize and secrete the substances that in the extracellular space comingle to form a composite material called osteoid. Osteoid is a gelatinous substance that contains a high percentage of collagen protein fibrils and lesser amounts of ground substance. Ground substance is a homogenous aqueous solution of proteoglycan molecules such as hyaluronic acid and chondroitin sulfate. Osteoid progressively develops into a mature bone matrix.

Organic and Inorganic Components of Bone Matrix
The collagen fibrils contained in osteoid polymerize to form collagen strands. Collagen strands and ground substance comprise the organic component of the extracellular matrix of bone. This organic component has a composition of 90% collagen and 10% ground substance. The inorganic component of the extracellular bone matrix is composed of calcium and phosphate hydroxide salts. Most of these salts are in the form of hydroxyapatite crystals. Hydroxyapatite is a mineral with a chemical formula of $Ca10(PO_4)6(OH)_2$.

Deposition

During the next phase of bone formation - deposition - small hydroxyapatite crystals condense along the surfaces of collagen strands. These small crystals prompt further hydroxyapatite crystallization and the content of hydroxyapatite increases. In mature bone matrix 70% of the matrix consists of the inorganic component - hydroxyapatite and other mineral salts. The remaining 30% of the matrix is composed of the organic component of the matrix - collagen strands and ground substance. The combination of collagen strands and hydroxyapatite crystals give the extracellular matrix remarkably high tensile and compressional strength.

Further bone formation can proceed by one of two general pathways. One is the pathway to cortical bone formation and the other is the pathway towards trabecular bone formation.

Cortical Bone

Cortical bone forms the outer layers of nearly all bones. It is a dense structure with has a white, smooth-appearing surface. Cortical bone has a complex and high regular microscopic structure. The formation of this structure begins with the formation of concentric layers of bone that surround a central cavity. These formations are called osteons.

Osteons

Osteons are the structural subunits that form cortical bone. Osteons are cylindrical columns that are tightly packed together in parallel arrangement in cortical bone and often extend for the entire length of individual bones. The central cavity of an osteon is called a Haversian canal. Haversian canals contain blood vessels and nerves. Volkmann's canals are passageways between adjacent Haversian canals. Together, Haversian and Volkmann canals provide an interconnected network of passageways throughout cortical bone. This network provides pathways for the flow of oxygen and nutrients to all regions of the bone.

The width of the osteon increases as osteoclast form additional concentric layer of bone. The collagen strands within these layers are highly organized into overlapping parallel fibers that extend parallel to the course of the central Haversian canal and alternating with fiber layers that encircle the canal. The result is concentric layers of bone with collagen fibers that are arranged at right angles to adjacent concentric layers. This highly organized and compact structure of cortical bone results in a very high strength to weight ratio.

Osteocytes

During cortical bone formation, a small percentage of osteoclasts become trapped within the extracellular matrix. These osteoclasts differentiate into osteocytes. The osteocytes remain within the cortical bone is small spaces called lacunae. The osteocytes within these lacunae are extremely long-lived cells that continue to reabsorb old bone tissue and produce new bone tissue for the lifetime of the bone. This process helps to maintain the structural and functional integrity of the bone often for as long as an individual's entire lifespan. Due to these structural features, cortical bone is also classified compact bone (due to its high density), and as lamellar bone - bone consisting of layers or lamina containing collagen fibers that are arranged in parallel sheets. Cortical bone is also classified as concentric bone due to the concentric structure of the parallel osteon subunits of cortical bone

Trabecular Bone

While the outer or superficial layers of most bones consist of very strong, very dense highly organized cortical bone, most bones also have adjacent underlying central regions composed of a different type of bone called trabecular bone. Trabecular bone is highly porous (filled with cavity spaces and passageways) with a fractal, coral-like structure that enormously increases the surface area of trabecular bone. Macroscopically a cross section of trabecular bone has a foamy appearance due to the myriad of spaces of varying sizes that are densely distributed throughout the bone matrix. Trabecular bone is also classified as spongy or cancellous (full of cavities) bone and as medullary (middle or centrally located) bone. Trabecular bone does not serve a significant structural function.

Hematopoiesis
The open architecture and high surface area of trabecular bone provide an ideal landscape for hematopoiesis. Hematopoiesis is the process that is required for the production of the cellular components of blood - red blood cells, granulocytic white blood cells (polymorphonuclear leucocytes (PMNLs) monocytes and macrophages, basophils, and eosinophils), lymphocytic white blood cells (B-cells and T-cells) and platelets.   Hematopoietic (blood forming) tissue consists of hematopoietic stem cells and their lineage of cells that progressively differentiated into mature red blood cells, white blood cells megakaryocytes. Fragments of megakaryocytes differentiate into platelets. Platelets circulate in large numbers in the bloodstream and are critical to thrombogenesis (clot formation) that is required for repair of leaks and tear in blood vessels. The hematopoietic function that occurs in the spaces within trabecular bone demonstrates that bone is much more than a connective tissue but is actually a complex organ that has other critical functions at least as important as the structural function. The substances within the cavities of trabecular bone is considered to be a particular type of connective tissue called myeloid tissue

Bone Marrow
The cavities within trabecular bone contain all of the cells that participate in erythropoiesis and also contain adipocytes and the other mixture of cells and organic and inorganic molecules typical of a loose connective tissue extracellular matrix. In many bones - the large long bone of the arms and legs in particular - there is a central or medullary cavity surrounded by trabecular bone. This central cavity is filled with the loose connective matrix associated with trabecular bone. This material within the medullary cavity is called bone marrow. Bone marrow has hematopoietic activity and also has a high content of adipocytes. This allows bone to perform an additional function by providing a energy reserve in the form of fats that are stored within bone marrow adipocytes. Bone marrow is also referred to as a type of myeloid tissue.

Bone Membranes
In addition to an outer layer of cortical bone and an inner layer of trabecular bone, bones also have an outer membrane - the periosteum and a membrane located between the cortical and trabecular bone layers - the endosteum. The periosteum contains numerous nerve fibers -pain fibers in particular. Even slight injury to the periosteum causes excruciating pain that is a primary protective mechanism of the body.

Bone Remodeling
Bone is a dynamic organ that is undergoing a continuous process of renewal and adaptation to the changing demands of the external environment. The mechanical forces acting on bones cause continual damage in the form of microfractures which must be repaired. Bone also responds to increased mechanical stress by increasing bone mass and reconfiguring the shape of bone to increase the bones ability to function at higher these levels of mechanical stress. Bone also serves as a crucial storage site of calcium and phosphate for all of the cells of the body. All of these functions -bone repair, growth and adaption to the mechanical demands of the external environment and the uptake and release of calcium and phosphate to and from the bloodstream and extracellular spaces within bone requires that there is a process to simultaneously break down bone matrix and create new bone matrix. This process is called bone remodeling. It occurs at the cortical surfaces of bones through the bone decomposing activities of cells called osteoclasts and the bone formation activities of osteoblasts. It is not clear how the relative activity of osteoblasts and osteoclasts is regulated to precisely remodel a bone or a region of bone. There is some evidence that increased mechanical stress at a bone regions generation small electrical currents that can be detected by osteoblasts and cause osteoblast activity to increase. Regardless of the precise manner in which remodeling is regulated, the overall process depends on the relative local activity of osteoblasts and osteoclasts. At regions where osteoblast activity

exceeds osteoclast activity the bone thickens and where the reverse is true bone is reabsorbed and the bone thins.

Metabolic Functions of Bone - Calcium and Phosphate Ion Levels
In addition to the production of osteoid, osteoblast also secrete an enzyme called alkaline phosphatase that promotes the mineralization of osteoid. This process removes calcium and phosphate ions from the blood and extracellular space and deposits the ions in newly formed bone in the form of hydroxyapatite crystals. The increased osteoblast activity therefore tends to decrease the levels of free calcium and phosphate ions in the body. Osteoclasts - which are derived from macrophages - have the capability to dissolve hydroxyapatite and disrupt collagen fibers in bone matrix. This activity releases calcium and phosphate ions into the circulation; therefore, increased osteoclast activity tends to increase the levels of free calcium and phosphate ions in the body.

In order for bone to function in its role of releasing or absorbing calcium and phosphate ions to maintain optimum levels of body calcium and phosphate ion levels, osteoclasts and osteoblast have to be responsive to the hormones that are designed to regulate these levels. There are numerous factors that influence calcium and phosphate levels in the body and numerous methods of monitoring these levels and numerous hormones that form a network of activities that influence these levels. When the overall activity of osteoblasts exceeds the overall activity of osteoclasts, the overall bone mass of the body increases and the levels of calcium and phosphate in the body decreases. The reverse is true when overall osteoclast activity exceeds overall osteoblast activity. Ultimately the hormones that directly determine the relative activity of osteoblasts and osteoclasts are the thyroid hormone **calcitonin** and **parathyroid hormone** (PTH). Calcitonin binds to membrane receptors and osteoclasts resulting in inhibition of osteoclast activity. Calcitonin therefore tends to increase levels of body calcium ion. Parathyroid hormone stimulates the activity of osteoblasts, resulting in decreased levels of body calcium ion.

Osteoblasts can also be stimulated growth hormone by the pituitary, thyroid hormone (T3 and T4), the sex hormones testosterone and estrogen and by Vitamin D. The result is an overall increase in the bodies total bone mass.

Structural Functions of Bone
In the musculoskeletal system, bone acts as the primary structural component of the system, acting as anchoring points for skeletal muscles and as pivot points for body movement at bony joints. Moveable bony joints are articulations (meeting points) of the two bones that allow a variable range of motion depending on the type of joint.

Synovial Joints
There are 206 major bones in the adult human body and many other smaller bones called sesamoid bones. Nearly all of the major bones form articulations with adjacent bones (the patellae and the hyoid bone are notable exceptions). The widest range of motion occurs at synovial joints which consist of a fibrous joint capsule that encloses the ends of two articulating bones. Ligaments between the articulating bone ends surround the exterior of the fibrous capsule and bind the joint together. The ends of the bones within the joint capsule are covered by pads of cartilage called articular cartilage which provide mechanical protection to the ends of the bone and also are slippery, allowing ease of movement of the bones within the synovial capsule.

Synovial fluid
The interior surfaces of the synovial capsule are covered with specialized connective tissue that forms a synovial membrane. Fibroblasts within the synovial membrane secrete components of synovial fluid. These contributions to synovial fluid consist of long chain sugar polymer molecules called hyaluronic acid and

another molecule called lubrin. Both hyaluronic acid and lubrin provide lubrication to the joint structures within the synovial capsule Additional elements of synovial fluid include water and dissolved oxygen and nutrients that diffuse out of capillaries within the synovial capsule.

Types of Synovial Joints

The synovial joints with the greatest range of motion are the ball and socket joint of the pelvic girdle and the shoulders (glenohumeral joints). Hinge joints -such as those found at the elbow and knee allow a range of motion limited to primarily one plane or one axis motions of this type are usually the flexion-extension and abduction adduction movements. Most synovial hinge joints are pure hinge joints but are compound or modified joints that allow limited additional ranges of motion such as pronation and supination. Ellipsoid or condylar joints - such as those found in the wrist and ankles have greater range of motion than hinge joints and less range of motion than ball and socket joints These allowed motions include two-axis - both flexion/extension and abduction/adduction. Simultaneous motions in both axes can generate circular motions or circumduction at the ankle and wrist. Gliding or plane joints allow only gliding or sliding movements of the articulating bone surfaces. Gliding joints are located in the carpals of the wrist and between spinal vertebral articulations. Pivot joints allow one bone to rotate around another bone on an axis at the articulation of the bones. The radioulnar joints and the atlantoaxial (first and second cervical vertebrae) joints are pivot joints. Saddle joints are saddle-shaped and allow the same types of motion as ellipsoid joint but with a greater range of motion. The thumb joint and the sternoclavicular joint are saddle joints.

Fibrous Joints and Sutures

Fibrous joints are much simpler in structure compared to synovial joints. Fibrous joints consist of varying proportions of cartilage and or collagen and elastic fibers and allow very limited mobility. Fibrous joints are typically located between the edges of two adjacent bones, forming a seam between the bone borders similar to the mortar between bricks or masonry stones. Joint movement is limited to hinge-like flexion and extension at the fibrous seam between adjacent bone edges. The sternomanubrial joint and the sacroiliac joints are fibrous joints that have a moderated amount of flexibility. Suture joints have very little fibrous content and almost not range of motion. They are the strongest joints and are analogous to seam welds between adjacent bone edges. The bones of the skull (except for the mandible) articulate with suture joints.

Bone Classification by Shape

The bones of the human body can be classified by shape into one of five general categories - long bones, short bones, flat bones, irregular bones and sesamoid bones.

Long Bones

Long bones possess a tubular shape with a long axis several times greater than cross-sectional diameter. The longest section of long bones is the bone shaft or diaphysis. The ends of long bones are called epiphyses. They are located at either end of the shaft (diaphysis) and have expanded and often complex geometries that are beautifully designed to allow the particular types of motion that occur with their articulations with adjacent epiphyses of within a synovial joint. The major bones of the upper and lower arms and legs - the humerus, femur, radius, ulna, tibia and fibula are long bones. The phalanges (finger and toe bones) and the clavicles (collar bones) are also long bones. Most long bones have medullary cavities and are a major site of erythropoiesis.

Epiphyseal Plates

The cartilaginous epiphyseal plates of the upper and lower extremities are a primary site for growth resulting in increased bone length. The adult height of an individual is determined by the amount of growth that occurs at the epiphyseal plates of these long bones and in the vertebrae of the spine. When the cartilage of the epiphyseal plates of long bones and vertebrae become fully mineralized into bone, no further increase in height can occur in an individual. The closure of these epiphyseal plates is a primary indication that an individual has reach adulthood.

Short Bones
Short bones have variable shapes, often cuboidal with dimensions of length width and height that are roughly equivalent.

The Wrist and Ankle Bones
The bones of the wrists and ankles metacarpals and the metatarsals and the middle bones of the hands and feet - the carpals and tarsals are short bones. There are eight carpal bones per hand and seven tarsal bones per foot. These bones are closely packed and have multiple interfaces with adjacent carpals or tarsals, At the ankle and wrist with some tarsal or carpal bones articulate with metacarpals or metatarsals. Metacarpals and metatarsals also articulate with adjacent long bone epiphyses of the radius and ulna or the tibia and fibula. Some tarsal and carpals also articulate or with epiphyses of phalanges in the hands these are the "knuckle" joints.

Due to their multiple articulations with adjacent bones carpal and metacarpal and tarsals and metatarsal have a complex surface geometry and a somewhat irregular overall three dimensional shape. These bones are designed to function as a group of subunits that allow very complex and subtle rearrangements of the contours of the palms of the hands and soles of the feet. These continuous alterations in the contours of the palms and soles are required particularly when walking on uneven surfaces or when grasping and manipulating objects. While these multi bone systems allow remarkable adaptability during walking and running activities and exceptional dexterity of the hands, even seemingly minor injuries to an individual ankle or wrist bone can destabilize the entire wrist or ankle system leading to severe impairment of function.

Irregular Bones
Irregular bones as a general category have complex three dimensional geometries. the range of irregularity varies greatly. By far the most irregular bones are two of the bones of the skull - the vomer and the sphenoid bones. These bones have complex three dimensional overall and local structures consisting of bony walls, partitions, shelves, protuberances, compartments, passageways and openings that accommodate a variety of contents, the sphenoid in particular is designed for a broad range of structural and functional purposes. Many anatomists have opined that the sphenoid is "a bone whose structure is so complex that it defies description". Several other bones of the cranium and the face are irregular bones or have regions that are irregular. These include the ethmoid, mastoid and maxillary bones. The bones of the pelvis - the ilium, ischium pubis and sacroiliac bones are irregular bones

The bones of the middle ear - the incus, malleus and stapes (anvil, hammer and stirrup) are irregular in the sense that they do not have a simple shape, but they each have a very specific shape which allows them to function together as a unit. These three middle ear bones form a linked bony mechanical system that transduces sound waves arriving at the tympanum (eardrum) in the outer ear canal to fluid waves within the canals of the inner ear.

The Spinal Vertebrae
The individual vertebrae of the spine are classified as irregular bones but they are comparable in structure and in their articulations with adjacent vertebrae to the short bones of the ankle and wrists. Their "irregularity" consists of their vertebral foramen, left and right transverse processes and dorsal midline single spinous processes.

The central canal of a vertebra is a tubular passage that aligns with the vertebral foramen of adjacent vertebrae. In the spine these central canals form a continuous tube called the spinal canal. The spinal cord is contained within the spinal canal. The dorsal spinous process of a vertebra is a single long projection of the dorsal surface of a vertebra. The tips of spinous processes can as a group be seen and felt as the longitudinal arrangement of bumps that define the location of spine underlying the skin in the midline of the dorsal surface of the torso.

These additional features of a vertebrae are actually very regular and differ slightly but regularly between vertebrae primarily in the length and thickness of the spinous processes in the cervical, thoracic and lumbar sections of the spine and in the mass of the main body of the vertebrae from smallest at the first cervical vertebrae (C1 and C2) to largest at the most caudal lumbar vertebrae (L4 and L5). The vertebrae function as subunits of the overall spine. Although the range of motion between adjacent vertebrae is limited, when these motions are coordinated along the entire length of the spine, they cumulatively can produce a remarkable range of bending and twisting spinal movements. As a result, the human body can adopt a vast number of specific postures in three dimensions and can coordinate changing postures to create extremely complex dynamic choreographies of continuous body movements.

Intervertebral Discs
A unique feature of the spinal vertebrae is the intervertebral disc. These are shock-absorbing structures consisting of a tough outer fibrous capsule that encases a gel-like substance called the nucleus pulposus. The discs act as a fibrocartilaginous joint between adjacent vertebrae

Flat Bones and Sesamoid Bones
Flat bones are thin with a high surface area. They have an outer layer of cortical bone and a thin central layer of trabecular bone. Most of the bones of the cranium are flat bones. flat bones have a primary protective function - protection of the brain in particular- and have little if any role in erythropoiesis. Sesamoid bones are formed with muscle tendons. They have a mechanical function related to the amount of leverage that a muscle can generate on an attached bone. Most sesamoid bones are relatively small, a notable exception is patella which is located anterior to the synovial joint of the knee.

Bone and Joint Disorders
There are a number of diseases and other pathological conditions of bones and joints that are notable for their frequency and/ or severity in humans. Joint disorders are so common there is a medical specialty - rheumatology - that focuses exclusively on the diagnosis and treatment of these conditions.

Disorders of the Synovial Joints
The two most important synovial joint disorders are rheumatoid arthritis and osteoarthritis. Rheumatoid arthritis is an autoimmune disorder that attacks synovial joints, resulting in progressive, painful disfigurement and loss of function of joints throughout the body. Modern treatment involves monoclonal antibody and other immunological therapies that can prevent the progression of the disease if the condition is diagnosed in its early stages.

Osteoarthritis is a result of the wear and tear damage to articular cartilage in synovial joints. The mechanical forces acting on joints over decades of physical activity eventually wear away the cartilage in synovial joints resulting in the loss of the protection the cartilage provides to underlying bone. The unprotected articulating bones grind against each other and cause severe pain and eventually loss of function. Most middle-aged to elderly males have some degree of osteoarthritis. The condition is most serious when the knee and hip joints are involved. Damage due to osteoarthritis is the number one reason for hip and knee replacements in the U.S.

Infection, Inflammation and Physical Injury

Synovial fluid is susceptible to accumulations of uric acid crystals resulting in the excruciatingly painful inflammatory condition known as gout. Bacteria that enter the bloodstream often settle in synovial joints causing infection or septic arthritis. Many viral and autoimmune diseases also attack synovial joints and causing a sterile or aseptic arthritis. The joints are common sites of severe physical injuries including ligament and tendon tears and ruptures and joint sprains and dislocations. The deep tendon reflexes are a specialized local neuromuscular reflex that has evolved to limit these types of injuries.

A particularly significant class of joint disorders are those of the intervertebral discs. herniated vertebral discs usually occur due to awkward and or strenuous lifting and twisting activities. Degenerative disc disease (DJD) is a progressive deterioration of the intervertebral discs. Both conditions are very common - in fact, lower back pain associated with these disorders is the number one reason for persons to seek medical attention.

Disorders of the Bone

Osteoporosis is the most common serious bone disorder and most commonly occurs in postmenopausal women. The condition is a loss of bone density and disruption of bone structure primarily due to inadequate calcium content. Persons with osteoporosis are at greatly increased risk of bone fractures, most seriously fractures of pelvic bones or the femur. Estrogen replacement therapy in postmenopausal women can greatly reduce the incidence of osteoporosis but this form of treatment must be balanced against the risks of such replacement therapy including increased risk of cardiovascular disease. Regular physical activity and weight bearing exercise reduces the risk of osteoporosis.

Although rare in developed countries, rickets is a common bone disorder elsewhere. It is caused by vitamin D deficiency. Untreated, rickets results in deterioration of bone tissue, bones become increasingly brittle and fracture easily. Osteomalacia (vitamin D resistant rickets) causes disease similar to rickets including bone weakness, but also abnormal bone formation. The condition is the result of a defect in vitamin D metabolism.

Paget's disease is characterized by abnormal structural development including enlargement and thickening of bones that are brittle and easily broken. The condition results from abnormalities of osteoblast and osteoclast functions. Perthes' Disease occurs primarily in children. It is a disorder of the femoral head of the tibia at the ball-and socket joint of the hip. The condition is caused by inadequate blood supply to the femoral head and results in pain an impaired ability to walk or run.

Osteogenesis Imperfecta (brittle bone disease) is a autosomal dominant genetic disorder caused by defects in the enzymes involved in collagen production. The result is brittle bones that fracture easily. Acromegaly is condition caused by excess of growth hormone and continued growth hormone production after individuals have completed puberty. Most commonly the abnormal growth hormone production is due to a benign tumor of the pituitary gland. Untreated, acromegaly results in progressive enlargement of facial bones and of the bones of the hands and feet. This process can continue over the entire li8fe of an individual.

Bone Marrow Disorders

Bone marrow suppression and bone marrow failure is an often life-threatening condition that is relatively common. The hematopoietic cells of bone marrow are particularly sensitive to a wide variety of drugs - antibiotics, anti-inflammatories and anti-cancer and many other commonly used drugs. Bone marrow cells are also easily damaged by environmental toxins - such as cleaning agents, heavy metals and insecticides and herbicides. Bone marrow is also very vulnerable to radiation induced injuries from medical and dental X-ray imagery and from artificial and naturally occurring radioactive compounds in the environment.

As these conditions worsen and persist, the granulocytes and lymphocyte cell production drops or even ceases resulting in profound impairment of the immune system. Impaired red cell production results in severe anemia and impaired platelet production results in spontaneous hemorrhages. All of these effects can be rapidly fatal if not corrected promptly. Most blood cancers - leukemias and lymphomas originate from abnormal cells in the bone marrow.

The Aerodigestive Tract

The outer surfaces of the body are nearly completely covered by a protective layer of skin and associated cells and tissues known as the integument. The aerodigestive tract begins at the entryways of the mouth and nose. This tract is a complexly branching and diversely specialized tube that passes through the neck, thorax and abdomen/pelvic cavities and exits at the anal sphincter. Air, solid food, water and other ingested liquids enter the tract at the nose (hopefully air only) and mouth then begin a passage through the tract beginning at the common continuation of the oral and nasal cavities known as the pharynx. Lymphoid tissues -the tonsils and adenoids - ring the entry to the pharynx within the pharyngeal walls. The pharynx, as it begins to descend through the neck, bifurcates (branches into two pathways) into the respiratory and digestive tracts.

The Respiratory System
The Respiratory Tract

The initial segment of the respiratory tract is the trachea. The initial segment of the digestive tract is the esophagus. A specialized hinged plate structure - the epiglottis- can drop across the top of the trachea during swallowing. This prevents ingested solids and liquids from entering the trachea. The tracheal tube consisting of rings of cartilage and descends through the anterior region of the neck (the trachea can be felt with one's fingers beneath the surface of the anterior neck). At the midpoint of the neck, a specialized region of the trachea - the larynx - can be seen as the Adam's apple. The larynx contains the vocal cords and associated structures involved in the production of speech.

The trachea continues to the base of the neck where it enters the thoracic cavity. At about the mid-sternum level, the trachea bifurcates into a left and right main-stem bronchus. The right and left main-stem bronchi then enter their respective right and left lungs. The main-stem bronchi undergo numerous subsequent branchings into smaller and smaller and increasingly numerous air passages. This results in a dense tree-like network of airways that infiltrate the entirety of the lung tissues. The thinnest terminal branches of this respiratory airway tree are called bronchioles. At the terminal ends of the bronchioles, grape-like clusters of spherical air sacs called alveoli serve as the site of oxygen and carbon dioxide exchange between the blood contained in capillaries that encircle the alveoli and inspired air in the alveoli.

The Respiratory System

Along with the respiratory tract anatomy that has already been described, the respiratory system is composed of the lungs, internal spaces of the thoracic cavity and the muscular diaphragm that forms the floor of the thoracic cavity. The lungs are composed of separate lobes, two on the left and three on the right. The heart is positioned between the left and right lungs and is directly adjacent to the medial surfaces of the lower lobe of the left lung. Individual secondary bronchi branch off of the main-stem bronchi and enter the lobes of the lung. The diaphragm is a dome shaped muscle that is convex into the thoracic cavity. The superior surface of the diaphragm is adjacent to the inferior surfaces of the left and right lower lobes of the lungs. Importantly, the left and right phrenic nerves pass from the cervical spine through the center of the thoracic cavity and innervate the diaphragm. Damage to these nerves can paralyze the diaphragm, making the act of breathing impossible. The nasal sinuses also serve a role in the respiratory system. These are located in cavities within the facial and occipital bones of the skull.

Respiratory Physiology

The primary functions of the respiratory system are to deliver oxygen from the air to the bloodstream and to remove carbon dioxide from the bloodstream into air in the lungs and then out of the body during expiration (exhalation). The primary tissues and structures of the respiratory system are the respiratory airway -

trachea, bronchi and alveoli, the lung tissue and the diaphragm. Breathing is usually involuntary, but can be under voluntary control for short periods of time.

Nervous System Control of Respiration
The basal breathing rate is driven by the medulla oblongata. Peripheral sensory receptors in major arteries and veins and within the brain itself monitor oxygen and pH levels and report this information to the hypothalamus and the medulla. Breathing depth and rate is modified as necessary to maintain optimum levels of oxygen and blood PH.

The smooth muscle cells in bronchial airways are also innervated by the sympathetic and parasympathetic nervous system Sympathetic signals cause relaxation of bronchial smooth muscle and this results in dilation of the bronchial airways. Parasympathetic signals have the opposite effect.

There is also a protective gag reflex that functions at the epiglottic region to prevent inhalation of solids or liquids

Cilia
The epithelial cells lining the bronchial airways secrete mucous and also have numerous densely packed cilia on their membranes that are in constant coordinated motion to propel mucus and inhaled particulate matter out of the lungs through the trachea.

Breathing Mechanics
When the epiglottis is open, the respiratory airways are continuous with the outside air. The flow of air is determined by the relative air pressures inside of the airway and the outside air. When the diaphragm contracts, the convex surface of the diaphragm within the thoracic cavity flattens; this increases the volume of the thoracic cavity surrounding the lungs. This causes a drop of pressure inside the thoracic cavity below that of the outside air. The resulting pressure differential between the airways within the lung and the outside air drives air from the outside through the respiratory airways and ultimately to the alveolar air sacs.

Inspiration
Lung tissue expands during the inspiratory phase of the breathing cycle. Lung tissue is elastic and the expansion that occurs during inspiration dynamically stretches lung tissue. This process requires energy in the form of muscular work that is done by the diaphragm to increase the volume of the thoracic cavity and to decrease the pressure in the thoracic cavity.

Expiration
When the diaphragm relaxes, the elastic tissue in the lung relaxes to its normal level of relaxation. Air pressure within the lung then increases and exceeds that of the outside air. Air within the airways is then driven out of the lungs by the differences in pressure inside and outside of the lung. This term for this portion of the breathing cycle is expiration. Expiration - in contrast to inspiration - is a passive process that does not require energy utilization by the body.

Gas Exchange - Diffusion
At the microscopic level, gas exchange between the bloodstream and the alveolar air is driven by diffusion. Diffusion is movement of particles from one region to another region that is driven by difference in the concentration of particle in one region compared to the other region. The blood arriving at the capillaries surrounding the alveoli is pulmonary arterial blood - which is deoxygenated blood. The oxygen concentrations in this blood are much lower and the carbon dioxide concentrations are much higher in this capillary blood than the air contained in nearby alveolar air sacs.

Microscopic Physiology
The microscopic physiology of the capillary/alveolar region provides the optimum possible conditions for diffusion to occur - very short diffusion distances with a minimum of physical barriers to the diffusion movements. Oxygen molecules must diffuse through a one-cell- layer thick alveolar wall then through a one-cell-layer-thick capillary wall and then through a cell membrane of a red blood cell. The reverse is true for carbon dioxide molecules, which are diffusing in the opposite direction - from the blood and into the alveolar air sacs. In the red blood cell, oxygen molecules bind to hemoglobin molecules.
This process re-oxygenates the capillary blood and rids the blood of carbon dioxide. This blood is then delivered back to the heart for recirculation throughout the body.

The Digestive System
The Digestive Tract
The digestive tract, beginning as the esophagus, follows along the same path as the trachea, immediately posterior or dorsal to the trachea. At the bifurcation of the trachea, the esophagus continues inferiorly to the base of the thoracic cavity, where it passes through an opening in the muscular diaphragm and enters the abdomen. Just after entering the abdomen, the esophagus connects to the stomach. A muscular sphincter - the gastroesophageal (GE) sphincter - seals the passage of the digestive tract at the junction of the esophagus and the stomach. The GE sphincter opens only during the passage of ingested material from the esophagus into the stomach.

At the distal end of the stomach the digestive tract continues as the small intestine. The region of the small intestine that accepts the contents of the stomach is the duodenum. Another muscular sphincter - the pyloric sphincter - seals the passageway between the stomach and the duodenum. The sphincter will open at appropriate intervals to allow stomach contents to pass into the duodenum. Also, substances produced by the liver and the pancreas that are involved in the digestive process are secreted into the duodenum through the common bile duct. The digestive process continues as nutrients and water continue through the small intestine, beginning at the duodenum then through two subsequent segments of the small intestines, the jejunum and then the ileum. The ileum connects to the first segment of the large intestine - the cecum.

 At this point, all of the nutrients and most of the water passing through the digestive tract have been absorbed. Indigestible bulk material continues to pass through the sequential segments of the large intestine, beginning with the cecum, and next the ascending, then the transverse and then the descending colon. Most of the remaining water in the material within the large intestine is absorbed and feces are formed during this stage of the journey through the digestive tract. The feces pass into the terminal segments of the large intestine - the sigmoid colon and the rectum - and then pass out of the body via defection through the anal sphincter.

The Digestive System
Along with the digestive tract anatomy that has already been described, the digestive system also consists of salivary glands, the liver, the gallbladder, the pancreas and a specialized regional venous circulatory system - the hepatic portal circulatory system - that carries blood from capillary beds in the intestines to capillary beds located in the liver. The salivary glands are located in the oral cavity. The liver is located on the right upper quadrant of the abdominal cavity, directly below the inferior surface of the diaphragm. The gallbladder is connected to the liver and is nestled between liver lobes at the inferior surface of the liver. The pancreas is located in the left upper quadrant of the abdomen. Partially retroperitoneal (buried) in the dorsal abdominal wall. The pancreatic duct and the gallbladder duct merge to form the common bile duct. Recall that common bile duct connects with the duodenum. An additional important anatomical relationship is that the stomach is anterior to the pancreas and inferior and to the left of the liver.

Digestive System Physiology
The function of the digestive system is to bring macronutrients, micronutrients, electrolytes and water into the body. The macronutrients are carbohydrates, fats and proteins. Electrolytes, when they are dissolved in body fluids, are the elemental ions Na+, K+, Ca++, Mg++ and Cl- The micronutrients are vitamins and trace minerals. The digestive system also functions best when the diet includes indigestible plant fiber, which is composed primarily of cellulose.

An often unappreciated fact regarding the digestive system is that, although the lumen (or canal) of the digestive tract is surrounded by the tissues and organs of the thorax and abdomen, the contents within the lumen of the digestive tract are literally outside of the body. Nothing that has been consumed orally and that is subsequently within the digestive lumen has been either absorbed by a cell of the body, nor has it passed through a surface epithelial cell layer into internal body regions.
The nutritional requirements of the body are the solid and liquid substances that must be consumed and then absorbed into the body. These are water, macronutrients and micronutrients.

Macronutrients
Proteins
Proteins are composed of one or more chains of amino acids. The human body requires 22 specific amino acids in order to assemble the tens of thousands of different proteins that the body uses for a myriad of structural and enzymatic functions. Seven of these amino acids are classified as essential amino acids because they cannot be synthesized from other molecular compounds by biochemical processes that occur within the body. In a typical American diet, most protein is acquired by eating meat, but all amino acid requirements can be supplied by a properly selected vegetarian diet. Excess dietary proteins can be converted to fat by the body. Inadequate protein intake during early childhood development can result in the starvation state known as kwashiorkor.

Carbohydrates
Carbohydrates are sugars or starches (polysaccharides). Starches are polymer sugar molecules. The primary role of carbohydrates in the body is to serve as a source of chemical energy. The product of these energy extraction reactions is the molecule ATP and a few other molecules (NADH and NADPH). These molecules are used primarily in anabolic biochemical reactions.

Aerobic Metabolism
 Anabolic metabolism is the construction of larger and more complex molecules such as proteins, from smaller and simpler molecules. Anabolic chemical processes by themselves are energetically unfavorable. When ATP molecules are coupled with (participate in) these reactions, the overall reaction is energetically favorable and therefore these anabolic reactions tend to proceed spontaneously.

Anaerobic Metabolism
In aerobic (where oxygen participates) cellular respiration, carbohydrates in the form of the sugar glucose and oxygen are converted to carbon dioxide, water and ATP molecules. This type of respiration is also known as oxidative phosphorylation. The body can also extract chemical energy from carbohydrates by anaerobic (Where no oxygen participates) respiration. In humans, when insufficient oxygen is available for oxidative phosphorylation, anaerobic metabolic chemical reactions convert glucose to lactic acid and ATP. This occurs primarily in skeletal muscle cells during intense physical activity.

Structural Roles of Carbohydrates
Sugars also are used in the synthesis of various complex molecules, including glycoproteins and glycolipids. The sugars ribose and deoxyribose are critical structural components of DNA and RNA molecules. Wheat

flour products and refined sugars - sucrose and fructose - are the primary source of carbohydrates in American diets. A diet of fruits and vegetables can provide all carbohydrate needs of the body.

A limited amount of excess dietary carbohydrates can be converted to glycogen - a glucose polymer molecule that is stored in the liver. Alternatively, carbohydrates can be converted to fats that are subsequently stored in adipose (fat) cells.

Fats
Dietary fat consists of long chain fatty acid molecules. The fatty-acid molecule structure is primarily a hydrocarbon chain. Fats are essential structural elements in cell membranes and are components of many other important biological molecules. Fats are readily convertible to glucose in the body and stored fat in adipocytes (fat cells) serves as the major reserve of stored energy in the body.

Saturated and Unsaturated Fats
A fat is a saturated fat if all of the carbon-carbon bonds of the hydrocarbon portion of the fatty acid molecule are single bonds; the fat is an unsaturated fat if the hydrocarbon portion of the molecule contains one or more carbon-carbon double bonds. Most animal fats are saturated fats. Most vegetable fats are unsaturated fats.

Triglycerides and Cholesterol
Triglycerides are a form of fat consisting of three fatty acids bonded to a small molecule called glycerol. Cholesterol is a 4-ring-structure derivative of fatty acids. Cholesterol is also an important component of cell membranes and it is also the molecule that is used by the body to synthesize the steroid hormones.

HDL and LDL Cholesterol
Cholesterol that is circulating in the bloodstream is bound with various proteins into lipoprotein particles. The most significant of these are the high-density lipoprotein (HDL) and low-density lipoprotein (LDL) particles.

High levels of LDL cholesterol in the bloodstream are associated with increased risk for the atherosclerosis related diseases - coronary artery disease (CAD) and stroke. High levels of HDL cholesterol in the bloodstream are associated with a decreased risk for CAD and stroke. In humans the most desirable blood cholesterol profile in terms of an associated lowest risk for cholesterol associated disease is a high HDL: LDL blood cholesterol ratio, conversely the greatest risk for cholesterol associated disease is a low HDL: LDL blood cholesterol ratio.

Vitamins
Vitamins are small molecules that are critical participants is a wide variety of biochemical processes, usually as cofactors for various enzymes. Although they are required is relatively small amounts, they cannot be synthesized by the body and therefore must be obtained through the diet. Most vitamins are water-soluble, but the vitamins A, D, E and K are fat soluble.

Vitamin Deficiencies
Vitamin D is essential for the absorption of calcium from the digestive tract. Vitamin D deficiency results in osteoporosis - brittle bones that are prone to fracture under minor stress. Vitamin C is critical to maintaining the strength of collagen - the major connective structural protein in the body. Vitamin C deficiency results in scurvy, a condition that leads to tooth loss, visual impairment and easy bruisability. When uncorrected by increased vitamin C intake, scurvy is eventually fatal. Vitamin B12 is essential for cell growth and maturation. Vitamin B12 deficiency results in anemia- a deficiency of red blood cells.

Minerals

Minerals are required for a vast array of body functions. They include the elements sodium potassium, magnesium, chlorine, calcium, phosphorus, sulfur and iron. Relative to vitamin requirements, most of the minerals are required in significantly larger amounts - calcium and phosphorus in particular. Zinc, selenium, copper and a few other elements are also required but in relatively tiny amounts. For this reason, they are often called the" trace" dietary elements.

Osteoporosis and Iron Deficiency Anemia

Calcium and phosphorus are major components of bone. Deficiency of calcium and phosphorous results in osteoporosis and impairment of muscle and nervous system functions. Iron is an essential component of hemoglobin - the molecule that binds oxygen in red blood cells. Iron deficiency results in anemia.

Digestion

Macronutrients must be broken down (digested) into individual small molecules before they can be absorbed from the digestive tract by intestinal epithelial cells. Starches and other polysaccharides must be broken down into simple 5 or 6 carbon sugars - primarily the sugars glucose and fructose.

Proteins must be broken down into individual amino acids. Fatty acids can be absorbed directly, but they need to be emulsified (separated into tiny droplets) prior to absorption. A variety of enzymes are required for the breakdown of polysaccharides and proteins. These enzymes are synthesized by cells located in the digestive system.

The digestive process begins in the mouth with the mechanical pulping of solids through the act of chewing. During this process the enzyme salivary amylase - which is synthesized by cells of the salivary glands - is mixed into the food mass where it begins to break down any starches that may be present in the food mass.

Peristaltic Motion

During swallowing, in the pharynx, the pulped food mass is compressed into a doughy consistency food-ball called a bolus. The bolus then passes into the esophagus. Beginning at the esophagus - and for the remainder of the journey through the digestive tract - the solid material in the food bolus will be propelled along by rhythmic contractions of the digestive tract called peristalsis. This peristaltic motion is produced by smooth muscle cells located in the walls of the digestive tract (esophagus, stomach, small intestines and large intestines).

Intraluminal Barriers - The GE and Pyloric Sphincters

At the terminal (distal) portion of the esophagus, the food bolus must pass through a muscular sphincter. In biology, sphincters are rings of muscle tissue that can contract - as the iris of the eye contracts - and thereby seals off a lumen (passageway) such as the lumen of the digestive tract. This process is called constriction, the relaxation of the sphincter reverses this action and opens the pathway - this process is called dilation.

Normally, except when a food bolus is passing from the esophagus into the stomach, this sphincter - the gastroesophageal (GE) sphincter - is tightly constricted. This is because the contents of the stomach are strongly acidic - roughly equivalent to the pH of battery acid. This stomach fluid will cause severe damage to any unprotected body tissues. Heartburn occurs when stomach contents leak through the GE sphincter. A second muscular sphincter - the pyloric sphincter - is located at the distal end of the stomach cavity, where it where it seals off the entryway to the initial segment of the small intestinal tract - the duodenum.

The Stomach

The stomach protects its inner wall lining from acidic injury by secreting large amounts of mucous onto the inner surface of the gastric lumen. The stomach creates this acidic environment by synthesizing and secreting hydrochloric acid. This highly acidic fluid by itself causes widespread chemical breakdown of proteins and carbohydrates, but the stomach also synthesizes and secretes a powerful proteolytic (protein cutting) enzyme called pepsin. Pepsin is the first enzyme that engages in the enzymatic breakdown of all proteins.

Chyme
The stomach also engages is a considerable amount of mechanical digestion. The Stomach walls are thick and constructed of several heavy muscle layers. This allows the stomach to generate powerful contractions that reduce food boluses into slurry of water and partially digested lipids, proteins and carbohydrates referred to as chyme.

Intrinsic Factor
Another notable substance secreted by the stomach is intrinsic factor. Intrinsic factor is a substance that the small intestinal epithelial cells require for the absorption of vitamin B12.

The Small Intestine
At a time determined by the demands of the body, the stomach will release its contents into the adjacent distal segment of the digestive tract, the duodenum of the small intestine. The duodenum is the first of three continuous segments of the small intestine. The second segment is the jejunum and the third and final segment is the ileum.

The Duodenum
The duodenum contains cells that synthesize and secrete the hormones secretin and cholecystokinin (CCK). Prior to the release of the stomach contents into the duodenum, these hormones are secreted into the bloodstream. The absorption of dietary iron occurs exclusively in the duodenum

Bile
When CCK arrives at the gallbladder, it stimulates the release of bile that is stored in the gallbladder into the gallbladder duct. The gallbladder duct connects to the common bile duct; Bile travels from the gall bladder duct into the common bile duct and then empties into the lumen of the duodenum. Bile that enters the duodenum will be used to emulsify fats that are present in the digestive contents of the stomach once these contents are delivered into the duodenum.

Pancreatic Enzymes and Bicarbonate Ion
Secretin stimulates the pancreas to release a volume of bicarbonate-ion-rich solution into the lumen of the duodenum. The bicarbonate solution is a moderately-strong basic solution which serves a critical role in the digestive tract, namely the neutralization of the highly acidic stomach contents as they are delivered into the duodenum. The pancreas also secretes a number of other digestive enzymes into the duodenum. For the TEAS, the only specific digestive pancreatic enzyme that one need be aware of is the proteolytic enzyme trypsin.

Absorption of Water and Nutrients
The absorption of water and nutrients begins in the small intestine. Whether through simple diffusion or facilitated or active transport, the rate of the absorption of substances is primarily dependent on the surface area through which absorption occurs. This is true for all diffusion based transport. The transport of gases across the body -airway interface in the lungs is greatly increased by segmentally increasing the surface area of the airways - at the level of alveoli; the diffusional surface area is approximately the area of a tennis court.

Villi, Microvilli and the Brush Border

The total surface area of the small intestine is approximately 250 square meters (interestingly, this is about the same area as the surface area of the alveoli in the lungs).

In the small intestines, surface area is increased first by the intestinal villi - finger like projection of the inner surface of the intestines into the intestinal lumen. Next, the outer surfaces of villi are covered in microscopic finger-like extensions called microvilli. The microvilli layer forms the brush-border of the intestinal epithelial cell lining. The brush border is where the absorption of water and nutrients from the intestinal lumen and into the body occurs.

Anatomical Sites and Details of Absorption

Amino acids from the enzymatic breakdown of proteins, and fats that have been reduced to fatty acids are absorbed through the brush borders of intestinal epithelial cells The sugars present in the intestine often require further breakdown by enzymes (disaccharidases) located in the brush border prior to absorption. Amino Acids and sugars are transported out of the epithelial cell and are absorbed by nearby capillaries. Absorbed fatty acids within the epithelial cells are processed into specialized particles and are then transported out of the cell and into lacteals - lymphatic vessel structures located in the core of villi. Water is absorbed from the intestine by passive diffusion

The majority of nutrients are absorbed through the jejunum. Vitamin B12 and bile salts - components of bile - are absorbed in the terminal ileum. 80 percent of ingested water is absorbed in the small intestine.

The remainder of intestinal water is absorbed through the large intestine. There are no other significant digestive events other than fecal formation and defecation through the anal sphincter that occur in the large intestine.

The Liver

The liver serves numerous vital roles in the body and although considered an organ of the digestive system has roles in other organ system at least as if not more important than the digestive role.

Detoxification and Drug Metabolism

The liver receives the venous blood that from the intestines via the hepatic portal circulatory system liver cells are capable of carrying out thousands of complex chemical reactions are responsible for the majority of the catabolic chemical functions of the body. This includes the detoxification of harmful molecules in the bloodstream, the processing of drugs that are present on the bloodstream and conversion of waste products produced by the turnover of cells -red blood cells in particular - and other organic debris that is generated by the continual metabolic activities of the cells of the body. All of the cells in the body are subject to damage and lethal injury and all of the cells of the body are generating waste products from the metabolic activities that are occurring within the cells on a continual basis.

In particular, the lifespan of red blood cells is 120 days, so the entire volume of red blood cells in the body must be recycled every four months. These waste products include large amounts of fragmented cell membrane, DNA, RNA hemoglobin and products resulting from chemically degradation of hemoglobin, and other cell proteins.

Cholesterol Metabolism

The degradation of cholesterol and related molecules is accomplished by the liver through the conversion of these molecules into bile acids. These are further processed into bile and secreted to the gall bladder and then to the duodenum. In addition to emulsification of fat, bile is also required for the uptake of the fat soluble vitamins A, D, E and K. Excess body cholesterol is removed from the body in bile acids that remain in the feces.

Nitrogenous Wastes and Production of Urea

Of particular significance are the nitrogen containing (nitrogenous) waste products resulting from protein and nucleic acid degradation. These waste products are highly toxic to cells and the liver converts these nitrogenous waste products into the molecule urea, which is a small, highly water-soluble, nontoxic nitrogen-containing molecule. Urea is easily filtered out of the bloodstream and transferred into urine by the kidneys. Urine is subsequently excreted from the body during urination.

Carbohydrate Metabolism

The liver regulates glucose levels in the blood by absorbing excess glucose from the bloodstream and then converting this excess glucose into long highly branched molecular chains of glucose. This glucose polymer molecule is call glycogen. Glycogen is stored in liver cells. If the level of glucose in the bloodstream falls below normal levels the liver cells can rapidly convert glycogen back into glucose and release this glucose into the bloodstream thereby restoring low blood glucose levels to normal levels. When glycogen reserves are exhausted, the liver can synthesize new glucose molecules from proteins and lipids. This process is termed gluconeogenesis.

Lipoprotein Synthesis

Liver cells also receive fats and cholesterol absorbed through the small intestine and process these fats and cholesterol molecules into lipoprotein particles, most notably the HDL and LDL lipoprotein-cholesterol complex particles. These particles are then released into the bloodstream by the liver cells.

Water distribution

An additional important role of the liver is the production of the protein albumin. This protein is synthesized by liver cells and subsequently secreted into the bloodstream. Albumin molecules remain in the bloodstream and act as osmotic particles that favor retention of water within the bloodstream. This is a critical role that maintains the proper balance of water distribution between the intravascular spaces and the extravascular compartment of the body.

The Nervous System

The nervous system can be anatomically divided into the central nervous system and the peripheral nervous systems.

The Central Nervous System

The central nervous system, as previously noted, consists of the brain - located in the cranial cavity and the spinal cord - located in the vertebral canal of the spine. Also mentioned was that the outermost or most superficial region of the terminal end of the brain, the cerebral cortex, consists of five regions or lobes. The frontal, parietal temporal and occipital lobes that underlie the cranial bones of the corresponding designations. The cerebral cortex is divided into two hemispheres, right and left, that are connected by large nerve tracts. The largest of these tracts is the corpus callosum. Each hemisphere consists of the five cerebral cortical lobes - thus there are right and left frontal, parietal temporal and occipital lobes.

The regions of the brain between the cerebral cortex and the spinal cord include the midbrain, the cerebellum and the brainstem. The brainstem is the brain region that is continuous with the spinal cord as it enters the brain at the base of the skull. More specific notable brain regions include the medulla oblongata, located in the brainstem and the hypothalamus, located in the midbrain at the base of the skull. The pituitary gland is an important endocrine structure that is located adjacent to and inferior to the hypothalamus. The spinal cord is the distal continuation of the brain stem and is contained within the vertebral canal. Beginning at the base of the occipital region of the skull, the spinal cord continues to its terminus at the junction of the first and second lumbar vertebrae. The spinal cord has relatively few neuron cell bodies; it consists mainly of nerves that relay information between the brain and neurons of the peripheral nervous system. The 31 pairs of spinal nerves exit the spinal cord at the interspaces between adjoining vertebrae - one pair per intervertebral junction.

The 12 pairs of cranial nerves and 31 pairs of spinal nerves become important elements of the peripheral nervous system once they have exited from the cranial or vertebral cavities.

The Peripheral Nervous System

All elements of the nervous system - neurons, nerves (axons of neurons), sensory cells, effector cells (muscle cells and glands) and supporting cells and structures - that are not located either inside of the skull or the spinal column - are classified as elements of the peripheral nervous system.

It is very important to understand that this is a purely anatomical definition. All of the neurological activity in the body is ultimately under the control of central nervous system and all of the neurons in the peripheral nervous system have nerve pathways that connect to the brain.

There are two broad divisions of the peripheral nervous system; 1) the voluntary or somatic nervous system, and 2) the involuntary or autonomic nervous system.

The Somatic (Voluntary) Nervous System

The somatic nervous system, as previously mentioned, consists of 12 pairs of cranial nerves and 31 pairs of spinal nerves. These nerves carry sensory information from sensory receptor cells located throughout the body to the brain, and carry instructions - in the form of electrical impulses - from to brain to effector cells located throughout the body. In most cases the effector cells are skeletal muscle cells or glands - endocrine glands and exocrine glands. The sensory information provided by the peripheral nervous system is integrated with other conscious thought processes and allow one to make a voluntary decision to carry out physical actions. These decisions are translated into actions beginning with the generation and transmission of electrical signals through the somatic nerves to skeletal muscles. Skeletal muscles relax and contract in a fashion that results in the desired body movements. Very often these highly complex movements occur in the muscles of the vocal cords to produce speech.

Somatic Ganglia

An important anatomical feature of the somatic nervous system is that the spinal peripheral nerves originate from collections of neuron cell bodies located in discrete regions of the vertebrae but outside of the vertebral canal. Collections of neuron cell bodies not located in the central nervous system are classified as "ganglia" The sensory ganglia are in dorsal regions of vertebrae and are called dorsal root ganglia. Neurons in the dorsal ganglia contribute the sensory nerve fibers to spinal nerves. In ventral regions of the vertebrae, ventral root ganglia neurons contribute the nerve fibers that send signals to effector cells. These types of nerves are called motor nerves.

The Autonomic (Involuntary) Nervous System

Most of the neural regulatory activity of the body is not under voluntary control. The central nervous system regulates the majority of the body's functions through the involuntary or autonomic nervous system. The two divisions of the autonomic nervous system are the sympathetic and the parasympathetic nervous systems. These are commonly described as - for the sympathetic division - the "fight or flight" nervous system and - for the parasympathetic division - as the "rest and digest" nervous system. Again, it is important to realize that both systems are directly connected to specific regions of the brain. They are not an independent peripheral nervous system, rather they have an extensive peripheral component and they have a highly complex central component as well.

One general anatomical feature of note is that the autonomic nerve fibers are usually not organized into separate specific nerves, but often are nerve fibers that that follow the course of and may even be adherent to blood vessels or somatic nerves.

The Sympathetic Nervous System

The peripheral component of the sympathetic nervous system begins with the neuron cell bodies located in the sympathetic ganglia. Most of these ganglia are located in pairs just lateral to the spinal cord and are therefore often referred to as the sympathetic "chain" ganglia. These ganglia send nerve fibers throughout the body, in particular to the organs, glands and blood vessels of the body.

The Parasympathetic Nervous System

The peripheral component of the parasympathetic nervous system begins with the neuron cell bodies located in the parasympathetic ganglia. In contrast to the sympathetic ganglia, the parasympathetic ganglia are usually located close to the organs and local anatomic regions that they innervate (supply nerves to). The Vagus nerve or tenth (X) cranial nerve is of particular importance in the parasympathetic nervous system. This nerve carries parasympathetic nerve fibers to most of the major organs of the body, including the heart, lungs and much of the digestive system.

Neurophysiology
Neurons

At the cellular level the production, transmission and processing or integration of information in the form of electrical impulses is carried out by neurons. Neurons are electrically excitable cells (muscle cells are also electrically excitable cells). All cells in the body maintain concentration levels of ions inside of the cell - Na+, K+ and Na+ and Cl- in particular, that are different than the ion concentrations outside of the cell. This causes a voltage difference across the cell membrane. Electrically excitable cells have specialized membrane pores and ion pumps that can use this voltage difference to generate a voltage spike called an action potential that travels along the cell membrane.

Axons, Dendrites and Synapses

The neuron has in, most cases, a very long membrane extension that looks like a tail called the axon. The nerves of the body are composed of these neuron axons. The sciatic nerve, which extends from the spine to the toes, can consist of numerous individual neuron axons that are each several feet in length. Action potentials generated by the neuron at the base of the axon travel along the axon to its terminal end.
At the end of the axon there is usually a dendrite - a branch like extension of another neuron. The action potential in the first neuron axon causes the release of neurotransmitters - small molecules that diffuse across the gap between the axon and the dendrite of the second neuron. The neurotransmitter molecules bind to receptors on the second neuron's dendritic membrane. This can cause the second neuron to generate its own action potential which again travels down the second neuron's axon.

By this method electrical impulses can be transmitted from one neuron to another. The location where the diffusion of neurotransmitters between two neurons occurs is called a synapse. There are estimated to be over 100 trillion synapses in the human brain

General Functions of the Nervous System
Sensory functions

The function of the nervous system is to monitor, regulate and coordinate all other body functions and to adapt to the external environment as needed. The nervous system attempts to maintain the optimum internal and external environment for the survival of the organism. In humans, these include uniquely high-level thinking abilities that allow us to exert unprecedented levels of voluntary control over our environment. This begins with the sensory functions of the nervous system. The nervous system collects an enormous amount of information about the internal conditions of the body and about the outside environment. This collection process begins with sensory receptor cells. Sensory receptor cells are specialized to detect many types of stimuli. When they detect the things they were designed to detect, they report this information to the brain through electrical signals that they generate and then transmit to the brain via sensory nerves.

The Visual System

The eyes are sensory organs designed to collect visual wavelength photons. In the retina of the eye, rods and cones - the visual sensory receptor cells - absorb photons that enter the eye. The rod and cone cells generated electrical signals that are sent through the optic nerve. The optic nerves are the cranial nerve II (2) pair of the 12 pairs of cranial nerves of the somatic nervous system. This information is processed at many areas in the brain. Final processing of visual information occurs in the occipital lobes of the cerebral cortex for this reason the occipital cortex is also called the visual cortex). Presumably this is where the conscious visual perception of the world is generated.

The Auditory and Vestibular System

Sound waves generated by movements in the environment around us are received at the ear and are converted to electrical signals by hair cells located in the cochlea of the inner ear. These signals are transmitted to the brain via the acoustic nerves - cranial nerves XIII (8) of the somatic nervous system. These signals are also widely processed throughout the brain and ultimately are integrated into a conscious perception of sound in the temporal lobes of the cerebral cortex - also known as the auditory cortex.

The vestibular sense is the set of sensations perceived when one's body is it is undergoing acceleration. The accelerations in all three translational dimensions - back-forward, up-down and side to side are detected by vestibular sensory cells. Rotation (which is always an acceleration) in any of the three rotational axes is also detected by vestibular sensory cells. Vestibular sensory cells are located in the semicircular canals. The semicircular canals are located in the cochlea of the inner ears. Vestibular information also travels through the acoustic nerve. Much of the processing of vestibular information occurs in the cerebellum of the brain

The Somatosensory System

The sense of touch actually consists of many types of sensory information light touch, pressure vibrations heat, cold and pain and a sense of body posture and relative positions of the parts of the body. These sensations are collectively classified as somatosensory information. Various types of sensory receptors located primarily near the surface of skin but also in deep structures of the body transmit somatosensory information via the cranial and spinal somatic nerves to a sub-region of the parietal lobes of the cerebral cortex. This region is designated as the sensory division of the somatic cortex. This is where the conscious perceptions of touch, heat, cold and pain are generated.

The Olfactory and Gustatory Systems

The sense of taste (olfaction) begins with the detection - by taste buds located in tongue - of molecules contained in the foods and beverages that are dissolved in saliva in the mouth. The types of taste we can detect are; salty, sweet, sour, bitter and umami. Umami is a recently identified taste category that is - no kidding - defined as the "delicious" taste.

For the sense of smell, the odor receptors in the nose are capable of detecting thousands and perhaps millions of different odors corresponding to molecules that are present in the air that we breathe. No further level of detail is required by the HESI for the neurophysiology of the taste and smell sensations.

Motor Functions

The somatic sensory cortex is adjacent and lateral to the somatic motor division of the somatic cortex. When a conscious decision is made to carry out voluntary movements, the electrical signal to do so are first generated by neurons in the somatic motor cortex. These signals are then transmitted ultimately to voluntary skeletal muscles via the peripheral somatic nerves.

Notice that the peripheral somatic nerves transmit sensory information to the brain and instructions in the form of electrical signals from the brain to the muscles of the body. They are not purely sensory nerves or purely motor nerves; they are therefore designated as "mixed nerves".

The motor cortex signals to initiate movement and the myriad of involuntary movements that occur continuously in the body require huge amounts of processing at lower brain levels before they can be expressed as actual signals to the muscles. Most notably, precise and complex movements and maintenance of balance and body posture in particular are heavily dependent on processing that occurs in the cerebellum. The basal ganglia and substantia nigra are also crucial in the generation of movement. Degeneration of the substantia nigra results in the progressive movement disorder Parkinson's disease.

Integrative Functions

Overall the nervous system functions as an information processing system of incredible complexity. The functions can be generalized as sensory functions, motor functions and integrative functions. The somatic systems sensory and motor functions are described above, but there is an integrative function that bridges the sensory and motor functions. These integrative functions involve cognitive awareness and intellectual and emotional thought processes that generate organized strategies of actions and complex behaviors that when operating properly enhance one's ability to survive in a complex society.

These integrative processes are deeply connected to processing that occurs in the frontal cortices and also depend on continuous input from regions of the brain crucial to maintaining homeostasis, and to regions that are central in memory processing and those involved in generating primitive drives such as hunger thirst and nurturing behaviors and basic emotions such as anger, fear and happiness.

Homeostasis and Vital Baseline Body Functions

At the most vital and fundamental needs level; the nervous system must strive to maintain the minimum levels of oxygen and glucose for cell survival. Equally important is the maintenance of the proper pH levels of fluids, and the proper concentrations of electrolytes in body fluids. Finally, survival is critically dependent on maintaining a proper core body temperature. The nervous system accomplishes this by establishing set points for blood pressure, oxygen, pH, glucose, osmolality (electrolyte concentration) and temperature. Levels that diverge from these set point values can be fatal within minutes to hours. Specialized detector cells in the peripheral body and also in the hypothalamus are able to determine the real time values for all of these set point criteria. The maintenance of these key chemical and physiological parameters represents homeostasis at the level of the entire human body with respect to the external environment.

Blood Pressure and Oxygen Levels

A continuous supply of oxygen and nutrients requires a continuous breathing and heart rate and an adequate blood pressure to drive the circulation of oxygen and nutrients to all cells in the body. When the nervous system detects inadequate blood pressure or oxygen levels it sends signals to increase breathing rate and breathing volume, increase the output of blood by increasing the force and rate of heart contractions and by adjusting the resistance of blood vessel by constriction or relaxation of smooth muscle cells in blood vessel walls.

Osmolality

Inadequate blood pressure and unacceptably high osmolality triggers thirst leading to single-minded activities devoted to the acquisition of drinkable water. The nervous system also triggers the endocrine system to signal the kidney to retain water and to concentrate the urine and to secrete electrolytes to lower osmolality. Low osmolality when detected results in nervous signals and hormone level adjustments to cause the kidneys to remove water by producing dilute urine and to reabsorb electrolytes to increase osmolality.

Glucose

Low glucose levels trigger signals that directly or through hormonal effect increase the production of glucose and the delivery of glucose to the circulation. High glucose levels are similarly readjusted most notably by adjustments of level of the hormone cortisol. Low glucose also triggers the drive state sensation of intense hunger, leading to behaviors devoted to the acquisition of food.

Core Body Temperature

Temperature adjustments are generated by signals to the blood vessels in the skin to constrict or dilate and thereby either decrease or increase blood flow to the skin. Increased blood flow to the skin results in transferal of internal heat from the blood to the body exterior. Blood vessel constriction has the opposite effect. The primitive drive state sensations of excessive heat or cold generate voluntary actions to seek warmth and shelter or find cooler local environments.

ph

There are no particular drive state sensations associated with excessively high or low blood pH, but the nervous system carefully monitors and adjusts pH to maintain an optimum pH level between 7.35 and 7.45. The primary means of compensation for low pH is signals to release hormones that cause the kidney to secrete hydrogen ion. Chemically this results in the production of bicarbonate ion by the kidney that then enters the bloodstream. Hydrogen ion is excreted in the form of carbonic acid and free hydrogen ion. The respiratory system can increase blood pH by increasing breathing rate and thereby decrease the levels of CO_2 in the blood. This lowers the levels of blood carbonic acid and increases the levels of blood bicarbonate ion. This increased breathing rate is also generated by the nervous system in response to excessively low blood pH.

The Medulla Oblongata

The medulla oblongata is among the most ancient regions of the brain. It is located in the brainstem adjacent to the spinal; cord. The medulla is responsible for maintaining heart rate, breathing rate and blood pressure and plays other key roles in homeostatic control of all body systems.

The Hypothalamus

The hypothalamus is a midbrain structure located at the base of the skull. The hypothalamus is a critical region in homeostatic regulation. It either detects directly or indirectly blood pH and osmolality levels, oxygen levels and numerous other biochemical and physiological metrics. Most of the drive state sensations including hunger, thirst and excessive heat and cold are generated by the hypothalamus. The hypothalamus is integrated with other brain regions to respond to homeostatic needs via activation of the sympathetic and parasympathetic nervous system and through the secretion of hypothalamic hormones that directly influence the activity all other endocrine glands throughout the body

The Autonomic Nervous System

The autonomic nervous system, consisting of the sympathetic and parasympathetic nervous systems, is activated through complex processing at all levels of the central nervous system. The homeostatic control systems of the central nervous system often exert regulatory control over a wide variety of biochemical and physiological function through a combination of sympathetic and parasympathetic induced physiological and biochemical responses. The sympathetic response can be nearly instantaneous, particularly with the effects on the cardiovascular system.

The Sympathetic Nervous System

Sympathetic nerves release neurotransmitters to cardiac muscle and smooth muscle located in bronchial walls, intestinal tract walls, and the walls of blood vessels that generate rapid response to environmental circumstances that require aggressive and highly energetic responses (fight or flight responses). The sympathetic effects in such circumstances include increased force of heart contractions, increase heart rate, increased blood pressure, redirection of flow of blood from the intestines to the skeletal muscles, suppression of peristalsis and dilation of the bronchial airways.

The sympathetic system also innervates the adrenal medulla and can cause the release of epinephrine and norepinephrine into the bloodstream. This creates a maximal and persistent overall state of dynamic alertness and physiological readiness to engage in pursuit of prey, physical combat, or escape from life threatening situations.

The Parasympathetic Nervous System

The parasympathetic nervous system innervates most of the same glands, cardiac muscle and smooth muscle cells as the sympathetic system. The effects of the parasympathetic system are the opposite if the sympathetic effects in most cases. The parasympathetic system predominates during periods when the body requires rest and regeneration and digestion of food. Perhaps most importantly, the body requires a continuously adjusting balance between the sympathetic and parasympathetic states. This is referred to as the autonomic tone of the body and it is essential for the continuous optimal performance of all body systems.

Protective Reflexes

 A Very important class of specialized nervous system function is the protective reflex class of functions. There are other primitive reflexes such as the Babinski reflex the root reflex and others that are rather complex and beyond the scope of the TEAS. The simple protective reflexes, most notably the deep tendon reflexes, are extremely simple two- or three-neuron circuits that are completely outside of the central nervous system.

These reflexes respond instantaneously to stimuli that represent potentially dangerous forces acting on the body. Examples include the instantaneous withdrawal of a body part from a hot surface. The deep tendon reflexes are usually the reflexes involved in this type of reflex, but they are also very important when the limbs and joints are experiencing possibly catastrophic mechanical forces. The deep tendon reflexes have mechanoreceptors that trigger impulses when a dangerous level of mechanical stress is detected. The mechanoreceptor signal travels through one or two neurons and synapses on a skeletal muscle that contracts to counteract the forces that are threatening injury at a bone or joint region. A specific example of a deep tendon reflex is the patellar tendon reflex that is elicited by tapping the patellar tendon of the knee with a reflex hammer.

The Endocrine System

The endocrine system is the system that synthesizes and secretes hormones in the body. Hormones exert a vast array of effects on the body. The endocrine system includes purely endocrine glands, whose sole function is the synthesis and secretion of hormones and also other tissues and organs that, in addition to their primary or co-functions, also synthesize and secrete hormones.

There is an important anatomical distinction between the two general types of glands, endocrine glands and exocrine glands. Exocrine glands do not necessarily secrete hormones; they can secrete many other substances. The anatomical distinction for exocrine glands is that all exocrine glands secrete substances through a duct. A duct is a tube that leads to an anatomical surface, such as the surface of the skin or the surface of the intestinal tract. The common bile duct is an example.

All endocrine glands secrete hormones and by anatomical definition, all endocrine glands secrete hormones directly into the bloodstream or the lymphatic system. Also by anatomical definition, no purely endocrine gland contains secretory ducts. This is why the endocrine glands are sometimes referred to as "ductless" glands.

The Hypothalamus and the Pituitary Gland

The hypothalamus and the pituitary gland are closely related anatomically. Together these two structures serve as master controllers of the endocrine system through the secretion of hormones that regulate the levels of other hormones. The hypothalamus is a region of the brain but it also synthesizes and secretes many critically important hormones. It is located in the inferior midbrain directly above the central region of the base of the cranial cavity. The pituitary gland is attached to the inferior portion of the hypothalamus by a connective stalk. The pituitary gland occupies a small depression or crater in the base of the skull called the sella turcica. The pituitary secretes a wide variety of hormones. An Important anatomical feature of the pituitary gland is that the posterior pituitary synthesizes only two hormones - oxytocin and vasopressin - and all other pituitary hormones are synthesized by the anterior pituitary.

The Pineal Gland

The pineal gland is located within the midbrain and is essentially at the anatomical center of the brain. The pineal gland produces melatonin, which regulates sleep patterns and circadian rhythms.

The Thyroid and Parathyroid Glands

The thyroid glands are located superficial and to either side of the midline of the tracheal cartilage - Many anatomists classify the thyroid as a single gland with left and right lobes. The parathyroid glands are notable for being, in a sense, glands within glands. There are usually four parathyroid glands, buried deeply in the thyroid gland, usually two per lobe. The thyroid glands secrete thyroid hormones and calcitonin. The parathyroids secrete parathyroid hormone (PTH).

The Pancreas

The pancreas is not a purely endocrine gland, it also has critical exocrine gland function as a part of the digestive system, but its endocrine function is even more important. The pancreas secretes the hormones glucagon and - most importantly - insulin. The pancreas as previously described, is located in the upper right quadrant of the abdomen, in a partially retroperitoneal position, immediately below the diaphragm and posterior to the stomach.

The Adrenal Glands

As we have discussed, the adrenal glands rest upon the superior surface of the kidneys, one gland per kidney. The anatomical structure of the adrenal gland is significant in that the adrenal cortex (the surrounding outer layer) synthesizes the corticosteroid hormones, including cortisol and aldosterone and the adrenal medulla (the central region) synthesizes epinephrine, norepinephrine and dopamine

The Gonads

The gonads have two important co-functions; the production of male or female gametes and the synthesis of sex hormones. The gonads in males are the testicles and are located externally within the testicular pouches. They synthesize the male sex hormone testosterone. The gonads in females are the ovaries, which are located lateral to and at the level of the superior region of the uterus, one ovary one the left and one on the right. The distal entry into either the left or right fallopian tube is closely adjacent to the left or right ovary. The fallopian tubes provide a passageway into the uterine cavity. The uterus is a midline pelvic organ that is posterior to the urinary bladder and anterior to the rectum. The ovaries synthesize the female sex hormone estrogen.

Endocrine Physiology

While a large majority of the central nervous systems responses are rapid in the form of electrical signals and muscular responses. The nervous system also exerts profound control over all aspects of the body through its influences on the endocrine system. In contrast to direct nervous- signal-mediated control, which generally produce rapid but short-lived effects; hormonal effects are usually much slower in their actions and their effects are often cumulative over longer periods of time - in some cases years or even decades. Many hormonal systems also function relatively independently of the central nervous system. Also there are many other hormones or hormone-like molecules that are produced and secreted by virtually all tissues and organs of the body. For instance, the duodenum synthesizes and secretes the locally active hormones CCK and secretin.

The Hypothalamic Hormones

As we have discussed, the hypothalamus is a critical brain region for the maintenance of homeostasis within the body. A Primary mode of this regulation of homeostasis by the hypothalamus is through the release of hypothalamic hormones.

Primary hormones secreted by the hypothalamus include:

Thyrotropin releasing hormone (TRH) - This hormone acts on the anterior segment of the pituitary gland and stimulates the release of thyroid-stimulating hormone (TSH)

Corticotropin-releasing hormone - This hormone also acts on the anterior segment of the pituitary gland and stimulates the release of adrenocorticotropin hormone (ACTH)

Growth hormone releasing hormone (GHRH) - This hormone stimulates the release of growth hormone (GH) from the anterior segment of the pituitary gland

Gonadotropin-releasing hormone (GnRH) - This hormone stimulates the release of follicle-stimulating hormone (FSH) from the anterior segment of the pituitary gland

Somatostatin (also known as growth-hormone-inhibiting hormone - GHIH) - This hormone inhibits the release of growth hormone (GH) and follicle-stimulating hormone from the anterior segment of the pituitary gland

The Pituitary Gland hormones

The pituitary gland is directly connected to the hypothalamus and the two structures together regulate nearly all body functions via hormonal control. The two major functional/anatomical regions of the pituitary gland are the posterior pituitary and the anterior pituitary

The Posterior Pituitary Gland Hormones

Many authorities consider the posterior pituitary to be part of the hypothalamus. The posterior pituitary secretes two hormones; oxytocin and vasopressin (also known as antidiuretic hormone - ADH).

Oxytocin
Oxytocin triggers the milk letdown reflex in nursing mothers.

The Pancreatic Hormones -Glucagon and Insulin
In addition to its exocrine function in the synthesis and release of digestive hormones and bicarbonate ions, the pancreas in its endocrine gland role, synthesizes and releases two hormones, glucagon and insulin. Both hormones are vital to maintaining proper levels of blood glucose. Insulin also is essential to most cells for the uptake of glucose into the cell. Insulin is produced by pancreatic islet cells. In type 1 diabetes, islet cells are attacked and destroyed by the body's own immune system. A total lack of insulin is fatal within hours to days.

The Adrenal Cortical (Steroid) hormones - Cortisol and Aldosterone
The adrenal cortical hormones are steroid hormone. Steroid hormones are molecules that are modified versions of the cholesterol molecule. Other hormones are either small water-soluble molecules or polypeptides - amino acid chains that are the same type of chains that are assembled from mRNA transcribed to form the protein products of genes.
Since the steroid hormones are based on a lipid type molecule -cholesterol-they are fat-soluble, rather than water-soluble. Steroid hormones are secreted into lymphatic vessels rather than blood vessels. The principle cortical hormones are the glucocorticoid steroid hormone cortisol and mineral corticosteroid hormone aldosterone. The adrenal cortex also produces the precursor molecules that are transformed by the gonads into the male hormone testosterone and the female sex hormone, estrogen.

Cortisol
Cortisol release is stimulated by the pituitary hormone ACTH. Cortisol has a wide range of actions including regulating the metabolism of fats, proteins and carbohydrates. Cortisol also plays an important role in the immune system -generally this involves suppression of the immune response. Cortisol also is involved in the regulation of glucose levels. Cortisol stimulates the liver to synthesize new glucose molecules by a process termed gluconeogenesis.
Baseline levels of cortisol are essential to life. An absence of cortisol is fatal within weeks to months.

Aldosterone
Aldosterone is a critical hormone in the regulation of blood pressure and electrolyte concentrations in the body. This regulation mechanism is highly complex and involves several other hormones in what is termed the renin-aldosterone-angiotensin hormone axis.

The Gonadal Hormones - Testosterone and Estrogen
The gonadal hormones - testosterone and estrogen - are synthesized in the testes in males and in the ovaries in females. The sex hormones are synthesized from cholesterol based precursors that are produced in the adrenal cortex. During the prenatal stage, testosterone is responsible for the development of male external genitalia. During adolescence, the sex hormones are responsible for the development of secondary sexual characteristics - pubic hair, testicular maturation, and breast development. Estrogen also appears to provide protection from coronary artery disease and osteoporosis in premenopausal females.

The Cardiovascular System

The anatomy of the cardiovascular circulatory system begins with the heart, which is located at the base of the thoracic cavity directly superior to the diaphragm and centered slightly to the left of the midline of the sternum. The lower lobes of the left and right lungs are immediately lateral to the lateral walls of the heart.

The heart consists of muscular walls that enclose four chambers, the thin-walled right and left atria and the thick-walled right and left ventricles. The right and left ventricles share a common medial wall - the interventricular septum - as do the right and left atria - the interatrial septum. The right atrium is directly superior to the right ventricle and the left atrium is directly superior to the left ventricle. The atria and ventricles are separated by a common septum - the atrioventricular septum - which forms the bases or floors of the atria and the ceilings of each atrium's underling ventricles.

Cardiovascular Blood Flow

Deoxygenated blood from all other regions arrives at the heart from the body via veins. The smaller veins eventually pass blood through to either the superior or inferior vena cava - the largest veins of the body. The superior and inferior vena cavae empty into the right atrium. Blood then passes from the right atrium through a three-leaflet valve - the tricuspid valve- into the right ventricle. Subsequently, this blood is pumped out of the right ventricle through a two leaflet valve - the pulmonic valve - into the main pulmonary artery. Blood in the main pulmonary artery continues to either the left or right pulmonary arteries, which then enter either the left or the right lung.

Pulmonary Blood Flow

The pulmonary arteries branch into increasingly smaller and more numerous arteries. The smallest terminal arterial branches are the arterioles. From the arterioles, blood passes into capillaries - one-cell-thick-walled vessels. Blood passing through these capillaries exchange oxygen from inspired air in alveolar airspaces. Carbon dioxide diffuses out of the blood in the capillaries and into the alveolar airspaces. This carbon dioxide it is then expelled from the body through respiratory airways during exhalation (expiration).

The capillary blood, now oxygenated, passes to venules, then to larger veins and finally returns to the heart via the main pulmonary veins. The main pulmonary veins (usually there are four of these) empty into the left atrium. Blood from the left atrium passes into the left ventricle through a two leaflet valve - the mitral valve. The blood is then pumped out of the heart from the left ventricle through a two leaflet valve - the aortic valve - into the aorta.

The aorta is the largest artery in the body. From the aorta, oxygenated blood is delivered through a network of branching arterial trees to all regions of the body. Oxygen and nutrients are transferred to tissues and carbon dioxide and other waste products are absorbed at capillary beds. Capillary blood, now deoxygenated, returns to the heart through networks of veins as already described.

Portal Vein Systems

An important anatomical concept in the cardiovascular system is that blood that is pumped out of the heart, either via the left or the right ventricle always first enters a main artery, then travels to sequentially smaller arteries then to the smallest arteries - arterioles and then into capillaries. From capillaries this blood next travels to the smallest veins - venules and then to larger veins. Most of this blood travels to sequentially larger veins and directly back to the heart, but some of the blood is routed through a second set of capillary beds, most notably this occurs with venous blood travelling from capillary beds located in the intestines to capillary beds located in the liver. This type of circulatory anatomy is classified as a "portal system or portal circulation".

Cardiovascular (Circulatory) Physiology

The primary functions of the cardiovascular system are 1) to deliver oxygen from the lungs to all of the cells of the body along with water, electrolytes, glucose, and other essential substances. 2) To transport waste products to the organs responsible for detoxifying and excreting waste products from the body. Carbon dioxide is delivered to the lungs and other wastes are delivered either directly to the kidneys or indirectly to the kidneys through the liver. To accomplish these functions, the circulatory vessels must maintain a large, driving blood-pressure differential between the arterial side of the heart (the left heart) and the venous side of the heart (the right heart).

Mechanics of Cardiac Pressure and Blood Flow

The heart is a muscular organ composed primarily of cardiac muscle. The atria of the heart are thin-walled compared to the ventricles of the heart. This is because the atria receive low pressure venous blood from the body and do not need to generate high blood pressure to pump blood to the ventricles. The ventricles are comparatively thick-walled and are designed to generate high blood pressures that drive blood through the arterial vessels.

The direction of blood flow within the heart is accomplished by the arrangement of one-way valves within the heart and by the sequence in which various regions of the heart contract during a cardiac cycle.

Veins to Atria

Venous blood enters the atria through one way valves. When the atria are relaxing, pressures inside the atria are lower than venous pressures. This drives venous blood through the one way valves and into the atria. When the atria begin to contract, pressure within the atria rises. When this pressure exceeds venous pressure, blood attempts to flow back into the veins, but the one-way valves slam shut as this begins to occur, sealing the blood route between atria and veins.

Atria to Ventricles

As the atria continue to contract, pressure continues to rise until the pressure exceeds the pressure in the underlying ventricles. This forces open the one-way valves between atria and ventricle. In the right side of the heart, this is the tricuspid valve; on the left side of the heart, this is the mitral valve. As blood is driven into the ventricles from the atria, the ventricles begin to contract. When ventricular pressures exceed atrial pressure the initial reversal of blood flow causes the tricuspid and mitral valves to slam shut, preventing blood flow from the ventricles back into the atria.

Ventricles to Arteries

The ventricles continue to contract and blood pressure rises until it exceeds blood pressure in the arterial outflow tracts of the ventricle - the main pulmonary artery for the right ventricle and the aorta for the left ventricle. The higher pressure inside the ventricles force open the one-way valves between the ventricles and the arterial outflow tracts. These valves are the pulmonic valve of the right ventricle and the aortic valve of the left ventricle. The ventricles continue to contract and drive all of the blood within the ventricular chambers past the one-way valves and into the arterial circulation.

This pressure corresponds to the highest blood pressures that the heart produces and this pressure is sufficient to drive blood through the entire circulatory pathway back to the atria, where the cardiac cycle repeats. As the ventricles relax, pressure within the ventricle drops below the arterial outflow tract pressure. The reversal of blood flow from the arteries back into the ventricles is prevented when this backflow causes the pulmonic and aortic valves to slam shut, sealing off the arterial-ventricular blood flow routes.

The Electrical Activity of the Heart

Cardiac muscle cells do not require nervous impulses to trigger contraction. An isolated cardiac muscle cell will rhythmically contract on its own. In the heart, cardiac muscle cells have open connections with adjacent cardiac muscle cells that allow the cell cytoplasm to flow between cells. This type of cellular organization is called a syncytium. This syncytium arrangement of cardiac muscle cells allows electrical signals to freely pass from one cell to another.

The Sinoatrial (SA) Node
The heart must contract in a precisely synchronized fashion to cause blood to be pumped in the proper manner and direction throughout the circulatory system. The atria must begin to contract from top to the base of the atrioventricular septum. This squeezes blood toward the tricuspid and atrial valves. Next the ventricles must contract beginning at the base of the ventricles and progressing toward the pulmonic and aortic valves.

This coordinated contraction pattern begins with the sinoatrial node tissue located in the wall of the right ventricle. This tissue has an intrinsic (inbuilt) ability to generate electrical signal at a rate on average of 60-80 signals per minute. For this reason, the sinoatrial node is referred to as the "pacemaker" of the heart. The electrical signals generated at the SA node are conducted through the cardiac muscle of the atria with a geometrical progression that automatically produces the desired contraction pattern of the atria.

The Atrioventricular (AV) Node and Purkinje Fibers
The electrical signals in the atria are blocked from progressing to the ventricles by the atrioventricular (AV) septum, which is constructed from non-conducting tissue. The atrioventricular node - located just above the AV septum - conducts electrical signals from the atria through the AV septum and into large conductive fibers called purkinje fibers located in the walls of the ventricles. These fibers rapidly transmit electrical signals throughout the ventricular cardiac muscle walls. The specific arrangement of the purkinje fibers results in the desired contraction pattern of the ventricles.

Arteries
Arteries are designed to withstand the high pressure generated by the ventricles of the heart. Arteries also must to be able to stretch when blood flow volumes increase greatly during ventricular contractions and to contract to maintain adequate blood pressures in the intervals between ventricular contractions. This requires that thick arterial walls that contain elastic protein fibers and a layer of smooth muscle cells.

Arterioles
As the arterial vasculature progresses from the heart, large arteries undergo numerous branchings into smaller diameter arteries. The final arterial branches are the arterioles. Arterioles are the smallest diameter arteries and they connect to capillaries. The arteriole walls contain smooth muscles that can relax or contract in response to numerous types of stimuli, some local and some in the form of hormonal or electrical to signals from the nervous system. Arteriolar contraction can completely close off blood flow to capillary beds and arteriolar relaxation increases blood flow to capillary beds. It is at this level that many systems of the body regulate blood distribution and organ function based on the needs of the body at any given time.

Capillaries
Capillaries are designed to maximize the diffusion of substances into and out of the circulatory system. This is accomplished by minimizing the structures and distances that substances must cross when passing through capillary walls. This is the reason that capillaries are only one-cell layer in thickness.

Fluid Compartments of the Body
There are three major fluid compartments of the body - the intravascular space - inside of blood vessels and the heart; the extracellular space - the space outside of the blood vessel, heart and all cells of the body; and the intracellular space - the total space within all the cells of the body. Oxygen, nutrients water and waste products and all other water-soluble biological substances diffuse between the intravascular space and the extracellular space and between the extracellular space and the intracellular space. Water diffuses freely

between all three spaces; the distribution of water is determined by the osmolality of the fluid compartments. The major osmotic particles in fluid compartments are proteins - which do not diffuse across cell membranes that separate fluid compartments (except by active transport processes).

When the arterioles feeding capillaries are open, the blood pressure within capillaries is higher than the fluid pressure in the extracellular compartment; this drives water out of the capillaries. The proteins in blood inside of capillaries limit the water loss from the intravascular space by osmotic pressure effects. Oxygen, nutrients and other essential biological substances diffuse down concentration gradients out of the capillaries and into the extravascular space. The reverse process occurs for waste products in the extracellular space.

Veins

Excess water is reabsorbed by lymphatic vessels and by the venules - the venous vessels at the other end of capillaries. These are the terminal branches of the venous side of the circulatory system. Veins return blood to the heart (except in portal systems). Venules converge on large veins and these to still larger veins, eventually converging into the superior and inferior vena cava. The blood pressure in veins is much lower than on the arterial side, consequently veins are thin-walled since they are not subject to high arterial pressure. Venous blood flow from the extremities is greatly aided by skeletal muscle contractions and associated limb movements. Veins also have internal one-way valves that allow blood to flow freely towards the heart but prevent blood flow in the opposite direction (backflow).

Autonomic Effects on the Heart and Blood Vessels

The activation of the sympathetic nervous system can have profound effects on the circulatory system Cardiac muscle cells responds with increased force of contractions which increases blood pressure, the sinoatrial node responds with increased electrical impulse rate resulting in increased heart rate. Major arteries constrict resulting in higher blood pressures and other arteries and arterioles relax or constrict so that blood flow is directed away from the digestive system, away from the skin (to reduce bleeding that may occur during strenuous activity) and toward the skeletal muscles. The actions of the parasympathetic nervous system generally have the opposite of theses sympathetic effects.

The Urinary System

The urinary system consists of the kidneys, renal arteries and veins (renal is an adjective meaning "related to the kidney" or "of the kidney"), ureters, urinary bladder and urethra. The kidneys are bean-shaped and are located, as previously mentioned, within the walls of the abdomen in a dorsolateral position on either side of the lumbar spine. This "buried in abdominal wall tissue" location is referred to as a retroperitoneal position, (The pancreas is also in a partial retroperitoneal position).

The renal arteries carry blood to the kidney where it eventually arrives at capillaries surrounding microscopic filtering units called nephrons. Blood filtration occurs at these sites. Filtered blood from nephrons moves through venous networks and emerges from the kidneys within the renal vein. Filtered products from the nephrons pass through tubules that empty into a central collecting cavity in the kidney known as the renal pelvis.

The ureters (one per kidney) are thin tubes connecting the renal pelvis to the urinary bladder. The ureters transport the kidney's' filtered liquid wastes - urine - from the renal pelvis to the urinary bladder. The urinary bladder is a distensible (inflatable) bag-like structure which is located in the central anterior pelvic region of the abdominal/pelvic cavity. The bladder stores urine until it is released through another tube - the urethra.

The urethra carries the urine outside of the body, exiting at the meatus (outer opening) of the glans penis in males and immediately anterior the entrance of the vagina in women. An additional important anatomical relationship of the urinary system is that the adrenal glands, which secrete many essential hormones as part of the endocrine system, are located directly adjacent to the superior surfaces of the kidneys - one adrenal gland per kidney.

The Kidneys

The Kidneys have several critical functions in the human body. Obviously the kidneys produce urine but this is only the final stage of kidney function. The production of urine and its transport to the urinary bladder is the excretory function of the kidneys. This excretory function reflects the other functions of the kidney which include maintaining an optimum volume of total body water and optimum concentrations of electrolytes within the fluid compartments of the body. Additionally, the kidneys play a crucial role in maintaining an optimal pH of body fluids and in maintaining an optimum blood pressure. The kidney removes soluble waste products from the body, most notably urea, bilirubin, organic acids including uric acid and ammonia. The kidney also has direct endocrine functions. These are the production of the hormones renin, erythropoietin and calcitriol.

Gross Anatomy

There are two kidneys, each located to anterior and laterally - either the left or right - of the spine in a retroperitoneal (buried in abdominal wall) position in the posterior wall of the abdominal cavity. Both kidneys are immediately inferior to the diaphragm. The left kidney is adjacent to and posterior to the spleen. The right kidney is adjacent to and posterior to the liver. The adult human kidneys are bean-shaped organs with an average size of about 10 to 13 cm in length, 5 to 7.5 cm in width and 2 to 2.5 cm in thickness The long axis of the kidney parallels the long axis of the body The lateral surfaces of the kidneys have a convex curvature and the medial surfaces have a concave curvature The upper region of the kidney is called the superior pole and the lower region is called the inferior pole, An adrenal gland is located adherent to the superior pole of each kidney.

Each kidney's outer surface is enclosed by a tough fibrous layer of tissue called the renal capsule. A layer of fat called the perinephric fat surrounds the renal capsule. The perinephric fat is surrounded by a connective tissue membrane called the renal fascia. The renal fascia is surround by a second layer of fat - the paranephric fat layer. The renal hilum is a recessed region. In the center of the medial surface of the kidney. The hilum contains the major blood vessels that supply the kidney - the renal artery and two renal veins -and the proximal end of the ureter.

The solid tissue of the kidneys is divided into two anatomical regions. The outer region is the renal cortex. The inner region is the renal medulla. The kidney is also subdivided into ten to fifteen renal lobes. The lobes are arranged sequentially as the wedges of an orange to produce the overall kidney structure. Each lobe consists of an upper or outer layer of renal cortex and a medial or deep cone-shaped region of renal medulla called a renal pyramid. The apex of each renal pyramid is called a papilla. Several adjacent renal papillae project into a cavity called a minor calyx. Several adjacent minor calyxes fuse medially into a larger cavity called a major calyx. The major calyces empty into a central cavity called the renal pelvis. The renal pelvis narrows into a tube that becomes the ureter. The ureter exits the kidney through the renal hilum and continues inferiorly to merge with the urinary bladder. The renal pelvis and the major and minor calyxes together form a continuous cavity called the renal sinus.

Microscopic Anatomy

The functional unit of the kidney is a microscopic structure called a nephron. There are approximately one million nephrons in the human kidney. The nephron consists of two subunits - a tuft or tangled cluster of capillary loops called a glomerulus, and a one-to-two cell - thick-walled renal tubule. The renal tubule consists of four segments. These are Bowman's capsule, the proximal convoluted renal tubule, the loop of Henle and the distal convoluted renal tubule. Bowman's capsule forms the distal end of the renal tubule. It is a balloon -like expansion of the tubule contains a deep invagination that is occupied by a single glomerulus. The glomerulus and the Bowman's capsule that surrounds the glomerulus together are referred to as a renal corpuscle. The renal corpuscle appears as a small tangled ball of yarn - the glomerulus -that is tightly positioned as an object within a vase that has a spherical body and a very short narrow neck - Bowman's capsule. The body of the capsule encloses the entire glomerulus except for the stalk of the glomerulus which consists of the afferent and efferent stems of the glomerular capillary.

General Anatomy of Renal Blood Vessels, Renal Tubules and Collecting Tubules
The afferent capillary stem connects the glomerulus to an arteriole supplied by blood from an interlobular artery. The interlobular arteries are branches of arcuate arteries. Arcuate arteries are located in the boundary region between the renal medulla and the renal cortex. Arcuate arteries are branches of interlobar arteries that are located between renal pyramids. Interlobar arteries are branches of segmental arteries and segmental arteries are branches of the main renal artery. the arcuate artery.

The efferent stem of the capillary continues to follow a course alongside the remainder of the renal tubule. The efferent capillaries form numerous loops that encircle the renal tubule along its course. These sections of capillaries are called peritubular capillaries. The peritubular capillary finally connects to a venule located in the renal cortex near the boundary of the renal cortex and the renal medulla.

The course of the renal tubule continues from Bowman's capsule- within the renal cortex - as the proximal convoluted tubule. The distal end of the proximal tubule then forms a sharp bend and dives deep into the renal medulla. At the apex of the renal pyramid, near the boundary with the renal pelvis, the tubule forms a tight 180-degree U-turn and reverses its course, continuing very closely alongside the descending portion of the tubule. This long, thin u-shaped portion of the renal tubule is called the loop of Henle. Adjacent peritubular capillaries form a netlike structure that surround the loop of Henle called the vasa recta. The distal segment of the loop of Henle reenters the cortex and continues within the cortex as the distal convoluted tubule. The distal tubule terminates at a renal collecting tubule. Numerous other distal tubules from adjacent nephrons also connect with the collecting tubule. Collecting tubules dive directly through the renal medulla and terminate into minor renal calices.

Microscopic Structure of the Renal Corpuscles
The capillary walls of glomeruli in renal corpuscles have small gaps in the junctions of adjacent endothelial cells called fenestrations. This feature is a major difference in structure compared to most other capillaries. In the majority of capillaries, the endothelial cells that form the capillary walls have very tight intercellular junctions. Water, nutrients, electrolytes, oxygen, carbon dioxide and cellular waste products must diffuse through the endothelial cell bodies to move between the intravascular space of the capillaries and the extravascular space surrounding the capillaries. between endothelial cells, as a result the walls of the capillary tufts are uncharacteristically permeable to water and dissolved solutes such as electrolytes, glucose amino acids urea, uric acid and other substances. The fenestrations are essentially tiny pores in the glomerular capillary wall. Consequently, glomerular capillary walls are very leaky, and their intravascular fluid contents readily pass through these fenestrations. Substances which are usually not able to pass from the capillary through fenestrations are macromolecules such as proteins and other polypeptides, lipid molecules - triglycerides and free fatty acids, and the cellular components of blood - red and white blood cells and platelets

The glomerular capillary walls are pressed tightly against an adjacent section of the glomerular membrane wall. The membrane of Bowman's capsule separates the interstitial spaces of the renal tissues from the internal lumen of the capsule. This membrane consists of a single-cell-thick parietal outer layer of very thin squamous epithelial cells and an underlying single-cell-thick visceral layer of cuboidal epithelial cells called podocytes.

A basement membrane separates the capillary endothelium from the squamous epithelium of Bowman's capsule. The podocytes have extended segments called foot processes or pedicels that press tightly against the internal surface of the outer layer of squamous epithelial cells. There is a small gap between adjacent foot processes. These gaps are called filtration slits or filtration diaphragms and consist of two layers of podocyte cell membrane separated by a very thin layer of cytoplasm.

Consequently, at the interface between glomerular capillary walls and the wall of Bowman's capsule there is a very small distance separating the lumen of the capillary from the lumen of Bowman's capsule. There are also very few physical barriers separating the intravascular contents of glomerular capillary and the lumen of Bowman's capsule.

Blood Pressure and Renal Filtration

Most non-cellular Contents within the capillaries can pass freely through the capillary fenestration then can diffuse a short distance across the basement membrane. These diffusing contents then pass through the very thin outer squamous epithelial cells of bowman's capsule, across an adjacent filtration slit between podocyte foot process and finally into the lumen of Bowman's capsule. This fluid is now called a renal filtrate. As the filtrate continues through the renal tubule and the renal collecting tubule it will be continuously processed by active and passive reabsorption of water, electrolytes, glucose, bicarbonate ions and amino acids and small polypeptide (oligopeptides) from the tubule and into the interstitial spaces of the kidney and from there reabsorbed into the peritubular capillaries. A few substances will be actively secreted from the interstitial spaces of the kidney into the renal and collecting tubules.

While a major force that drives fluid components of capillaries into the surrounding extravascular space in most capillaries is osmotic pressure - the movement of water and dissolved particles from regions of high concentration to regions of lower concentration, another critical driving force is the pressure gradient between the fluid within capillaries and the fluid is the extracellular space surrounding capillaries.

The higher the differential pressure gradient the greater to driving force in the direction of high pressure to low pressure, In most regions of the body the pressure differential favors the movement of fluids from capillaries into the interstitial space for the first half of the length of the capillary - that originating from an arteriole, and favors the movement of fluid from the extracellular space into capillaries and the remaining half-length of the capillary - the segment that connects to a venule. The balance between these two processes determines how much fluid volume occupies the extracellular space. Increasing blood pressure tends to drive this balance toward the extracellular space and increases extracellular fluid volume.

Blood pressure continues to decrease as blood flows from major arteries to progressively smaller arteries and finally to arterioles and capillaries. It may seem that pressure should increase because arterioles and capillaries are much narrower than the large arteries that they originate from, but there are so many arterioles and capillaries that their cumulative lumen diameters are much larger than the parent artery diameter. The resistance to fluid flow within a closed fluid channel decreases as the diameter of the channel increases. The fluid pressure within the channel increases as the resistance to fluid flow increases. Therefore, at the arteriolar/capillary level the resistance to blood flow is much less than in the parent artery and the blood pressure is much lower than in the parent artery.

Glomerular Filtration Rate (GFR)

In the renal corpuscles, the effects of blood pressure on the movement of fluids from the capillary into the lumen of bowman's capsule are much greater than the movement of fluids out of capillaries elsewhere in the body. The fluid pressure within the lumen of Bowman's capsule is potentially much lower than in the extracellular spaces elsewhere in the body. It is almost exclusively the pressure gradient between the capillary interior and the lumen of bowmans space that drives fluids from the capillary into the lumen of Bowman's space. The amount of fluid that passes from capillaries into bowman's capsule is called the glomerular filtration rate (GFR). By far the most important determinant of GFR is the body's arterial blood pressure.

Determinants of Blood Pressure

There are three primary determinants of arterial blood pressure: 1) the total volume of blood in the cardiovascular system, 2) the force of contraction of the left ventricle of the heart and 3) the resistance of the arterial vessels to arterial blood flow. The force of ventricular contraction can be influenced by the autonomic nervous system by increasing or decreasing the contractive force of cardiac myocytes in the cardiac tissue. Sympathetic stimulation increases the force of ventricular contraction and also increases contraction of smooth muscles within arterial wall. By contracting smooth muscle within arterial walls, pressure increases on the blood within the arteries and increases blood pressure. The degree of contraction of arterial smooth muscle is called arterial tone. When arterial tone increase arterial blood pressure increases.

Determinants of Total Body Water

The remaining major determinant of blood pressure is the total volume of blood within the blood vessels. Most of this volume is due to the volume of water within the blood. The volume of water is directly determined by the amount of water that is ingested through the digestive tract and the amount of water that is lost through urine and through insensible water loss. Insensible water loss occurs through sweating, evaporation from the lungs and by chemical reactions in the body. There is an absolute minimum water loss that cannot be prevented through these processes. Water loss through sweat can be almost eliminated by regulation of sweat production by the autonomic nervous system. Water loss through evaporation through the lung, by consumption in chemical reactions and by the limit imposed by the maximum capacity of the kidney to concentrate urine cannot be prevented and must be replaced by oral fluid intake. Euvolemia is the state where there is normal a volume of total body water. Hypovolemia is the state where there is inadequate volumes of total body water. Hypervolemia is the state where there abnormally high volumes of total body water

If total body water volume falls below a critical level, there is insufficient blood volume in the circulatory system to maintain a minimum survivable blood pressure. This occurs when the heart is contracting as strongly and rapidly as possible, when the blood vessels are at maximum tone and the kidney is concentrating urine at the highest possible level. As we will discuss, the maximum urine concentrating capacity of the kidney is directly dependent on the osmolality of the extracellular fluid in the renal medulla.

Intravascular Volume and Sodium Ion Concentrations

The volume of water that is confined to the intravascular and extracellular spaces is determined primarily by the concentration of sodium ion in the intravascular and extravascular fluids. When sodium ion concentrations fall below optimum levels (hyponatremia) The volume of water within blood vessels decrease and can be inadequate to maintain a minimum blood pressure even when there is a normal or even excessive volume of total body water. The kidney's response to this is to reabsorb the maximum possible amount of sodium ion from fluids that are filtered by the kidney.

While the kidney plays a crucial role in maintaining adequate blood pressure, in large part this is related to the requirement of a minimum blood pressure for adequate kidney function. Since glomerular filtration rate depends on blood pressure, inadequate blood pressure results in inadequate glomerular filtration rate. The rate of production of soluble waste products such as organic acids and urea then exceeds the rate that they can be secreted by the kidney. Urea, ammonia levels then rise and pH levels fall to fatal levels if an adequate blood pressure is not restored. The kidney has the capacity to directly adjust the blood pressure within glomerular capillaries within a range of 80-180 mmHg through a process called autoregulation.

Another critical role of the kidney is to directly maintain the optimum osmolarity of the blood and indirectly the osmolality of the intravascular fluid space and the osmolarity of the fluid within cells - the intracellular fluid space. This is also accomplished by regulating the excretion of water and sodium from the body.

A third critical function of the kidney is to maintain an optimal blood pH. This requires that the kidney have a mechanism to get rid of hydrogen ions when pH is too low and to retain hydrogen ions when blood pH is too high. This is accomplished by regulating the amount of bicarbonate ion in the bloodstream. Blood pH is also decreased by organic acid waste products produced by the body. The kidney does not regulate the levels of these organic acids, but strives to excrete all of these as well as all other soluble waste products with the exception of small amounts of urea that is concentrated in the renal medulla.

All of these functions require a complex interaction with other organ systems including systems and with systems that can detect the levels of water sodium blood osmolarity and blood pH. This information then needs to be transmitted to the kidney. This is usually in the form of hormones secreted elsewhere in the body or by signals sent via the autonomic nervous system.

The kidney also is involved in maintaining adequate levels of red blood cells in blood vessels and in maintaining the optimum level of calcium ions and phosphate in the body. Again these require detectors for calcium and red blood cell levels and signals to the kidney relaying this information. In many cases it is the kidney itself that directly or indirectly detect the levels of the physiological parameters that it is responsible for optimizing.

The kidney requires a complex suite of structural and cellular functions that can respond to these signals. In the case of red blood cell levels this is the synthesis and secretion of the hormone erythropoietin. For calcium levels it includes the synthesis and secretion of calcitriol - the activated form of vitamin D. For other functions it includes the synthesis and secretion of the hormone renin. Of course the kidney must have receptors for hormones that participate in maintaining optimum fluid electrolyte and pH . These include the hormones aldosterone, atrial natriuretic hormone, and antidiuretic hormone (ADH or vasopressin). Finally, the kidney uses specialized cells and specialized local environment regions that can respond in a manner that maintains these optimum levels.

An important feature of the renal collection system - the renal tubules, collecting ducts calyces and renal pelvis is that the lumens of these structures are continuous - they are all connected and continuous with the lumens of the ureters, with the internal cavity of the urinary bladder and with the lumen of the urethra. The distal opening of the urethra - the urethral meatus in the glans of the penis in males and in the vulvar surface in females - is potentially open to the external environment. This means the entire internal space of this system is literally outside of the body. Anything that passes into Bowman's capsule from the body has been excreted from the body. And must be reabsorbed through the renal tubules or the renal collecting ducts in order to return to the interior of the body.

Reabsorption
Filtration and reabsorption are the primary processes utilized by the kidney to perform its numerous functions. By definition - in the kidney - reabsorption is the movement of a substance out of the lumen of a renal or collecting tubule into the extracellular space surrounding the tubule or into a peritubular capillary. When this movement is down a substance's concentration gradient it is usually a passive diffusion process - a process that does not require energy. In the case of water this commonly is simple diffusion through segments of the renal tubule whose tubular walls are permeable to water. After substances are filtered into Bowman's capsule from glomerular capillaries, they almost always must be reabsorbed through specialized transmembrane transport systems located in the cell membranes of the cells that form the interior wall of renal tubules. These are simple cuboidal epithelial cells called parafollicular cells. parafollicular cells have

dense microvilli located on their apical borders - the surface of the cells that are exposed to the tubule lumen. This creates a brush border similar to the brush border of the small intestine. As is the case with the intestinal epithelia cells' brush border - the parafollicular cells brush border vastly increases the cells' absorptive surface area. This greatly enhances the ability of parafollicular cells to reabsorb substances from the lumen of renal tubules.

Different segments of the renal tubule - The proximal convoluted tubule, the loop of Henle and The distal convoluted renal tubule - have unique complements of transmembrane transporters and permeabilities to water and other substances. The loop of Henle has several sub regions that have very different membrane permeabilities (by simple diffusion) to various substances and have very different abilities to passively transport substances by facilitated diffusion or to reabsorb substances by actively transport.

Both glucose and amino acids are filtered from capillaries into Bowman's capsule. It is detrimental to the body to lose these crucial molecules through the urine and under normal circumstances the kidney is able to nearly completely reabsorb all of the glucose and amino acid molecules that are filtered into the renal tubules. It is logical for the kidney to reabsorb these substances as rapidly as possible and consequently nearly all of the active transporters for the reabsorption of glucose and amino acids are located in the walls of the proximal convoluted tubule (PCT) which is the tubular segment directly adjacent to Bowman's capsule. the transporter for amino acids is a sodium ion cotransporter.

The transporter for glucose - a sodium ion glucose cotransporter - can be saturated when the concentration of glucose in tubular fluid exceeds a critical level corresponding to a plasma glucose level 350 mg/dL. Glucose in tubular fluid cannot be completely reabsorbed and glucose is lost from the body in the urine (glucosuria). The presence of glucose in the urine is an indication that an individual is experiencing excessive blood glucose levels (hyperglycemia) usually due to diabetes mellitus.

Most bicarbonate ion (90%) is indirectly reabsorbed in the PCT, about 65% of sodium and chloride ions, 65% of water. Angiotensin II stimulates the reabsorption of sodium ion and bicarbonate ion from the PCT. The increased reabsorption of sodium ion also indirectly increases the diffuse of water out by decreasing the osmotic pressure of tubular fluid. of the PCT, and Most of the phosphate ions of tubular fluid is also reabsorbed is reabsorbed in the PCT. Parathyroid hormone(PTH) which is secreted when blood phosphate ions levels in the body are too high - inhibits the reabsorption of phosphate ion. The distal convoluted tubule is the site of most of the reabsorption of calcium ions. Parathyroid hormone (PTH) increases the reabsorption of calcium ion at this site. The levels of sodium ion in the blood are fine-tuned by variable reabsorption of sodium ions. This is usually about 10% of the total amount of sodium ion that is reabsorbed by the kidney.

Reabsorption in the Loop of Henle
One of the most critical features of the kidney is the creation of a very high osmolality within the extracellular compartment of the renal medulla. The renal medulla is composed mostly of loops of Henle. The tips or papillae of renal pyramids are adjacent to the renal calyces and are the deepest region of the renal medulla The papillae are composed primarily of the sharp bend or u turn in the loops of Henle. The renal collecting duct importantly also travel from the renal cortex through the adrenal medulla to their termination at the renal calices. The segment of the loop of Henle that originate at the PCT and descends to the U-turn of the loop in the renal papilla is the descending limb of the loop of Henle, The adjacent limb of the loop is the ascending loop of Henle. The lower segment of the ascending loop, originating from the u turn is called the thin ascending segment. The second segment of the ascending limb is called the thick segment of the ascending limb. The thick ascending limb terminates at the DCT.

It is the loop of Henle's function to create the hyperosmolar environment of the renal medulla. The osmolarity of the adrenal medulla steadily increases as one [proceeds from the superficial regions nearest to the adrenal cortex to the region of maximal hyperosmolarity at the renal papillae. The loop of Henle accomplishes this by virtue of the manner in which various regions have variable permeability to water and by which various regions have variable permeability to sodium and variable ability to reabsorb sodium ion.

The lower end of ascending limb of the loop - the thin ascending segments - is lined by simple squamous epithelium. The distal portion of the ascending limb - the thick ascending segment - and is lined by simple cuboidal epithelium. Water is reabsorbed in the medulla at the descending loop of Henle. This region is permeable to water consequently water diffuses out of the descending limb into the extracellular medullary space due to the high osmotic pressure of the medullary space. This process increases the osmolarity of the tubule fluid. The thin segment of the ascending limb is also permeable to water and consequently water continues to be reabsorbed by passive diffusion. The ascending thick segment of the loop is impermeable to water and actively reabsorbs sodium from the tubular fluid. This is the process that creates the high osmolarity of the renal medulla and simultaneously decreases the osmolarity of the tubular fluid. This tubular fluid continues through to the DCT and then to a collecting tubule. The tubular fluid in the DCT is maximally dilute. The osmolarity of this fluid corresponds to the minimum osmolarity of the urine that can be produced by the kidney and therefore corresponds to the maxim limit to the ability of the kidney to excrete excess water.

Reabsorption of Water from Collecting Tubules
Tubular Fluid flows from the DCT in the renal cortex into a collecting tubule at a level within the renal cortex. As the fluid the descends through the collecting tubule, it again passes through the adrenal medulla. Although collecting tubules are generally impermeable to nearly all substances, they are remarkable for their ability to alter their permeability to water. The walls of collecting tubules - in the absence of antidiuretic hormone (ADH) - are completely impermeable to water. When ADH molecules bind to receptors on collecting tubules, specialized water pores called aquaporins are inserted into the walls of the tubule.

the number of aquaporins that are inserted into the collecting tubule walls - and correspondingly the permeability of collecting tubules to water - increases as the levels of ADH that bind to collecting tubules increases. This is a critical mechanism in the kidney's ability to adjust the osmolality of urine - from maximally concentrated to maximally dilute. It is important to note that water is still diffusing down its concentration gradient from the collecting tubule into the surrounding extracellular space. The human body does not possess any transmembrane systems that can actively transport water against its concentration gradient.

The maximum urine concentrating ability of the kidney is about equal to the osmolarity of the renal medulla. Additional water cannot be reabsorbed by passive diffusion from the collecting tubule once the osmolarity of the tubular fluid is equal to the osmolarity of the surrounding extracellular space within the renal medulla.

Integration of Renal functions
It is remarkable that there are some many factors that influence the kidney's functions as the body attempts to maintain optimal levels of total body water of blood osmolarity of blood pressure by regulating intravascular blood volume and arterial tone and contractility of the heart. There are cells and structures that detect the osmolality of the blood - osmoreceptors in the hypothalamus and kidney and blood pressure - baroreceptors - in blood vessels. that interact with hormone systems consisting of renin produced and secreted by the kidney, aldosterone produced and secreted by the adrenal cortex, angiotensin I and II, and ADH produced and released by the posterior pituitary.

It is helpful in the understanding of how these systems interact to first consider that ADH causes the kidney to maximally reabsorb water. Renin aldosterone and angiotensin II causes the kidney to maximally reabsorb sodium ion. Next, consider that there is a baseline state where all of these systems have optimized levels of blood pressure, of total body water and of blood osmolality. This corresponds to the baseline levels of renin, aldosterone, angiotensin II and ADH that are maintaining these levels. In this state the kidneys roles are primarily to excrete waste products and to maintain an optimum blood pH. In this scenario the kidney will produce the minimum amount of urine required to excrete waste products. Additionally, it will produce a urine with an osmolality that is equal to the blood osmolality. this minimizes the loss of body water and sodium ion and maintains the desired osmolality of the blood. this corresponds to maximal levels of ADH and intermediate levels of other hormones. When the body is hypervolemic with high osmolality (corresponding to hypernatremia), the kidney will maximize the excretion of both water but will also maximally excrete sodium. In this case, the kidney will produce a maximum volume of urine with a maximum osmolality (most maximally concentrated urine). If the body is hypovolemic and hyponatremic - too little body water and too little sodium, the kidney will produce a minimum volume of urine with a minimum or most dilute osmolality - this conserves body water and sodium. This state corresponds to a maximum level of ADH and a maximum level of other hormones -renin, aldosterone and angiotensin II. The same logical analysis can be applied to determine how the kidney should respond to any combination of abnormal levels of body water and Blood osmolarity.

The Immune System and the Lymphatic System

The immune system is a complex and widely distributed network of cells, organs and other structures. The lymphatic system is a body-wide circulatory system that includes lymphatic vessels, lymph nodes and lymphoid organs. The lymphatic vascular system is closely associated in both structure and distribution to the blood vessels of the cardiovascular system. The lymphatic system functions include the removal of excess fluids and debris from the extracellular or interstitial compartments of the body (the area surrounding cells not including spaces inside blood vessels). The lymphatic system is also a major component of the immune system.

Capillary-size lymphatic vessels are found throughout the body. They are terminal branches of the lymphatic vascular system. Lymphatic fluid moves from interstitial spaces into the lymphatic capillaries, then to progressively larger vessels and then to lymph nodes. Lymph nodes are nodular structures that are widely distributed throughout the body. Lymphatic fluid is filtered at lymph nodes and continues in vessels leaving the lymph nodes to reach one of the two major lymphatic vessels; either the right lymphatic duct or the thoracic duct. The right lymphatic duct delivers lymph fluid into the right subclavian vein and the thoracic duct delivers lymphatic fluid into the left subclavian vein.

The lymphatic circulation is also responsible for the absorption of fats and fat soluble vitamins (vitamins A, C, D and E) in the small intestines and subsequently for transport to the bloodstream.

Lymph Nodes

For the TEAS, the anatomy of lymph nodes is significant in that the cortex of the lymph node is a site where T-cells accumulate and interact with B-cells and that the medulla of lymph nodes is one of the anatomical regions where the maturation of B-cells occurs.

The Spleen

The spleen is the largest lymphoid organ in the body and one of the largest organs of the body in general. It is located in the left upper quadrant of the abdomen just superior to the stomach and just inferior to the diaphragm. The spleen has structures similar to lymph nodes that contain B- and T-cells. The spleen filters blood that arrives via the splenic artery arteries. The spleen contains macrophages that consume damaged and elderly red blood cells and recycles iron to the liver. The spleen also contains a large volume of white blood cells that serve as a readily accessible reserve for immune activities that may be required by the body.

The Thymus

The thymus is an organ located in the midline of the thoracic cavity immediately posterior to the sternum and anterior to the trachea, directly between the lungs. The thymus is the organ where the maturation of T-cells occurs.

The Appendix and the Tonsils

The appendix, an appendage of the cecum of the large intestine and the tonsils, located in the lateral walls of the pharynx are also lymphoid organs that contain B- and T-cell functional regions.

Bone Marrow

The medulla (central region) of most skeletal bones - and in particular the long bones of the arms and legs and the pelvic bones - contain bone marrow. Both red blood cells and white blood cells (including immature T-and B-cells) are produced in the bone marrow.

Immune System Physiology

Most authorities would agree that the nervous system is probably the most complex system of the human body, but the human immune system is vastly complex and decades of research remain to answer large gaps in our knowledge about this system. The immune system functions to protect the human body from foreign disease causing biological and chemical agents. These include viruses, bacteria, and other single and multi-cellular organisms. The immune system also protects the body from chemical products produced by disease causing organisms such as toxins. Finally, the immune system attempts to identify and contain or destroy cells of the body that are dysfunctional or cancerous.

There are various ways to categorize the immune system one is to define functions as either innate or adaptive immune system response.

Innate Immune system

The innate immune system is a non-specific or generic immune system - it responds to infection by disease causing agents - pathogens- and to any other event that cause injuries to the body. In contrast to active immunity, innate immunity does not provide long-lasting resistance to repeated infection by the same organism.

Anatomical Barriers

The innate immune consists of anatomical barriers and a variety of chemicals and cell types. The skin provides a physical barrier to pathogens and also rids the skin surface of pathogens by desquamation (skin flaking) by sweating and by the production of organic acids that create an unfavorable skin pH for the proliferation of pathogens. The continuous transport of mucus out of the respiratory tract by the motion of cilia provides physiological barriers to pathogens in the respiratory tract. The peristaltic motion of the intestines transports pathogens out of the digestive tract and gastric and bile acids and digestive enzyme create a very hostile environment to most living organisms. Those organisms that do thrive in the digestive tract create a bio community that resists intrusion of other organisms. Saliva, mucous and other bodily secretions contains a potent antibacterial compound called lysozyme.

Natural Killer Cells

If the barriers to a pathogen are breached, there are several innate defenses that are triggered. If the pathogen infects a cell of the body - usually in the form of a virus - the infected cell will alter its surface membrane molecules to alert natural killer (NK) cells that the cell is injured or infected. The NK cells attacks the unhealthy cell by releasing perforins - small molecules that assemble on the target cell membrane and create holes or pores in the cell membrane. This can be sufficient to kill the cell but the NK cells also uses the perorations created in the cell membrane to pass a potent toxin into the cell. The toxin has rapidly fatal effects on the unhealthy cell.

Recent evidence has shown that NK cells do recognize antigens - small molecules that trigger antibody-dependent responses. The assumptions before had been that NK cells do not require any antibody related processes to recognize and attack an unhealthy cell. This view is no longer considered to be true.

Sentinel Cells and Cytokines
Pathogens that are not confined to the interior of cell - those are eliminated primarily by NK cells are identified by monitoring cells of the innate immune system. These are also called sentinel cells or surveillance cells. They recognize a limited number of molecular features common to most biological pathogens - bacterial and other cellular pathogens. As these pathogens enter the body sentinel cells - usually macrophages - identify them and in response release a number of molecules called cytokines.

Inflammation and the Complement Cascade
Cytokines are a class of intercellular signaling molecules that have a wide range of actions One category of action - the inflammatory reaction- is the generation of fever, vasodilation and activation of the complement cascade -a series of chemical reactions that produce large amount of protein products that can directly kill pathogens or can bind to pathogens and make them highly susceptible to destruction by macrophages.

Interferons
Interferons are a class of a number of specific molecules released by many cells that among other effects - progressively restrict the ability of viruses to continue infectious cycles within the body. These effects tend to peak at between five to ten days.

Macrophages
Macrophages are cells of the immune system that literally consume other cells - pathogens and injured or dead cells of the body. The term for this process is phagocytosis. Fever raises body temperature to levels that are unfavorable for viral infection processes. Swelling and increased blood flow begins the process of drawing a variety of types of immune cells to infection sites where an increasingly complex battle is waged to wall off the pathogens from further entry into the body and ultimately to kill the pathogens and then to remove the cellular debris that results from this immunological warfare.

Histamine
Another class of effects that greatly enhances the local inflammatory reactions is the triggering of the release of the molecule histamine - this molecule causes local pain, increases fluid leakage from blood vessels a at the infection site resulting in swelling and causes vasodilation that results in increased blood flow to the infected region - resulting in redness and increased temperature at the infection site. These are the four primary indicators of an infected region of the body; heat, redness, pain and swelling.

The Reproductive System
The male and female human reproductive systems are responsible for the generation of human offspring. The first stage of this process begins with the production of male and female gametes. Recall that gametes are the haploid (N) cells that result from meiotic cell division. In males the gamete is a sperm cell and in females the gamete is a mature ovum.

The second stage of this process is fertilization, where male gametes are transported to the female reproductive system and a sperm cell fuses with an ovum to produce a diploid (2N) cell - a zygote. The zygote is a hybrid cell that contains one set of chromosomes 1 through 21 (the human autosomal chromosomes) and one sex chromosome (chromosome 22) either an X or a Y chromosome from the sperm cell and one set of chromosomes 1 through 21 and one X sex chromosome (chromosome 22) from the ovum. The resultant zygote has a full set of 21 pairs of autosomes and two sex chromosomes - either an X or a Y chromosome or two X chromosomes. Zygotes with an X and a Y chromosome develop into male human offspring and those with two X chromosomes develop into female offspring.

The zygote then begins the process of cell division and cell differentiation that eventually leads to the production of a mature human fetus that is capable of independent survival outside of the female reproductive system. At this stage the fetus is born from the mother to the outside world through the process of labor and delivery.

The synthesis and secretion of the sex hormones - testosterone in the male and estrogen in the female also occurs in the gonads of the reproductive system.

The Male Reproductive System

The male reproductive system consists of the external male genitalia - the penis, the scrotum and the testis, and the internal male genitalia - The distal segment of the urethra, the seminal vesicles, and the prostate gland, bulbourethral glands and the Cowper's gland. The penis consists of a central canal - the urethra - which also serves as the passageway for the delivery of urine from the bladder to the exterior of the body, and the distensible surrounding erectile tissue - the corpus cavernosum. The distal end of the penis forms the head or glans of the penis which contains the external opening of the urethra - the meatus and surrounding tissue called the foreskin.

The scrotum is an external anatomical pouch or sack consisting of skin and smooth muscle. The scrotum is divided into two chambers. Each chamber contains a single testis along with the associated structures of the testis - the epididymis and the ductus deferens. The scrotum allows the testis to experience a slightly lower temperature environment than internal body temperature. This is necessary to allow the proper functioning of spermatogenesis (sperm production) that occurs within the testis.

The testes are ovoid shaped organs that are responsible for the first stages of the production of sperm cells. The testes are enclosed by a tough outer membrane - the tunica albuginea. The interior of the testis consists of a collection of thin coiled tubules called the seminiferous tubules. The cells lining the interior of the seminiferous tubules include specialized epithelial cells called Sertoli cells and germ cells that are capable of undergoing cell division and differentiation to produce sperm cells (spermatozoa).

The seminiferous tubules connect proximally to the **rete testis** - a short stalk of common connecting tubules were developing sperm cells are concentrated before they proceed to **efferent ducts** and into the epididymis. The epididymis is a highly convoluted tubule that forms a mass at the superior surface of the testis. Developing sperm cells are retained within the epididymis for 2-3 months. During this time the developing sperm cell reach maturity.

The distal end of the epididymis is continuous with the vas deferens. The vas deferens are short -length segments of tubules that connect the epididymis to the ejaculatory ducts located in the interior of the pelvic cavity. The ejaculatory ducts connect to the urethra and also have connections with ducts of the prostate gland, the bulbourethral glands and Cowper's glands. These glands provide contributions to the seminal fluid that serves as the fluid medium that nourishes and supports the transportation of sperm cells during ejaculation.

Testosterone production

A primary function of the male gonads - the testis - is the production of the male sex hormone testosterone. Testosterone is a steroid hormone whose synthesis and secretion is regulated by the hypothalamus through the release of gonadotrophin releasing hormone (GnRh) which regulates the synthesis and release of luteinizing hormone (LH) and follicle-stimulating hormone (FSH) by the anterior pituitary.

Both FSH and LH stimulate the testes to synthesize and release testosterone. Luteinizing hormone directly stimulates the production of testosterone. Testosterone production occurs in Leydig cells. Leydig cells interstitial cells (located in loose connective tissue) that are located alongside the seminiferous tubules of the testis. Testosterone produced by the Leydig cells stimulates the sexual maturation of prepubescent males and during puberty stimulate the development of male secondary sexual characteristics. Secondary male sexual characteristics include the development of pubic and facial hair, an increase in muscle and bone mass, a deepening of the voice and the maturation of the gonads and external male genitalia. After puberty, testosterone plays critical roles in the maturation of sperm cells.

Spermatogenesis
The production of mature sperm cells begins with male diploid germ cells called spermatogonia. Spermatogonia cells are located on the basement membrane of seminiferous tubules. Spermatogonia are surrounded by specialized epithelial cells called Sertoli cells. As sperm cell development proceeds from spermatogonia, the developing sperm cells move upward through the Sertoli cells. During this process the Sertoli cells provide critical functions that support the development of the sperm cells. The functions of sertoli cells are under the direct influence of the hormone FSH.

Spermatogonia mitoticly divide to form daughter cells called primary spermatocytes. These primary spermatocytes undergo meiotic division to produce haploid gamete cells called spermatids. Under the influence of testosterone, spermatids begin to mature into spermatozoa. As this maturation process continues, the developing spermatozoa move upward through their surrounding Sertoli cells and are released into the lumen of the seminiferous tubules. The spermatozoa are then transported by peristaltic action to the lumens of the tubules of the epididymis where they undergo final maturation and attain the ability of independent locomotion via a flagellum or tail located on each spermatozoa.

The Female Reproductive System
 The female reproductive system consists of the external and internal female genitalia. The functions of the female reproductive system are the production of female gametes the support of the fertilization of the fusion of female and male gametes to create a human zygote, and the physical support, protection and nourishment of the development of the zygote to a mature human fetus and the subsequent delivery of the fetus to the outside world. The gonads of the female reproductive system are also responsible for the synthesis and release of the female sex hormone estrogen.

The External Female Genitalia
The external female genitalia as a group are called the vulva. The vulva consists of the mons pubis which is a mound of fatty tissue overlying the pubic bone that forms the anterior segment of the vulva. The mons pubis consists of the labia majora. The labia majora are outer folds or lips that are divided into right and left labia by the pudendal cleft. The two folds of the labia majora are lateral to the underlying labia minora, clitoris, vaginal introitus (external opening), urethral meatus, the greater and lesser vestibular glands (Bartholin's glands and Skene's glands) and the vulvar vestibule

The labia minora are similar in structure to the labia majora and are laterally located adjacent to and inferomedial to the labia majora and adjacent and lateral to the central regions of the vulva. The central vulvar regions include the midline superiorly located clitoris and the centrally located vulvar vestibule. The urethral meatus and the vaginal introitus or orifice is located in the midline of the vulvar vestibule. The urethral meatus is located immediately superior to the vaginal orifice. The greater vestibular glands or Bartholin's glands and the lesser vestibular glands or Skene's glands are located lateral to the vaginal orifice.

The Bartholin's glands secrete mucous which provides lubrication of the vagina and the surrounding vestibular regions

The Female Internal Reproductive System
The female internal reproductive system consists of four major components, the vagina, uterus, fallopian tubes and the ovaries. In contrast to the male reproductive system, the female urethra does not communicate with any female reproductive structures and has no role in the female reproductive system.

The Vagina
The vagina is an anatomical tube consisting of muscular and fibrous tissue. The lumen of the vagina begins at the vaginal orifice and extends internally to the pelvic cavity where it terminates at the cervix of the uterus. The cervix is the inferior portion of the uterus and protrudes into the lumen of the vagina. The walls of the vagina encircle the cervix and the interior lining of the vaginal lumen is continuous with the external surfaces of the cervix.

The Uterus
The functions of the uterus are to serve as a site for the implantation of a developing embryo and to provide a continuous supportive, nurturing and protective environment for the continued development of the embryo into a viable human fetus. When the fetus is sufficiently developed to survive outside of the uterus, the uterus undergoes a series of muscular contractions that expel the fetus from the internal uterine cavity through the cervical canal and into the lumen of the vagina.

The uterus is a pear-shaped muscular organ located in the pelvic cavity in a position immediately adjacent and dorsal to the urinary bladder and immediately adjacent and ventral to the rectum. The four major anatomical regions of the uterus are the cervix or neck of the uterus, the internal os, the corpus or body of the uterus and the fundus or superior region of the uterus. The cervix or neck of the uterus is the conically shaped inferior segment of the uterus that extends into the vagina forming the cap to the internal end of the vagina. In the central region of the cervix is a passageway that is continuous with the lumen of the vagina and extends into the central cavity of the uterus.

The Walls of the uterus consist of three layers. The innermost layer, which includes the internal surface of the central uterine cavity, is the endometrium. The endometrium includes an innermost epithelial layer which in turn consists of a basal layer and an overlying functional layer. The functional layer includes the surface layer cells that are exposed as the lining of the central uterine cavity. The functional layer consists of epithelial cells, mucous glands and blood vessels that are responsive to a number of hormones.

The Functional layer undergoes an approximately once-per-month cycle of growth, degeneration and regeneration (menstrual cycle) that occurs in response to the variations in the levels of hormones that regulate the menstrual cycle. The middle layer of the uterus is called the myometrium. The myometrium is composed of several thick layers of smooth muscle tissue. The outermost encapsulating layer of the uterus - the parametrium - consists of a continuation of the peritoneum, the epithelial surface layer of the abdominal cavity. The Uterus is structurally supported in its position within the pelvic cavity by the three pairs of suspensory ligaments the uterosacral, cardinal and round ligaments.

The Fallopian Tubes
The fallopian tubes are a pair of structures that extend from superior-lateral positions on the uterus, one on the left and one on the right - medial to a position directly opposite of the respective left or the right ovary. The fallopian tubes contain a central lumen that is lined with ciliated epithelium. One end of the lumen is continuous with the central cavity of the uterus and the other end is open to the pelvic cavity and faces the respective ovary. There is a short gap between the ovary and the lateral opening of the lumen of the

fallopian tube. During ovulation -when a mature follicle within the ovary ruptures and releases a mature ovum (female gamete) - the ovum is drawn into the fallopian tube by local peritoneal fluid currents generated by the motion of cilia within the fallopian tube. Once inside the tube, the ovum is carried by the same ciliary motions into the central cavity of the uterus. Fertilization of the ovum by a sperm cell (which sometimes occurs within the fallopian tubes) triggers a set of reactions that allow the developing embryo to implant within the wall of the endometrium of the uterus.

The Ovaries

The ovaries are the female gonads. Ovaries are 3-to-4 cm in size and ovoid shaped. There are two ovaries in females, one located in the pelvic cavity on either the left or right side just medial to distal end of the respective left or right fallopian tube. The ovaries are connected to the uterus by a ligament - the ovarian ligament and to the peritoneal wall of the pelvis by another ligament - the suspensory ligament.

In addition to their role as the primary estrogen producing glands the ovaries also are the organs that contain all of a female's germ cells that will eventually mature and be released by the ovaries during ovulatory cycles. All of these progenitor germ cells are present at birth in a human female's ovaries.
The general structure of an ovary includes an outer region called the cortex and an inner region called the medulla. The medulla of the ovary contains loose connective tissue that surrounds the blood vessels that provide the blood supply the ovary

The Ovarian Cortex

The ovarian cortex is composed of dense connective tissue including fibroblast cells that can change functionally in response to various hormone levels. The cortex also has an outer layer of cuboidal epithelial cells called the germinal layer. As female germ cells mature into functional gametes (eggs) they acquire an organized collection of cells called granulosa cells. The granulosa cell mass and the embedded germ cell together are called an ovarian follicle. The ovarian follicles at all stages of development are located in the ovarian cortex.

Oogenesis

The process of producing human female gametes is called oogenesis. The process begins during fetal development with female primordial germ cells. These cells appear in the fetal ovaries. Primordial germ cells then differentiate into oogonia. Oogonia are diploid germ cells that undergo further mitotic divisions and differentiation into primary oocytes. Primary oocytes then enter meiotic division and progress to the prophase 1 stage of meiosis.

Primary Follicles and Maturation Arrest

Prior to the onset of puberty, all primary oocytes remain in the prophase 1 stage of meiosis. This is called maturation arrest. These primary oocytes acquire a collection of granulosa cells and together they comprise a primary ovarian follicle. No primary oocytes within a female's ovaries will proceed to subsequent phases of meiosis until the female reaches puberty. At puberty, the cyclic processes of ovarian follicular development and the menstrual cycle of the uterine endometrial tissue begins. The onset of this process at puberty is called menarche.

Hormonal Regulation during the Menstrual Cycle

With the onset of puberty, the hypothalamus begins to release GnRH in a controlled fashion that varies throughout the menstrual cycle. For the first half of the cycle GnRH is released in increasing amounts. This triggers the anterior pituitary to release FSH and LH also in increasing amounts. FSH stimulates the ovaries to begin the next stage of oogenesis. Some of the primary follicles randomly begin to mature into secondary follicles.

During this process, the primary oocytes of the developing secondary follicle emerge from maturation arrest and proceed from the prophase 1 stage of meiosis and complete the first round of meiosis. This results in the production of a haploid (N) daughter cell called a secondary oocyte. The other daughter cell of this first round of mitosis degenerates into a structure called a polar body.

ENGLISH LANGUAGE

The organic way to expand your vocabulary is to read everything you can get your hands on. That means blogs, articles and social media, but also physical books, posted signs and even the labels on your shampoo bottle. Start looking for opportunities to read a little bit more every day, from now until the day of the test.

Of course, you do have that test coming up, so you don't have much time to go au naturale. We got your back. Here is your first and most crucial vocabulary hack: identifying root words.

What is the What?

Many words are little stories in and of themselves, which is to say that they have a beginning, middle and end. These parts are, respectively, the prefix, the root word and the suffix.

Not all words have all three parts. Sometimes it's just the prefix and root, sometimes just the root and suffix, and sometimes there are multiple roots. But—and this is important—a word is never made up only of prefixes and suffixes. There is always at least one root word, because that's the main idea of the word. You can't have a complete, grammatically correct sentence without a subject, and you can't have a complete word without a main idea, or root word.

For example, here's a word that's close to your heart lately: *reviewing*. It means viewing something again. Here are its parts:
Prefix = re
Root = view
Suffix = ing

Re is a prefix that basically means again. *View* means *see* or look. *Ing* is a suffix that tells you the root word is happening. So, if you're reviewing, you're viewing something again. Thus, the root word, or main idea, is view.

Let's get concrete: If you went up to one of your friends and just said, "Again," they would give you a funny look and say, "What again?"

It's the same idea if you went up to them and said, "Doing." They would say, "Doing what?"

If you went up to them and just said, "Look," they would look where you're looking to determine what you're seeing. They may not know what to look for, but they get the idea.

Almost every vocabulary word on the test will be some combination of prefixes, roots and suffixes. If you run into one that you don't know, the first question to ask yourself is, "What is the what?"

Here is another example: *unemployment*
Prefix = un
Root = employ

Suffix = ment

You can't just say "un" or "ment" and expect to be understood, but when you add the main idea, *employ*, the word makes sense. It means the state of not having a job.

Where It Gets Messy

Of course, we speak the English language, which is a marvelous, madcap collage of many other languages, but mostly Latin, German and Greek. That means many root words are not English words. On top of that, there are no hard-and-fast rules for how prefixes and suffixes will change root words, so each root may look a little different depending on which prefixes and suffixes are used.

However, you can usually get the gist by breaking off the parts that you know are prefixes and suffixes and asking yourself what the remaining part reminds you of.

In order to break things down, you need to have a grasp of the most common prefixes, suffixes and root words you'll encounter on the test (these are outlined below).

Prefixes
Here are your opposite prefixes, which you'll encounter a lot on the test:

Prefix	Variations	What it Means	Examples
Anti-	Ant-	Against or opposite	Anti-inflammatory, antagonist
De-		Opposite	Decontaminate, deconstruct
Dis-		Not or opposite	Disagree, dis (slang for insult)
In-	Im-, Il-, Ir-	Not	Incapable, impossible, illegitimate, irreplaceable
Non-		Not	Noncompliant, nonsense
Un-		Not	Unfair, unjust

Here is a quick list of some other common prefixes:

Prefix	Variations	What it Means	Examples
En-	Em-	Cause	Enlighten, empower
Fore-		Before	Foresee, foretell
In-		Inside of	Inland, income
Inter-		Between	Interrupt, interaction
Mid-		In the middle of	Midair, midlife
Mis-		Wrong	Mistake, misdiagnose
Pre-		Before	Pregame, prefix
Re-		Again	Review, recompress
Semi-		Half or partial	Semitruck, semiannual
Sub-		Under	Subconscious, subpar
Super-		Above	Superimpose, superstar
Trans-		Across	Translate, transform

Suffixes

Here are some common suffixes you'll encounter on the test:

Suffix	Variations	What it Means	Examples
-Able	-Ible	Can be accomplished	Capable, possible
-Al	-Ial	Has traits of	Additional, beneficial
-En		Made of	Molten, wooden
-Er		More than	Luckier, richer
-Er	-Or	Agent that does	Mover, actor
-Est		Most	Largest, happiest
-Ic		Has traits of	Acidic, dynamic
-Ing		Continues to do	Reviewing, happening
-Ion	-Tion, -Ation, -Ition	Process of	Occasion, motion, rotation, condition
-Ity		The state of	Ability, simplicity
-Ly		Has traits of	Friendly, kindly
-Ment		Process/state of	Enlightenment, establishment
-Ness		State of	Happiness, easiness
-Ous	-Eous, -Ious	Has traits of	Porous, gaseous, conscious
-Y		Has traits of	Artsy, fartsy

Common Root Words

If you can't identify a word because it seems like it's in another language, that's most likely because it is. This isn't always true, but a good general rule is that our longer, more academic words tend to have their roots in Latin and Greek, while our shorter words tend to have their roots in German. For example, *amorous* and *loving* are synonyms, but one has its roots in the Latin *amor* and the other in the German *lieb*.

Latin/Greek

Because vocabulary words on the test tend toward the longer, more academic variety, you'll get the most out of studying some common Latin and Greek roots:

Root	Variations	What it Means	Examples
Aster	Astro	Star	Astronomy, disaster
Aqua		Water	Aquatic, aquarium
Aud		Hear	Auditorium, audience
Bene		Good	Benevolent, benign
Bio		Life	Biology, autobiography
Cent		Hundred	Century, cent (money)
Chrono		Time	Chronological, synchronize
Circum	Circa	Around	Circumspect, circumnavigate
Contra	Counter	Against or conflict	Contraband, encounter
Dict		Speak or say	Dictate, dictation
Duc	Duct, duce	Lead or leader	Produce, conduct
Fac		Make or do	Manufacture, facsimile (fax)
Fract	Frag	Break	Fraction, defragment
Gen		Birth or create	Genetics, generate
Graph		Write	Telegraph, calligraphy
Ject		Throw	Inject, projection
Jur	Jus	Law	Juror, justice
Log	Logue	Concept or thought	Logo, dialogue
Mal		Bad	Maladaptive, malevolent
Man		Hand	Manuscript, manual
Mater		Mother	Maternal, material
Mis	Mit	Send	Mission, submit
Pater	Pat	Father	Paternal, patriot
Path		Feel	Sympathy, empathetic
Phile	Philo	Love	Philosophy, anglophile
Phon		Sound	Telephone, phonetic
Photo		Light	Photograph, photosynthesis
Port		Carry	Transport, portable
Psych	Psycho	Soul or spirit	Psychiatrist, psyche
Qui	Quit	Quiet or rest	Acquittal, tranquility
Rupt		Break	Rupture, interrupt
Scope		See, inspect	Telescope, microscopic
Scrib	Script	Write	Describe, transcription
Sens	Sent	Feel	Sensory, consent
Spect		Look	Spectate, circumspect
Struct		Build	Construct, obstruction
Techno	Tech	Art or science	Technical, technology
Tele		Far	Teleport, television
Therm		Heat	Thermometer, thermal
Vac		Empty	Vacation, evacuate
Vis	Vid	See	Visual, video
Voc		Speak or call	Vocal, vocation

Vocabulary Practice Test

For items 1-5, try to identify the root and write an English translation or synonym for it. We did the first one for you as an example.

#	Word	Root	Translation/Synonym
Ex	Description	Script	Something written
1	Irresponsible		
2	Entombment		
3	Professorial		
4	Unconscionable		
5	Gainfully		

For items 6-10, identify the prefix and write an English translation or synonym for it.

#	Word	Prefix	Translation/Synonym
Ex	Prepare	Pre	Before
6	Proceed		
7	Misapprehend		
8	Antibiotic		
9	Hyperactive		
10	Cacophony		

For items 11-15, identify the suffix and write an English translation or synonym for it.

#	Word	Suffix	Translation/Synonym
Ex	Lovable	Able	Can be accomplished
11	Tedious		
12	Absolution		
13	Cathartic		
14	Merriment		
15	Inspector		

Now, it's time to test your current vocabulary:

1. Achromatic most nearly means:
a. full of color
b. fragrant
c. without color
d. vivid

2. Cursory most nearly means:
a. meticulous; careful
b. undetailed; rapid
c. thorough
d. expletive

3. Hearsay most nearly means:
a. blasphemy
b. secondhand information that can't be proven
c. evidence that can be confirmed
d. testimony

4. Magnanimous most nearly means:
a. suspicious
b. uncontested
c. forgiving; not petty
d. stingy; cheap

5. Terrestrial most nearly means:
a. of the earth
b. cosmic
c. otherworldly/unearthly
d. supernatural

Let's see how you did:

1. c. without color
2. b. undetailed; rapid
3. b. secondhand information that can't be proven
4. c. forgiving; not petty
5. a. of the earth

When reading through a chapter in a book or a passage on a test, you will sometimes encounter a word you've never seen before. You may not know what it means, but don't worry! You can still figure out a basic definition of the word, even if you don't have a dictionary in hand (or if you don't want to get off the sofa and get one).

In every sentence, any given word is surrounded by clauses, phrases and other words. When you find a word you don't recognize, you can learn more about it by studying the context surrounding it. These surrounding words, phrases and clauses are called context clues. Using these, you can determine the definition for almost every unfamiliar word you encounter. This is a skill that will become especially helpful when you start reading higher-level texts with fancy words or training manuals with lots of jargon.

Types of Context Clues

As you read, you can use several different types of context clues to help you discover the meaning of unknown words. Some important and common types of context clues are outlined below. Try to use the specific context clue to determine the meaning of the bolded word.

Root Word & Affix

This is a context clue that uses your existing knowledge of common root words.

Example: Scientists who dig up dinosaur bones are experts in **paleontology**.

This context clue assumes you have knowledge of dinosaurs and can relate that to the study of "paleontology."

Compare/Contrast

This is a context clue that signals a similarity or difference by using words or phrases that denote a comparison or contrast. Words that imply similarity (or comparison) include *like, also, just as, too,* etc. Words that imply difference (or contrast) include *whereas, opposed to, unlike, versus,* etc.

Example: A comet, like an **asteroid**, is made from leftover matter in the universe.

This context clue compares an "asteroid" with a comet to imply a similarity to the given definition of a comet.

Logic

This is a context clue wherein you must infer the definition of the unknown word by using the relationships within the sentence.

Example: Builders routinely use **fasteners** that will   help hold their structures and buildings in place.

This context clue describes the job that "fasteners" do.

Definition

This is a context clue that includes a basic definition of the unknown word.

Example: New biological species can be formed through a process called **speciation**.

This context clue defines "speciation" outright.

Example or Illustration
This is a context clue that uses an example or illustration of the unknown word.

Example: Animals classified in the phylum porifera live in a **marine** habitat like the Atlantic and Pacific Oceans.

This context clue uses Atlantic and Pacific Oceans as examples of "marine" habitats.

Homographs
Now that you've had a refresher on context clues, let's talk about homographs. A homograph is a word that is spelled exactly like another word, but has a different meaning. For example, "bass" can mean "a low, deep sound" or "a type of fish." Here's a more complex homograph: "minute" can mean "a unit of time" or "something very small."

Although questions with homographs aren't necessarily difficult, you'll need to pay extra attention to the context clues. If you're rushing or don't read the entire sentence, you can accidentally mark an incorrect answer by mistaking the homograph for the wrong meaning. As long as you take your time and use the context clues, you'll most likely have no problem.

Here's something to consider when you take the exam. Within the question, replace the vocabulary term with your selected answer choice. Read the sentence and check whether or not it makes sense. This won't guarantee a correct answer, but it will help identify an incorrect one.

Another point to keep in mind is that sometimes there will not be an answer choice that exactly fits into the sentence. Don't panic! You probably did not misread the context clues or come up with an incorrect meaning. Many times, questions will ask you to select the *best* word from the given answer choices, even though that correct answer choice may not be the best *possible* answer overall. These types of questions want you to choose the *most* correct answer choice. These can be tricky to tackle, but expect to see questions like this on the exam. Just remember the tip above and you'll do fine.

Vocabulary-in-Context

Vocabulary-in-Context questions ask you for the definition of a word as it is used within the context of the passage. The format of these questions is similar to that of Word Knowledge questions. You will be given a word and asked to select the closest meaning from a list of four choices. The difference, though, is that where Word Knowledge questions test straightforward vocabulary, the words chosen for Vocabulary-in-context questions are often words that can have more than one meaning. You will need to use context clues from the passage in order to figure out which meaning is correct.

It's also important to note that many questions on the exam will not always ask you to simply determine the meaning of a vocabulary word. Many times, instead of asking you for a synonym or definition of a vocabulary word, the question will ask you what the vocabulary word "most nearly means". For these types of questions, you'll need to use context clues and your existing vocabulary knowledge to determine which answer choice has a meaning that is closest to that of the vocabulary word.

To answer these questions, reread the sentence from the passage that the word is taken from. Come up with a prediction—your own definition or synonym of what the word means as used in that sentence. Then, look at the answer choices and choose the one that best matches your prediction. If you do not see your prediction among the answer choices, read each of the answer choices as part of the sentence, replacing the original word, and choose the one that makes the most sense.

Let's look at some examples.

Some of the questions you'll encounter will ask you to fill in the blank in a sentence. For the questions below, select the word that fits best in the sentence.

1. The bolt was _____. It took a lot of effort to loosen the fastener.
A. Rusted
B. Shiny
C. Loose
D. Strong

Answer: A.
Using the context clues in the sentence, you can assume that the missing word is somehow related to the phrase "loosen the fastener". Something about the bolt made it difficult to remove. You can immediately eliminate "shiny" since it is not related to the action of removing a fastener. Likewise, "loose" is not correct because if the bolt were loose, it wouldn't be difficult to remove it. "Strong" could possibly fit if there wasn't a better answer choice, but it's not typically used to describe how difficult a fastener is to remove. The word that best fits in the sentence is "rusted" because rust directly increases the difficulty of removing a fastener.

2. As the commanding officer's eyes widened and his face turned red, he proceeded to _____ the lance corporal.

A. Tease

B. Scold

C. Compliment

D. Correct

Answer: B.

Using the context clues in the sentence, you can assume that the missing word is somehow linked to widened eyes and a red face, which are associated with anger. You can immediately eliminate "tease" and "compliment" since those words connote lightheartedness and sincerity, not exactly similar to the demeanor described in the sentence. "Correct" could possibly fit if there wasn't a better answer choice, but it's not necessarily associated with widened eyes and a red face. The word that best fits in the sentence is "scold" because scolding connotes anger or irritation, which correlate with widened eyes and a red face.

Sure, those were fairly easy, but those are just one type of vocabulary-in-context questions you'll probably encounter on the exam. For the questions below, select the word that MOST NEARLY means the same as the underlined word.

1. The chairman of the board <u>abandoned</u> his position after a damaging scandal.

A. Squandered

B. Resigned

C. Ignored

D. Neglected

Answer: B.

All the answer choices connote negative characteristics of the position of chairman of the board, but only "resigned" most closely matches the underlined word. "Squandered" suggests a wasted opportunity. "Ignored" means deliberately taking no notice of. "Neglected" signifies a failure to pay attention to. "Resigned" indicates voluntarily leaving a job, which MOST nearly means the same as "abandoned", leaving permanently.

2. Sarah considered herself a <u>parsimonious</u> shopper. She loved finding great shopping deals.

A. Cheap

B. Frugal

C. Economical

D. Thrifty

Answer: A.

All the answer choices reflect the general meaning of "parsimonious", being careful with money, but only one choice has a negative association. "Frugal", "economical" and "thrifty" are all adjectives with a positive connotation, but "cheap" is usually used as a negative description.

Those were a bit more difficult, but let's try a few more. For the questions below, select the word that LEAST LIKELY means the same as the underlined word.

1. The evidence of the murder was <u>destroyed</u> before the trial.
A. Devastated
B. Obliterated
C. Ruined
D. Incinerated

Answer: D.
While all the answer choices can be used in place of "destroyed", "incinerated" suggests a specific type of damage: destruction by fire. Technically, "incinerated" is a logical answer, but the question isn't asking which choice is not logical. It's asking which choice LEAST likely means the underlined word. This was a tough one, but you should expect to see some questions like this on the exam.

2. While trying to negotiate a peace treaty, one side was being entirely <u>hostile</u> to the other.
A. Belligerent
B. Threatening
C. Averse
D. Combative

Answer: C.
While all the choices are mostly synonyms of "hostile", only one choice excludes a violent implication in its definition. "Averse" means strongly opposed to, but "belligerent", "threatening" and "combative" all suggest harm or death, as does "hostile".

Sometimes, you will need to read a passage before answering the questions. Let's look at some examples of those questions.

"American elections consist of citizens voting for their government representatives. Today, this includes members of the U.S. Senate, but this was not always the case. When the United States Constitution was first written, the people did not get to elect their senators directly. Instead, the senators were appointed by state legislators (who are elected directly by the people in their respective states). This changed in 1913, however, with the 17th Amendment to the Constitution. This amendment allows for the direct election of U.S. Senators by the citizenry. While this election process can make the senators more accountable to their constituents, since the citizens will decide whether a senator will keep his or her job at the next election, it diminishes the voice that state legislatures have in the federal government."

1. The word <u>constituents</u> in the passage most nearly means:
A. Elements
B. Employees
C. Senators
D. Voters

Answer: D.
By reading the choices back into the sentence, you can see that the best synonym for "constituents" is "voters". It is the voters who decide whether or not to reelect the senators. The word "constituents" on its own can have several meanings, including voters, elements, members, components and parts. In the context of this passage, however, "voters" is the best definition.

2. The word <u>amendment</u> in the passage most nearly means:
A. Rule
B. Principle
C. Alteration
D. Truth

Answer: C.

By reading the choices back into the sentence, you can see that the best synonym for "amendment" is "alteration". The passage states how the Constitution originally provided for senator selection. However, the passage explains the difference in process after the 17th amendment. Because "alteration" means "change", it is the best choice.

READING PRACTICE TEST

Passage 1

The United States Treasury operates a subsidiary, the Bureau of Engraving and Printing (BEP), where the nation's supply of paper money is designed and manufactured. But to call American currency "paper" money is a slight misnomer that understates its unperceived complexity and intrinsic technological sophistication. The Treasury goes to extraordinary lengths to safeguard cash from counterfeiters. One of the most fundamental ways is by printing not on paper, per se, but on a proprietary blend of linen and cotton. American money is more akin to fabric than paper, and each bill that is printed is a phenomenal work of art and masterful craftsmanship.

The most frequently counterfeited denominations are the 20-dollar bill, preferred by domestic counterfeiters, and the 100-dollar note, which is the currency of choice for foreign forgers. To make the copying of twenties more difficult, the BEP uses color-shifting ink that changes from copper to green in certain lights. Evidence of this can be seen in the numeral "20" located in the lower right corner on the front of the bills. A portrait watermark – which is a very faint, rather ethereal image of President Jackson – is also juxtaposed into the blank space to the right to his visible and prominent portrait. Additionally, there is a security ribbon, adorned with a flag and the words "USA Twenty," printed on and embedded into the bill. When exposed to ultraviolet light, the thread glows with a greenish hue. Twenties also include an almost subliminal text that reads "USA20;" this micro-printed text is well-camouflaged within the bill. With the use of a magnifying glass, it can be found in the border beneath the Treasurer's signature.

The 100-dollar bill utilizes similar security features. These include color-shifting ink, portrait watermarks, security threads and ribbons, raised printing, and micro-printing. These units of currency, dubbed "Ben Franklins" in honor of the president whose face graces it, also boast what the BEP describes as a 3-D security ribbon. The ribbon has bells and numbers printed on it. When the currency is tilted it appears that the images of bells transform into the numeral 100 and, when tilted side to side, the bells and 100s seem to move in a lateral direction.

Security threads woven into each different denomination have their own respective colors, and each one glows a different color when illuminated with ultraviolet light. Fine engraving or printing patterns appear in various locations on bills too, and many of these patterns are extremely fine. The artists who create them for engraving also incorporate non-linear designs, as the waviness can make it exponentially more difficult to successfully counterfeit the currency. The surface of American currency is also slightly raised, giving it a subtly, but distinct, tactile characteristic.

1. Which of the following conclusions may logically be drawn from the first paragraph of the passage?
   a) Linen and cotton are more expensive printing materials than paper.
   b) The current process of printing money is reflective of decades of modifications.
   c) Counterfeiting of American money is an enormous problem.
   d) The artistry inherent in the making of American money makes it attractive to collectors.

2. What sentence, if added to the end of the passage, would provide the best conclusion to both the paragraph and the passage?
   a) It is clear from all these subtly nuanced features of the various bills that true artistry is at work in their making.
   b) Yet, despite all of these technological innovations, the race to stay ahead of savvy counterfeiters and their constantly changing counterfeiting techniques is a never- ending one.
   c) Due to the complexities involved in the printing of money, these artists are consequently well-paid for their skills.
   d) Thus, many other countries have begun to model their money-printing methods on these effective techniques.

3. The passage is reflective of which of the following types of writing?
   a) Descriptive
   b) Narrative
   c) Expository
   d) Persuasive

4. This passage likely comes from which of the following documents?
   a) A pamphlet for tourists visiting the United States Treasury
   b) A feature news article commemorating the bicentennial of the Bureau of Engraving and Printing
   c) A letter from the US treasury Secretary to the President
   d) A public service message warning citizens about the increased circulation of counterfeit currency

5. Which of the following is an example of a primary source document?
   a) A pamphlet for tourists visiting the United States Treasury
   b) A feature news article commemorating the bicentennial of the Bureau of Engraving and Printing
   c) A letter from the US treasury Secretary to the President
   d) A public service message warning citizens about the increased circulation of counterfeit currency

6. Which of the following describes the word intrinsic as it is used in the first paragraph of the passage?
   a) Amazing
   b) Expensive
   c) Unbelievable
   d) Inherent

Passage 2
In the Middle Ages, merchants an artisans formed groups called "guilds" to protect themselves and their trades. Guilds appeared in the year 1000, and by the twelfth century, analogous trades, like wool, spice, and silk dealers had formed their own guilds.
_____ , towns like Florence, Italy, boasted as many as 50 merchants' guilds. With the advent of guilds, apprenticeship became a complex system. Apprentices were to be taught only certain things and then they were to prove they possessed certain skills, as determined by the guild. Each guild decided the length of time required for an apprentice to work for a master tradesman before being admitted to the trade.

7. The topic sentence of the above passage is
   a) In the Middle Ages, merchants an artisans formed groups called "guilds" to protect themselves and their trades.
   b) Guilds appeared in the year 1000, and by the twelfth century, analogous trades, like wool, spice, and silk dealers had formed their own guilds.
   c) With the advent of guilds, apprenticeship became a complex system.
   d) Apprentices were to be taught only certain things and then they were to prove they possessed certain skills, as determined by the guild.

8. The main idea of the passage is that
   a) wool, spice and silk dealers were all types of merchant trades during the Middle Ages.
   b) Florence, Italy was a great center of commerce during the Middle Ages.
   c) merchant guilds originated in the Middle Ages and became extremely popular, eventually leading to a sophisticated apprenticeship system.
   d) apprenticeships were highly sought after, therefore merchants had many skilled workers to choose from to assist them in their trade.

9. From the content of the passage, it reasonably be inferred that
   a) prior to the inception of guilds, merchants were susceptible to competition from lesser skilled craftsmen peddling inferior products or services.
   b) most merchants were unscrupulous business who often cheated their customers.
   c) it was quite easy to become an apprentice to a highly skilled merchant.
   d) guilds fell out of practice during the Industrial Revolution due to the mechanization of labor.

10. As it is used in the second sentence, "analogous" most nearly means
    a) obsolete
    b) inferior
    c) similar
    d) less popular

11. Which of the following is the best signal word or phrase to fill in the blank above?
    a) Up until that time,
    b) Before that time,
    c) By that time,
    d) After that time,

Passage 3
Certainly we must face this fact: if the American press, as a mass medium, has formed the minds of America, the mass has also formed the medium. There is action, reaction, and interaction going on ceaselessly between the newspaper-buying public and the editors. What is wrong with the American press is what is in part wrong with American society. Is this,_____, to exonerate the American press for its failures to give the American people more tasteful and more illuminating reading matter? Can the American press seek to be excused from responsibility for public lack of information as TV and radio often do, on the grounds that, after all, "we have to give the people what they want or we will go out of business"?
--Clare Boothe Luce

12. What is the primary purpose of this text?
    a) To reveal an innate problem in American society
    b) To criticize the American press for not taking responsibility for their actions
    c) To analyze the complex relationship that exists between the public and the media
    d) To challenge the masses to protest the lack of information disseminated by the media

13. From which of the following is the above paragraph most likely excerpted?
    a) A newspaper editorial letter
    b) A novel about yellow journalism
    c) A diary entry
    d) A speech given at a civil rights protest

14. Which of the following is an example of a primary source document?
    a) A newspaper editorial letter
    b) A novel about yellow journalism
    c) A diary entry
    d) A speech given at a civil rights protest

15. As it is used in sentence 4, "illuminating" most nearly means
    a) intelligent
    b) sophisticated
    c) interesting
    d) enlightening

16. Which of the following is the best signal word or phrase to fill in the blank?
    a) so
    b) however
    c) therefore
    d) yet

17. What is the author's primary attitude towards the American press?
    a) admiration
    b) perplexity
    c) disapproval
    d) ambivalence

18. Which of the following identifies the mode of the passage?
    a) expository
    b) persuasive/argumentative
    c) narrative
    d) descriptive

19. Based on the passage, which of the following can most likely be concluded?
    a) The author has a degree in journalism
    b) The author has worked in the journalism industry
    c) The author is seeking employment at a newspaper
    d) The author is filing a lawsuit against a media outlet

Passage 4
The game today known as "football" in the United States can be traced directly back to the English game of rugby, although there have been many changes to the game. Football was played informally on university fields more than a hundred years ago. In 1840, a yearly series of informal "scrimmages" started at Yale University. It took more than twenty-five years,_____, for the game to become a part of college life. The first formal intercollegiate football game was held between Princeton and Rutgers teams on November 6, 1869 on Rutgers' home field at New Brunswick, New Jersey, and Rutgers won.

20. Which sentence, if added to the end of the paragraph, would provide the best conclusion?
    a) Despite an invitation to join the Ivy League, Rutgers University declined, but later joined the Big Ten Conference instead.
    b) Football was played for decades on school campuses nationwide before the American Professional Football Association was formed in 1920, and then renamed the National Football League (or the NFL) two years later.
    c) Women were never allowed to play football, and that fact remains a controversial policy at many colleges and universities.
    d) Football remains the national pastime, despite rising popularity for the game of soccer, due to increased TV coverage of World Cup matches.

21. Which of the following is the best signal word or phrase to fill in the blank above?
    a) however
    b) still
    c) in addition
    d) alternatively

Passage 5
Modernism is a philosophical movement that arose during the early 20th century. Among the factors that shaped modernism were the development of modern societies based on industry and the rapid growth of cities, followed later by the horror of World War I. Modernism rejected the science-based thinking of the earlier Era of Enlightenment, and many modernists also rejected religion. The poet Ezra Pound's 1934 injunction to "Make it new!" was the touchstone of the movement's approach towards what it saw as the now obsolete culture of the past. A notable characteristic of modernism is self-consciousness and irony concerning established literary and social traditions, which often led to experiments concerned with HOW things were made, not so much with the actual final product. Modernism had a profound impact on numerous aspects of life, and its values and perspectives still influence society in many positive ways today.

22. According to the passage, what is the overarching theme of the modernist movement?
    a) Rejection of the past and outmoded ideas
    b) Appreciation of urban settings over natural settings
    c) A concentration on method over form
    d) A focus on automated industry

23. As it is used in the passage, "touchstone" most nearly means
    a) Challenge
    b) Basis
    c) Fashion
    d) Metaphor

24. Which of the following statements from the passage can be described as an opinion?
   a) Among the factors that shaped modernism were the development of modern societies based on industry and the rapid growth of cities, followed later by the horror of World War I.
   b) The poet Ezra Pound's 1934 injunction to "Make it new!" was the touchstone of the movement's approach towards what it saw as the now obsolete culture of the past.
   c) A notable characteristic of modernism is self-consciousness and irony concerning established literary and social traditions, which often led to experiments concerned with HOW things were made, not so much with the actual final product.
   d) Modernism had a profound impact on numerous aspects of life, and its values and perspectives still influence society in many positive ways today.

Passage 6

The modern Olympics are the leading international sporting event featuring summer and winter sports competitions in which thousands of athletes from around the world participate in a variety of competitions. Held every two years, with the Summer and Winter Games alternating, the games are a modern way to bring nations together,_____ allowing for national pride, and sportsmanship on a global scale. Having withstood the test of time over many centuries, they are the best example of the physical achievements of mankind.

The creation of the modern Games was inspired by the ancient Olympic Games, which were held in Olympia, Greece, from the 8th century BC to the 4th century AD. The Ancient Games events were fewer in number and were examples of very basic traditional forms of competitive athleticism. Many running events were featured, as well as a pentathlon (consisting of a jumping event, discus and javelin throws, a foot race, and wrestling), boxing, wrestling, pankration, and equestrian events. Fast forward to the modern state of this ancient athletic competition, and we see that the Olympic Movement during the 20th and 21st centuries has resulted in several changes to the Games, including the creation of the Winter Olympic Games for ice and winter sports, which for climate reasons, would not have been possible in ancient Greece. The Olympics has also shifted away from pure amateurism to allowing participation of professional athletes, a change which was met with criticism when first introduced, as many felt it detracted from the original spirit and intention of the competition.

Today, over 13,000 athletes compete at the summer and Winter Olympic Games in 33 different sports and nearly 400 events. The first, second, and third-place finishers in each event receive Olympic medals: gold, silver, and bronze, respectively. And every country hopes to be able to go home with many of these medals, as they are truly still a point of pride for each nation to be recognized for some outstanding achievement on the world stage, however briefly.

25. Which of the following is the best signal word or phrase to fill in the blank in the first paragraph?
   a) despite
   b) however
   c) instead of
   d) as well as

26. Which of the following words from the last sentence of paragraph 2 has a negative connotation?
   a) Shifted
   b) Allowing
   c) Change
   d) Detracted

27. Which of the following statements based on the passage would be considered an opinion?
    a) The ancient Olympic games were held in Olympia, Greece.
    b) The Olympic games are the best example of humanity's physical prowess.
    c) When the games were changed from pure amateurism to allowing professional athletes to participate, this change displeased many people.
    d) Today, 33 different sports are represented at the Olympic games.

Passage 7

A day or two later, in the afternoon, I saw myself staring at my fire, at an inn which I had booked on foreseeing that I would spend some weeks in London. I had just come in, and, having decided on a spot for my luggage, sat down to consider my room. It was on the ground floor, and the fading daylight reached it in a sadly broken-down condition. It struck me that the room was stuffy and unsocial, with its moldy smell and its decoration of lithographs and waxy flowers
– it seemed an impersonal black hole in the huge general blackness of the inn itself. The uproar of the neighborhood outside hummed away, and the rattle of a heartless hansom cab passed close to my ears. A sudden horror of the whole place came over me, like a tiger-pounce of homesickness which had been watching its moment. London seemed hideous, vicious, cruel and, above all, overwhelming. Soon, I would have to go out for my dinner, and it appeared to me that I would rather remain dinnerless, would rather even starve, than go forth into the hellish town where a stranger might get trampled to death, and have his carcass thrown into the Thames River.

28. Based on the passage above, the author's attitude toward his experience in London can best be described as:
    a) Awe
    b) Disappointment
    c) Revulsion
    d) Ambivalence

29. Which type of document is this passage likely excerpted from?
    a) A travel guide
    b) A diary entry
    c) A news editorial
    d) An advertisement

30. Which of the following documents would likely NOT be considered a primary source document?
    a) A travel guide
    b) A diary entry
    c) A news editorial
    d) An advertisement

31. Based on the content of the passage, which of the following is a reasonable conclusion?
    a) The author is quite wealthy.
    b) The author has been to London before.
    c) The author is traveling to London based on the recommendation of a friend.
    d) The author will not be traveling to London again.

1.   C. Counterfeiting of American money is an enormous problem.
Rationale: C is the best option as we are told that "The Treasury goes to extraordinary lengths to safeguard cash from counterfeiters."

2.   B. Yet, despite all of these technological innovations, the race to stay ahead of savvy counterfeiters and their constantly changing counterfeiting techniques is a never- ending one.
Rationale: B is the best as the main point of the passage is to emphasize the extent of counterfeiting and detail the technology used to counteract such constantly changing fraudulent activity.

3.   C. Expository
Rationale: C. An expository essay is one in which an idea is investigated and expounded upon, and an argument is set forth presenting evidence concerning that idea in a clear and concise manner. In this case the idea being investigated and expounded upon is anti- counterfeiting techniques.

4.   A. A pamphlet for tourists visiting the United States Treasury
Rationale: A. The style and specific subject matter all indicate that it is most likely from an informational pamphlet written for visitors to the Bureau of Engraving and Printing.

5.   C. A letter from the US treasury Secretary to the President
Rationale: C. A primary source document is one which was created and serves as a first- hand source of information or evidence about a particular time period. Only the personal letter would meet the criteria of a primary source.

6.   D. Inherent
Rationale: D. Technological sophistication is inherent, (or naturally found) in the making of American money, so much so that to call it "paper" does not fully reveal how complex a product it really is.

7.   A. In the Middle Ages, merchants an artisans formed groups called "guilds" to protect themselves and their trades.
Rationale: A. The first sentence is the topic sentence because it introduces the main idea of the paragraph.

8.   C. merchant guilds originated in the Middle Ages and became extremely popular, eventually leading to a sophisticated apprenticeship system.
Rationale: C. The guild system's origins and development is the main idea of the paragraph. The other options are too narrow to constitute a main idea.

9.   A. prior to the inception of guilds, merchants were susceptible to competition from lesser skilled craftsmen peddling inferior products or services.
Rationale: A. It can be inferred that if guilds were instituted, there must have been a need for merchants to safeguard themselves from threats to their livelihood.

10.   C. similar
Rationale: C. The sentence conveys to us that the spice, silk and wool dealers were similar tradesman to that of other merchants who had set up guilds.

11.   C. By that time,

Rationale: C. The passage introduces the inception of guilds and their development over time, chronologically. From the previous sentence, it is clear that guilds grew in popularity over the centuries, until towns like Florence had 50 guilds by the twelfth century. "By that time" most clearly states this increase and development over time.

12.   B. To criticize the American press for not taking responsibility for their actions Rationale: B. Luce is clearly criticizing the press for not taking responsibility to disseminate enlightening information to the public, and instead are blaming the public for not asking for reading matter which is "tasteful and more illuminating".

13.   A. A newspaper editorial letter
Rationale: A. Given the paragraph's opinionated style and serious, critical tone, it most likely excerpted from a longer letter printed in the op/ed section of a newspaper.

14.   C. A diary entry
Rationale: C. The diary entry (which would likely provide firsthand thoughts, feelings and opinions about current life or world events as witnessed by the author) would qualify as a primary source document of evidence or information of a particular time period.

15.   D. enlightening
Rationale: D. Illuminating reading matter is that which would be enlightening and provide necessary information to the public.

16.   C. therefore
Rationale: C. Luce is using a cause and effect argument here, but she is questioning the excuse of the press to not do their job as a result of certain demands of the public, which would "therefore exonerate the American press for its failures to give the American people more tasteful and more illuminating reading matter".

17.   C. disapproval
Rationale: C. Luce clearly disapproves of the press and their practice of serving up a lack of news to the public, "on the grounds that, after all, "[they] have to give the people what they want or [they] will go out of business".

18.   B. persuasive/argumentative
Rationale: B. Luce utilizes several modes of writing here, but overall, she is critical of the American press, and is arguing that they are at fault for not giving the American public useful information or "illuminating reading matter".

19.   B. The author has worked in the journalism industry
Rationale: B. The author clearly has an understanding of the business of the media, as well as its public responsibility to inform citizens, so it can be concluded that she likely has worked in the journalism industry. None of the other statements can reasonably be concluded based on the content of the passage.

20.   B. Football was played for decades on school campuses nationwide before the American Professional Football Association was formed in 1920, and then renamed the National Football League (or the NFL) two years later.
Rationale: B. This statement adds additional information to the paragraph about the progression of the game of football in the US and therefore, appropriately concludes the paragraph. The other statements discuss topics not directly related to football, or add additional information that is slightly off topic.

21.   A. however
Rationale: A. The sentence is explaining that, despite the appearance of football as a sport on some college campuses, and annual scrimmages occurring at Yale, 25 years passed before it became a regular activity in college life. "However" shows this contrast best.

22.   A. Rejection of the past and outmoded ideas
Rationale: A. From the paragraph it is clear that modernism is mainly concerned with rejecting the ideas of the past -- like the science of the enlightenment, and old ideas about religion –and instead focusing on creating what was "New".

23.   B. Basis
Rationale: Pound's suggestion to "Make it new" was the basis, or touchstone of the Modernist movement's outlook and approach to interpreting the world and society.

24.   D. Modernism had a profound impact on numerous aspects of life, and its values and perspectives still influence society in many positive ways today.
Rationale: D. The author's description of Modernism's influence as being "positive" is clearly an opinion about the nature of the influence. The other statements are factually based, providing general information about the Modernist movement.

25.   D. as well as
Rationale: D. This sentence discusses all of the positive benefits that result from the continuation of the Olympic games in the present day, so "as well as" is the correct signal phrase to convey this idea, in a list form.

26.   D. Detracted
Rationale: D. The idea that allowing professional athletes to participate in the games would cause people to believe it "detracted" from the intentions of the original, is a negative notion, as it suggests that this would take away from the games, instead of adding something positive.

27.   B. The Olympic games are the best example of humanity's physical prowess. Rationale: B. This statement is the opinion of the author, as there is no indication that this idea has been tested or proven in any way, but is simply what the author believes or feels.

28.   C. Revulsion
Rationale: C. The author uses words like "moldy smell" and "black hole" to describe his rented room in the inn, and "heartless" and "hideous" to describe the environment of London, adding that he "would rather even starve" than go out to find himself a meal in the "hellish town where a stranger might get trampled to death". These are very strong negative sentiments that clearly indicate his revulsion to the city.

29.   B. A diary entry
Rationale: B. The personal and frank tone that the author uses to describe his hotel room and his private fears about going out into the city of London for dinner suggest that this would have been written in a journal or diary.

30.   D. An advertisement
Rationale: D. A primary source document is one which was created from first-hand experience under a period of study of a particular event, moment in time, situation etc. A travel guide, diary entry and news editorial could all potentially be primary sources which chronicle one of the aforementioned. The only one that would likely NOT qualify as a primary source is the advertisement, as usually advertisements are meant to persuade

one to engage in an experience, purchase a product or the like, and are often not completely based in personal experience and may not even be factual.

31.   D. The author will not be traveling to London again.
Rationale: D. It is clear that the author is unhappy with his lodging and finds London a generally disagreeable place, so it is likely that he would not travel to London again. The other statements are not reasonable conclusions which can be made from the content of the passage.

MATHEMATICS PRACTICE TEST

1. Change to an improper fraction: 2 1/3
    a) 5/3
    b) 3/7
    c) 7/3
    d) 8/3

2. Which of the following is equivalent to 60% of 90?
    a) 0.6 x 90
    b) 90 ÷ 0.6
    c) 3/5
    d) 2/3

3. Convert the improper fraction 17/6 to a mixed number.
    a) $1\frac{7}{6}$
    b) $2\frac{5}{6}$
    c) 6/17
    d) $2\frac{7}{6}$

4. The decimal value of 7/11 is _____?
    a) 1.57
    b) 0.70
    c) 0.6363...
    d) 0.77

5. The decimal value of 5/8 is _____?
    a) 0.625
    b) 0.650
    c) 0.635
    d) 0.580

6. The fractional value of 0.5625 is ___ ?
    a) 7/15
    b) 11/23
    c) 5/8
    d) 9/16

7. The fractional value of 0.3125 is_____?
    a) 5/16
    b) 4/24
    c) 6/19
    d) 9/25

8. What is the value of this expression if a = 10 and b = –4: $\sqrt{b^2 - 2 \times a}$

    a) 6
    b) 7
    c) 8
    d) 9

9. What is the greatest common factor of 48 and 64?

    a) 4
    b) 8
    c) 16
    d) 32

10. Solve for x: $X = \frac{3}{4} \times \frac{7}{8}$

    a) 7/8
    b) 9/8
    c) 10/12
    d) 21/32

11. Find the value of $a^2 + 6b$ when a = 3 and b = 0.5.

    a) 12
    b) 6
    c) 9
    d) 15

12. What is the least common multiple of 8 and 10?

    a) 80
    b) 40
    c) 18
    d) 72

13. What is the sum of 1/3 and 3/8?

    a) 3/24
    b) 4/11
    c) 17/24
    d) 15/16

14. Solve this equation: $-9 \times -9 = $ ___?

    a) 18
    b) 0
    c) 81
    d) −81

15. Which of the following is between 2/3 and 3/4?
    a) 3/5
    b) 4/5
    c) 7/10
    d) 5/8

16. Which digit is in the thousandths place in the number: 1,234.567
    a) 1
    b) 2
    c) 6
    d) 7

17. Which of these numbers is largest?
    a) 5/8
    b) 3/5
    c) 2/3
    d) 0.72

18. Which of these numbers is largest?
    a) −345
    b) 42
    c) −17
    d) 3^4

19. Find 4 numbers between 4.857 and 4.858
    a) 4.8573, 4.85735, 4.85787, 4.8598
    b) 4.857, 4.8573, 4.8578, 4.8579,
    c) 4.8571, 4.8573, 4.8578, 4.8579
    d) 4.8572, 4.8537, 4.8578, 4.8579

20. Which number is between 4 and 5?
    a) 11/3
    b) 21/4
    c) 31/6
    d) 23/5

21. Which number is not between 7 and 9?
    a) 34/5
    b) 29/4
    c) 49/6
    d) 25/3

22. If $\frac{4}{9}x - 3 = 1$, what is the value of x?
    a) 9
    b) 8
    c) 7
    d) −4½

23. What value of q is a solution to this equation: 130 = q(−13)
    a) 10
    b) −10
    c) 1
    d) 10^2

24. Solve this equation: x = −12 ÷ −3
    a) x = −4
    b) x = −15
    c) x = 9
    d) x = 4

25. Solve for r in the equation p = 2r + 3
    a) r = 2p − 3
    b) r = p + 6
    c) r = (p - 3) / 2
    d) r = p − 3/2

26. Solve this equation: x = 8 − (−3)
    a) x = 5
    b) x = −5
    c) x = 11
    d) x = −11

27. Evaluate the expression $7x^2 + 9x - 18$ for x = 7
    a) 516
    b) 424
    c) 388
    d) 255

28. Evaluate the expression $x^2 + 7x - 18$ for x = 5
    a) 56
    b) 42
    c) 38
    d) 25

29. Evaluate the expression $7x^2 + 63x$ for x = 27
    a) 5603
    b) 4278
    c) 6804
    d) 6525

30. Sam worked 40 hours at d dollars per hour and received a bonus of $50. His total earnings were $530. What was his hourly wage?
    a) $18
    b) $16
    c) $14
    d) $12

31. The variable X is a positive integer. Dividing X by a positive number less than 1 will yield
    a) a number greater than X
    b) a number less than X
    c) a negative number
    d) an irrational number

32. Amanda makes $14 an hour as a bank teller and Oscar makes $24 dollars an hour as an auto mechanic. Both work eight hours a day, five days a week. Which of these equations can be used to calculate how much they make together in a five-day week?
    a) $(14 + 24) \bullet 8 \bullet 5$
    b) $14 \bullet 24 \bullet 8 \bullet 5$
    c) $(14 + 24)(8 + 5)$
    d) $14 + 24 \bullet 8 \bullet 5$

33. Seven added to four-fifths of a number equals fifteen. What is the number?
    a) 10
    b) 15
    c) 20
    d) 25

34. If the sum of two numbers is 360 and their ratio is 7:3, what is the smaller number?
    a) 72
    b) 105
    c) 98
    d) 108

35. Jean buys a textbook, a flash drive, a printer cartridge, and a ream of paper. The flash drive costs three times as much as the ream of paper. The textbook costs three times as much as the flash drive. The printer cartridge costs twice as much as the textbook. The ream of paper costs $10. How much does Jean spend altogether?
    a) $250
    b) $480
    c) $310
    d) $180

36. The area of a triangle equals one-half the base times the height. Which of the following is the correct way to calculate the area of a triangle that has a base of 6 and a height of 9?
    a) $(6 + 9)/2$
    b) $\frac{1}{2}(6 + 9)$
    c) $2(6 \times 9)$
    d) $(6)(9)/2$

37. Calculate the value of this expression: $2 + 6 \bullet 3 \bullet (3 \bullet 4)^2 + 1$
    a) 2,595
    b) 5,185
    c) 3,456
    d) 6,464

38. A rectangle of length and width 3x and x has an area of $3x^2$. Write the area polynomial when the length is increased by 5 units and the width is decreased by 3 units. $(3x+5)(x-3)$
    a) $3x^2 + 14x - 15$
    b) $3x^2 - 4x - 15$
    c) $3x^2 - 5x + 15$
    d) $3x^2 + 4x - 15$

39. A triangle of base and height 4x and 7x has an area of $14x^2$, which is equal ½ times the base times the height. Write the area polynomial when the base is increased by 2 units and the height is increased by 3 units. $\frac{1}{2}(4x+2)(7x+3)$
    a) $14x^2 + 14x + 6$
    b) $14x^2 + 14x + 3$
    c) $14x^2 + 13x + 3$
    d) $14x^2 + 28x + 3$

40. Momentum is defined as the product of mass times velocity. If your 1,250 kg car is travelling at 55 km/hr, what is the value of the momentum?
    a) 68,750 kg m/s
    b) 19,098 kg m/s
    c) 9,549 kg m/s
    d) 145,882 kg m/s

41. In her retirement accounts, Janet has invested $40,000 in stocks and $65,000 in bonds. If she wants to rebalance her accounts so that 70% of her investments are in stocks, how much will she have to move?
    a) $33,500
    b) $35,000
    c) $37,500
    d) $40,000

42. Brian pays 15% of his gross salary in taxes. If he pays $7,800 in taxes, what is his gross salary?
    a) $52,000
    b) $48,000
    c) $49,000
    d) $56,000

43. In a high school French class, 45% of the students are sophomores, and there are 9 sophomores in the class. How many students are there in the class?
    a) 16
    b) 18
    c) 20
    d) 22

44. Marisol's score on a standardized test was ranked in the 78th percentile. If 660 students took the test, approximately how many students scored lower than Marisol?
    a) 582
    b) 515
    c) 612
    d) 486

45. The population of Mariposa County in 2015 was 90% of its population in 2010. The population in 2010 was 145,000. What was the population in 2010?
    a) 160,000
    b) 142,000
    c) 120,500
    d) 130,500

46. Alicia must have a score of 75% to pass a test of 80 questions. What is the greatest number of question she can miss and still pass the test?
    a) 20
    b) 25
    c) 60
    d) 15

47. A cell phone on sale at 30% off costs $210. What was the original price of the phone?
    a) $240
    b) $273
    c) $300
    d) $320

48. In the graduating class at Emerson High School, 52% of the students are girls and 48% are boys. There are 350 students in the class. Among the girls, 98 plan to go to college. How many girls do not plan to go to college?
    a) 84
    b) 48
    c) 66
    d) 72

49. The number of students enrolled at Two Rivers Community College increased from 3,450 in 2010 to 3,864 in 2015. What was the percent increase?
    a) 9%
    b) 17%
    c) 12%
    d) 6%

50. Produce is usually priced to the nearest pound. A scale for weighing produce has numerical values for pounds and ounces. Which of the following weights would you expect to be priced for 15 pounds?
    a) 15 pounds 14 ounces
    b) 15 pounds 10 ounces
    c) 14 pounds 4 ounces
    d) 14 pounds 14 ounces

51. Which number is rounded to the nearest ten-thousandth?
    a) 7,510,000
    b) 7,515,000
    c) 7,514,635.8239
    d) 7,514,635.824

52. Measuring devices determine the precision of our scientific measurements. A graduated cylinder is used that has a maximum of 10 cc's but has ten increments in between each whole number of cc's. Which answer is a correct representation of a volume measurement with this cylinder?
    a) 7 cc's
    b) 7.1 cc's
    c) 7.15 cc's
    d) 7.514 cc's

53. If a man can unload about 50 pounds in a time of 15 minutes, estimate the time and labor force to unload 2.5 tons of 50 pound blocks from a truck working 8 hours per day.
    a) 1 man for 10 days
    b) 2 men for 1 day
    c) 4 men for 1 day
    d) 5 men for 5 days

54. In rush hour, you can usually commute 18 miles to work in 45 minutes. If you believe that you can travel an average of 5 miles per hour faster in the early morning, how much time would you estimate for the early commute to work?
    a) 50 minutes
    b) 40 minutes
    c) 30 minutes
    d) 20 minutes

55. You are taking a test and you are allowed to work a class period of 45 minutes. 20 problems are multiple choice and 30 of the problems are true / false. If they have equal value, how much time would you estimate for each type of problem if you believe you are twice as fast at multiple choice problems?
    a) 90 seconds per m/c; 45 seconds per t/f
    b) 60 seconds per m/c; 30 seconds per t/f
    c) 70 seconds per m/c; 35 seconds per t/f
    d) 80 seconds per m/c; 40 seconds per t/f

56. Your interview is scheduled for 8:00 in the morning and you need to allow 20 minutes for your trip to the interview. You oversleep and leave 10 minutes late. How fast will you travel to get there on time?
    a) half as fast
    b) twice as fast
    c) three times as fast
    d) four times as fast

57. A square meter is a square with sides that are one meter in length. If a meter is 1000 millimeters, how many square millimeters are in a square meter.
    a) 100
    b) 1000
    c) 10,000
    d) 1,000,000

58. In four years, Tom will be twice as old as Serena was three years ago. Tom is three years younger than Serena. How old are Tom and Serena?
    a) Serena is 28, Tom is 25
    b) Serena is 7, Tom is 4
    c) Serena is 18, Tom is 15
    d) Serena is 21, Tom is 18

59. Amy drives her car until the gas gauge is down to 1/8 full. Then she fills the tank by adding 14 gallons. What is the capacity of the gas tank?
    a) 16 gallons
    b) 18 gallons
    c) 20 gallons
    d) 22 gallons

60. Two rectangles are proportional; that is, the ratio of length to width is the same for both rectangles. The smaller rectangle has a length of 8 inches and a width of 3 inches. The large rectangle has a length of 12 inches. What is the width of the larger rectangle?
    a) 4 inches
    b) 4.5 inches
    c) 6 inches
    d) 8.5inches

61. The perimeter of a rectangle is 24 inches, and the ratio of the length to the width is 2:1. What is the area of the rectangle?
    a) 60 square inches
    b) 18 square inches
    c) 32 square inches
    d) 48 square inches

62. The tree near your house casts a shadow of 27 feet. At the same time of day, your house which is 40 feet tall at the peak of the roof casts a shadow of 68 feet. The tree height must be   .
    a) 100 feet tall
    b) 16 feet tall
    c) 45 feet tall
    d) 20 feet tall

63. Five students volunteered to paint a room in the community center. If the painters estimated they would finish the job with 2 ½ man-days, how long should it take the students?
    a) Two days
    b) One day
    c) Half a day
    d) One quarter of a day

64. Your car can maintain 23 miles per gallon on the freeway. If you are travelling to Oklahoma City, which is about 500 miles north, how much gasoline will be required for the trip?
    a) 37 gallons
    b) 53 gallons
    c) 105 gallons
    d) 22 gallons

65. On your trip, you find that it takes you 8.5 hours to get to Oklahoma City which is 500 miles north. How much more time should it take to get to Wichita, Kansas (640 miles total)
    a) 7 hours
    b) 5 hours
    c) 11 hours
    d) 2.5 hours

66. Eight machines can produce 96 parts per minute. How many parts could 12 identical machines produce in 3 minutes?
    a) 144
    b) 288
    c) 256
    d) 432

67. At Pleasantville College, the ratio of female to male students is exactly 5 to 4. Which of the following could be the number of students at the college?
    a) 8,200
    b) 2,955
    c) 3,500
    d) 3,105

68. When you add two numbers, the sum is 480. The ratio of the two numbers is 5:1, what is the smaller number?
    a) 60
    b) 70
    c) 72
    d) 80

69. Four friends plan to share the cost of a retirement gift equally. If one person drops out of the arrangement, the cost per person for the other three would increase by $12. What is the cost of the gift?
    a) $144
    b) $136
    c) $180
    d) $152

70. It took Charles four days to write a history paper. He wrote 5 pages on the first day, 4 pages on the second day, and 8 pages on the third day. If Charles wrote an average of 7 pages per day, how many pages did he write on the fourth day?
    a) 11
    b) 8
    c) 12
    d) 9

71. How much weight must you lose each week if you are determined to lose 63 pounds in 6 months?
    a) 0.4 lbs. per week
    b) 2.4 lbs. per week
    c) 1.4 lbs. per week
    d) 0.64 lbs. per week

72. How much money must you save each week if you are determined to have
$375 in the next 7 months?
    a) $12.38 per week
    b) $11.50 per week
    c) $13.75 per week
    d) $7. 75 per week

73. If you think that you can save $450 out of your monthly pay check, how long will it take for you to save
    $3995 for your car down payment?
    a) 8 months
    b) 10 months
    c) 9 weeks
    d) 9 months

74. You have read that your car is losing value at a rate of $55 per month. You are asking $1790 and a
    potential buyer has offered you $1450. How many months will it take before you can accept that offer?
    a) 8 months
    b) 6 months
    c) 15 weeks
    d) 4 months

75. The product of two numbers is 6 more than the sum of the two numbers. Which of these equations
    describes this relationship?
    a) $X \bullet Y + 6 = X + Y$
    b) $X \bullet Y = X + Y + 6$
    c) $X + Y = X + Y - 6$
    d) $X \bullet Y = X + Y - 6$

76. There are 3 more men than women on the board of directors of the Big Box Retail Company. There are 13
    members of the board. How many are women?
    a) 3
    b) 4
    c) 5
    d) 6

77. The average of 25, 35, and 120 is 10 more than the average of 40, 45, and which value?
    a) 60
    b) 65
    c) 70
    d) 76

78. What is the smallest positive integer that is evenly divisible by 5 and 7 and leaves a remainder of 4 when divided by 6?
    a) 35
    b) 70
    c) 105
    d) 140

79. The ratio of female to male nurses in a hospital is 9:1. If there are 144 female nurses, how many male nurses are there?
    a) 12
    b) 14
    c) 16
    d) 18

80. Of the patients admitted to an ER over a one-week period, 14 had heart attacks, 15 had workplace injuries, 24 were injured in auto accidents, 12 had respiratory problems, 21 were injured in their homes, and 34 had other problems. What percent of patients had respiratory problems?
    a) 10%
    b) 12%
    c) 15%
    d) 18%

81. Alan commutes 18 miles to work. Bob's commute is 4 miles shorter. Ted's commute is 6 miles shorter than Bob's. Rebecca's commute is shorter than Alan's but longer than Bob's. Which of the following could be the length of Rebecca's commute?
    a) 12 miles
    b) 14 miles
    c) 15 miles
    d) 18 miles

82. At a lunch cart there are 2 orders of diet soda for every 5 orders of regular soda. If the owner of the lunch cart sells 112 sodas a day, how many are diet and how many are regular?
    a) 28 diet, 84 regular
    b) 32 diet, 80 regular
    c) 34 diet, 82 regular
    d) 36 diet, 84 regular

83. The three teams with the best records in the division are the Bulldogs, the Rangers, and the Statesmen. The Bulldogs have won nine games and lost three. The Rangers have won ten games and lost two. The Statesmen have also won ten games and lost two. Each team has one game left before the playoffs. The Bulldogs will be playing the Black Sox, and the Rangers will be playing the Statesmen. The team with the best record will win a spot in the playoffs. Which of the following statements is true?
    a) The Statesmen will definitely be in the playoffs.
    b) The Bulldogs will definitely not be in the playoffs.
    c) The Rangers will definitely not be in the playoffs.
    d) The Statesmen will definitely not be in the playoffs.

84. At Pleasantville College, the ratio of female to male students is exactly 5 to 4. Which of the following could be the number of students at the college?
    a) 8,200
    b) 2,955
    c) 3,500
    d) 3,105

85. Which equation is shown on this graph?

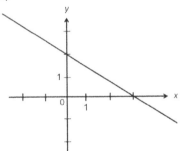

    a) y = 2x + 1
    b) y = −2/3x + 2
    c) y = −3x + 1
    d) y = 3x + 2

86. If the y-intercept of the line on this graph was reduced by 1, what would be the slope of the line?

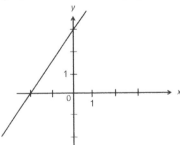

    a) −1
    b) −2
    c) 2
    d) 1

87. Each figure (ß) is valued at $450 . Which of the following is valued closest to $6,500?
    a) ß/2
    b) ß ß ß ß ß ß ß ß ß
    c) ß ß ß ß ß ß ß ß ß ß ß ß ß ß ß/2
    d) ß ß ß ß ß

88. Kevin has his glucose levels checked monthly. These are the results:

January	February	March	April	May	June	July
98	102	88	86	110	92	90

In which month was his glucose level equal to the median level for these seven months?
    a) January
    b) March
    c) April
    d) June

89. The average weight of five friends (Al, Bob, Carl, Dave, and Ed) is 180 pounds. Al weighs 202 pounds, Bob weighs 166 pounds, Carl weighs 190 pounds, and Dave weighs 192 pounds. How much does Ed weigh?
    a) 180 pounds
    b) 172 pounds
    c) 186 pounds
    d) 150 pounds

90. What is the mode in this set of numbers: 4, 5, 4, 8, 10, 4, 6, 7
    a) 6
    b) 4
    c) 8
    d) 7

91. Find the median in this series of numbers: 80, 78, 73, 69, 100.
    a) 69
    b) 73
    c) 78
    d) 80

92. Your scholarship requires a 93% average in your Medical Terminology class. Your grades so far are in this class are 88, 90, 95, 92, 87, 89, 90, 95. With two grades left, what average do you need to have for those two grades to maintain your scholarship?
    a) 97
    b) 99
    c) 101
    d) 102

93. The x/y values for your data look like the following table:

X:	3	5	7	9	11	13	15	17
Y :	22	19	16	13	10	7	4	1

The y-intercept is defined as the y value when x = 0. The y-intercept for the data table in this problem is:
a) 8
b) 19.7
c) 25
d) 26.5

94. Which of the following represents the relationship between x and y in this table?

X	Y
0	7
3	13
5	17
7	21
8	23

a) $y = x + 7$
b) $y = 4x + 1$
c) $y = 2x + 10$
d) $y = 2x + 7$

95. If a patient's weight is recorded each day for a two-week period, a graph of this data would most likely be presented with:
a) y axis with height and x axis with date
b) y axis with weight and x axis with time
c) y axis with dates and x axis with weight
d) y axis with weight and x axis with date

96. The weather channel says that the temperature will be 45 degrees on Monday and increasing 5 degrees each day for the Tuesday through Sunday. With this description, which best describes the dependent and independent variables?
a) The day depends on the temperature
b) Days are the independent variable
c) Temperature is the independent variable
d) There is no correlation between day and temperature

97. A critical care patient has lost 15 pounds during the hospital stay. In terms of the mathematical model of this data, it is labelled as a(n)
a) positive covariation
b) negative covariation
c) independent variable covariation
d) random covariation

98. A rectangle has a length of 8 and a width of 6. What would be the side of a square with the same perimeter?
    a) 5
    b) 6
    c) 7
    d) 8

99. Which of the following can be the lengths of the sides of a triangle?
    a) 1,2,4
    b) 2,4,8
    c) 2,3,4
    d) 4,5,9

100. A square 8 inches on a side is cut into smaller squares 1 inch on a side. How many of the smaller squares can be made?
    a) 8
    b) 16
    c) 24
    d) 64

101. What is the perimeter of this figure?

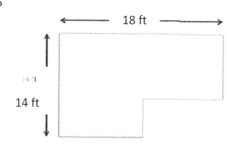

    a) 64 ft.
    b) 72 ft.
    c) 84 ft.
    d) 96 ft.

102. If the radius of the circle in this diagram is 4 inches, what is the perimeter of the square?

    a) 24 inches
    b) 32 inches
    c) 64 inches
    d) 96 inches

103. A rectangle's length is three times its width. The area of the rectangle is 48 square feet. How long are the sides?
    a) length = 12, width = 4
    b) length = 15, width = 5
    c) length = 18, width = 6
    d) length = 24, width = 8

104. Danvers is 8 miles due south of Carson and 6 miles due west of Baines. If a driver could drive in a straight line from Carson to Baines, how long would the trip be?
    a) 8 miles
    b) 10 miles
    c) 12 miles
    d) 14 miles

105. Carmen has a box that is 18 inches long, 12 inches wide, and 14 inches high. What is the volume of the box?
    a) 44 cubic inches
    b) 3,024 cubic inches
    c) 216 cubic inches
    d) 168 cubic inches

106. Which of the following is equal to 0.0065?
    a) 6.5×10^{-2}
    b) 6.5×10^{-3}
    c) 6.5×10^{-4}
    d) 6.5×10^{-5}

107. If one inch is equal to 25.4 millimeters, how many millimeters are in a 20 foot long steel beam?
    a) 6506
    b) 6906
    c) 6609
    d) 6096

108. Medical doses are often measured in cubic centimeters or cc's. A rectangular volume that has a volume of 100 cc's and a square base with 4 inches on each side must must be how tall?
    a) 9.7 millimeters
    b) 6.5 centimeters
    c) 103 centimeters
    d) 10.3 millimeters

109. Small motorcycles often have a displacement of 100 cc's or less. This represents ___ cubic inches?
    a) 61 cubic inches
    b) 15.5 cubic inches
    c) 6.1 cubic inches
    d) 39.4 cubic inches

110. A medical dose is listed as 25 milligrams for each capsule. If there are thirty capsules in the bottle. How many kilograms of the drug are in the bottle?
    a) 0.00075 kg
    b) 750 g
    c) 250 g
    d) 0.00050 kg

<u>1 – C. 7/3</u>
Rationale: An improper fraction is a fraction whose numerator is greater than its denominator. To change a mixed number to an improper fraction, multiply the whole number (2) times the denominator (3) and add the result to the numerator. Answer C is the correct choice.

<u>2 – A. 0.6 x 90</u>
Rationale: To find 60% of 90, first convert 60% to a decimal by moving the decimal point two places to the left. Then multiply this decimal, 0.6, times 90. Answer A is the correct choice.

<u>3 – B. 2 5/6</u>
Rationale: To convert an improper fraction to a mixed number, divide the numerator by the denominator. In this case, you get 2 with a remainder of 5. 2 becomes the whole number and the remainder is the numerator. Answer B is the correct choice.

<u>4 – C. 0.6363…</u>
Rationale – The ratio 7/11 implies division, so the decimal value can be determined by the long division problem of 7 divided by11. The long division results in the repeating decimal 0.6363… There may be a simpler method to find this decimal. The ratio 7/11 is the product of 7 times 1/11. The ratio 1/11 is the repeating decimal 0.0909… so multiplying that decimal by 7 is 0.6363… provides the same answer. If it seems like the same amount of effort, remember that every fraction with 11 in the denominator can be determined in the same way. Answer C is the correct choice.

<u>5 – A. 0.625</u>
Rationale – The ratio implies division, so 5/8 can be determined by the long division problem of 5 divided by 8. The long division results in the decimal 0.625. There is a simpler method to find this decimal. The ratio 5/8 is the product of 5 times 1/8. The ratio 1/8 is the decimal 0.125 so multiplying that decimal by 5 is 0.625, which is the same answer. If it seems like the same amount of effort, remember that every fraction with 8 in the denominator can be determined in the same way. Answer A is the correct choice.

<u>6 – D. 9/16</u>
Rationale – The numerator in the correct ratio will be equal to the given decimal times the correct denominator. It is simply a result of cross multiplying. But first, these problems can be greatly simplified if we eliminate incorrect answers.

For example, answers A and B can both be eliminated because they are both less than 0.5 or ½. If you can't see that, then multiply .5 times 15 and .5 times 23. In answer A, .5 times 15 is 7.5 so 7/15 is less than the fractional value of 0.5625. In B, .5 times 23 is 11.5 so 11/23 is less than the fractional value of 0.5625.

Now, evaluating fractional answers this way, you may look at answer C and realize that since 0.6 times 8 equals 4.8. Since 4.8 is less than the numerator and 0.6 is larger than the given decimal value, C can be eliminated. Answer D is the correct choice.

<u>7 – A. 5/16</u>
Rationale – The numerator in the correct ratio will be equal to the given decimal times the correct denominator. It is simply a result of cross multiplying. But first, the problem can be simplified if we eliminate impossible answers.

For example, answer B can be eliminated because it simplifies to 1/6 which is much less than 0.3125. If you can't see that, then divide 1 by 6 which becomes 0.167.

For answer D, the ratio 9/25 is a simplified form of 36/100 or 0.36. 0.36 is greater than 0.3125, so answer D can be eliminated.

Now, evaluating fractional answers this way, you may eliminate answer C for a very simple reason. 19 times 0.3125 will always leave a value of 5 in the ten-thousandths place because 19 times 5 equals 95. That means the product can never be the whole number 6, so answer C can be eliminated.

The correct answer is D because you have logically eliminated all the other possible choices.

8 – A. 6
Rationale: If a = 10, then 2a = 20. Now compute the value of b2
$b^2 = (b) \bullet (b)$
$b^2 = (-4) \bullet (-4)$
$b^2 = 16$

So now you have: 16 + 20 or 36

The square root of 36 is 6. Answer A is the correct choice

9 – C. 16
Rationale: The greatest common factor of two numbers is the largest number that can be divided evenly into both numbers. The simplest way to answer this question is to start with the largest answer (32) and see if it can be divided evenly into 48 and 64. It can't. Now try the next largest answer (16), and you see that it can be divided evenly into 48 and 64. 16 is the correct answer. The other answers are also factors but the largest of them is 16. Answer C is the correct choice

10 – D. 21/32
Rationale: To multiply fractions, multiply the numerators and the denominators. In this case, multiply 3 times 7 and 4 times 8. The answer is 21/32. Answer D is the correct choice.

11 – A. 12
Rationale: Replace the letters with the numbers they represent and then perform the necessary operations.

$3^2 + 6(0.5)$

$9 + 3 = 12$

Answer A is the correct choice.

12 – B. 40
Rationale: The least common multiple is used when finding the lowest common denominator. The least common multiple is the lowest number that can be divided evenly by both of the other numbers.

Here is a simple method to find the least common multiple of 8 and 10. Write 8 on the left side of your paper. Then add 8 and write the result. Then add another 8 to that number and write the result. Keep going until you have a list that looks something like this:
8 16 24 32 40...

This is a partial list of multiples of 8. (If you remember your multiplication tables, these numbers are the column or row that go with 8.)

Now do the same thing with 10.

10 20 30 40…
This is the partial list of multiples of 10.

Eventually, the numbers will be found in both rows. That smallest common number is the least common multiple. There will always be more multiples that are common to both rows, but the smallest number is the least common multiple.

Answer B is the correct choice

13 – C. 17/24
Rationale: To add 1/3 and 3/8, you must find a common denominator. The simplest way to do this is to multiply the denominators: 3 x 8 = 24. So 24 is a common denominator. (This method will not always give you the lowest common denominator, but in this case it does.)

Once you have found a common denominator, you need to convert both fractions in the problem to equivalent fractions that have that same denominator. To do this, multiply each fraction by an equivalent of 1.

1/3 ● 8/8 = (8●1) / (8●3) or 8/24

3/8 ● 3/3 = (3●3) / (8●3) or 9/24.
8/24 + 9/24 = 17/24

Adding 8/24 and 9/24 is the solution to the problem. Answer C is the correct choice.

14 – C. 81
Rationale: When two numbers with the same sign (both positive or both negative) are multiplied, the answer is a positive number. When two numbers with different signs (one positive and the other negative) are multiplied, the answer is negative. Answer C is the correct choice.

15 – C. 7/10
Rationale: The simplest way to solve this problem is to convert the fractions to decimals. You do this by dividing the numerators by the denominators.

2/3 = 0.67 and 3/4 = 0.75, so the correct answer is a decimal that falls between these two numbers.

3/5 = 0.6 (too small) 4/5 = 0.8 (too large)
7/10 = 0.7 (correct choice between 0.67 and 0.75 5/8 = 0.625 (too small)

Answer C is the correct choice

16 – D. 7
Rationale: In this number:
1 is in the thousands place. 2 is in the hundreds place. 3 is in the tens place.
4 is in the ones place 5 is in the tenths place.

6 is in the hundredths place. 7 is in the thousandths place.

Answer D is the correct choice.

17 – D. 0.72
Rationale: The simplest way to answer this question is to convert the fractions to decimals. To convert a fraction to a decimal, divide the numerator (the top number) by the denominator (the bottom number).
5/8 = 0.625
3/5 = 0.6
2/3 = 0.67

So the largest number is 0.72. Answer D is the correct choice.

18 – D. 3^4
Rationale: All positive numbers are larger than the negative numbers, so the possible answers are 42 or 3^4. 3^4 equals 81 (3 • 3 • 3 • 3). Answer D is the correct choice.

19 – C. 4.8571, 4.8573, 4.8578, 4.8579
Rationale: The numbers 4.857 and 4.858 have an unlimited set of numbers between them and the simplest method is to start with another number after the last digit of 4.857. Therefore 4.8571 and 4.8572 are both greater than 4.857 and less than 4.858. Choices A, B, and D, include numbers that are equal to or greater than the larger of the two or less than the two numbers. Only C has all numbers between. Answer C is the correct choice

20 – D. 23/5
Rationale: The numbers 4 and 5 can be multiplied by the denominators in the answer set to see which answers are correct. Only D is correct because 20/5 and 25/5 are the numbers that are less than and greater than the answer 23/5. Answer D is the correct choice.

21 – A. 34/5
Rationale: The numbers 7 and 9 can be multiplied by the denominators in the answer set to see which answers are correct. A is correct because 34/5 is less than 35/5 and 45/5, so it can't be in between. Answer A is the correct choice.

22 – A. 9
Rationale: Begin by subtracting −3 from both sides of the equation. (This is the same as adding +3). Then:

$$\frac{4}{9}x = 4$$

Now to isolate X on one side of the equation, divide both sides by 4/9. (To divide by a fraction, invert the fraction and multiply).

$$\frac{9}{4} * \frac{4}{9}X = \frac{4}{1} * \frac{9}{4}$$

You are left with $x = \frac{36}{4} = 9$. Answer A is the correct choice.

23 – B. −10
Rationale: To find the value of q, divide both sides of the equation by −13. When a positive number is divided by a negative number, the answer is negative. Answer B is the correct choice.

<u>24 – D. x = 4</u>
Rationale: When you multiply or divide numbers that have the same sign (both positive or both negative), the answer will be positive. When you multiply or divide numbers that have different signs (one positive and the other negative), the answer will be negative. In this case, both numbers have the same sign. Divide as you normally would and remember that the answer will be a positive number. Answer D is the correct choice.

<u>25 – C. r = (p - 3) / 2</u>
Rationale: Begin by subtracting 3 from both sides of the equation. You get:

p – 3 = 2r

Now to isolate r on one side of the equation, divide both sides of the equation by 2. You get:
r = (p-3) / 2

Answer C is the correct choice

<u>26 – C. x = 11</u>
Rationale: Subtracting a negative number is the same as adding a positive number. So 8 – (–3) is the same as 8 + 3 or 11. Answer C is the correct choice.

<u>27 – C. 388</u>
Rationale – The value can be expanded as 7 x 49 added to 9 x 7 with 18 subtracted from the total. That becomes 343 + 63 -18 with the answer equal to 388. Answer C is the correct choice.

<u>28 – B. 42</u>
Rationale – The value can be expanded as 25 added to 5 x 7 with 18 subtracted from the total. That becomes 25 + 35 -18 with the answer equal to 42. There is another simple way to evaluate this expression. The expression can be rewritten as the product of two expressions (x+9)(x-2). If we substitute 5 for x then this product becomes 14 x 3 which is also 42. Answer B is the correct choice.

<u>29 – C. 6804</u>
Rationale – The simplest way to evaluate this expression is to rewrite it as the product of two expressions. Factoring common factors out the given expression becomes 7x(x + 9). "7x" becomes 189 and x+9 becomes 36. The product of 189 and 36 becomes 6804. In the interest of eliminating incorrect answers, the product of the values in the "ones" column is 6x9 which is 54. The correct answer must end in 4 so the correct answer must be C. Answer C is the correct choice.

<u>30 – D. $12</u>
Rationale: Use the information given to write an equation: 530 = 40d + 50

When you subtract 50 from both sides of the equation, you get: 480 = 40d

Divide both sides of the equation by 40.

12 = d, Sam's hourly wage Answer D is the correct choice.

31 – A. a number greater than X

Rationale: When a positive number is divided by a positive number less than 1, the quotient will always be larger than the number being divided. For example, 5 ÷ 0.5 = 10. If we solve this as a fraction, 5÷ (1/2) is the same as 5 x (2/1) or 10 since dividing by a fraction is the same as multiplying by the reciprocal. Answer A is the correct choice.

32 – A. (14 + 24) • 8 • 5

Rationale: In the correct answer, (14 + 24) • 8 • 5, the hourly wages of Amanda and Oscar are first combined, and the total amount is multiplied by 8 hours in a day and five days in a week. One of the other choices, 14 + 24 • 8 • 5, looks similar to this, but it is incorrect because the hourly wages must be combined before they can be multiplied by 8 and 5. Answer A is the correct choice

33 – A. 10

 Rationale: Use the facts you are given to write an equation:

7 + 4/5n = 15

First subtract 7 from both side of the equation. You get:

4/5n = 8

Now divide both sides of the equation by 4/5. To divide by a fraction, invert the fraction (4/5 becomes 5/4) and multiply:

(5/4)4/5n = 8•5/4

n = 40/4 or 10. Answer A is the correct choice

34 – D. 108

Rationale: The ratio of the two numbers is 7:3. This means that the larger number is 7/10 of 360 and the smaller number is 3/10 of 360.

The larger number is 7 • 360/10 or 7 • 36 or 252
The smaller number is 3 • 360/10 or 3 • 36 or 108 Answer D is the correct choice.

35 – C. $310

Rationale: The costs of all these items can be expressed in terms of the cost of the ream of paper. Use x to represent the cost of a ream of paper. The flash drive costs three times as much as the ream of paper, so it costs 3x. The textbook costs three times as much as the flash drive, so it costs 9x. The printer cartridge costs twice as much as the textbook, so it costs 18x. So now we have:
x + 3x + 9x + 18x = 31x

The ream of paper costs $10, so 31x, the total cost, is $310. Answer C is the correct choice

36 – D. $\frac{(6)(9)}{2}$

Rationale: The area of a triangle is one-half the product of the base and the height. Choices A and B are incorrect because they add the base and the height instead of multiplying them. Choice C is incorrect because it multiplies the product of the base and the height by 2 instead of dividing it by 2. Answer D is the correct choice.

<u>37 – A. 2,595</u>
Rationale: The steps in evaluating a mathematical expression must be carried out in a certain order, called the order of operations. These are the steps in order:

Parentheses: The first step is to do any operations in parentheses.

Exponents: Then do any steps that involve exponents Multiply and Divide: Multiply and divide from left to right Add and Subtract: Add and subtract from left to right

One way to remember this order is to use this sentence:
Please Excuse My Dear Aunt Sally.
To evaluate the expression in this question, follow these steps: Multiply the numbers in Parentheses:
3 • 4 = 12
Apply the Exponent 2 to the number in parentheses: 12^2 = 144
Multiply: 6 • 3 • 144 = 2,592
Add: 2 + 2,592 + 1 = 2,595

Answer A is the correct choice.

<u>38 – B. $3x^2$ - 4x - 15</u>
Rationale – The words in the problem tell us that the new expression for the length is 3x+5 and the new width is represented by the expression x-3. The area is represented by the product of (3x+5) (x-3). Multiplying the two binomials together with FOIL means that the first term is the product of x and 3x or $3x^2$. All of the multiple choices have the correct first term. However, the last term is the product of 5 and -3, or -15, which means that answer C is an incorrect answer.

Since the middle term is the difference of 5x and -9x, which is -4x, answer B is the only correct answer. If you choose to use the box method to solve these products, you will see the same results and the same factors. Answer B is the correct choice.

<u>39 – C. $14x^2$ +13x + 3</u>
Rationale – The words in the problem tell us that the new expression for the base is 4x+2 and the new height is represented by the expression 7x+3. The area is represented by the product of 1/2(4x+2) (7x+3). Multiplying the two binomials together with FOIL means that the first term is the product of 4x and 7x and ½ or $14x^2$.

However, the last term is the product of 2 and 3 and 1/2, or 3, which means that answer A is an incorrect answer.

The middle term is ½ the sum of 14x and 12x which is 26/2 x or 13x. Therefore answer C is the only correct answer.

<u>40 – B. 19,098 kg m/s</u>
Rationale – Momentum is defined as the product of mass times velocity. The conversion of 55 km/hr to meters per second means multiplying by one thousand and dividing by 3600. (seconds per hour). That value,15.28, must be multiplied by the 1,250 kg mass. That answer is 19,098 kg m/s. Answer B is the correct choice.

41 – A. $33,500
Rationale: Janet has a total of $105,000 in her accounts. 70% of that amount, her goal for her stock investments, is $73,500. To reach that goal, she would have to move
$33,500 from bonds to stocks. Answer A is the correct choice.

42 – A. $52,000
Rationale: Convert 15% to a decimal by moving the decimal point two places to the left: 15% = 0.15. Using x to represent Brian's gross salary, you can write this equation:

0.15 x = $7,800

To solve for x, divide both sides of the equation by 0.15. $7,800 divided by 0.15 is
$52,000. Answer A is the correct choice.

43 – C. 20
Rationale: To solve this problem, first convert 45% to a decimal by moving the decimal point two place to the left: 45% = .45. Use x to represent the total number of students in the class. Then: .45x = 9
Solve for x by dividing both sides of the equation by 0.45.
9 divided by .45 is 20. Answer C is the correct choice.

44 – B. 515
Rationale: Marisol scored higher than 78% of the students who took the test. Convert 78% to a decimal by moving the decimal point two places to the left: 78% = .78. Now multiply .78 times the number of students who took the test:

.78 x 660 = 514.8 or 515 students (whole number answers) Answer B is the correct choice.

45 – D. 130,500
Rationale: The population of Mariposa County in 2015 was 90% of its population in 2010. Convert 90% to a decimal by moving the decimal point two places to the left: 90%
= .90. Now multiply .90 times 145,000, the population in 2010.

.90 • 145,000 = 130,500

Answer D is the correct choice.

46 – A. 20
Rationale: Alicia must have a score of 75% on a test with 80 questions. To find how many questions she must answer correctly, first convert 75% to a decimal by moving the decimal point two places the left: 75% = .75.
Now multiply .75 times 80:

.75 • 80 = 60.

Alicia must answer 60 questions correctly, but the question asks how many questions can she miss. If she must answer 60 correctly, then she can miss 20. Answer A is the correct choice.

47 – C. $300
Rationale: If the phone was on sale at 30% off, the sale price was 70% of the original price.
So $210 = 70% of x
where x is the original price of the phone. When you convert 70% to a decimal, you get:

$210 = .70 \cdot x$

To isolate x on one side of the equation, divide both sides of the equation by .70. You find that x = $300. Answer C is the correct choice

48 – A. 84
Rationale: First, find the number of girls in the class. Convert 52% to a decimal by moving the decimal point two places to the left:

52% = .52

Then multiply .52 times the number of students in the class:

$.52 \cdot 350 = 182$

$182 - 98 = 84$

Of the 182 girls, 98 plan to go to college, so a total of 84 do not plan to go to college. Answer A is the correct choice

49 – C. 12%
Rationale: To find the percent increase, you first need to know the amount of the increase. Enrollment went from 3,450 in 2010 to 3,864 in 2015. This is an increase of
414. Now, to find the percent of the increase, divide the amount of the increase by the original amount:

$414 \div 3,450 = 0.12$

To convert a decimal to a percent, move the decimal point two places to the right:

0.12 = 12%

When a question asks for the percent increase or decrease, divide the amount of the increase or decrease by the original value. Answer C is the correct choice.

50 – D. 14 pounds 14 ounces
Rationale: When rounding measurements to the whole number value, the measurement is usually rounded up to the next larger whole number if that measurement is halfway or closer to the next higher value. In this case, since there 16 ounces in a pound, D is the correct answer.

51 – C. 7,514,635.8239
Rationale: When rounding a number to a given place value, the next lower place value is used to determine if the number is rounded up or down. The rounded value has its last significant digit in that place. Answer C has a number 9 in the ten thousandths place. Notice the difference between ten-thousands and ten-thousandths. Answer A is rounded to the ten-thousands place!

52 – C. 7.15 cc's
Rationale: When rounding a measurement, the value includes a precision of plus or minus half of the smallest increment measured. The lines on the cylinder would have the values of 7.00, 7.10, 7.20, or each tenth of a cc. The actual value of the meniscus that reads between tenths would be 7.15 cc. Answer C has a number with the correct precision.

53 – C. 4 men for 1 day

A. 1 man for 10 days
B. 2 men for 1 day
C. _____
D. 5 men for 5 days

Rationale: When estimating, it is helpful to round before estimating. The summary of this problems solution includes a rate of 200 pounds per hour (15 minute each). Two and one-half tons is 5000 pounds. 5000 pounds divided by 200 pounds per hour means 25 hours of labor is required. Answer C is the best estimate of 25 hours of labor (32).
Answer A is 800 hours, B is 16 hours, and D is 200 hours.

54– B. 40 minutes
 Rationale: When estimating this answer, the basic formula of distance equal to rate multiplied by time applies. So the time required for the trip is the distance divided by the rate. 18 miles divide by ¾ (45 minutes is ¾ of an hour), is 24 miles per hour. The new rate would be 29 miles per hour (increase of 5). 18 divided by 29 is about 60% of an hour or close to 40 minutes. 30 minutes is a close answer, but that is only possible if the rate is 36 miles per hour! Estimating may require that you eliminate answers that are close to the correct answer. Answer B is the correct choice

55 – C. 70 seconds per m/c; 35 seconds per t/f
Rationale: An estimate often means that you will need to check possible answers to see if they are correct. In this example, the basic assumption is that the time for m/c problems will be twice the value for the t/f. Trying one minute for m/c and one half minute for t/f comes out to 35 minutes. So answer B is not correct. The next closest one is answer C which comes out to 1400 seconds and 1050 seconds for the total 2450 seconds. That is close to the allowable 2700 seconds (45 minutes). If you try answer D, the total comes out to 1600 plus 1200 or a total of 2800 seconds. That's more than the allowable total of 2700. Answer C is the correct choice.

56 – B. twice as fast
Rationale: When estimating this answer, the formula of distance equal to rate multiplied by time applies. So the speed required for the trip is the distance divided by the time. In this example 10 minutes late means half the amount of time. Dividing by one-half means that the rate must be doubled. Answer B is the correct choice.

57 – D. 1,000,000
Rationale: The number of square units in this square meter is determined by 1000 rows of 1000 squares of 1 millimeter square units each. 1000 multiplied by 1000 is 1,000,000 units. Answer D is the correct choice.

58 – B. Serena is 7, Tom is 4
Rationale: Use S to represent Serena's age. Tom is 3 years younger than Serena, so his age is S–3. In 4 years, Tom will be twice as old as Serena was 3 years ago. So you can write this equation:

Tom + 4 = 2(Serena – 3) Now substitute S for Serena and S–3 for Tom.
(S–3) + 4 = 2(S–3)

Simplify the equation.

S + 1 = 2S – 6

Subtract S from both sides of the equation:

1 = S – 6

Add 6 to both sides of the equation:

7 = S. Serena's age

4 = S-3, Tom's age
Answer B is the correct choice.

<u>59 – A. 16 gallons</u>
Rationale: Amy drives her car until the gas tank is 1/8 full. This means that it is 7/8 empty. She fills it by adding 14 gallons. In other words, 14 gallons is 7/8 of the tank's capacity. Draw a simple diagram to represent the gas tank.

You can see that each eighth of the tank is 2 gallons. So the capacity of the tank is 2 x 8 or 16. Answer A is the correct choice.

<u>60 – B. 4.5 inches</u>
Rationale: The length of the larger rectangle is 12 inches and the length of the smaller rectangle is 8 inches. So the length of the larger rectangle is 1.5 times the length of the smaller rectangle. Since the rectangles are proportional, the width of the larger rectangle must be 1.5 times the width of the smaller rectangle.

1.5 • 3 inches = 4.5 inches Answer B is the correct choice.

<u>61 – C. 32 square inches</u>
Rationale: The perimeter of the rectangle is 24 inches. This means that the length plus the width must equal half of 24, or 12 inches. The ratio of length to width is 2:1, so the length is 2/3 of 12 and the width is 1/3 of 12. The length is 8 inches and the width is 4 inches. The area (length times width) is 32 square inches. Answer C is the correct choice.

<u>62 – B. 16 feet tall</u>
 Rationale: The ratio of the shadow length and the actual height is a constant determined by the sun. The ratios that apply are tree height / 27 equals 40 / 68. We solve these ratios by multiplying 27 times 40 divided by 67. The correct answer is B.

<u>63 – C. Half a day</u>
Rationale: The rate for the room is 2.5 man-days per room. The students can apply 5 man-days in one day. One half of a day (answer C) is the required amount of time.

<u>64– D. 22 gallons</u>
Rationale: The rate is defined by 23 miles per gallon. The distance divided by the rate is about 21.7 gallons. Answer D is the correct choice.

<u>65 – D. 2.5 hours</u>
Rationale: The rate is defined by 500 miles per 8.5 hours. That rate means that 140 more miles will require about 2.38 hours (cross multiply 140 • 8.5 and divide by 500). Answer D is the correct choice.

<u>66 – D. 432</u>
Rationale: Each machine can produce 12 parts per minute (96 ÷ 8). Multiply 12 times 12 (12 machines) times 3 (minutes). Answer D is the correct choice.

<u>67 – D. 3,105</u>
Rationale: The ratio of female to male students is exactly 5 to 4, so 5/9 of the students are female and 4/9 of the students are male. This means that the total number of students must be evenly divisible by 9, and 3,105 is the only answer that fits this requirement. Answer D is the correct choice.

<u>68 – D. 80</u>
Rationale: If we call the smaller number x, then the larger number is 5x. The sum of the two numbers is 480, so:
x + 5x = 480 6x = 480
x = 80

Answer D is the correct choice.

<u>69 – A. $144</u>
Rationale: When one person dropped out of the arrangement, the cost for the other three went up by $12 per person, for a total of $36. This means that each person's share was originally $36. There were four people in the original arrangement, so the cost of the gift was 4 x $36 or $144.
Let 4x equal the original cost of the gift. If the number of shares decreases to 3 then the total cost is 3(x+12). Then those expressions must be equal, so :

4x = 3(x+12)
4x = 3x +36

Subtracting 3x from both sides:
X = 36

Then the original price of the gift is 4 time 36 of $144. Answer A is the correct choice.

<u>70 – A. 11</u>
Rationale: If Charles wrote an average of 7 pages per day for four days, he wrote a total of 28 pages. He wrote a total of 17 pages on the first three days, so he must have written 11 pages on the fourth day. Answer A is the correct choice.

<u>71 – B. 2.4 lbs. per week</u>
Rationale – Six months is half of a year and a year is 52 weeks. The rate will be determined by dividing the total amount by 26 weeks. The rate is therefore 63/26 or about 2.4 pounds per week. Answer B is the correct choice.

72 – A. $12.38 per week
Rationale – Seven months out of a year is (52 • 7) / 12 weeks. The rate will be determined by dividing the total amount by 30.3 weeks. The rate is therefore $375/ 30.3 weeks or about $12.38 per week. Answer A is the correct choice.

<u>73 – D. 9 months</u>
Rationale – $3995 divided by $450 per month will provide an answer in months. Numerically the value of that ratio is about 8.88. Since that partial month can't be used, it means that a full nine months will be required to get the full amount. Answer D is the correct choice.

<u>74 – B. 6 months</u>
Rationale – The difference between the offer and your asking price is $1790 – $1450 or
$340. Dividing that value by the monthly decrease equals 340/55 or about 6.18 months. Rounding that value to 6 months, you can now evaluate the acceptability of the reduced offer. Since the partial month can be used as part of your decision process, rounding down to the six months is somewhat a judgment for the seller on the value of the money compared to the value of the car. Answer B is the correct choice.

<u>75 – B. X • Y = X + Y+ 6</u>
Rationale: The product of the two numbers is X times Y or X • Y. Therefore,
X • Y equals the sum of the two numbers (X + Y) plus 6. Answer B is the correct choice.

<u>76 – C. 5</u>
Rationale: Use x to represent the number of women on the board. Then the number of men is x + 3. So:
x + (x + 3) = 2x +3 = 13

To isolate 2x on one side of the equation, subtract 3 from both sides.

2x = 10
x = 5
Answer B is the correct choice.

<u>77 – B. 65</u>
Rationale: The average of 25, 35, and 120 is 60. 60 is 10 more than the average of the second set of numbers, so the average of the second set of numbers must be 50. The three numbers in the second set of numbers must add up to 150. Subtract 40 and 45 from 150 to get the answer of 65. Answer B is the correct choice.

<u>78 – B. 70</u>
Rationale: Try each of the answers to see if it fits the requirements in the question. The numbers divisible by both 5 and 7 are 35, 70, 105, 140, 175...
The multiples of 6 are 6, 12, 18, 24, 30, 36, 42, 48, 54, 60, 66, 72, 78... Since 70 – 66 = 4; the correct number is 70. Answer B is the correct choice

<u>79 – C. 16</u>
Rationale: There are 9 times as many female nurses as male nurses. To find the number of male nurses, divide the number of female nurses by 9: 144 ÷ 9 = 16. Answer C is the correct choice

<u>80 – A. 10%</u>
Rationale: First find the total number of patients admitted to the ER by adding the number admitted for all the reasons given in the question. A total of 120 patients were admitted. To find the percent that were admitted for respiratory problems, divide the number admitted for respiratory problems by the total number admitted:

12 ÷ 120 = .10

Convert this decimal to percent by moving the decimal point two places to the right: .10

= 10%. When you are asked what percent of a total is a certain part, divide the part by the whole. Answer A is the correct choice

81 – C. 15 miles
Rationale: Rebecca's commute is shorter than Alan's but longer than Bob's. Alan's commute is 18 miles and Bob's is 14 miles, so Rebecca's must be longer than 14 but shorter than 18. Neither 14 nor 18 is correct since the distances cannot be equal to either of the examples. So 15 is the only correct answer. Answer C is the correct choice

82 – B. 32 diet, 80 regular
Rationale: If the owner sells 2 diet sodas for every 5 regular sodas, then 2/7 of the sodas sold are diet and 5/7 are regular. Multiply these fractions times the total number of sodas sold:
2/7 x 112 = 32
5/7 x 112 = 80

Remember: when multiplying a fraction times a whole number, it is usually simpler to divide by the denominator first and then multiply by the numerator. Answer B is the correct choice

83 – B. The Bulldogs will definitely not be in the playoffs.
Rationale: The Rangers are playing the Statesmen in the final game, so one of these teams will finish with a record of eleven wins and two losses. Even if the Bulldogs win their game, their final record will be ten wins and three losses. So the Bulldogs will not be in the playoffs. Answer B is the correct choice

84 – D. 3,105
Rationale: The ratio of female to male students is exactly 5 to 4, so 5/9 of the students are female and 4/9 of the students are male. This means that the total number of students must be evenly divisible by 9, and 3,105 is the only answer that fits this requirement. Answer D is the correct choice

85 – B. y = –2/3x + 2
Rationale: The formula for a linear equation is y = mx +b. m is the slope of the line to be graphed and b is the y-intercept, the point where the line meets the y axis.

The slope of the line in this graph is negative because it is moving downward from left to right. So the number before the x will be negative. Answers A and D cannot be correct answers. The slope of the line is expressed as rise/run. The slope of this line is –2/3 run because it crosses the y axis at 2 and the x axis at 3. The y-intercept, the point where the line crosses the y axis, is 2. The correct equation must be y = –2/3x + 2. Answer B is the correct choice

86. D - 1
Rationale: If the y intercept of the line on this graph was reduced by 1, the line would cross the y axis at 2. The slope of a line is defined as rise/run. You might also describe the run slope of a line as "the change in y over the change in x". If the y intercept was changed to 2, the slope of the line would be 2/2 or 1. The slope of this line is positive because it is moving upward from left to right. Answer D is the correct choice

87 – C. ß ß ß ß ß ß ß ß ß ß ß ß ß ß ß/2
Rationale: If the figures are valued at $450, then dividing $6500 by $450 is 14.44 . C has 14.5 figures which is closest to $6500. Answer C is the correct choice.

<u>88 – D. June</u>
Rationale: To find the median in a series of numbers, arrange the numbers in order from smallest to largest. The number in the center, 92 in this case, is the median. Answer D is the correct choice

<u>89 – D. 150 pounds</u>
Rationale: The average weight of the five friends is 180 pounds, so the total weight of all five is 5 times 180 or 900 pounds. Add the weights of Al, Bob, Carl, and Dave. Together they weigh 750 pounds. Subtract 750 from 900 to find Ed's weight of 150 pounds.
Answer D is the correct choice

<u>90 – B. 4</u>
Rationale: The mode is the number that appears "most often" in a set of numbers. Since 4 appears three times, it is the "Mode". Answer B is the correct choice

<u>91 – C. 78</u>
Rationale: To find the median in a series of numbers, arrange the numbers in order from smallest to largest:
69, 73, 78, 80, 100

The number in the center is the median. Answer C is the correct choice NOTE: If there is an even number of values in the series, for example:
34, 46, 52, 54, 67, 81

then the median will be the average of the two numbers in the center. In this example, the median will be 53, the average of 52 and 54. Remember: the median is not the same as the average. Answer C is the correct choice.

<u>92 – D. 102</u>
Rationale: To find the mean or average, total all the values and divide by the number of values in the sample. In this example there will be 10 grades with an average of 93 points for a total of 930 points. Subtracting the total of points already scored, there are 204 points which are needed to maintain the average. 204 points divided by 2 grades is 102 points per grade. Answer D is the correct choice.

<u>93 – D. 26.5</u>
Rationale: To find the y-intercept, the patterns in the table must be extended until the x value of the table is equal to 0. Extending the data table to the left means the next two data entries will be 1 and -1. The next two y entries will be 25 and 28. Since 0 is midway between 1 and -1, the y-intercept is midway between 25 and 28. The correct value is 26.5. Answer D is the correct choice.

<u>94 – D. y = 2x + 7</u>
Rationale: The simplest way to answer this question is to see which of the equations would work for all the values of x and y in the table.

Choices A and D would work when x = 0 and y = 7, but A would not work for any other values of x and y. Choice B would work when x = 3 and y = 13, but it would not work for any other values of x and y. Choice C would not work for any of the values of x and y.

Only choice D would be correct for each ordered pair in the table

95 – D. y axis with weight and x axis with date
Rationale: The data recorded on a "daily" basis implies that the independent data is the time or date of the test. Independent data is normally recorded on the "x-axis".
Answers A and D are the two possible correct choices. Since the "weight" is the selected data to be recorded, Answer D is the correct choice.

96 – B. Days are the independent variable
Rationale: The weather data reported on a "daily" basis implies that the temperature data is independent. Since time or date is normally the independent data. Answer B is the correct choice.

97 – B. negative covariation
Rationale: The patient's weight data in this problem is a decreasing value in relation to time. Decreasing as a function of increasing x values is the definition of negative covariation. Answer B is the correct choice.

98 – C. 7
 Rationale: The perimeter of the rectangle is 28: 8 + 8 + 6 + 6. If the perimeter of a square is 28, each side is 7. Answer C is the correct choice.

99 – C. 2,3,4
Rationale: The two shorter sides of a triangle must always add up to a value greater than the longest side. Answer C is the correct choice.

100 – D. 64
Rationale: A diagram of the larger square, could be made with 8 rows of 8 smaller squares, so you can make a total of 64 squares. Answer D is the correct choice.

101 – A. 64 ft.
Rationale: We know the dimensions of the left side and the top side of this figure, but how can we find the dimensions of the other sides? Look at the two horizontal lines on the bottom of the figure. We know that together they are as long as the top side of the figure, so together they must total 18 ft. Similarly, the two vertical lines on the right side of the figure, must be as long as the left side of the figure and together they must be 14 ft. So now we know that the perimeter of the figure is 14 + 18 + 14 + 18 or 32 +32 =64. Answer A is the correct choice.

102 – B. 32 inches
Rationale: The radius of a circle is one-half the diameter, so the diameter of this circle is 8 inches. The diameter is a line passing through the center of a circle and joining two points on its circumference. If you study this figure, you can see that the diameter of the circle is the same as the length of each side of the square. The diameter is 8 inches, so the perimeter of the square is 32 inches (8+ 8 + 8 + 8). Answer B is the correct choice.

103 – A. length = 12, width = 4
Rationale: Use w to represent the width of the rectangle. The length is three times the width, so the length is 3w. The area of the rectangle is the length times the width, so the area is w • 3w, or $3w^2$.

$3w^2 = 48$

Divide both sides of the equation by 3. You get:

$w^2 = 16$

So the width of the rectangle is 4 and the length of the rectangle is 12. Answer A is the correct choice.

104 – B. 10 miles
Rationale: If you made a simple map with these three cities, it would look like this:

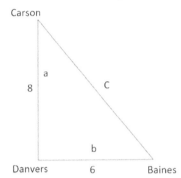

This is a right triangle. The longest side of a right triangle is called the hypotenuse. The two legs of the triangle are labeled a and b. The hypotenuse is labeled c. You can find the length of the hypotenuse (the distance between Caron and Baines) by using this equation: $a^2 + b^2 = c^2$

In this case, the equation would be:
$8^2 + 6^2 = c^2$

or

$64 + 36 = c^2$
$100 = c^2$

To find c, find which number times itself equals 100? The answer is 10. Answer B is the correct choice.

105   – B. 3,024 cubic inches
Rationale: The formula for the volume of a rectangular solid is length x width x height. So the volume of this box is:

18 x 12 x 14 = 3,024 cubic inches

Answer B is the correct choice.

106 – B. 6.5 x 10^{-3}
Rationale: Make a list of the negative powers of 10:

$10^{-2} = 1/100 = 0.01$
$10^{-3} = 1/1000 = 0.001$
$10^{-4} = 1/10000 = 0.0001$
$10^{-5} = 1/100000 = 0.00001$

Now multiply each of these numbers by 6.5 to see which one gives you 0.0065. The decimal must be moved 3 places to the left from 6.5 to 0.0065. Answer B is the correct choice.

107 – D. 6096

Rationale: Twenty feet multiplied by twelve inches per foot multiplied by 25.4 millimeters per inch gives a value of 6096 millimeters. Answer D is the correct choice.

108 – A. 9.7 millimeters

Rationale: The square base that is 4 inches on a side has an area of 4•4•2.54•2.54 or about 103 square centimeters. One hundred cubic centimeters divided by 103 square centimeters is approximately 0.97 centimeters or about 9.7 millimeters. Answer A is the correct choice.

109 – C. 6.1 cubic inches

Rationale: One inch is 2.54 centimeters. To convert centimeters to inches, divide by 2.54. Since a cubic centimeter is a centimeter times itself 3 times, to convert we divide by 2.54 three times. 100/2.54/2.54/2.54 equals about 6.1 cubic inches. Answer C is the correct choice.

110 – A. 0.00075 kg

Rationale: Twenty-five milligrams multiplied by 30 capsules is 750 milligrams. Dividing by 1000 is .75 grams. Dividing by 1000 again gives the answer in kilograms.

Answer A is the correct choice.

SCIENCE PRACTICE TEST

1. Which of the following is a primary functional difference between smooth endoplasmic reticulum (SER) and rough endoplasmic reticulum (RER)?
   a) smooth endoplasmic reticulum does not participate in synthesis of products that are destined for external secretion.
   b) smooth endoplasmic reticulum does not participate in synthesis of proteins.
   c) Rough endoplasmic reticulum does not participate in synthesis of products that are destined for external secretion.
   d) rough endoplasmic reticulum does not participate in synthesis of proteins

2. Which of the following is a universal feature of all living cells?
   a) an external cell membrane
   b) an external cell wall
   c) a nucleus
   d) mitochondria

3. Which of the following terms would NOT be used to define the relative position of one body structure to another?
   a) caudal
   b) coronal
   c) ventral
   d) inferior

4. Which of the following identifies the type of intracellular filament that generates the whip- like motion of the flagellum of a human sperm cell?
   a) Thick filaments
   b) microfilaments
   c) microtubules
   d) intermediate filaments

5. Which of the following is NOT a characteristic of voluntary muscle tissue?
   a) synaptic muscle membrane interfaces with neurons
   b) high extracellular matrix volume
   c) high intracellular actin content
   d) electrically excitable cell membranes

6. Which of the following could be a nitrogenous base sequence of both a single codon and a single anticodon?
   a) ACG
   b) GCT
   c) UTC
   d) AGU

7. Which of the following is NOT a product molecule generated by a complete round of the Krebs (citric acid) cycle?
- a) CO_2
- b) acetyl CoA
- c) NADH
- d) $FADH_2$

8. Which of the following is an event that occurs during the successful maturation of a human primary follicle into a human secondary follicle?
- a) the corpus luteum degenerates
- b) a human sperm cell fertilizes the primary follicle
- c) A polar body is generated
- d) Increasing estrogen levels trigger a second luteinizing hormone (LH) peak.

9. Which of the following pairs of terms correctly completes the statement below?
In the human male reproductive system _____ cells produce _____.
- a) tunica albuginea; primary spermatids
- b) Sertoli; follicle stimulating hormone (FSH)
- c) spermatogonia; luteinizing hormone (LH)
- d) Leydig; testosterone

10. Which of the following pairs of terms correctly completes the statement below?
In humans, the _____ joint has a greater range of motion than the _____ joint.
- a) elbow; knee
- b) sacroiliac; atlanto axial
- c) elbow; shoulder
- d) knee; hip

11. Which of the following choices lists three organs that are all, to the greatest extent, derived from the same primary germ layer?
- a) heart, lung and kidney
- b) brain, heart and lung
- c) pancreas, liver, kidney
- d) lung, liver and pancreas

12. Which of the following is the primary function of pulmonary surfactant?
- a) prevention of rupture of alveoli during maximal inspiratory effort
- b) prevention of collapse of alveoli during exhalation
- c) increased solubility of oxygen in solution between alveoli and capillary endothelium
- d) decreased viscosity of bronchiolar luminal mucous secretions

13. Which of the following most likely does NOT increase during a maximal inspiratory effort compared to a normal (tidal) inspiratory effort?
- a) intrathoracic volume
- b) diffusion of CO_2 into alveolar airspaces
- c) pulmonary artery pressure
- d) diffusion of O_2 out of alveolar airspaces

14. Which of the following events occurs simultaneously with the end of systole?
    a) The aortic valve opens.
    b) The right ventricular pressure reaches a minimum value.
    c) The atrio-ventricular (A-V) node generates an electrical impulse.
    d) The mitral valve closes.

15. Among the choices below, within the cardiovascular system, which of the following in general has the lowest electrical conductivity?
    a) the atrioventricular septum
    b) intercalated discs
    c) Purkinje fibers
    d) The AV node

16. Which of the following is the most likely site for the origin of a blood clot that travels to and then lodges within the right main pulmonary artery?
    a) a peripheral vein located in the leg
    b) the aorta
    c) the left atrium
    d) a main pulmonary vein

17. Which of the following is by definition a lymphocyte lineage cell type?
    a) eosinophils
    b) plasma cells
    c) monocytes
    d) basophils

18. Dedicated or professional antigen presenting cells present antigens on their cell surfaces to T-cells in conjunction with which of the following types of cell membrane molecules?
    a) HLA class I antigens
    b) ABO glycoproteins
    c) Rh-factor proteins
    d) cadherin-class cell-adhesion molecules

19. Which of the following is NOT a cellular feature of enterocytes located in the small intestine?
    a) microvilli
    b) tight junctions
    c) desmosomes
    d) lacteals

20. Which of the following is most likely to lead to a suppression of the secretion of the hormone glucagon?
    a) high protein content of chyme in the stomach
    b) activation of the sympathetic nervous system
    c) a meal with high simple carbohydrate content
    d) the release of the hormone cholecystokinin (CCK)

21. Which of the following is a correct cause and effect sequence of events during the digestive process?
    a) CCK secretion→↑somatostatin secretion→↑pancreatic amylase secretion
    b) CCK secretion→↑bile secretion→↑fat emulsification
    c) secretin secretion→↑gastric mucous secretion→↑pepsin secretion
    d) secretin secretion→↑gastric HCL secretion→↑pepsin activation

22. Which of the following identifies the process responsible for the late hyperpolarization phase of an action potential?
    a) sodium ion (Na+) diffusion into a neuron
    b) sodium ion (Na+) diffusion out of a neuron
    c) potassium ion (K+) diffusion into a neuron
    d) potassium ion (K+) diffusion out of a neuron

23.   Which of the following does not occur as a step in the physicochemical sequence that triggers sarcomere contraction within a myofibril?
    a) The release of norepinephrine (NE) into the neuron-myofibril gap of a neuromuscular junction
    b) The propagation of an electrical signal along a myofibril outer membrane into a T-tubule
    c) the release of CA++ ion from the sarcoplasmic reticulum of a myofibril
    d) the crosslink-binding of actin molecules and the "heads" of myosin molecules.

24. Which of the following pairs of cell types produce myelin sheaths?
    a) Schwann cells and oligodendroglia
    b) oligodendroglia and astrocytes
    c) astrocytes and Schwann cells
    d) microglia and neurons

25. Electrical signals to voluntary muscles most likely originate in which of the following locations in the central nervous system?
    a) the temporal lobes of the cerebral cortex
    b) the parietal lobes of the cerebral cortex
    c) the basal ganglia of the midbrain
    d) The cerebellum

26. Which of the following is most likely to directly result in the accumulation of lactic acid in muscle tissue?
    a) activation of the sympathetic nervous system
    b) depletion of glycogen stored in the liver
    c) inadequate amounts of O_2 delivered to muscle tissue
    d) inadequate levels of pyruvate within muscle tissue.

27. Which of the following is an effect of activation of the parasympathetic nervous system?
    a) increased activity of the sinoatrial node
    b) decreased activity of smooth muscle contractions in the wall of the digestive tract
    c) direct inhibition of deep tendon reflexes
    d) contraction of smooth muscle in the walls of arterioles in voluntary muscle tissue

28. On the outer membrane of a neuron, which of the following local regions would most likely contain the highest concentration of ligand-gated transmembrane ion channels?
   a) axon terminals
   b) junctional region of the axon and the main cell body (soma) of the neuron
   c) dendrites
   d) longitudinal mid-portion of the axon

29. Which of the following is the most precise anatomical location of the first stage of human spermatogenesis?
   a) the corpus spongiosum
   b) the seminiferous tubules
   c) the epididymis
   d) the seminal vesicles

30. Which of the following is the most precise location of the Bartholin's glands?
   a) immediately lateral to the labia majora
   b) medial to the labia majora and lateral to the labia minora
   c) medial to the labia minora and inferolateral to the vaginal introitus
   d) medial to the labia minora and superolateral to the urethral meatus

31. Which of the following correctly describes the course of a typical apocrine gland duct beginning at the duct's glandular origin and proceeding to the distal orifice of the duct?
   a) gland→hypodermis→basement membrane→dermis→shaft of hair follicle
   b) gland→dermis→basement membrane→epidermis→shaft of hair follicle
   c) a gland→hypodermis→basement membrane→dermis→external surface of the epidermis
   d) gland→dermis→basement membrane→epidermis→external surface of the epidermis

32. Which of the following describes the primary function of integumentary Langerhans cells?
   a) immune - antigen presentation
   b) somatosensory reception
   c) thermoregulation
   d) structural adherence

33. Which of the following identifies the primary tissue type of the hypodermis and a primary function of the main cellular component of the hypodermis?
   a) epithelial; mechanical barrier
   b) epithelial energy storage
   c) connective; mechanical barrier
   d) connective; energy storage

34. Which of the following is NOT a hormone synthesized by the pituitary gland?
   a) prolactin
   b) melatonin
   c) oxytocin
   d) adrenocorticotropic hormones (ACTH)

35. Which of the following hormones has rapid effects that are similar to effects associated with the activation of the sympathetic nervous system?
  a) insulin
  b) thyroid hormone (T3 and T4)
  c) testosterone
  d) aldosterone

36. Which of the following cell types initially secrets the majority of the hydroxyapatite component of lamellar bone?
  a) osteoblasts
  b) osteoclasts
  c) osteocytes
  d) fibroblasts

37. Which of the following is not a feature of or within trabecular (cancellous) bone?
  a) red blood cell progenitor cells
  b) white blood cell progenitor cells
  c) haversian canals
  d) adipocytes

38. Among the following, which choice identifies a join whose most general type is different from the other three?
  a) frontal-sagittal joint
  b) temporomandibular joint
  c) sternomanubrial joint
  d) sacroiliac joint

39. The initial filtration of blood by the kidney occurs at which of the following anatomical locations?
  a) the renal pelvis
  b) the adrenal cortex
  c) the collecting ducts
  d) the glomeruli

40. Which of the following is the kidney's response to exposure to antidiuretic hormone?
  a) increased secretion of urea
  b) decreased osmolality of extracellular fluid in the renal medulla
  c) Increased renal tubule permeability to water
  d) decreased secretion of glucose

41. Which of the following is the primary hormonal response of the central nervous system to an undesirably high plasma osmolarity?
  a) increased secretion of corticotropin releasing hormone
  b) decreased secretion of corticotropin releasing hormone
  c) increased secretion of antidiuretic hormone
  d) decreased secretion of antidiuretic hormone

42. Which of the following correctly completes the statement below?
   The effect of_____on the kidney is the release of _____by the kidney.
   a) an undesirably low plasma sodium ion concentration; renin
   b) an undesirably high plasma sodium ion concentration; renin
   c) an undesirably low plasma sodium ion concentration; aldosterone
   d) an undesirably high plasma sodium ion concentration; aldosterone

43. Under normal physiological circumstances, which of the following is completely reabsorbed by the kidney?
   a) glucose
   b) sodium
   c) bicarbonate ion
   d) urea

44. Which of the following is a physiological purpose of the sodium ion reabsorption-secretion cycle in the loop of Henle?
   a) sodium ion conservation
   b) potassium ion excretion
   c) concentration of urine
   d) acidification of urine

45. Which of the following is a DIRECT consequence of decreasing blood pressure on kidney function?
   a) decreased reabsorption of sodium ions
   b) decreased glomerular filtration rate (GFR)
   c) decreased secretion of renin
   d) increased secretion of aldosterone

46. Which of the following is a DIRECT physiological effect of angiotensin II?
   a) increased blood pressure
   b) increased renal medullary osmolality
   c) decreased renal tubule permeability to water
   d) redistribution of gastrointestinal blood flow

47. Which of the following are structurally required for the formation of a membrane attack complex (MAC)?
   a) perforins
   b) antigen specific antibodies
   c) platelet adhesion factors
   d) complement proteins

48. Which of the following does not participate in the immune response to viral infection?
   a) T-cells
   b) interferons
   c) chief cells
   d) plasma cells

49. Which of the following describes the mechanism of action of antivenom in snakebite victims?
    a) blockade of cell membrane molecular targets of snake venom toxin
    b) proteolytic destruction of the snake venom toxin molecules
    c) Non-enzymatic deamination of the snake venom toxin molecules
    d) deactivation of the snake venom toxin molecules by antigen-specific antibody binding

50. Which of the terms below correctly completes the following sentence?
The influenza vaccine provides _____ immunity to the influenza virus.
    a) active innate
    b) active humoral
    c) passive cellular
    d) passive innate

51. Which of the pairs of terms below correctly completes the following sentence?
Human T-cells originate from cells located in the_____ and reach maturity in the_____
    a) bone marrow; cortex of the spleen
    b) bone marrow; thymus
    c) thymus; cortex of the spleen
    d) cortex of the spleen, thymus

52. Among the four cardinal signs of localized infection, which of the following is/are NOT the DIRECT result of increased vascular permeability?
    a) redness and swelling only
    b) redness and heat only
    c) swelling and pain only
    d) pain and heat only

53. Which of the following is most clearly an autoimmune disease in humans?
    a) type 1 diabetes mellitus
    b) cystic fibrosis
    c) sickle cell anemia
    d) peptic ulcer disease

54. Which of the following identifies a direct causative sequence that results in the typical symptoms of seasonal pollen/mold allergies?
    a) antigen→mast cell release of peroxidase
    b) antigen→mast cell release of histamine
    c) antigen→Langerhans cell release of peroxidase
    d) antigen→Langerhans cell release of histamine

55. Which of the following diagrams the chemical reaction that results in the formation of a peptide bond between two amino acids, AA1 and AA2?
    a) $AA_1 + AA_2 \rightarrow AA1\text{-}AA_2 + H_2O$
    b) $AA_1 + AA_2 \rightarrow AA1\text{-}AA_2 + CO_2 + NH_3$
    c) $AA_1 + AA_2 \rightarrow AA1\text{-}AA_2 + 2\ glucose$
    d) $AA_1 + AA_2 + NAD^+ \rightarrow AA_1\text{-}AA_2 + CO_2 + NADH$

56. Which of the following is an initial non-specific interaction between infectious bacteria and immune system cells that triggers activation of the innate immune system?
   a) immune sentinel cell membrane toll-like receptor binding to bacterial pathogen associated molecular patterns (PAMPs)
   b) antibody dependent cytotoxicity antibodies detected by natural killer cell membrane receptors
   c) cell membrane injury triggers conversion of cell membrane lipids to arachidonic acid
   d) down-regulation (removal) of classI MHC molecules from the surface of infected cells is recognized by T-helper cells

57. Which of the following correctly diagrams the synthesis of a triglyceride molecule?
   a) glycerol + 3 fatty acid molecules → triglyceride + 3 H_2O
   b) glycerol + 3 alkanes → triglyceride + 3 CO_2
   c) 3 glycerol + 3 fatty acid molecules → triglyceride + 3H_2O
   d) 3 glycerol + 3 alkanes → triglyceride + 3CO_2

58. Which of the following correctly diagrammatically summarizes glycogenesis in the liver?
   a) glucose molecules→ linear configuration glucose monomers in linear polymer chain molecules
   b) glucose molecules→ cyclic configuration glucose monomers in linear polymer chain molecules
   c) glucose molecules→ linear configuration glucose monomers in branching chain polymer molecules
   d) glucose molecules→cyclic configuration glucose monomers in branching chain polymer molecules

59. Which of the following is a correct statement with regard to the molecular structure of human chromosomes?
   a) an individual chromatid always consists of one continuous single-strand form of a DNA molecule
   b) an individual chromatid always consists of one continuous s double-strand form of a DNA molecule
   c) an individual chromatid always consists of one continuous single-strand form of a DNA molecule
   d) an individual chromatid always consists of one continuous s double-strand form of a DNA molecule

60. Which of the following events could explain how a child could have three copies of chromosome 21 in all of his/her somatic cells?
   a) failure of separation of the chromosome 21 tetrad form during meiosis 1 division of gametogenesis
   b) failure of sister chromatid separation of chromosome 21 during a meiosis 2 division of gametogenesis
   c) failure of separation of the chromosome 21 tetrad form during the 2nd meiotic division of gametogenesis
   d) failure of sister chromatid separation of chromosome 21 during the first meiotic division of gametogenesis

61. Which of the following is NOT an error in the base pairing between two complementary strands of nucleic acid molecules?
   a) T-G
   b) G-A
   c) A-U
   d) C-T

62. Assume that there are a dominant and a recessive allele for each of two individual genes. The dominant gene alleles are P and Q and the recessive alleles are p and q. Which of the following are the predicted allelic inheritance frequencies of the two genes in offspring of parents where one parent is homozygous dominant for both genes and the other parent is homozygous recessive for both genes?
   a) 100% PpQq
   b) 50% PPQQ; 50% ppqq
   c) 50% PPqq; 50% ppQQ
   d) 25%PPQQ; 50%PpQq; 25% ppqq

63. The atoms of the elements argon and neon share which of the following characteristics?
   a) a complete n=3 electron energy shell
   b) positions located in the same period of the periodic table of the elements
   c) filled valence octets
   d) atomic diameter

64. The molecule CO2 has which of the following characteristics?
   a) approximately 109 degree bond angles.
   b) two sigma bonds and two pi bonds
   c) a molar weight of 24 atomic mass units (AMUs)
   d) two lone-pairs of electrons

65. Which of the following crystalline solids contain ionic bonds with the least covalent character?
   a) lithium fluoride (LiF)
   b) magnesium chloride ($MgCl_2$)
   c) potassium fluoride (KF)
   d) calcium chloride ($CaCl_2$)

66. Among the choices below, which atoms have the highest 2nd ionization energy?
   a) sodium
   b) potassium
   c) phosphorus
   d) chlorine

67. Which of the following reversible reactions is catalyzed by the enzyme carbonic anhydrase?
   a) R_1-COOH + H_2N-R_2 $\rightleftharpoons$ R1CONHR2 + H_2O
   b) acetyl CoA + CO_2 $\rightleftharpoons$ pyruvate
   c) CO_2 + H_2O $\rightleftharpoons$ H_2CO_3
   d) $C_6H_{12}O_6$ + $6O_2$ $\rightleftharpoons$ $6CO_2$ + $6H_2O$

68. The function of which of the following peripheral nerves is most immediately essential to human life?
    a) The vestibular nerves
    b) the median nerves
    c) the sciatic nerves
    d) the phrenic nerves

69. Which of the following is a molecular compound that is directly produced by the normal catabolic pathway for the breakdown of hemoglobin?
    a) bilirubin
    b) uric acid
    c) urea
    d) bile

70. Which of the following pair of terms correctly completes the statement below?
    reversible reactions are always _____ reactions.
    a) exergonic forward, heat-producing forward
    b) endothermic forward, heat consuming reverse
    c) exothermic forward, spontaneous forward
    d) endergonic forward, spontaneous reverse

71. Which of the following physical, phase-related properties of water is a deviation from the typical physical phase-related properties of other pure monomolecular substances?
    a) the ration of the substance's gas-phase density to its liquid-phase density is less than 1
    b) the ration of the substance's liquid-phase density to its solid-phase density is less than 1
    c) the ration of the substance's gas-phase density to its solid-phase density is less than 1
    d) the ration of the substance's plasma-phase density to its liquid-phase density is less than 1

72. Which of the following is NOT correct regarding the activation energy of a reversible reaction?
    a) The activation energy for the forward and reverse reactions is equal
    b) The rate of both the forward and reverse reactions increases when the activation energy decreases.
    c) The enthalpy for both the forward and reverse reactions is independent of the activation energy
    d) The entropy change for both the forward and reverse reactions is independent of the activation energy

73. Which of the following will tend to directly increase plasma pH levels?
    a) increased ventilation rate
    b) increased urinary excretion of bicarbonate ion
    c) increased anaerobic cellular respiration
    d) decreased tidal volume

74. In a sealed reaction vessel containing adequate volume to contain the volume of all liquid and gas components of a reaction, which of the following forward reactions of a reversible reaction will NOT be favored by increasing the volume of the reaction vessel? Note: (g) = gas phase, (l) = liquid phase and (s) = solid phase

   a) $A(g) + B(g) \rightleftharpoons C(g) + 2 D(g)$
   b) $A(g) + 4 B(s) \rightleftharpoons C(g) + D(g)$
   c) $2 A(g) + 2 B(g) \rightleftharpoons 4 C(s) + D(g)$
   d) $3 A(l) + 2 B(g) \rightleftharpoons 2 C(g) + D(g)$

75. Which of the following changes in the temperature of H2O at standard temperature and pressure requires the greatest input of heat energy?

   a) -3 Celsius to 0 Celsius
   b) -2 Celsius to 1 Celsius
   c) 97 Celsius to 100 Celsius
   d) 102 Celsius to 105 Celsius

76. In a sealed container filled only with gas molecules, where the container volume = V, the gas temperature = T and the gas pressure = P, which of the following expressions is directly proportional to the number of moles of gas in the container?

   a) (P)(V)/T
   b) (P)(T)/V
   c) (T)(V)/P
   d) V/(T)(P)

77. The addition of 100 ml of pure liquid water will lower the pH of a 1 liter volume of which of the following solutions by the greatest amount?

   a) a solution with a pH = 8
   b) a solution with a pH = 7
   c) a solution with a pH = 6
   d) a solution with a pH = 5

78. Which of the following statements is true regarding the reaction of 1 liter of a 0.1 molar strong acid (HA) aqueous solution with a one liter of a 0.1 molar weak base (BOH) aqueous solution?
Note: In this question the conjugate base A- and conjugate acid B+ do not form a salt (AB) that precipitates out of solution.

   a) the resultant solution will have a pH of 7
   b) the resultant solution will have a pH that is greater than 7
   c) the concentration of HA will be greater than the concentration of BOH in the resultant solution.
   d) The combined concentration of the conjugate base A- and conjugate acid B+ in the resultant solution will be greater than the combined concentration of conjugate acid B+ and OH- in the resultant solution

79. Which of the following MUST be true regarding two sealed samples of different monomolecular gases that have the same temperature?

   a) The gas molecules in both samples have the same molecular mass
   b) The gas molecules in both samples have the same average velocity
   c) The gas molecules in both samples have the same average ratio of mass to velocity
   d) The gas molecules in both samples have the same average kinetic energy

80. Which of the following choices represents as sample of a substance that consists of 6.022 x 1023 molecules?
   a) 1 liter of H_2O gas at standard pressure and temperature
   b) 20 liters of N2 gas at standard pressure and temperature
   c) 18 grams of liquid H_2O
   d) 8 grams of liquid CH_4

81-   Which of the following is the pressure at the bottom of the inside of a sealed cylindrical vessel with an internal cross-sectional area of $1\ m^2$ that is completely filled by a liquid substance with a mass of 1 kg?
   a) 9.8 pressure units
   b) $9.8/\pi^2$ pressure units
   c) $(4.9)\ \pi$ pressure units
   d) $(4.9)\ \pi^2$ pressure units

82. Which of the following is velocity (v) of a 100 kilogram (kg) object that has that has a kinetic energy (KE) of 500 joules (J)?
   a) 1 m/s
   b) 2 m/s
   c) 5 m/s
   d) 10 m/s

83. Which of the following is the density of a solid sphere with a radius of 1 meter (m) and a mass of 4 kg?
   a) (4)(9.8) density units
   b) $3/\pi$ density units
   c) $9.8\ \pi^3$ density units
   d) 4 density units

84. Which of the following is most nearly the sum of the masses of one proton, one neutron and one electron?
   a) 1×10^{-3} amu
   b) 2 amu
   c) 3 amu
   d) 1×10^3 amu

85. Which of the following pairs of atoms have the largest ratio of nuclear charge?
   a) helium to hydrogen
   b) nitrogen to carbon
   c) chlorine to magnesium
   d) krypton to potassium

86. In humans, the complete absence of which of the following hormones would represent the most immediate threat to life without medical treatment?
   a) oxytocin
   b) cortisol
   c) insulin
   d) melatonin

87. Which of the following has the lowest percentage content of collagen?
   a) compact bone
   b) ligaments
   c) tendons
   d) cartilage

88. In Humans, which of the following has the highest percentage content of protein arranged in helical structures?
   a) testosterone
   b) keratin
   c) hemoglobin
   d) DNA

89. Which of the following INCORRECTLY identifies one or both functional groups shown in the answer choices below? Note: "R" represents a hydrocarbon group. Note: The functional groups in some cases could instead be bonded to groups other than R groups - the indicated carbons of the functional groups all will bond to carbons of hydrocarbon R groups as represented in the answer choices.
   a) CH_4 → alkane; $R-CH_2OH$ → alcohol
   b) R-COOH → carboxylic acid; R-CO-R → ketone
   c) $R-NH_2$ → amine; R-CH=CH2 → alkene
   d) R-O-R → ether; R-COO-R → aldehyde

90. If the equilibrium constant (Keq) for a reversible chemical reaction is Keq=1, which of the following is a correct equation for the reaction if at equilibrium the concentrations of all of the participants in the reaction are equal?
   a) A + B ⇋ C
   b) A + B ⇋ 2C
   c) 2A + 2B ⇋ C
   d) 2A + 2B ⇋ 2C

91. Which of the following conditions would be MOST likely to increase to risk for osteoporosis?
   a) high testosterone levels in males
   b) vitamin E deficiency
   c) subnormal ovarian function
   d) hyperactive adrenal medullary gland function

92. Which of the following is an INCORRECT pairing of a disease and a major risk factor for the disease?
   a) myocardial infarction → high HDL cholesterol levels
   b) stroke → high blood pressure
   c) malignant melanoma → sunlight exposure
   d) bacterial pneumonia → surgical removal of the spleen (splenectomy)

93. Which of the following is the dominant/recessive type and chromosomal location of the gene that is responsible for the most common form of inherited color-blindness?
   a) chromosome 21, dominant
   b) chromosome 21, recessive
   c) X chromosome, dominant
   d) X chromosome, recessive

94. Which of the following vitamin deficiencies can cause anemia that does not improve with the administration of daily oral iron supplementation?
   a) vitamin B-12 deficiency
   b) vitamin C deficiency
   c) vitamin D deficiency
   d) vitamin K deficiency

95. Which of the following the nucleic acid type of the human immunodeficiency virus (HIV) and the cell target of the HIV virus in the human immune system?
   a) DNA virus; T-helper cells (CD4 cells)
   b) DNA virus; cytotoxic T-cells (CD8 cells)
   c) RNA virus; T-helper cells (CD4 cells)
   d) RNA virus; cytotoxic T-cells (CD8 cells)

96. Which of the following correctly completes the statement below?
The carotid and aortic bodies measure th3 _____ and relay this information to the   .
   a) partial pressure of arterial O_2: pons and medulla oblongata
   b) partial pressure of arterial CO_2: pons and medulla oblongata
   c) partial pressure of arterial O_2: hypothalamus
   d) partial pressure of arterial O_2: hypothalamus

97. Which of the following hormones regulates overall energy metabolism and modulates the body's immune system responses?
   a) thyroid hormone (T3 and T4)
   b) cortisol
   c) calcitonin
   d) parathyroid hormone (PTH)

98. Which of the following separate genetic traits are least likely to follow the mendelian law of independent assortment?
   a) traits resulting from genes located on the sex chromosomes (X and Y chromosomes)
   b) traits resulting from genes located on different autosomal chromosome pairs
   c) traits resulting from genes located at either terminal pole of the same chromosome
   d) traits resulting from genes located adjacent to each other on the same chromosome

99. Which of the following vessels normally experiences the highest levels of free amino acids in the bloodstream?
   a) the splenic vein
   b) the hepatic portal vein
   c) the renal glomerular capillaries
   d) the thoracic duct.

100. The term mycosis refers to which of the following?
   a) excessive myoglobin levels in the bloodstream
   b) a fungal infection
   c) an inherited abnormality of myosin proteins in muscle cells
   d) nearsightedness

1- B. smooth endoplasmic reticulum does not participate in synthesis of proteins.
Rationale: Smooth endoplasmic reticulum does not contain ribosomes. Rough endoplasmic reticulum does contain ribosomes. Ribosomes are required to synthesize proteins. Both RER and SER may be involved in the synthesis of products that are destined for transport and secretion out of the cell into the external environment.

2-   A. an external cell membrane
Rationale: An external cell membrane is a feature of all living cells. Many cells such as plant fungi and bacterial cells also possess at least one outer cell wall, but human and other animal cells do not. Bacterial cells do not possess a nucleus or mitochondria.

3-   B. coronal
Rationale: Coronal refers to an axial plane of the body. The other axial planes are the sagittal and the cross sectional planes. Caudal means nearer to the tail or the posterior part of the body.
Ventral means at or nearer to the frontal surface of the body. The term inferior means near to the feet.

4-   C. microtubules
Rationale: Human sperm flagellum are constructed from and internal bundle of microtubules that interact with a microtubule organizing structure at the base of the flagellum. The individual microtubules sequentially slide back and forth within the outer envelope of the flagellum causing a whipping motion that generates a forward motion of the sperm cells. Thick or myosin filaments are critical elements of muscle contraction and actin microfilaments are involved in many functions that require active purposeful movement of cells and within cells but neither are elements of the flagellum of human sperm cells. Intermediate filaments are generally structural elements of the cytoskeletal framework of a cell and do not contribute to the functioning of flagellum of human sperm cells.

5-   B. high extracellular matrix volume
Rationale: Muscle and nerve tissue have high cell volume compared to extracellular matrix volumes. In voluntary muscle the neuromuscular junction is an interface between the terminal endings of axons of neurons and cell membranes of muscle fibrils. Actin filaments are a component of the thin fibers of sarcomeres in voluntary muscle tissue. All muscle cells have electrically excitable membranes that can conduct electrical signals along the surface of muscle outer cellular membranes

6-   A. ACG
Rationale: The nitrogenous base thymine (T) occurs in DNA molecules but not in RNA molecules. The nitrogenous base uracil (U) occurs in RNA molecules but not in DNA molecules. The remaining nitrogenous basis of nucleic acids, adenine (A), cytosine (C) and guanine (G) occur in both RNA and DNA. Codons are DNA 3-base sequences and anticodons are RNA 3-base sequences. Among the choices only choice A has a three base sequence that does not include thymine or uracil. Therefore, this is the only choice that could occur in both an RNA and a DNA sequence.

7-   B. acetyl CoA
Rationale: Acetyl CoA is generated by conversion of pyruvate -an end product of glycolysis and by many other chemical pathways including the metabolism of lipids. It is a starting reactant molecule that enters at the beginning of a Krebs cycle. Two CO_2 molecules, 2 NADH molecules and one $FADH_2$ molecules are among the product molecules generated by each round of a Krebs cycle.
8-   C. A polar body is generated

Rationale: The successful maturation of a human primary follicle into a human secondary follicle occurs in response to the LH peak in the ovulatory cycle. During this maturation phase, the primary oocyte of the primary follicle undergoes a meiotic division resulting in a secondary oocyte and a polar body. The formation of the corpus luteum occurs after the rupture of the secondary follicle and the release of the secondary oocyte. Degeneration of the corpus luteum occurs a few days after ovulation if the secondary oocyte is not fertilized. Increasing estrogen levels trigger an initial luteinizing hormone (LH) peak during an ovulatory cycle but a second peak does not occur during a cycle.

9-   D. Leydig; testosterone
Rationale: Leydig cells of the testes produce testosterone in the male reproductive system. The tunica albuginea is a fibrous outer membrane of the testis and does not directly participate in the production of any particular type of cells. Sertoli cells produce various substances that support the development of sperm cell precursor cells, but they do not produce FSH. Spermatogonia are cells that are progenitors of mature sperm cells. Spermatogonia do not produce LH.

10-   A. elbow; knee
Rationale: The elbow and knee joints are both synovial hinge joints which allow flexion and extension. The elbow joint is a complex hinge joint that also allows the head of the radius to pivot at the articulation of the distal end of the humerus. This allows for additional range of motion in the form of supination and pronation of the lower arm and hand. This additional range of motion is much greater than that allowed by the knee joint. The sacroiliac joint connects the sacrum (triangular bone at the bottom of the spine) with the pelvis (iliac bone that is part of the hip joint) on each side of the lower spine. It is a non-synovial ligamentous joint that has very little range of motion, less than any of the other joints listed in the choices above. The elbow and shoulder joints are both synovial ball-and-socket joints which have a much greater range of motion than hinge joints such as the knee and elbow.

11-   D. lung, liver and pancreas
Rationale: The lung, liver and pancreas are all primarily derived from endoderm. The heart and the kidney are primarily derived from mesoderm. The brain is primarily derived from ectoderm.

12-   B. prevention of collapse of alveoli during exhalation
Rationale: Pulmonary surfactant decreases the surface tension of the fluid layer overlying the internal surfaces of alveoli. The surface tension of fluid layers of a concave surface such as the internal surface of a sphere increases as the radius of sphere decreases. Without pulmonary surfactant the surface tension of the aqueous layer within alveoli would increase as the alveoli deflate during exhalation to a point where the alveoli would completely collapse. This event would prevent reflation of the alveoli on a subsequent inspiratory effort.

13-   C. pulmonary artery pressure
Rationale: A maximal inspiratory effort increases intrathoracic volume by maximally decreasing the convexity of the diaphragm and by lifting the ribs upward and outward through contraction of intercostal muscles (accessory muscles of inspiration). Maximal inspiration increases the volume of lung that is both perfused and ventilated therefore the diffusion of CO_2 into the alveolar airspaces and the diffusion of O_2 out of alveolar airspaces will increase. With additional regions of the lung perfused during maximal inspiration, the total cross-sectional area of the pulmonary outflow tract of the heart increases. The total resistance to a fixed amount of blood delivered by the contraction of the right ventricle decreases and the pulmonary artery pressure most likely will decrease rather than increase.

14- B. The right ventricular pressure reaches a minimum value.
Rationale: Systole is the portion of the cardiac cycle where the ventricles are contracting. The end of systole corresponds with the completion of ventricular contraction. The pressures within ventricle reach a minimum value at the end of their contraction cycles. The aortic valve opens and the mitral valve closes at the beginning of systole. The AV node does not generate electrical impulses but will conduct electrical signals across the AV septum at the beginning of systole.

15- A. the atrioventricular septum
Rationale: the AV septum tissue is non-conductive and prevents the propagation of electrical signal from the atrium to the ventricles. The exception occurs at The AV node where electrical signals are intercalated discs possess gap junctions that allow electrical signals to propagate through cardiac muscle tissue. Purkinje fibers act as electrical conduction wires within the walls of ventricles.

16- A. a peripheral vein located in the leg
Rationale: the pulmonary arteries are components of the right cardiovascular circulation system. Blood clots of the pulmonary arteries (thrombotic pulmonary embolisms) must originate from sites within the right heart circulation unless there is an abnormal pathway from the left to the right circulation pathways such as a direct connection between the left and right atrium. Most commonly, thrombotic pulmonary embolisms originate as blood clots in large deep veins of the lower leg. The origins listed in the other choices are all located on the left side of the heart circulation.

17- B. plasma cells
Rationale: White blood cells or leukocytes include lymphocytes and non-lymphocytes Lymphocytes include T-cells, B-cells and the activated form of B-cells - the plasma cell Eosinophils, basophils, monocytes and polymorphonuclear leucocytes (PMNLs) are all non-lymphocyte lineage white blood cell types.

18- A. HLA class I antigens
Rationale: The major histocompatibility complex (MHC) class I human leukocyte antigens (HLA) are generally restricted to the cell membranes of dedicated or professional antigen presenting cells of the immune system. T-cells are activated when they bind with a class I molecule and an antigen on the surface of an antigen presenting cell. ABO and Rh factor molecules are generally restricted to red blood cell (RBC) membranes and can be a antigen that is identified as foreign by the immune system. Cadherin class cell adhesion molecules are involved primarily with structural functions related to binding with extracellular matrix molecules.

19- D. lacteals
Rationale: A common feature of non-glandular epithelial tissues, including the primary cell type of the epithelial lining of the intestines, is polarity. This refers to the separation of structure and functions of the top or apical region of the epithelial cell from lower or basal regions of the cell.
Enterocytes at their apical surface (the surface exposed to the contents of the lumen of the intestinal tract) have dense hair like extensions called microvilli. These microvilli vastly increase the surface area of the enterocytes that is exposed to the contents of the lumen of the intestines. This increases the efficiency of the enterocytes ability to absorb water and nutrients from the intestine. Tight junctions and desmosomes knit adjacent enterocytes together at or near their apical surfaces. This creates are relatively impermeable barrier to contents of the intestine, preventing the contents from diffusing between enterocytes. Lacteals are sealed terminals of lymphatic vessels that are located in the cores of intestinal villi that underlie enterocytes. They are responsible for receiving lipids from overlying enterocytes. Theses lipids are derived from lipids absorbed by the enterocytes from the intestine.

20-   C. a meal with high simple carbohydrate content

Rationale: The most common stimulus for the release of the hormone glucagon is low levels of glucose in the bloodstream. The primary effect of glucagon is on the liver, where it induces the liver to break down stored glycogen molecules into glucose molecules. The glucose molecules are secreted into the bloodstream and restore the blood glucose levels toward normal. Conversely, high blood glucose levels have the opposite effect, namely the suppression of the release of glucagon. A meal high in carbohydrates will generally result in high levels of blood glucose, because carbohydrates are composed primarily of glucose monomers. Simple carbohydrates are easily hydrolyzed by enzymes in the digestive tract to glucose molecules which in turn are rapidly absorbed into the circulation. This increases blood glucose levels and consequently tends to suppress glucagon secretion.

21-   B. CCK secretion→↑bile secretion→↑fat emulsification

Rationale: Cholecystokinin release from the duodenum triggers the release of bile from the gallbladder into the duodenal lumen. Bile emulsifies collections of lipids in the duodenum. Somatostatin is a hormone secreted by the duodenum and the pancreas (and anterior pituitary gland) that inhibits HCL secretion and gastrin secretion in the stomach. Secretin is a hormone released by the duodenum that inhibits HCl secretion in the stomach and stimulates the release of bicarbonate by the pancreas.

22-   D. potassium ion (K+) diffusion out of a neuron

Rationale: As the transmembrane potential reaches a positive peak during an action potential, voltage-gated potassium ion channels are activated and K+ ions, which have a higher intracellular concentration compared to extracellular concentration, diffuse out of the cell. This rapidly reverses the peak positive transmembrane potential of the action potential and generates a negative transmembrane potential that is more negative than the normal resting transmembrane potential. This is referred to as hyperpolarization. The effect of hyperpolarization is to cause the local cell membrane to become less likely to generate another action potential. The short period of time that corresponds to the persistence of the hyperpolarization of the local membrane region is called the refractory period of an action potential.

23-   A. The release of norepinephrine (NE) into the neuron-myofibril gap of a neuromuscular junction

Rationale: The choices from A through D summarize the process of contraction that occurs in sarcomeres within a myofibril beginning with the release of a neurotransmitter at a neuromuscular junction. The incorrect step is that the neurotransmitter that is released is not norepinephrine (NE). Acetylcholine (ACh) is the neurotransmitter released at neuromuscular junctions.

24-   B. oligodendroglia and astrocytes

Rationale: Both Schwann cells - in the peripheral nervous system - and oligodendroglia - in the central nervous system - produce myelin sheaths for axons of neurons. Astrocytes contribute to the blood-brain barrier of the central nervous system. Microglia provide metabolic support functions to neurons in the CNC. The axons of neurons can have myelin sheaths, but neurons do not produce myelin themselves.

25-   B. the parietal lobes of the cerebral cortex

Rationale: The primary motor cortices of the parietal lobes contain upper-motor neurons that initial the electrical signal sequence that ultimately triggers voluntary muscle movement. The parietal cortex processes auditory information. Both the basal ganglia and the cerebellum provide additional processing of voluntary muscle signals, but they do not initiate voluntary muscle movement signals.

<u>26-   C. inadequate amounts of O$_2$ delivered to muscle tissue</u>
Rationale: Lactic acid (lactate) production in muscle tissue results from the anaerobic conversion of pyruvate (predominantly as a product of glycolysis) to lactic acid. This process generates energy but is very inefficient compared to oxidative metabolism of glucose. Inadequate oxygen supplies shift energy production to the anaerobic pathway that generates lactic acid. Additionally, oxygen is required to reduce lactate back to pyruvate. In an oxygen deficient environment, muscle tissue cannot convert lactate back to pyruvate and consequently lactate levels rise within muscle tissue.

<u>27-   D. contraction of smooth muscle in the walls of arterioles in voluntary muscle tissue</u>
Rationale: Parasympathetic nervous system activation produces physiological changes that are associated with resting and digestive functions. Contraction of smooth muscle in the walls of arterioles in voluntary muscle tissue redirects blood flow from voluntary muscles where it can be utilized by the digestive system. Increased sinoatrial node activity results in an increase in heart rate; decreased activity of smooth muscle contractions in the wall of the digestive tract slows peristalsis and inhibits digestive processes. Both of these effects are the opposite one would expect of parasympathetic effects. There are no direct autonomic effects on deep tendon reflexes. These are independent reflex arc consisting of only a sensory receptor cell and one or two neurons in a sequence terminating on a voluntary muscle.

<u>28-   C. dendrites</u>
Rationale: Ligand-gated ion channels respond to the binding of a substance to it membrane receptor. In neurons, these ligands are usually neurotransmitter molecules. The site of release of neurotransmitters by neurons is usually at the synapse of two neurons or at a neuromuscular junction. Neurotransmitters are released by axon terminals of the presynaptic neuron into the synaptic cleft. The neurotransmitters diffuse across to the adjacent membrane region of the postsynaptic neuron. Most often this is the terminal region of a dendrite of the postsynaptic neuron. This is the reason that ligand-gated ion channels are usually most highly concentrated in the dendrites of neurons.

<u>29-   B. the seminiferous tubules</u>
Rationale: the first stage of spermatogenesis occurs in the walls of seminiferous tubules in the testis. Later stages of spermatogenesis occur within the lumen of the convoluted vessels that is the epididymis. The corpus spongiosum is highly vascularized region of the penis that comprises most of the tissue mass of the penis. The seminal vesicles are internal gland of the male reproductive system that provides most of the seminal fluid that nourishes and transports sperm within the genitourinary system. Neither the corpus spongiosum nor the seminal vesicles contain any sperm cells or progenitors of sperm cells.

<u>30-   C. medial to the labia minora and inferolateral to the vaginal introitus</u>
Rationale: The Bartholin's glands or greater vestibular glands are 1 to 2 cm length glands with a terminal ductal orifice located immediately inferolateral (one gland to the left and one to the right) to the vaginal introitus (external entrance). Bartholin's glands secrete mucus which provides lubrication of the vagina.

<u>31-   D. gland→dermis→basement membrane→epidermis→external surface of the epidermis</u>
Rationale: there are two general types of sweat glands located in human integument, apocrine and eccrine sweat glands. The eccrine sweat glands are by far the most numerous and excrete sweat onto the outer surface of the skin. The apocrine sweat glands are located in the lower dermis near the interface with the underlying hypodermal layer of the integument (also called the subcutaneous layer) apocrine sweat gland duct beginning at the origin to the body of the gland must sequentially pass through the overlying region of the dermis and then pass through the basement membrane which separates the dermis from the more superficial epidermis. In the epidermis the duct inserts into a hair follicle and excretes the apocrine glandular oily sweat solution into the space between the keratigenous hair shaft and the outer wall of the hair follicle

32-   A. immune - antigen presentation
Rationale: Langerhans cells are a form of dendritic cell that are located primarily in the epidermis (except for the most superficial layer - the stratum corneum) regions of the epidermis and superficial regions of the dermis. Langerhans cells are antigen presenting cell. In the integument they ingest debris resulting from skin infections and present them on their cell membranes for interaction with other immune system cells.

33-   D. connective; energy storage
Rationale: The hypodermis is the deepest of the three layers of the human integument. It is primarily loose connective tissue with a high content of adipocytes. One of the primary functions of the adipocytes is the storage of fat which serves as an energy reserve for the body. The adipocytes also provide some mechanical cushioning properties to the integument but they allow interstitial fluids and cells to freely pass through the hypodermis. This is the opposite of a barrier function

34-   B. melatonin
Rationale: There are no obvious methods to determine if a hormone is produced by the pituitary other than to memorize which are and which are not. Often this type of question can be answered by recognizing a hormone that is easily identified as the product of another endocrine gland. In this case, melatonin is the only significant hormone produced by the pineal gland and it is not a significant product of any other gland.

35 – B. thyroid hormone (T3 and T4)
Rationale: At the most general level the activation of the sympathetic nervous system induces a high level of overall alertness and priming of the body for high energy activities. Among these effects is an elevated metabolic state. Thyroid hormones in general also induce increased metabolic activity. It is often difficult to distinguish the difference is symptoms between persons with excessive levels of thyroid hormone (hyperthyroidism) and those with extreme activation of the sympathetic nervous system, as occurs with general anxiety disorders, and panic attacks.

36-   A. osteoblasts
Rationale: The non-cellular structural components of bones consist of a matrix of a calcium and phosphorous containing mineral called hydroxyapatite and collagen fibers. Collagen is produced by fibroblasts and the hydroxyapatite that is laid down during bone formation is secreted by osteoblasts. In mature bone, some osteoblasts differentiate into osteocytes' which are sparsely distributed within the center of osteons of bones. Osteocytes secrete small amounts of hydroxyapatite but this is after the bone has been formed. Osteoclasts break down bone matrix - usually during bone remodeling activities. Lamellar bone has well organized arrangements of collagen fibers within the bone matrix. In contrast, woven bone has randomly arranged collagen fibers. Lamellar bone possesses significantly greater mechanical strength compared to woven bone.

37-   C. haversian canals
Rationale: Trabecular or cancellous bone is one of two general types of bone, the other being cortical or hard bone. In contrast to cortical bone, trabecular bone has a porous, irregular structure that forms extensive cavities that contain adipocytes and the progenitor cells of both red blood cells (hematopoietic stem cells). Trabecular bone is diffusely and heavily vascularized.
Compact bone is comparatively poorly vascularized, with blood vessels primarily limited to haversian canals. Haversian canals are features of compact bone. Haversian canals are longitudinal passages that contain blood vessels that branch into smaller vessels that provide blood supplies to osteocytes located in lacunae (small hollow spaces) located in the center of osteons (structural subunits) of compact bone.

38-   B. temporomandibular joint

Rationale: Of the four choices, three are completely fused or relatively immobile non-synovial joints. The temporomandibular joint is a highly mobile synovial joint which allows for the chewing motions of the lower jaw (mandible).

39-   D. the glomeruli

Rationale: Arterial blood arrives for filtration by the kidney via the renal artery. The renal artery undergoes several branching to eventually form renal arterioles that extend throughout the renal cortex. Branches of these arterioles form tufts of capillaries that occupy an invagination of Bowman's capsule. Bowman's capsule is a balloon-like expansion of the proximal renal tubule. The combined region of capillary tufts and Bowman's capsule is called a glomerulus. There are over one million glomeruli in the renal cortex. The walls of the capillary tufts are uncharacteristically permeable to water and dissolved solutes such as electrolytes, urea and other substances. The blood pressure inside the capillaries exceeds the pressure of the surrounding extracellular space and of the fluid within the lumen of Bowman's capsule. This pressure gradient drives water and dissolved solutes out of the capillary tufts and into the lumen of Bowman's capsule. The solution that enters the capsule lumen is referred to as a filtrate.

40-   C. Increased renal tubule permeability to water

Rational: The effect of antidiuretic hormone on the kidney is to increase the permeability of the renal tubules and collecting ducts to water. This results in the diffusion of water out of the filtrate solution and into the renal medulla where it can be reabsorbed into the circulation by renal capillaries within the renal medulla. This concentrates urine and reduces the loss of additional water from the body that occurs through the excretory system.

41-   C. increased secretion of antidiuretic hormone

Rationale: Osmoreceptors in the hypothalamus and the pituitary gland directly detect plasma osmolality from adjacent capillaries. When plasma osmolality is undesirably high, the osmoreceptors relay this information to the pituitary. The pituitary response is to release antidiuretic hormone (ADH). As discussed in the rationale for question 40, the effect of antidiuretic hormone on the kidney is to increase the permeability of the renal tubules and collecting ducts to water. This results in the diffusion of water out of the filtrate solution and into the renal medulla where it can be reabsorbed into the circulation by renal capillaries within the renal medulla. This concentrates urine and reduces the loss of additional water from the body that occurs through the excretory system.

42-   A. an undesirably low plasma sodium ion concentration; renin

Rationale: The kidney is able to directly detect the sodium ion concentration of plasma within renal arterioles. A response of the kidney to an undesirably low plasma sodium ion concentration (and also to low blood pressure) is the release of the hormone renin. Renin in the bloodstream leads to the production of angiotensin II. Angiotensin II is a potent vasoconstrictor and also stimulates the release of aldosterone from the adrenal gland. The adrenal gland is not part of the kidney - although it does rest upon the superior pole of the kidney. Aldosterone causes the kidney to increase the reabsorption of sodium ion thereby helping to restore plasma ion concentrations to normal levels.

43-   A. glucose

Rationale: Under normal circumstances, glucose molecules that are filtered from the blood into a renal tubule are 100% reabsorbed from the filtrate. This process can be overwhelmed when blood levels of glucose are abnormally high. Glucose in the urine is an abnormal finding and often indicates the presence of type 1 or type 2 diabetes mellitus. The presence of sodium, urea and bicarbonate ion in the urine is normal so clearly these are not completely reabsorbed from renal tubule filtrates.

44-   C. concentration of urine

Rationale: The loop of Henle is a U-shaped segment of the renal tubules. It is the mid-portion of the renal tubule - located between the proximal convoluted tubule segment and the distal convoluted tubule segment of the renal tubules. The bottom of the "U" in the loops of Henle are located in the renal medulla. The distal or ascending limb of the loop excretes sodium ion from the tubule into the adjacent interstitium of the medulla. This creates a very high osmolality of the interstitial fluids in the adrenal medulla. The renal collecting tubules pass through the renal medulla on their pathway to the sinuses of the renal pelvis. The permeability of the renal collecting tubules to water can be adjusted by various hormonal influences. The collecting tubules are impermeable to sodium and other solutes. When the tubules are maximally permeable to water, water diffuses out of the tubules into the adrenal medulla interstitium. Since this is a process of diffusion, the maximal concentration of urine or the maximum osmolality of the urine that can be produced is slightly lower than the osmolality of the interstitium of the adrenal medulla. As water diffuses out of the tubule solution, the osmolality of the solution increases. When the osmolality of the two regions are nearly equal the driving force of the diffusion of water disappears as the concentration gradient between the two regions is eliminated.

45-   B. decreased glomerular filtration rate (GFR)

Rationale: The glomerular filtration rate of the kidney is the volume of fluid that is driven out of glomerular capillaries and into the lumen of Bowman's capsule per unit time. This rate is determined by the blood flow rate to the glomerular capillaries and the pressure gradient between blood within glomerular capillaries and the pressure within Bowman's capsule - the greater the pressure gradient the greater the filtration rate. Decreasing blood pressure decreases the magnitude of the pressure gradient and therefore reduces the kidney's glomerular filtration rate.

46-   A. increased blood pressure

Rationale: Angiotensin II is the activated form of angiotensin hormone. Activation of angiotensin begins with the release of the hormone renin from the kidney. Angiotensin II has a direct effect on circulatory vessels causing contraction of smooth muscle cells located in the walls of arteries and veins. This increases the force of the vessel walls on the blood within the vessels resulting in increased blood pressure. Angiotensin II has a direct effect on the proximal tubules to increase Na+ reabsorption. But this is not one of the answer choice options. Angiotensin II also stimulates the release of the hormone aldosterone which has additional effects on the kidney. These effects are indirect effects on the kidney.

47-   D. complement proteins

Rationale: the membrane attack complex is a multiprotein structure that attaches to the exterior cell membrane of disease causing bacteria that have invaded the human body. The MAC punctures the cell membrane allowing contents of the cell to escape and external substances to enter the interior of the cell (cell lysis). This results in the death of the cell. The MAC is formed from activated protein fragments of the complement proteins (the C5b-C6-C7-C8-C9 complement proteins and protein fragments). Complement proteins circulate continuously throughout the body. Over 30 proteins and protein fragments make up the complement system When the either the innate or active immune system is activated, complement proteins may be activated in a sequential cascade, where one activated complement protein or protein fragment catalyzes the activation of the next set of complement proteins. The activation of the complement cascade also produces activated proteins and protein fragment that the phagocytosis of cells and other substances and also act as cell signaling molecules that recruit immune cells to the site of an infection

48-   C. chief cells

Rationale: Chief cells are cells located in the stomach that secrete pepsinogen - a digestive proenzyme. The immune response to viral infection is generally an active immune response requiring the activation of B-cells by T-cells and the differentiation of B-cells -into plasma cells. Plasma cells then produce circulating antibodies that target the specific viral associated antigens. Interferons are circulating proteins that suppress the intracellular replication of viruses and have several other important antiviral functions.

49-   D. deactivation of the snake venom toxin molecules by antigen-specific antibody binding
Rationale: Antivenom to snake venom (and other biological venoms) is created by injecting the venom into lab animals and collecting the animal's blood serum afterwards. The injected animal will generate an active immune response to the venom that includes the production of antibodies that are targeted to antigens present on the venom molecules. In human patients, these antibodies bind to the venom molecules and in the process disrupt the venom's ability to cause injury either by altering the active sites of the venom molecule or by sequestering the venom molecules within antigen-antibody complexes which neutralize the antigen and enhance the clearance of the venom molecules from the body.

50-   B. active humoral
Rationale: The influenza virus contains viral shell proteins of the influenza virus that are recognized upon injection into the body by T-helper cells that have receptors complementary to the injected antigens. The T-cells activate B-cells with complementary antibody capability.
Activation induces B-cell differentiation into plasma cells which actively release antigen specific antibodies into the circulation. These antibodies are short lived and will not protect against influenza infection after a few days. The exposure to the vaccine proteins antigens also results in the differentiation of some of the activated B-cells into long-lived memory cell that can generate a much stronger and more rapid antibody response to a subsequent encounter with infectious influenza viral particles. This rapid response is sufficient to prevent the viral particles from infecting significant numbers of cells in the body. The antibody response is part of the active immune response (vs. the innate immune response) and is categorized as the humoral division of the active immune response (vs. the cellular cell-dependent active immune response).

51-   B. bone marrow; thymus
Rationale: All circulating red and white blood cell types of the human body originate from hematopoietic stem cells located in the bone marrow (and a few other regions in some circumstances in some individuals). Immature T-cells then migrate to the thymus early in life. These immature T-cells, as a group, have at least a few T-cells have the ability to respond to almost any possible specific molecular antigen including all of the antigens that are present in the host body. In the thymus, those T-cells that are capable of reacting to host antigens are detected and eliminated. Without this vital selection process, these T-cells would trigger immune system attacks against the body's own cells. This T-cell screening process continues into the early- to mid- teenage years. Afterwards the thymus progressively decreases in size and functionality.

52-   B. redness and heat only
Rationale: The four cardinal signs of localized infection are the result of the effects of various molecules that are generated by injured and infected cells and by immune cells that migrate to the site of infection. The most important of these molecules are histamines and prostaglandins. One of the effects of these molecules is to induce dilation of the local blood vessels - resulting in redness and increased heat due to increased local blood flow. Swelling is due to the accumulation of fluids and other substances that leak from the local blood vessels due to the increased permeability of the vessels induced by the infection-associated molecules. The pain associated with a localized infection is in part indirectly due to vascular permeability since increased swelling can trigger pain receptors. Pain is also a direct effect of the infection-associated molecules.

53-   A. type 1 diabetes mellitus
Rationale: Type 1 diabetes is a disease where the body produces either inadequate amounts of insulin or more commonly no insulin. In diabetes type 1, the immune system attacks the insulin- producing beta cells in the pancreas and destroys them. Cystic fibrosis and sickle cell disease are classic genetic diseases characterized by dysfunctional alleles of specific genes. Peptic ulcer disease is usually a result of chronic

infection of the stomach by the bacteria H. pylori. The Nobel Prize in medicine was awarded to the physician who proved this was true.

54-   B. antigen→mast cell release of histamine

Rationale: Seasonal pollen and mold allergies (hay fever) are a type I hypersensitivity reaction. Hypersensitivity reactions are caused by activation of the immune system in response to relatively harmless substances or excessively strong immune responses to relatively minor infectious or toxic chemical exposure. Hay fever is a hypersensitivity to airborne pollen or molds that are otherwise not harmful to the mucosal tissue of the upper airway epithelium. Mast cells are immune response cell that contain large amounts of histamine and other substances that can trigger inflammation processes. Mast cells are located within or just deep to the epithelial tissue of respiratory airways. Pollen or mold antigens that are inhaled subsequently diffuse into upper respiratory epithelial tissue and bind to receptors on mast that are complementary to these antigens. This triggers the release of histamine into the surrounding tissue. The effects of histamine are dilation and increased blood flow in local blood vessels, increased permeability of local blood vessels and direct and indirect chemical irritation of local sensory nerve fibers and adjacent cells within the epithelia tissues. These effects generate the typical signs and symptoms of hay fever including itching, nasal congestion sneezing, watery eyes and increased watery mucous secretion within the upper airways.

55-   A. $AA_1 + AA_2 \rightarrow AA_1$-$AA_2 + H_2O$

Rationale: Single chain proteins are linear amino acid polymers that are synthesized by formation of peptide bonds between individual amino acid monomers. Amino acids contain an amine group (-NH2) and a carboxylic acid group (-COOH) bonded to a central carbon atom. Peptide bonds are formed between adjacent amino acids in a polypeptide chain through a dehydration (condensation) reaction of the amine group of one amino acid and the carboxylic acid of an adjacent amino acid. Dehydration reactions produce a one or more H_2O molecules as a product of each individual dehydration reaction. Amino acids can form two peptide bond with other amino acids by forming one peptide bond through a dehydration reaction with their carboxylic acid group and the amine group of an adjacent amino acid and a second peptide bond through a dehydration reaction with their amine group and the carboxylic acid group of an adjacent amino acid.

56-   A. immune sentinel cell membrane toll-like receptor binding to bacterial pathogen associated molecular patterns (PAMPs)

Rationale: Infectious bacteria and other infectious agents have several common general patterns of molecular structure called pathogen associated molecular patterns (PAMPs) that are recognized by complementary membrane receptors of macrophages, dendritic cells and other immune surveillance cells in the body. These receptors come in several varieties and as a group are called toll-like receptors. Once the PAMP-toll-like receptor binding occurs, the immune surveillance cells release several types of cell signaling molecules that trigger the various cellular and chemical immune pathway responses to the infectious agent.

57-   A. glycerol + 3 fatty acid molecules → triglyceride + 3 H_2O

Rationale: A triglyceride can be directly synthesized from one glycerol molecule and three fatty acid molecules. A glycerol molecule has three hydroxyl groups (-OH) and fatty acids consist of a hydrocarbon chain (R group) with a terminal carboxylic acid group (-COOH). Each hydroxyl group on the glycerol molecule can undergo a dehydration (condensation) reaction with a carboxylic acid group on a tatty acid molecule. This creates an acyl group (-COO-) that connects the hydrocarbon R group of the former carboxylic acid to one of the three carbons of the former glycerol molecule. When this occurs at all three hydroxyl groups on a glycerol molecule the resulting molecule is a triglyceride. All condensation/dehydration reactions produce H_2O as a product of the reaction.

There are three condensation reactions required to produce a triglyceride from one glycerol molecule and three fatty acid molecules so three H_2O molecules are created by this synthesis reaction.

58-   D. glucose molecules→cyclic configuration glucose monomers in branching chain polymer molecules
Rationale: Glycogenesis in the liver - in general - is the formation of branching polymer chain molecules composed of glucose monomers. Most simple sugars, including glucose, can exist in a linear or a cyclic (ring) form. In glycogen, glucose monomers are locked in the cyclic configuration.

59-   A. an individual chromatid always consists of one continuous single-strand form of a DNA molecule
Rationale: DNA molecules in chromosomes are always in the double-strand form. A chromosome may consist of a single chromatid (following metaphase of mitosis and meiosis 2 and before the subsequent interphase stage of the cell cycle) or in the sister chromatid stage. An individual chromatid always consists of one continuous single-strand form of a DNA molecule. Chromosome in the sister-chromatid form have two identical sister chromatids and therefore have two continuous double-strand form DNA molecules.

60-   A. failure of separation of the chromosome 21 tetrad form during meiosis 1 division of gametogenesis
Rationale: Tetrads are paired autologous chromosomes. The tetrad form of chromosome 21 consists of the two copies of chromosome 21 arranged one alongside the other. Tetrad forms of chromosome pairs occur only during the first meiotic division of gametogenesis. Sister chromatid separation occurs only during the 2nd meiotic division of gametogenesis. Failure of separation of the chromosome 21 tetra during gametogenesis could result in a daughter cell with two copies of chromosome 21. If this cell matures to an ovum that is subsequently fertilized by a normal sperm cell (which contains one copy of chromosome 21), the zygote formed by this fertilization will have three copies of chromosome 21. All the progeny cells of subsequent mitotic divisions beginning with the mitotic division of the zygote will also have three copies of chromosome 21. All of the somatic cells in an individual's body are derived from mitotic divisions that began with the zygote. Therefore all somatic cells would have three copies of chromosome 21. Failure of sister chromatid separation would result in a gamete with single-chromatid-form chromosomes of all 22 autosomes except for chromosome 21 which would be a sister-chromatid form. Upon fertilization the resulting zygote would have one sister chromatid form of chromosome 21 from the sperm cell and one sister-chromatid form of chromosome 21 from the ovum. The result of subsequent mitotic divisions beginning with this zygote would be unpredictable but it is difficult to explain how this abnormality could produce progeny cells all of which have three copies of a normal chromosome 21. The condition described in the question actually occurs in humans and is one of the most common congenital chromosome abnormalities. It is known as trisomy 21 or Down's syndrome.

61-   C. A-U
Rationale: The correct nitrogenous base pairing between two complementary strands of DNA molecules is thymine (T) with adenine (A) and guanine (G) with cytosine (C). During transcription of a strand of a DNA molecule, the complementary strand of an RNA molecule substitutes uracil (T) for T. Therefore there is an additional correct complementary base pairing between a DNA and an RNA molecule, namely A-U. Overall there are three correct base pairings, A-T, G-C and A-U.

62-   A. 100% PpQq
Rationale: This question can be answered by constructing a Punnett square for a dihybrid cross of PPQQ X ppqq. The question is more easily answered by realizing that one parent is PPQQ (homozygous dominant) and the other is ppqq (homozygous recessive) for the two genes. Since every offspring will receive exactly one and only one allele of each gene from each parent, the only possible genetic profile for the two genes in any offspring is PpQq.

63-   C. filled valence octets

Rationale: Both argon and krypton have filled valence s and p orbital and these are the valence octet electrons that are filled for all group VIII elements. After the n=2 electron energy shell level, the correlation between the completion of the valence energy shell and the group VIII elements (the noble gases) is no longer valid. At the third period, there are eight elements. These eight elements, beginning with the group I element sodium (Na), sequentially add electrons to the 3s and then the 3p orbitals. The final element in the third period, the group VIII noble gas argon(Ar) has eight valence electrons - 2 in the 3s orbital and two each in each of the three 3p orbitals. For argon there are also five 3d orbitals available at the n=3 electron energy shell. Argon has no electrons in the 3d orbitals so it does not have a filled n=3 level. Argon is located in the third row of the periodic table. By definition this is the third period of the periodic table. Krypton is in the fourth period of the periodic table. The outer or valence electron shell diameter determines the atomic diameter of atoms. Krypton atoms have s and p valence electrons in the n=4 electron shell. Argon has no electrons in the n=4 electron shell. The n=4 shell is farther from the nucleus than the n=3 shell so krypton has a larger atomic radius than argon.

64-   B. two sigma bonds and two pi bonds

Rationale: to satisfy their respective valence octets, carbon seeks to acquire 4 additional electrons through sharing of electrons through the formation of 4 covalent bonds with other atoms and oxygen seeks to acquire 2 electrons that can be acquired in the form of electron sharing through the formation of two covalent bonds with an atom or atoms. This occurs in the molecule CO_2 where a single central carbon atom forms double bonds with each of two oxygen atoms. Double bonds are formed between two atoms by the formation of one sigma bond and one pi bond.

65 – A. lithium fluoride (LiF)

Rationale: Ionic bonds between cations and anions occur when there is a large difference in ionization energies of the parent neutral atoms of the cations and anions. The greater the difference in these ionization energies the less covalent or "electron sharing" character of the ionic bonds. The analysis is somewhat more complex for MgCl2 and MgCl2 since there are second ionization energies for Mg and Cl, but lithium is the least electronegative of all the atoms in the answer choices and fluorine is the most electronegative so there no doubt that this choice is the one where the largest difference in electronegativities exists.

66-   A. sodium

Rationale: Although the general trend for ionization energies in the periodic table is that ionization energies increase from right to left and decrease from top to bottom, sodium has only one valence electron. The second ionization energy would be the energy required to remove an electron from sodium's filled n=2 electron energy shell. This second ionization would break sodium's filled 2s 2p octet. This would always require a higher second ionization energy than the second ionization energy for any non-octet valence electron.

67-   C. $CO_2 + H_2O \rightleftharpoons H_2CO_3$

Rationale: One of the most important buffer (pH range stabilizer) systems in the human body is the carbon dioxide/H2O -carbonic acid-bicarbonate ion reactions that occurs primarily within the bloodstream and in the kidney. The reversible reaction sequence is
$CO_2 + H_2O \leftrightharpoons H_2CO_3 \leftrightharpoons HCO_3^- + H^+$

This is also the reaction sequence that is used by the pancreas to produce bicarbonate ion for secretion into the lumen of the duodenum for the neutralization of acidic chyme from the stomach. The enzyme carbonic anhydrase catalyzes the reversible reaction $CO_2 + H_2O \rightleftharpoons H_2CO_3$.

68-   D. the phrenic nerves

Rationale: the phrenic nerves are the nerves that innervate the thoracic diaphragm muscle. Without the function of theses nerves, contraction of the diaphragm is impossible and breathing cannot occur. Obviously this would result in death. The vestibular nerves transmit information from the vestibular system in the inner ear. Dysfunction of these nerves causes vertigo (dizziness) and difficulty maintaining balance, but this is not necessarily a fatal impairment. The median nerves are somatic nerves that innervate the muscles of the arms. Loss of median nerve function results in numbness and paralysis of portions of the arms. This is not a function that is absolutely essential to human life. The sciatic nerves are the major somatic nerves of the lower extremities. Loss of function results in numbness and paralysis of the legs. Again this is not necessarily an essential function for human life.

69-   A. bilirubin

Rationale: Red blood cells have an average lifespan of 120 days in the human body. When red blood cells die the hemoglobin within red blood cells must be broken down or catabolized to products that can be removed from the body or recycled by the body. This breakdown process begins with the conversion of hemoglobin to biliverdin. The second step is the conversion of biliverdin to bilirubin. Bilirubin is subsequently excreted in bile and urine. Uric acid is a breakdown product of purines from DNA. Urea is formed from ammonia (NH_3) which is a breakdown product from the catabolism of individual amino acids. Urea is synthesized by the liver and excreted through the kidneys.

70-   D. endergonic forward, spontaneous reverse

Rationale: for reversible reactions such as the general reaction $A + B \leftrightarrows C + D$ the convention is that the left to right reaction is the forward reaction and the right to left reaction is the reverse reaction. When it is not explicitly stated that the reaction is specifically the forward or the reverse reaction, it is assumed that the reaction refers to the forward, left to right reaction. If the reaction $A + B \leftrightarrows C + D$ is simply described as an endothermic or exothermic reaction or as an endergonic or exergonic reaction, it is assumed to refer to the forward reaction where A and B are the reactants and C and D are the products. The reverse reaction designations are always the opposite of the forward reactions for the exergonic vs. endergonic designation and the exothermic vs. endothermic designation. Exergonic reactions are always spontaneous reactions. For choice D if the forward reaction is endergonic, the reverse reaction must be exergonic and therefore the reverse reaction is spontaneous. For choice A, not all exergonic reactions are exothermic or heat- producing reactions. For choice B, all endothermic or heat consuming forward reactions are exothermic or heat producing -NOT heat consuming - reverse reactions. For choice C, not all exothermic reactions are exergonic or spontaneous reactions.

71-   B. the ration of the substance's liquid-phase density to its solid-phase density is less than 1

Rationale: Almost all monomolecular substances have a greater density in the solid phase compared to their density in the liquid phase. This correlates with a solid phase density to liquid phase density ratio (density of solid/density of liquid) that is greater than 1. Water is nearly unique in that it is a monomolecular substance that has a higher density in the liquid phase compared to the solid phase. Therefore the ratio of the solid phase density to liquid phase density that is less than 1. This is apparent in everyday life since anyone can observe that ice floats in liquid water. If the solid phase of water (ice) were denser than the liquid phase, ice would sink in liquid water.

72-   A. The activation energy for the forward and reverse reactions is equal

Rationale: The activation energy for a reaction is the amount of energy the reaction must invest to overcome an energy barrier to the reaction. This energy barrier is present in part because the reaction must reach a transition state where the reactants are spatially oriented and electrochemically primed to transform into the products of the reaction. Both the forward and reverse reactions must invest the energy required to achieve this peak energy transition state, but if the forward reaction is exergonic, it produces energy. This energy must also be added to the peak energy value of the transition state for the reverse reaction to occur. The converse is true for endergonic forward reactions. For example if the forward reaction produces 30 kJ per mole of reactant and must overcome a 10 kJ peak activation energy barrier. The activation energy for the reaction is only the 10 kJ transition state barrier. For the reverse reaction. The 30 kJ per mole energy must be expended as well as the additional 10 kJ to attain the peak transition state energy that exists between the right and left side participants in the chemical reaction. In this case the activation energy for the reverse reaction is 30 kJ + 10 kJ =40 kJ per mole.

73-   A. increased ventilation rate
Rationale: The most important buffer (pH range stabilizer) system in the human body is the carbon dioxide/H2O -carbonic acid-bicarbonate ion reactions that occurs primarily within the bloodstream and in the kidney. The reversible reaction sequence is:
$$CO_2 + H_2O \leftrightharpoons H_2CO_3 \leftrightharpoons HCO_3^- + H^+$$

When carbon dioxide is exhaled from the lungs plasma CO_2 concentrations decrease and the reaction is driven toward the left, reducing hydrogen ion concentrations in the plasma and by definition increasing the plasma pH. When the ventilation rate (volume of air exchanged through the lungs per unit time) increases, the amount of CO_2 that diffuses out of the blood stream and into the respiratory airways increases. This lowers CO_2 levels in the blood, and increases plasma pH. Excretion of bicarbonate ion (HCO_3^-) lowers the bicarbonate ion concentration of the plasma and shifts the reaction to the right, producing more hydrogen ion and by definition decreases the plasma pH. Anaerobic respiration produces lactic acid which increases hydrogen ion concentrations in the plasma. Again this by definition decreases PH. Tidal volume is the volume of air exchange during a normal cycle of one inhalation followed by an exhalation. Decreasing tidal volume decreases the amount of air exchanged per breath and this will reduce the rate of CO_2 diffusion from the bloodstream and will decrease plasma pH.

74-   C. 2 A(g) + 2 B(g) ⇌ 4 C(s) + D(g)
Rationale: Within a sealed reaction vessel increasing the volume of the vessel decreases the partial pressures of all of the gas-phase participants in the reaction. This reduces the pressure stress on the reaction and favors the reaction that produces higher amounts of gas- phase products from lower amounts of gas-phase reactants.. In reaction A, the forward reaction produces 3 moles of gas-phase products from 2 moles of gas-phase reactants. In reaction B, the forward reaction produces 2 moles of gas-phase products from 1 mole of gas-phase reactants. In reaction D, the forward reaction produces 3 moles of gas-phase products from 2 moles of gas- phase reactants. All three forward reactions produce greater amounts of gas-phase products than gas-phase reactants and are therefore favored by increasing the volume of the reaction vessel. In reaction C, the forward reaction produces 1 mole of gas-phase products from 4 moles of gas- phase reactants. The reverse reaction of choice C would be favored by increasing the volume of the reaction vessel.

75 –   B. -2 Celsius to 1 Celsius
Rationale: All of the temperature changes are increases of three degrees Celsius. Only choice B requires a phase change of H_2O - in this case from the solid to the liquid phase since the melting/freezing point of H_2O at standard temperature and pressure is 0 degrees Celsius. Phase changes require many times more heat energy to convert a given amount of a substance from a lower energy phase to a higher energy phase than is required to raise the same amount of the substance by a single degree in any of the 4 phases of matter.

76-   A. (P)(V)/T
Rationale: the ideal gas equation is (P)(V)=nRT

where the container volume = V, the gas pressure = P, n= the number of moles of gas (or another quantitative unit) in the container, R= universal gas constant and T = the temperature of the gas. To determine the proportional relationship of the number moles of gas within the container and the temperature and volume of the container , the ideal gas law can be rearrange to

n = (P)(V)/RT

Since R is a constant, it can be excluded from the equation and this gives the proportional relationship between n and the pressure volume and temperature of the system.
n $\propto$ (P)(V)/T.

The "$\propto$" symbol means "proportional to".

77-   A. a solution with a pH = 8
Rationale: Liquid water has a pH of 7 meaning it has a hydrogen ion (or H_3O+) concentration of 1×10^{-7} moles/liter concentration. Obviously addition of pure water will have on effect on the solution with the pH of 7 since both pure water and the solution have exactly the same hydrogen ion concentration. Since pH is equal to the negative log of the solution's hydrogen ion concentration, the higher the pH value, the lower the hydrogen ion concentration. For water to lower the hydrogen ion concentration of a solution it must increase the hydrogen ion concentration of the solution. Solutions which have a pH less than that of pure water (solutions with a pH less than 7) have a higher hydrogen ion concentration than pure water. The addition of water to these solutions will dilute the hydrogen ion concentration of the solution resulting in a new solution with a higher pH than the original solution. This eliminates choices C and D. Choice A has a pH of 8, and therefore has a hydrogen ion concentration of 1×10^{-8} moles/liter. The hydrogen ion concentration of pure water, (1×10^{-7} moles/liter) is ten time higher than the pH 8 solution. The addition of pure water to this solution must therefore increase the concentration of hydrogen ion in the resultant solution and by definition lower the pH of the resultant solution.

78-   D. The combined concentration of the conjugate base A- and conjugate acid B+ in the resultant solution will be greater than the combined concentration of conjugate acid B+ and OH- in the resultant solution
Rationale: strong acids (HA) by definition completely dissociate into hydrogen ions (H+) and the conjugate base (A-). Weak bases by definition only partially dissociate into hydroxide ions (OH-) ions (H+) and the conjugate acid (B+) Since the strong acid HA will completely dissociate into A- and H+ The H+ concentration of the solution will be equal to the HA concentration. 0.1 molar or 1×10^{-1} moles per liter. This is equivalent to a solution pH of 1. Basic aqueous solutions add OH- ions to an aqueous solution solutions and these can combine with H+ ions but less OH- ions add added to the solution because the weak base has an equal initial concentration to the strong acid but it does not completely dissociate so fewer OH- ions are contributed than H+ ions. By definition aqueous solutions with higher concentrations of H+ than OH- are acidic and by definition have a pH less than 7 and therefore choices A and B are incorrect. Since strong acids completely dissociate the concentration of HA in solution is zero. Weak bases do not completely dissociate so there is some BOH in solution therefore choice C is incorrect. For choice D the rational is lengthy but as an exercise one can use similar reasoning to verify that it is correct. This is an information overload type of question that is common in standardized testing. The key is to use a process of elimination since the other three choices are not difficult to exclude with simple one-step logical reasoning.

79-   D. The gas molecules in both samples have the same average kinetic energy
Rationale: The average kinetic energy of a gas particle is directly proportional to the temperature of the gas sample. Kinetic energy (KE) = ($\frac{1}{2}$)(mass)(velocity)^2. For choice A, gas molecules with different masses can have the same kinetic energy, as long as the square of their velocities times their masses are equal. The same argument is true for choice B. Choice C is incorrect, the different gas molecules must have the same ration of mass to velocity squared. This is usually not the same as the ratio of mass to velocity ratio. For example an

object with a mass of 2 kg and with a velocity of 4 m/s and an object with mass of 2 kg with a velocity of 8 m/s have the same mass to velocity ratio (1kg/(2 m/s) and 2 kg/(4 m/s) are both equal to 1/2 . the mass to velocity squared ratios are $1/2^2$ =¼ for the first object and $2/4^2$ = 2/16 = 1/8 for the other object

80-   C. 18 grams of liquid H_2O

Rationale: One mole is defined as the numerical value 6.022 x 10^{23} (Avogadro's number). One mole of any pure monomolecular substance has a mass equal to its molecular weight in gram units. For instance, the molecular weight of H_2 is 2 amu. One mole of H2 therefore has a mass of 2 grams. The molecular weight of H_2O is 18 AMU so one mole of H_2O has a mass of 18 grams.

Therefore, choice C is correct. For choice D, the molecular weight of CH4 is 16 AMU so one mole of CH_4 has a mass of 16 grams, not 8 grams. For choices A and B, at standard pressure and temperature one mole of ANY gas will occupy a volume of 22.4 liters, not 1 liter (choice A) and not 20 liters (choice B).

81 – A. 9.8 pressure units

Rationale: pressure is defined as force per unit area. Force is defined as mass times acceleration. The acceleration on the mass of fluid in the contained is the acceleration due to the force of gravity which is 9.8 m/s^2, therefore the force exerted on the bottom surface of the vessel due to the overlying column of liquid is equal to (1 kg)(9.8 m/s^2) = 9.8 newtons. The area of the bottom inside surface of the container is 1 m^2 since pressure is equal to force per unit area The pressure that is experienced at the bottom of the interior of the vessel is 9.8 newtons/1 m^2 = 9.8 pressure units. In this case the pressure units are kg-/m-sec^2. This pressure unit is called a Pascal (Pa). Another unit of pressure the atmosphere (atm) uses only units of height in millimeters of mercury in a barometric pressure tube.

82- D. 10 m/s

Rationale: the formula for the kinetic energy of an object is KE = (½)mv^2.
The calculation for the object described is therefore 500 = (½)(100)(v) ^{2}
v^2 = (2)(500)/100 kg
v^2 = 10,000/100 kg v^2 = 100
v = 10
The units of velocity are m/s, therefore the correct answer is 10 m/s.

83-   B. 3/π density units

Rationale: density is defined as mass per unit volume (m/v). The formula for the volume of a sphere is (4/3)$πr^3$ where r is the radius of the sphere. The density of sphere is therefore Density = mass/(4/3)($πr^3$) Density = 4 kg/(4/3)(π)(1 m) ^{3} Density = 3/ π kg/m^3

Notice that the density units are mass (in kilograms) per volume (in cubic meters).

84-   B. 2 amu

Rationale: The masses of both the proton and the neutron are both 1 amu to three significant figures - 1.007 amu for the proton and 1.008 amu for the neutron. The mass of the proton is thousands of times lower than 1 amu (0.0005 amu). The nearest of the four choices to the sum of the masses of the three subatomic particles to one significant figure is 2 amu.

85-   A. helium to hydrogen

Rationale: Since the atomic number of an element is equal to the number of protons in the nucleus of the elemental atoms and since the nuclear charge of an atom is equal to the number protons in the atom's nucleus, the correct answer will be the choice with the largest ratio of atomic numbers for the pairs of atoms The atomic numbers are usually displayed at the top of the elemental symbol on a periodic table of the elements. You will be provided with a periodic table during administration of the HESI. The atomic number for helium is 2 and for hydrogen is 1 so the ratio is 2 to 1 for choice A. By similar reasoning choice B ratio is 7 to 6, choice C ratio is 17 to 19 and choice D ratio is 36 to 19. It should be recognized that one need not calculate these ratios but rather to observe that for choices B,C and D the first value of the ratio is clearly not twice the value of the second value of the ratio, therefore none are as large as the 2 to 1 ratio of choice A.

86-   C. insulin
Rationale: Oxytocin triggers the milk let down reflex in nursing mothers and melatonin plays a role in the regulation of sleep wake cycles. There are other effects of both of these hormones but the complete absence of either has no obvious greater threat to life than the well documented fatal consequences of the absence of either insulin or cortisol from the body. While complete lack of cortisol is eventually fatal if untreated over several months. The complete absence of insulin makes the uptake of glucose from the bloodstream by most cells of the body impossible. Within days to a week or two this causes a severe and progressive derangement in the electrolyte and pH levels within the body that is 100% fatal unless insulin is replaced in the bloodstream.

87-   A. compact bone
Rationale: All of the choices above are composed of connective tissue with a high percentage of collagen content. Ligaments, tendons and cartilage are almost exclusively composed of collagen fibers or collagen molecules. Compact bone contains a significant fraction of hydroxyapatite mineral matrix and a comparatively smaller percentage of collagen content.

88-   B. keratin
Rationale: Keratin is a primary structural protein component of human hair and nails. It has predominantly secondary alpha helical structure and supercoiled helical tertiary structure. Most structural fibrous proteins have a helical structure. Testosterone and DNA have virtually no protein content. Testosterone is a steroid hormone. Steroid hormones are synthesized from cholesterol molecules which are lipids. DNA is composed of deoxyribose sugars, phosphate groups and nitrogenous bases. Hemoglobin is composed of four polypeptide chain proteins and has many regions that are helical but overall there is much less helical structure compared to keratin protein.

89-   D. R-O-R→ ether; R-COO-R→ aldehyde
Rationale: All of the functional groups are correctly identified with the exception of the R-COO-R group in choice D. The correct designation for this functional group is an ester, which consists of a carbon atom double-bonded to an oxygen atom (forming a carbonyl group), and single-bonded to another oxygen atom which in turn is single bonded to another carbon atom (in the example this would be a carbon of an R group - a hydrocarbon molecule or molecular segment). Finally, the central or carbonyl carbon is also bonded to a different R group carbon top another carbon of an R group. The correct structure for an aldehyde is R-COH, where the carbon atom is a terminal carbon of an R group and is double-bonded to an oxygen atom and single-bonded to a hydrogen atom.

90-   B. A + B ⇋ 2C
Rationale: When chemical reactions occur in a closed system they proceed toward chemical equilibrium. Chemical equilibrium occurs when there is no free energy to be gained by the reaction proceeding in either a net forward or reverse direction. At equilibrium the concentrations of the reactants and products remains constant and the reaction appears to stop. In reality both the forward and reverse reactions are occurring but at exactly the same rate so there is no apparent change in the concentrations of any of the participants of the reaction.
The equilibrium constant (K_{eq}) for a reversible chemical reaction is the ratio - when the reaction has reached equilibrium - of the product of the concentrations of the products of the forward reaction raised to the power of their stoichiometric coefficients to the product of the concentrations of the products of the forward reaction raised to the power of their stoichiometric coefficients. As with many attempts to explain

mathematical relationships in words, this statement is difficult to understand, but the general formula is much clearer. For the general chemical reaction $aA + bB \rightleftharpoons cC + dD$

When the reaction above reaches equilibrium, the equilibrium constant (K_{eq}) for the reaction is
$K_{eq} = [C]^c[D]^d /[A]^a[B]^b$

The bracket symbols such as [A] indicate "the concentration of " whichever participant is identified inside the brackets. The concentration units are usually moles/liter (mol/l)

Let us use the correct answer - answer "B" to illustrate. The chemical reaction for choice B is
$A + B \rightleftharpoons 2C$

Therefore, the equilibrium constant (K_{eq}) for the reaction is $K_{eq} = [C]^2/[A][B]$

For choice C the reaction is $2A + 2B \rightleftharpoons C$

Therefore, the equilibrium constant (K_{eq}) for the reaction is $K_{eq} =[C]/[A]^2 [B]^2$

Notice how the stoichiometric coefficients for each participant are the exponential values for the concentration of the participant in the K_{eq} equation.

The question states that equilibrium the concentrations of all participants are equal. This is usually not true for a particular reaction, but given that in this case it is we can substitute the value x for every participant's equilibrium concentration value (since they are all equal). For choice B
$A + B \rightleftharpoons 2C$

This gives an equilibrium constant (K_{eq}) for the reaction of
$K_{eq} = [C]^2/[A][B]$
$K_{eq} = [x]^2/[x][x]$
$Keq = [x]^2/[x]^2$
$K_{eq} = 1$

There are other stoichiometric values that can also give a $K_{eq} = 1$ for this scenario but none of the other answer choices options will; for example, choice C.
$2A + 2B \rightleftharpoons C$
$K_{eq} =[C]/[A]^2 [B]^2$
$K_{eq} = [x]/ [x]^2 [x]^2$ $Keq = [x]/[x]^4$
$K_{eq} = 1/[x]^3$

It is a lengthy explanation but once the concept is understood it can be applied quickly to similar questions in a test situation.

91-   C. subnormal ovarian function
Rationale: The leading cause of osteoporosis is a lack of certain hormones, particularly estrogen in women and testosterone in men. Menopause is accompanied by lower estrogen levels due to reduced secretion of estrogen by the ovaries and postmenopausal women are at greatly increased risk for osteoporosis. Excess cortisol secretion (hypercortisolism) can cause osteoporosis but cortisol is secreted by the adrenal cortex, not the adrenal medulla. Vitamin D deficiency can increase the risk for osteoporosis but vitamin E deficiency is not associated with increased risk for the condition.

92-   A. myocardial infarction → high HDL cholesterol levels

Rationale: High levels of HDL cholesterol are considered beneficial and are associated with a lower risk of atherosclerosis and coronary artery disease. LDL cholesterol levels are associated with increased risk for myocardial infarction (heart attack). High blood pressure is the other major risk factor for atherosclerosis and the diseases associated with atherosclerosis including stroke. Research indicates ANY amount of exposure to UV light -which occurs with any exposure to sunlight, even normal exposure - increases the risk for malignant melanoma. The spleen is a major lymphatic organ that plays an important role in the defense against infection by certain forms of bacteria. Most notably pneumococcus bacteria that cause pneumococcal pneumonia. Person who have their spleens removed are always administered pneumovax - a vaccine against the most common strains of pneumococcal bacteria that are responsible for bacterial pneumonia.

93-   D. X chromosome, recessive

Rationale: Male color blindness is one of the most common sex-linked abnormalities. The gene is located on the X chromosome. The Y chromosome is essentially an X chromosome that is missing one of the "legs" of the X chromosome. The gene for colorblindness is located on the leg of the X chromosome that is missing in the Y chromosome. Males therefore only have one copy of the gene and will develop the disease if they inherit the recessive form of the gene from their mothers. Females have two copies of the gene since they have two X chromosomes. It is much less likely that they will develop color-blindness because the gene is recessive and therefore the recessive form of the gene must be present on each of the two X chromosomes for the condition to occur.

94-   A. vitamin B-12 deficiency

Rationale: Vitamin B-12 is essential for the maturation of healthy red blood cells. Most forms of anemia (low red blood cell levels) are the result of iron deficiency, usually due to blood loss in menstruating women. Vitamin B-12 deficiency associated anemia cannot be corrected by additional intake of dietary or other sources of iron. One important cause of B-12 deficiency is the lack of production of intrinsic factor by the stomach. Intrinsic factor is required for the intestinal absorption of vitamin B-12 Vitamin. This type of anemia is called pernicious anemia and will not respond to increased oral intake of vitamin B-12. Persons with pernicious anemia require regular intravenous injections of vitamin B-12.

95-   D. RNA virus; cytotoxic T-cells (CD8 cells)

Rationale: The HIV virus is responsible for one of the deadliest pandemics in modern human history - acquired immunodeficiency syndrome (AIDS). The virus is also in part responsible for a revolutionary discovery in biology - that the paradigm that all life progresses from information stored in DNA molecules that is transcribed into RNA molecules and then translated into protein molecules was incorrect This was referred to as the central dogma of living organisms. The HIV virus violated this central dogma. HIV genetic information is stored in RNA molecules. The viral RNA codes for - among other proteins - a reverse transcriptase that transcribes the viral RNA into DNA in HIV infected cells. HIV is therefore categorized as an RNA virus. The most significant target of the HIV virus is human T-helper cells (CD4 T-cells). T-helper cells have an absolutely critical role in the active immune system. HIV infection kills T-helper cells and consequently cripples the body's active immune system. Prior to modern antiviral therapy, HIV infection was nearly 100% fatal.

96 –   A. partial pressure of arterial O_2; pons and medulla oblongata

Rationale: Specialized structures located in the walls of aorta and the carotid arteries called the aortic and carotid bodies respectively are able to measure the partial pressure of oxygen (PaO_2) contained in the arterial blood flowing past these structures. Sensory cells in the carotid and aortic bodies relay this information to the pons and hypothalamus which adjust the ventilation rate of the lungs to adjust and maintain an optimum level of oxygen within the arterial blood. The partial pressure of CO_2 is measured directly in the medulla and pons and indirectly as corresponding cerebrospinal fluid pH in the medulla.

97-   B. cortisol

Rationale: Cortisol is the primary glucocorticoid hormone of the human body. It has wide ranging effects on virtually all of the functions of the human body but in particular regulates energy metabolism in the body by stimulating gluconeogenesis, by increasing the breakdown of stored fats into substrates that can used as substrates for new glucose formation and by shifting the usage of amino acids from protein synthesis to pathways that can generate new glucose molecules. In the immune system cortisol participates in a feedback system that limits the inflammatory processes that occur due to activation of the immune system. The name "glucocorticoid" derives from early observations that these hormones were involved in glucose metabolism. In the fasted state, cortisol stimulates several processes that collectively serve to increase and maintain normal concentrations of glucose in blood.

98-   D. traits resulting from genes located adjacent to each other on the same chromosome

Rationale: the law of independent assortment refers to traits that appear to be inherited independent of other traits. Traits due to genes located on separate chromosome will occur in a parental gamete with frequencies that are not linked - in other words the fact that one of the trait genes is present in a parental gamete has no correlation to the probability that the other trait gene will also be present in the same parental gamete other than that the probability is that expected by random chance. Linked genes occur together at frequencies higher than predicted by random chance. When g these genes are located on the same chromosome it is much more likely that they be distributed to the same gamete. This correlation would be 100% if crossing over between homologous chromosomes did not occur during meiosis I of gametogenesis. If one of the genes located on the same chromosome is on a segment of the chromosome that is exchanged for the corresponding segment of the other homologous chromosome by crossing over during meiosis. The two genes would then be on separate chromosomes that could assort independently. The further apart two genes are on a single chromosome the more likely it is that they could be separated by crossing over events. The least likely separation of the two genes due to cross over occurs when the two genes are adjacent to each other on the chromosome. In this case the crossover would have to occur exactly between the two genes.

99-   B. the hepatic portal vein

Rationale: Proteins are absorbed from the intestine in the form of single amino acids and small di- and tripeptides that result from the enzymatic cleavage of protein s by proteolytic enzymes in the small intestines. Theses amino acids and small amino acids segments are absorbed by intestinal enterocyte and then are transported into the hepatic portal vein where they are carried to the liver for further processing. This is the reason that the highest concentrations of free amino acids occur in the hepatic portal vein. Free amino acids are found in lower concentrations in the general circulation, lower on the venous side than the arterial side since arterial blood is the route that transports amino acids to cells. The thoracic duct is a major lymphatic vessel that can have high protein content but not individual amino acid content.

100-   B. a fungal infection

Rationale: "Myco"" is the prefix of "related to organisms of the kingdom fungi; "osis" means "abnormal condition" In the case of an abnormal fungal condition of the human body this is synonymous with fungal infection. Excessive myoglobin levels in the bloodstream occur due to excessive breakdown of muscle tissue resulting in myoglobinemia - myoglobin is a hemoglobin - like molecule found primarily in muscle tissue. The medical term for nearsightedness is myopia.

ENGLISH LANGUAGE PRACTICE TEST

1. Which of the following choices best completes this sentence?

When asked if the sleeping pill had _____ him at all, the man replied that it had had no _____; nonetheless, he realized that he _____ not attempt to drive his car that evening.
   a) affected; effect; ought
   b) affected; effect; aught
   c) effected; affect; ought
   d) effected; affect; aught

2. Which sentence makes best use of grammatical conventions for clarity and concision?
   a) Hiking along the trail, the birds chirped loudly and interrupted our attempt at a peaceful nature walk.
   b) The birds chirped loudly, attempting to hike along the nature trail we were interrupted.
   c) Hiking along the trail, we were assailed by the chirping of birds, which made our nature walk hardly the peaceful exercise we had wanted.
   d) Along the nature trail, our walk was interrupted by loudly chirping birds in our attempt at a nature trail.

3. Which word from the following sentence is an adjective?

A really serious modern-day challenge is finding a way to consume real food in a world of overly processed food products.
   a) really
   b) challenge
   c) consume
   d) processed

4. To improve sentence fluency, how could you state the information below in a single sentence?

My daughter was in a dance recital. I attended it with my husband. She received an award. We were very proud.
   a) My daughter, who was in a dance recital, received an award, which made my husband and I, who were in attendance, very proud.
   b) My husband and I attended my daughter's dance recital and were very proud when she received an award.
   c) Attending our daughter's dance recital, my husband and I were very proud to see her receive an award.
   d) Dancing in a recital, my daughter received an award which my husband and I, who were there, very proud.

5. Which sentence is punctuated correctly?
   a) Since the concert ended very late I fell asleep in the backseat during the car ride home.
   b) Since the concert ended very late: I fell asleep in the backseat during the car ride home.
   c) Since the concert ended very late; I fell asleep in the backseat during the car ride home.
   d) Since the concert ended very late, I fell asleep in the backseat during the car ride home.

6. Which of the choices below best completes the following sentence? Negotiations with the enemy are never fun, but during times of war_____ a necessary evil.
   a) its
   b) it's
   c) their
   d) they're

7. Which of the verbs below best completes the following sentence?
The a cappela group   looking forward to performing for the entire student body at the graduation ceremony.
   a) is
   b) are
   c) was
   d) be

8. What kind of sentence is this? I can't believe her luck!
   a) Declarative
   b) Imperative
   c) Exclamatory
   d) Interrogative

9. Identify the error in this sentence:
Irregardless of the expense, it is absolutely imperative that all drivers have liability insurance to cover any personal injury that may be suffered during a motor vehicle accident.
   a) Irregardless
   b) Imperative
   c) Liability
   d) Suffered

10. Which of the following sentences is grammatically correct?
   a) Between you and me, I brang back less books from my dorm room than I needed to study for my exams.
   b) Between you and I, I brought back less books from my dorm room then I needed to study for my exams.
   c) Between you and me, I brought back fewer books from my dorm room than I needed to study for my exam.
   d) Between you and me, I brought back fewer books from my dorm room then I needed to study for my exams.

11. Choose from the answers to complete this sentence with the proper verb and antecedent agreement:
Neither of _____ _____able to finish our supper.
   a) we; were
   b) we; was
   c) us; were
   d) us; was

12. Which word in the following sentence is a noun? The library books are overdue.
   a) The
   b) library
   c) books
   d) overdue

13. Which of the following is a simple sentence?
   a) Mary and Samantha ran and skipped and hopped their way home from school every day.
   b) Mary liked to hop but Samantha preferred to skip.
   c) Mary loved coloring yet disliked when coloring was assigned for math homework.
   d) Samantha thought Mary was her best friend but she was mistaken.

14. Which of the following is NOT a simple sentence?
   a) Matthew and Thomas had been best friends since grade school.
   b) Matthew was tall and shy, and Thomas was short and talkative.
   c) Matthew liked to get Thomas to pass notes to the little red-haired girl in the back row of math class.
   d) Matthew and Thomas would tease Mary and Samantha on their way home from school every day.

15. Which of the following sentences is punctuated correctly?
   a) "Theres a bus coming so hurry up and cross the street!" yelled Bob to the old woman.
   b) "There's a bus coming, so hurry up and cross the street", yelled Bob, to the old woman.
   c) "Theres a bus coming, so hurry up and cross the street,"! yelled Bob to the old woman.
   d) "There's a bus coming, so hurry up and cross the street!" yelled Bob to the old woman.

16. Which of the following sentences is punctuated correctly?
   a) It's a long to-do list she left for us today: make beds, wash breakfast dishes, go grocery shopping, do laundry, cook dinner, and read the twins a bedtime story.
   b) Its a long to-do list she left for us today; make beds; wash breakfast dishes; go grocery shopping; do laundry; cook dinner; and read the twins a bedtime story.
   c) It's a long to-do list she left for us today: make beds; wash breakfast dishes; go grocery shopping; do laundry; cook dinner; and read the twins a bedtime story.
   d) Its a long to-do list she left for us today: make beds, wash breakfast dishes, go grocery shopping, do laundry, cook dinner, and read the twins a bedtime story.

17. Which of the following sentences is written in the first person?
   a) My room was a mess so my mom made me clean it before I was allowed to leave the house.
   b) Her room was a mess so she had to clean it before she left for the concert.
   c) You had better clean up your room before your mom comes home!
   d) Sandy is a slob and never cleans up her own room until her mom makes her.

18. Which sentence follows the rules for capitalization?
    a) My second grade Teacher's name was Mrs. Carmicheal.
    b) The Pope gave a very emotional address to the crowd after Easter Sunday mass.
    c) The president of France is meeting with President Obama later this week.
    d) My family spent our summer vacations at grandpa Joe's cabin in the Finger Lakes region.

19. The girl returning home after her curfew found the _____up the stairs to her bedroom maddening as it seemed every step she took on the old staircase yielded a loud _____.
Which of the following completes the sentence above?
    a) clime; creak
    b) clime; creek
    c) climb; creek
    d) climb; creak

20.By this time next summer, _____my college coursework. Which of the following correctly completes the sentence above?
    a) I did complete
    b) I completed
    c) I will complete
    d) I will have completed

21. Which of the following choices best completes this sentence?
The teacher nodded her _____to the classroom_____ who was teaching a portion of the daily lesson for the first time.
    a) assent; aide
    b) assent; aid
    c) ascent; aide
    d) ascent; aid

22. Which of the following sentences is grammatically correct?
    a) No one has offered to let us use there home for the office's end-of-year picnic.
    b) No one have offered to let we use their home for the office's end-of-year picnic.
    c) No one has offered to let ourselves use their home for the office's end-of-year picnic.
    d) No one has offered to let us use their home for the office's end-of-year picnic.

23. Which choice most effectively combines the information in the following sentences? The tornado struck. It struck without warning. It caused damage.
The damage was extensive.
    a) Without warning, the extensively damaging tornado struck.
    b) Having struck without warning, the damage was extensive with the tornado.
    c) The tornado struck without warning and caused extensive damage.
    d) Extensively damaging, and without warning, struck the tornado.

24.   Which word in the sentence below is a verb?
Carrying heavy boxes to the attic caused her to throw out her back.
   a) Carrying
   b) to
   c) caused
   d) out

25. Which choice below most effectively combines the information in the following sentences?
His lecture was boring. I thought it would never end. My eyelids were drooping. My feet were going numb.
   a) His never-ending lecture made my eyelids droop, and my feet were going numb.
   b) My eyelids drooping and my feet going numb, I thought his boring lecture would never end.
   c) His lecture was boring and would not end; it made my eyelids droop and my feet go numb.
   d) Never-ending, his boring lecture caused me to have droopy eyelids and for my feet to go numb.

26. Which choice below correctly completes this sentence?
   Comets_____balls of dust and ice,
   _____ leftover materials that
   _____ planets during the formation of
   _____ solar system.
   a) Comets is balls of dust and ice, comprised of leftover materials that were not becoming planets during the formation of its solar system.
   b) Comets are balls of dust and ice, comprising leftover materials that are not becoming planets during the formation of our solar system.
   c) Comets are balls of dust and ice, comprised of leftover materials that became planets during the formation of their solar system.
   d) Comets are balls of dust and ice, comprised of leftover materials that did not become planets during the formation of our solar system.

Questions 27-35 are based on the following passage about Penny Dreadfuls.

Victorian era Britain experienced social changes that resulted in increased literacy rates. With the rise of capitalism and industrialization, people began to spend more money on entertainment, contributing to the popularization of the novel. Improvements in printing resulted in the production of newspapers, as well as, Englands' more fully recognizing the singular concept of reading as a form of leisure; it was, of itself, a new industry. An increased capacity for travel via the invention of tracks, engines, and the coresponding railway distribution created both a market for cheap popular literature, and the ability for it to be circulated on a large scale.

The first penny serials were published in the 1830s to meet this demand. The serials were priced to be affordable to working-class readers, and were considerably cheaper than the serialized novels of authors such as Charles Dickens, which cost a shilling (twelve pennies) per part. Those who could not afford a penny a week, working class boys often formed clubs sharing the cost, passed the booklets, who were flimsy, from reader to reader. Other enterprising youngsters would collect a number of consecutive parts, then rent the volume out to friends.

The stories themselves were reprints, or sometimes rewrites, of gothic thrillers, as well as new stories about famous criminals. Other serials were thinly-disguised plagiarisms of popular contemporary literature. The penny dreadfuls were influential since they were in the words of one commentator the most alluring and low-priced form of escapist reading available to ordinary youth.

In reality, the serial novels were overdramatic and sensational, but generally harmless. If anything, the penny dreadfuls, although obviously not the most enlightening or inspiring of literary selections, resulted in increasingly literate youth in the Industrial period. The wide circulation of this sensationalist literature, however, contributed to an ever greater fear of crime in mid-Victorian Britain.

27. Which of the following is the correct punctuation for the following sentence from paragraph 1?
    a) NO CHANGE
    b) Improvements in printing resulted in the production of newspapers, as well as England's more fully recognizing the singular concept of reading as a form of leisure; it was, of itself, a new industry.
    c) Improvements in printing resulted in the production of newspapers, as well as Englands more fully recognizing the singular concept of reading as a form of leisure; it was, of itself, a new industry.
    d) Improvements in printing resulted in the production of newspapers as well as, England's more fully recognizing the singular concept of reading as a form of leisure; it was, of itself, a new industry.

28. In the first sentence of paragraph 1, which of the following words should be capitalized?
    a) era
    b) social
    c) literacy
    d) rates

29. In the last sentence of paragraph 1, which of the following words is misspelled?
   a) capacity
   b) via
   c) coresponding
   d) cheap

30. In the first sentence of the paragraph 2, "this demand" refers to which of the following antecedents in paragraph 1?
   a) travel
   b) leisure
   c) industry
   d) market

31. Which of the following sentences is the clearest way to express the ideas in the third sentence of paragraph 2?
   a) A penny a week, working class boys could not afford these books; they often formed sharing clubs that were passing the flimsy booklets around from one reader to another reader.
   b) Clubs were formed to buy the flimsy booklets by working class boys who could not afford a penny a week that would share the cost, passing from reader to reader the flimsy booklets.
   c) Working class boys who could not afford a penny a week often formed clubs that would share the cost, passing the flimsy booklets from reader to reader.
   d) Sharing the cost were working class boys who could not afford a penny a week; they often formed clubs and, reader to reader, passed the flimsy booklets around.

32. Which word in the first sentence of paragraph 3 should be capitalized?
   a) stories
   b) gothic
   c) thrillers
   d) criminals

33. Which of the following versions of the final sentence of paragraph 3 is correctly punctuated?
   a) The penny dreadfuls were influential since they were in the words of one commentator; the most alluring and low-priced form of escapist reading available to ordinary youth.
   b) The penny dreadfuls were influential since they were, in the words of one commentator, "the most alluring and low-priced form of escapist reading available to ordinary youth".
   c) The penny dreadfuls were influential since they were, in the words of one commentator, the most alluring and low-priced form of escapist reading available to ordinary youth.
   d) The penny dreadfuls were influential since they were in the words of one commentator "the most alluring and low-priced form of escapist reading available to ordinary youth."

34. In this first sentence of paragraph, which of the following words is a noun?
   a) serial
   b) novels
   c) sensational
   d) generally

35. In the last sentence of paragraph, which of the following words is an adjective?
    a) circulation
    b) literature
    c) however
    d) greater

36. The author wants to add a sentence to the passage that would list some of the books which were plagiarized into penny dreadfuls. Which paragraph would be the best place to add this information?
    a) Paragraph 1
    b) Paragraph 2
    c) Paragraph 3
    d) Paragraph 4

Questions 37-43 are based on the following passage about Martin Luther King Jr.

Martin Luther King Jr. was an American baptist minister and activist who was a leader in the African-American Civil Rights Movement. He is best known for his role in the advancement of civil rights using non-violent civil disobedience based on his Christian beliefs. In the United States, his racial equality efforts, and his staunchly advocating civil rights is among, undoubtedly, culturally the most important contributions made by King to last century's society.

King became a civil rights activist early in his career. In 1955, he led the Montgomery bus boycott, and in 1957 he helped found the Southern Christian Leadership Conference (SCLC), serving as its first president. With the SCLC, King led an unsuccessful 1962 struggle against segregation in Albany, Georgia, and helped organize the 1963 nonviolent protests in Birmingham, Alabama. King also helped to organize the 1963 March on Washington where he delivered his famous I Have a Dream speech. There, he established his reputation as the greatest orator in American history.

On October 14, 1964, King justly received the Nobel Piece Prize for combating racial inequality through nonviolent resistance. In 1965, he helped to organize the famous Selma to Montgomery marches, and the following year he and SCLC took the movement north to Chicago to work on eliminating the unjust and much-despised segregated housing there. In the final years of his life, King expanded his focus to include opposition towards poverty and the Vietnam War, and he gave a famous speech in 1967 entitled "Beyond Vietnam". This speech alienated many of his liberal allies in government who supported the war, but to his credit King never allowed politics to dictate the path of his noble works.

In 1968, King was planning a national occupation of Washington, D.C., to be called the Poor People's Campaign, when he was assassinated on April 4 in Memphis, Tennessee. His violent death was, not surprisingly, followed by riots in many U.S. cities.

King was posthumously awarded the Presidential Medal of Freedom and the Congressional Gold Metal. Martin Luther King, Jr. Day was established as a holiday in numerous cities and states beginning in 1971, and eventually became a U.S. federal holiday in 1986. Since his tragic death, numerous streets in the U.S. have been renamed in his honor, and a county in Washington State was also renamed for him. The Martin Luther King, Jr. Memorial on the National Mall in Washington, D.C., was dedicated in 2011.

37. In the first sentence of paragraph 1, which of the following words should be capitalized?
   a) baptist
   b) minister
   c) activist
   d) leader

38. Which is the best rewording for clarity and concision of this sentence from paragraph 1?
   a) His efforts to achieve racial equality in the United States, and his staunch public advocacy of civil rights are undoubtedly among the most important cultural contributions made to society in the last century.
   b) His efforts achieving equality in the United States, and to staunchly advocate civil rights are undoubtedly among the most important contributions culturally and societally made in the last century.
   c) Racial equality and civil rights, staunchly advocated by King in the United States, are, without a doubt, last century's greatest contributions, in a cultural way, to society.
   d) Last century, King made cultural contributions to racial equality and civil rights, which are undoubtedly the greatest made in the previous century.

39. Which of the following found in paragraph 2 should be placed inside quotation marks?
   a) Montgomery bus boycott
   b) Southern Christian Leadership Conference
   c) March on Washington
   d) I Have a Dream

40. In the first sentence of paragraph 3, which of the following words is misspelled?
   a) received
   b) Piece
   c) combating
   d) racial

41. In the first sentence of paragraph 5, which of the following words is misspelled?
   a) Posthumously
   b) Presidential
   c) Medal
   d) Metal

42. Which of the following sentences from the passage provides context clues about the author's feelings in regard to King?
   a) He is best known for his role in the advancement of civil rights using non-violent civil disobedience based on his Christian beliefs. (P. 1)
   b) King also helped to organize the 1963 March on Washington where he delivered his famous I Have a Dream speech. (P. 2)
   c) This speech alienated many of his liberal allies in government who supported the war, but to his credit King never allowed politics to dictate the path of his noble works. (P. 3)
   d) King was posthumously awarded the Presidential Medal of Freedom and the Congressional Gold Metal. (P. 5)

43. The author is considering adding a paragraph about King's family to the passage. Should he or she do this?
   a) Yes, because it adds needed personal details to the passage.
   b) Yes, because it would elaborate on information already provided in the passage.
   c) No, because the passage is about King's public life and works, and information about his family would be irrelevant.
   d) No, because information about his family has already been included and an additional paragraph on that topic would be redundant.

44. Which of the following sentences uses correct punctuation for dialogue?
   a) "Hey, can you come here a second"? asked Marie.
   b) She thought about his offer briefly and then responded. "I think I will have to pass".
   c) "I am making pancakes for breakfast. Does anybody want some?" asked mom.
   d) The conductor yelled "All aboard"! and then waited for last minute travelers to board the train.

45. Which of the following is a compound sentence?
   a) She and I drove to the play together.
   b) I woke up early that morning and began to do long-neglected household chores.
   c) The long-separated cousins ran and jumped and sang and played all afternoon.
   d) I trembled when I saw him: his face was white as a ghost.

46. Which of the following is the best order for the sentences below in forming a logical paragraph?
   a) A, B, C, D, E
   b) A, C, E, B, D
   c) A, D, B, D, E
   d) A, C, E, D, B
A. Walt Disney was a shy, self-deprecating and insecure man in private but adopted a warm and outgoing public persona.
B. His film work continues to be shown and adapted; his studio maintains high standards in its production of popular entertainment, and the Disney amusement parks have grown in size and number to attract visitors in several countries.
C. However he had high standards and high expectations of those with whom he worked.
D. He nevertheless remains an important figure in the history of animation and in the cultural history of the United States, where he is considered a national cultural icon.
E. His reputation changed in the years after his death, from a purveyor of homely patriotic values to a representative of American imperialism.

47. Which of the choices below is the meaning of the word "adopted" in the following sentence? *Walt Disney was a shy, self-deprecating and insecure man in private but adopted a warm and outgoing public persona.*
   a) took
   b) began to use
   c) began to have
   d) legally cared for as one's own child

48. Which of the following sentences is written in the second person?
    a) You had better call and RSVP to the party right away before you forget.
    b) She had every intention of calling with a prompt reply to the invitation, but the week got hectic and she forgot.
    c) I am utterly hopeless at remembering things, so I will set up a calendar reminder for myself to call Jan about the party.
    d) "Did you forget to RSVP to the party?!" asked her exasperated roommate.

49. Which of the following sentences shows proper pronoun-antecedent agreement?
    a) The author published several best-selling novels; some of it was made into films that were not as popular.
    b) Everyone should bring their parents to the town-wide carnival.
    c) Smart companies will do what it takes to hold onto its best employees.
    d) Parents are reminded to pick up their children from school promptly at 2:30.

50. Which of the following sentences shows proper subject-verb agreement?
    a) Danny is one of the only students who have lived up to his responsibilities as a newspaper staff member.
    b) One of my friends are going to be on a TV series starting this fall.
    c) Rice and beans, my favorite meal, reminds me of my native country Puerto Rico.
    d) Most of the milk we bought for the senior citizens' luncheons have gone bad.

51. Which sentence below illustrates proper use of punctuation for dialogue?
    a) "I have a dream", began Martin Luther King, Jr.
    b) "Can you believe that I have been asked to audition for that part," asked Megan excitedly?
    c) "You barely know him! How can she marry him?" was the worried mother's response at her teenager's announcement of marriage.
    d) "Remain seated while the seatbelt signs are illuminated." Came the announcement over the airplane's loud speaker system.

52. Which of the sentences below is NOT in the second person?
    a) "I have a dream", began Martin Luther King, Jr.
    b) "Can you believe that I have been asked to audition for that part," asked Megan excitedly?
    c) "You barely know him! How can you marry him?" was the worried mother's response at her teenager's announcement of marriage.
    d) "Remain seated while the seatbelt signs are illuminated." Came the announcement over the airplane's loud speaker system.

53. Which of the following sentences is an example of an Imperative sentence?
    a) "I have a dream", began Martin Luther King, Jr.
    b) "Can you believe that I have been asked to audition for that part," asked Megan excitedly?
    c) "You barely know him! How can she marry him?" was the worried mother's response at her teenager's announcement of marriage.
    d) "Please remain seated while the seatbelt signs are illuminated." Came the announcement over the airplane's loud speaker system.

54. Which of the following means "the act of cutting out"?
    a) Incision
    b) Concision
    c) Excision
    d) Decision

55. Which of the following refers to an inflammation?
    a) Appendectomy
    b) Colitis
    c) Angioplasty
    d) Dermatology

56. Which of the following refers to a cancer?
    a) Neuropathy
    b) Hysterectomy
    c) Oncology
    d) Melanoma

57. Which of the following conditions is associated with the nose?
    a) Hematoma
    b) Neuralgia
    c) Rhinitis
    d) Meningitis

58. Which of the following refers to the study of something?
    a) Gastroenterology
    b) Gastritis
    c) Psychosis
    d) Psychopath

English Language Practice Test – Answer Key

1.   A. affected; effect; ought
Rationale: Since a verb is needed in the first blank, "affected" not "effected" (a noun) will work; but the noun "effect" is correct in the second blank. "ought", meaning "should" correctly completes the sentence, indicating he should not drive. "aught", meaning zero, or nothing, or none, does not make sense in this context.

2.   C. Hiking along the trail, we were assailed by the chirping of birds, which made our nature walk hardly the peaceful exercise we had wanted.
Rationale: Who was hiking along the trail? "we" were, so only option C works. The other options are dangling participles: in option b, the birds were not attempting to hike, so that doesn't make sense; in option a, again, the birds were hiking along the trail, so that makes no sense; option d is just poorly constructed and makes the meaning overall unclear.

3.   D. processed
Rationale: "Processed" modifies "food products" so that is the adjective; "really" is an adverb modifying the adjective "serious"; "challenge" is a noun, which is a person, place or thing; "consume" is a verb, a word that shows action.

4.   B. My husband and I attended my daughter's dance recital and were very proud when she received an award.
Rationale: The most clear and concise sentence is option b; all the information is included, it is presented logically, it flows smoothly off the tongue, and it is not overly wordy.

5.   D. Since the concert ended very late, I fell asleep in the backseat during the car ride home.
Rationale: Option d is correct. "Since the concert ended very late" is a dependent clause which explains why "I fell asleep…"; since they are dependent, the only proper way to link them is with a comma.

6.   D. they're
Rationale: This question asks you make pronoun and antecedent agree; in this sentence the antecedent is "negotiations"; since this is a plural noun, the pronoun must also be plural, but the blank is also missing a verb. The only option with a plural pronoun and a verb is the contraction "they're".

7.   A. is
Rationale: "Group", a singular noun, is the subject of the sentence, so a singular verb is needed. Also needed is a present tense helping verb for "looking forward". The only option that satisfies both is "is".

8.   C. Exclamatory
Rationale: An exclamatory sentence is a type of sentence that expresses strong feelings by making an exclamation. Therefore, the above sentence is an exclamatory sentence.

9.   A. Irregardless
Rationale: "Irregardless" is incorrect as it is a double-negative: the suffix "less" already indicates a lack of regard, so the addition of the negative "ir" before the correct word, regardless, is unnecessary.

10.   C. Between you and me, I brought back fewer books from my dorm room than I needed to study for my exam.
Rationale: C. "Brought" is the correct past tense form of bring; "fewer" is the correct word to describe an exact number of items, whereas "less" is used to refer to an amount of something that cannot be exactly counted, like sand or air or water; and "than" is the correct spelling of the word that shows a comparison between two things.

11.   D. us; was
Rationale: D. Words that follow prepositions are considered to be in the objective case, therefore "us" is the correct word here; "Neither", a single pronoun, is the subject of the sentence, so a singular verb, "was" is needed to properly complete it.

12.   C. books
Rationale: C. A noun is a person, place or thing. While a "library" is usually used as a noun to denote a place where people can go to borrow books, or look up information, in this sentence it is used as an adjective to modify "books", which is the only true noun in the sentence.

13.   A. Mary and Samantha ran and skipped and hopped their way home from school every day.
Rationale: A. A simple sentence is one which has one subject and one verb, though both the subject and verb can be compound. In this case, option a is a simple sentence, with the one subject being compound ("Mary and Samantha") and the one verb also being compound ("ran and skipped and hopped"). The other options either have more than one subject or more than one verb.

14.   B. Matthew was tall and shy, and Thomas was short and talkative.
Rationale: B. A simple sentence is one which has one subject and one verb, though both the subject and verb can be compound. Linked by the conjunction "and", sentence B is the only compound sentence above because it links the first sentence "Matthew was tall and shy" with the second sentence "Thomas was short and talkative".

15.   D. "There's a bus coming, so hurry up and cross the street!" yelled Bob to the old woman.
Rationale: D. "There's" is the subject and verb of the sentence written as a contraction so the apostrophe is needed; a comma is needed before "so" because what follows it is a dependent clause which must be separated from the single sentence with a comma. When writing dialogue, the punctuation is included inside the quotation marks; in this case an exclamation is appropriate because Bob is warning the old woman to get out of the way of the oncoming bus; the use of the verb "yelled" is a clue that the statement by Bob is exclamatory.

16.   C. It's a long to-do list she left for us today: make beds; wash breakfast dishes; go grocery shopping; do laundry; cook dinner; and read the twins a bedtime story.
Rationale: "It's" is the subject and verb joined together in a contraction, so an apostrophe is needed. The sentence introduces a list, so it must be preceded by a colon; because the list is comprised of phrases instead of single words, a semicolon is needed to separate each item.

17.   A. My room was a mess so my mom made me clean it before I was allowed to leave the house.
Rationale: The use of the possessive pronoun "my" and the singular pronoun "I" indicates that the sentence is written from the first person perspective. "You" and "your" are second person; "her" or "him" are third person.

18.   C. The president of France is meeting with President Obama later this week.
Rationale: C. When referring to the "president of France", "president" is just a noun denoting his position, so it is not capitalized. In the case of "President Obama", "President" is the title by which he is addressed, so it is a proper noun and requires capitalization. The other options are incorrectly capitalized.

19.   D. climb; creak
Rationale: "Climb" is the proper spelling to denote ascending the stairs; "clime" refers to climate. "Creak" denotes a squeaky sound; "creek" denotes a stream or small moving waterway.

20.   D. I will have completed
Rationale: D. The FUTURE PERFECT TENSE indicates that an action will have been finished at some point in the future. This tense is formed with "will" plus "have" plus the past participle of the verb (which can be either regular or irregular in form). "By this time next summer" is the clue that lets you know the coursework will be done some time in the future.

21.   A. assent; aide
Rationale: A. The word "Assent" means approval, which is what the teacher wants to do to show encouragement to novice teacher who is currently her "aide" or assistance in the classroom. "Ascent" denotes a climb; "aid" is a verb denoting the action of helping.

22.   D. No one has offered to let us use their home for the office's end-of-year picnic.
Rationale: D. "No one", a singular pronoun, requires a singular verb, "has". "Us" is the objective case pronoun which is needed to follow the verb "to let"; "ourselves" is the reflexive case which is not needed in this sentence; "we" is subjective. "Their" shows possession of "home"; spelled "there", this word denotes location (e.g. here or there).

23.   C. The tornado struck without warning and caused extensive damage.
Rationale: C. Incorporating all of the information from the four sentences logically and concisely, option C is the best choice.

24.   C. caused
Rationale: C. "Caused" is the verb in this sentence; "Carrying" is the subject. Though it may look like a verb, it is actually a gerund (a verb acting as a noun) which is the subject. Deleting extraneous words will help see this, so let's rewrite the sentence in its most basic form: "Carrying caused her to throw out her back." This way it is clear to see that "carrying" is the subject, and is not a verb.

25.   B. My eyelids drooping and my feet going numb, I thought his boring lecture would never end.
Rationale: B. This sentence most clearly concisely conveys all of the information in the four above sentences; structure is parallel and no awkward or extraneous words are included.

26.   D. Comets are balls of dust and ice, comprised of leftover materials that did not become planets during the formation of our solar system.
Rationale: D. "Comets" (a plural subject requiring a plural verb) "are" "comprised of" (meaning: made up of) leftover materials that "did not" (in the past) become planets during the formation of "our" solar system.

27.   B. Improvements in printing resulted in the production of newspapers, as well as England's more fully recognizing the singular concept of reading as a form of leisure; it was, of itself, a new industry.
Rationale: B. The sentence is a compound sentence (two complete subject and verb phrases), so these should be separated by a comma after newspapers. The possession of recognition of the singular concept of reading by England needs to be shown with an apostrophe plus "s": "England's".

28.   A. era
Rationale: A. The Victorian Era is a two-word proper noun referring to a time period in history so "era" should be capitalized. The other words should not be capitalized.

29.   C. coresponding
Rationale: C. The correct spelling is corresponding.

30.   D. market
Rationale: D. "this demand" refers back to the "market (for cheaper literature)" in the last sentence of paragraph 2.

31.   C. Working class boys who could not afford a penny a week often formed clubs that would share the cost, passing the flimsy booklets from reader to reader.
Rationale: C. This sentence most clearly and concisely expresses the idea of book sharing amongst working boys who could not afford to spend a penny every week to buy the penny dreadfuls.

32.   B. gothic
Rationale: B. The word Gothic is a proper adjective referring to a specific genre of literature. None of the other words in this sentence should be capitalized.

33.   D. The penny dreadfuls were influential since they were in the words of one commentator "the most alluring and low-priced form of escapist reading available to ordinary youth."
Rationale: D. The independent clause "in the words of one commentator" needs to be set off by commas on either end; and since it is a direct quote, the last part of the sentence needs to be in quotation marks. The period at the end of the sentence needs to be inside the quotation marks.

34.   B. novels
Rationale: B. A noun is a person, place or thing. "Novels" is a plural noun which denotes a thing
that can be read. "Serial" and "sensational" are adjectives; "generally" is an adverb.

35.   D. greater
Rationale: D. An adjective is a word which describes a noun. In this sentence, "greater" is an adjective describing fear. "Circulation" and "literature" are nouns; "however" is a pronoun.

36.   C. Paragraph 3
Rationale: C. Paragraph mentions that penny dreadfuls were often plagiarized versions of other popular literature at the time, so this would be the best place to add a sentence of supporting detail about this.

37.   A. baptist
Rationale: A. As the word identifies King's religion, "Baptist" should be capitalized.

38.   A. His efforts to achieve racial equality in the United States, and his staunch public advocacy of civil rights are undoubtedly among the most important cultural contributions made to society in the last century.
Rationale: A. Using parallel structure and no extraneous verbiage, option A is the most clear and concise of the versions.

39.   D. I Have a Dream
Rationale: D. "I Have a Dream" is the title of a speech and should therefore be put inside quotation marks.

40.   B. Piece
Rationale: B. In this sentence, "Piece" should be spelled Peace, as in harmony or an absence of fighting.

41.	D. Metal

Rationale: D. In this sentence, "Metal" should be spelled "Medal", as an award or honor, not "metal" as in a naturally occurring element or raw material.

42.	C. This speech alienated many of his liberal allies in government who supported the war, but to his credit King never allowed politics to dictate the path of his noble works. (P. 3)

Rationale: C. The phrase "to his credit" and the description of his works as "noble" provide clues that the author has a positive perspective about Martin Luther King and the role his activism played in American history.

43.	C. No, because the passage is about King's public life and works, and information about his family would be irrelevant.

Rationale: C. The focus of the passage is about King's work as a minister and activist, so details about his family are unrelated to this focus, and therefore should be left out.

44.	C. "I am making pancakes for breakfast. Does anybody want some?" asked mom.

Rationale: Only option C correctly includes sentence punctuation for quoted statements: punctuation for dialogue should be inside quotation marks, as is illustrated with mom asking if anyone wants pancakes; the question mark is within the quotation marks.

45.	B. I woke up early that morning and began to do long-neglected household chores.

Rationale: Option B contains two simple sentences, which when combined make a compound sentence:" I woke up early than morning" AND "I began to do long-neglected household chores."

46.	D. A, C, E, D, B

Rationale: D. The most logical progression of ideas is in option D. The topic of Disney's public persona is introduced, and is then contrasted with his treatment of people at work, and then the transformation of his persona from that of an American patriot to an imperialist. Finally, the paragraph is wrapped up with statements about the importance of his work and his current legacy in popular culture.

47.	C. began to have

Rationale: C. The sentence is discussing the contrast between Disney's private and public personas, stating that he began to have a public persona which was very different than the way he was in private.

48.	A. You had better call and RSVP to the party right away before you forget.

Rationale: A. Statements which show direct address, and use the pronoun "you" are referred to as the second person. Though the exclamation uses the pronoun you, it is a quoted statement, so it is really in the third person. Only choice A is an example of second person writing.

49.	D. Parents are reminded to pick up their children from school promptly at 2:30.

Rationale: D. Only D makes proper use of pronouns and their antecedents: in A, novels and it do not agree; in B, everyone is singular, so instead of their, the pronoun should be him or her; in C, companies and it do not agree.

50.	C. Rice and beans, my favorite meal, reminds me of my native country Puerto Rico.

Rationale: Choice C is the only sentence in which subject (rice and beans/meal) and verb (reminds) agree: in A, one and have lived do not agree; in B, one and are going do not agree; and in D, most (of the milk OR it) does not agree with have gone.

51.   C. "You barely know him! How can she marry him?" was the worried mother's response at her teenager's announcement of marriage.
Rationale: C. Sentence punctuation always is inside quotation marks; therefore, option C is punctuated correctly for dialogue.

52.   A. "I have a dream", began Martin Luther King, Jr.
Rationale: A. Second person uses the pronoun "you" or features direct address. Though punctuated incorrectly, it is clear that only the first sentence is not written in the second person; the use of "I" illustrates first person.

53.   D. "Please remain seated while the seatbelt signs are illuminated." Came the announcement over the airplane's loud speaker system.
Rationale: D. An Imperative statement is one which gives a command. Though punctuated incorrectly, it is clear that option D is imperative: the announcement is commanding the passengers to remain seated.

54.   C. Excision
Rationale: C. The prefix "ex" means out, so that is our clue here. "Excision" refers to a surgical procedure done to cut out something unwanted or unnecessary.

55.   B – Colitis
Rationale: B. The suffix "itis" is one which refers to inflammation, so "colitis" is an inflammation of the colon.

56.   D. Melanoma
Rationale: The suffix "oma" refers to a tumor or cancer, so "melanoma" refers to a cancer of the skin (coming from melanin, that which gives our skin its color). "Oncology" is the study of cancer, but it does not refer to cancer itself.

57.   C. Rhinitis
Rationale: The root "rhino" refers to the nose or nasal area, so "rhinitis" is an inflammation of the nasal passages.

58.   A. Gastroenterology
Rationale: A. The suffix "logy" refers to the study of some discipline or area, therefore gastroenterology is the study or examination of the gastrointestinal area of the body.

Made in the USA
Coppell, TX
04 June 2021